Winning the War on War

Winning the

DUTTON

JOSHUA S. GOLDSTEIN

War on War

THE DECLINE OF ARMED CONFLICT WORLDWIDE

DUTTON
Published by Penguin Group (USA) Inc.
375 Hudson Street, New York, New York 10014, U.S.A.
Penguin Group (Canada), 90 Eglinton Avenue East, Suite 700, Toronto, Ontario M4P 2Y3, Canada
(a division of Pearson Penguin Canada Inc.); Penguin Books Ltd, 80 Strand, London WC2R 0RL,
England; Penguin Ireland, 25 St Stephen's Green, Dublin 2, Ireland (a division of Penguin Books Ltd);
Penguin Group (Australia), 250 Camberwell Road, Camberwell, Victoria 3124, Australia (a division of
Pearson Australia Group Pty Ltd); Penguin Books India Pvt Ltd, 11 Community Centre, Panchsheel
Park, New Delhi—110 017, India; Penguin Group (NZ), 67 Apollo Drive, Rosedale, Auckland 0632,
New Zealand (a division of Pearson New Zealand Ltd); Penguin Books (South Africa) (Pty) Ltd,
24 Sturdee Avenue, Rosebank, Johannesburg 2196, South Africa

Penguin Books Ltd, Registered Offices: 80 Strand, London WC2R 0RL, England

Published by Dutton, a member of Penguin Group (USA) Inc.

First printing, September 2011
10 9 8 7 6 5 4 3 2 1

REGISTERED TRADEMARK—MARCA REGISTRADA

LIBRARY OF CONGRESS CATALOGING-IN-PUBLICATION DATA
has been applied for.

ISBN 978-0-525-952534

Printed in the United States of America
Set in ITC Cheltenham Std
Designed by Amy Hill

For Solomon, whose name means peace

"We the peoples of the United Nations
Determined
to save succeeding generations
from the scourge of war . . ."

—*UN Charter, 1945*

Contents

Prologue   ix

1 War on the Street Outside
   Beirut, 1980   1

2 The Long-Term Trend
   A Trip in a Time Machine, 2011 to Prehistoric Times   12

3 Palestine to Congo
   The Invention of Peacekeeping, 1947–61   45

4 Angola to Mozambique
   Failures and Successes of the Early 1990s   73

5 The Kofi Annan Reforms
   Consolidation and Expansion, 1997–2006   109

6 The Sierra Leone Model
   Multidimensional Peace Operations, 1998–2011   136

7 The Unarmy
   Nonmilitary Forces Supporting Peace   177

8 Peace Movements
   If You Want Peace, Work for Peace   203

9 Assessing Progress
   Is Peace Increasing since 1945?   229

10 Three Myths
   *Finding the Truth When Conventional
   Wisdom Is Wrong*   253

11 Wars of the World
    The Fires Still Smoldering   275

12 What We Can Do
    A New Global Identity   308

    Notes   329
    References   353
    Acknowledgments   373
    Index   375

Prologue

This book asks readers to break out of a dominant way of thinking about world affairs that focuses on negativity and drowns out progress. If we turn off the screech of alarmist "news" and overblown political rhetoric for a moment and look at hard evidence objectively, we find that many people in the world are working hard for peace, and in fact the world is becoming more peaceful. For this shocking idea to sink in requires either a paradigm shift or at least a broken TV set.

For those who are sure wars are getting worse all the time and that peace is an illusion, and will not believe any amount of evidence I produce to the contrary, I have one question: "Compared to what?" Take the situation in Iraq in 2011—a terrible mess, Americans still getting killed by insurgents, civilians dying, the population unhappy, the government needing eight months to get organized after an election, the potential for civil war after the departure of U.S. forces. All true, and more, but "compared to what?" Compared to a few years ago when Sunni-Shiite sectarian violence ravaged the country? Compared to the period of the U.S. invasion in 2003, the looting, and the insurgency? Or compared to how Iraq *would* be if the United States had not botched the invasion? Or how it would be if fairies sprinkled magic dust over the country to end sectarian strife, corruption, and electricity shortages?

The ability to distinguish between bad (Iraq today) and worse (Iraq a few years ago) unlocks a profound understanding of today's world situation. The world is going from worse to bad, from the fire to the frying pan. Good news—unless you are freaked out by the frying pan and so upset by the "bad" coming at you constantly in the news that you cannot compare it with anything.

With the frying pan still pretty hot, it is easy to assume that war is getting worse, and can never get better, because everyone knows that war is inevitable. But if we look past the heat and smoke, a radical notion emerges in this book. War among human beings is not inevitable. Rather, the end of war, though also not inevitable, is possible. The possibility of an end to war is not something to be ridiculed, but to be pursued.

I hope that this story, one that tours some of the most awful war-torn places on earth but that is ultimately about peace, will inspire readers to see—through the continuing fog of war—our best qualities as human beings: our ability to communicate, to empathize, to cooperate, and to create a safer, freer, more prosperous world for our children.

Winning the War on War

1

WAR ON THE STREET OUTSIDE

Beirut, 1980

I have studied war as a professor for decades, but have been in a war zone only once. It was April 16, 1980, and I was driving into Beirut, Lebanon, from the airport with Black Panther founder Huey P. Newton and a half dozen of his friends to visit the Palestine Liberation Organization (PLO) and meet its leader, Yasser Arafat. I was a white, Jewish, nonviolent twenty-seven-year-old who had met Huey just a few times but had worked on Black Panther community programs in the party's "put down the gun" phase in the early 1970s. The PLO was bringing in foreign big-shots to see its state-within-a-state in Beirut, and evidently did not know that the Black Panthers had fallen apart years ago and that Huey personally was on a cocaine-strewn path to self-destruction that would kill him within the decade—shot on the streets of Oakland.

When the PLO invited Huey to assemble a delegation for an expenses-paid visit, he took his wife, brother-in-law, secretary, and a white supporter who was a friend of mine. I got myself invited along because there was extra space and I hoped to (and did) help Huey visit Israel afterward, as he had expressed a desire to do. We rode in from the Beirut airport and through the city in two cars, Huey's inner circle in the first and me with two other people in the second.

When I heard popping sounds ahead, I thought fireworks. After all, there was a lull in the civil war. Our airport arrival had been smooth (for one thing, the PLO seemed to bypass the Lebanese authorities altogether) and nobody mentioned trouble. True, the city was traumatized still from its recent years of civil war, and whole buildings gaped open from unrepaired shell damage. But there was a stable dividing line and cease-fire between the Muslim side, where we were, and the Christian side. If you stayed away from the dividing line and the Israeli border you were safe—unless the crazy traffic killed you, but that's another story. So the popping sounds did not alarm me at first.

As we continued, though, the shots got louder and it became clear they were not fireworks but automatic weapons fire in the city streets. A gun battle was soon taking place a block ahead of us and our driver, completely calm, said, "OK, something's happening; we'll go another way," and turned the car around. He said, "Don't worry," and I commented, "I *am* worried." He remarked of the fighting, "You get used to it," and I replied, "I hope *I* never get used to it." I remember slouching down in the backseat of the car so that a stray bullet would have less chance to hit me if one came our way. But none did.

When we got to our hotel, Huey and his friends showed a certain amusement with the street fighting. "Did you see that guy running along with the AK-47 nipping at his heels?" they laughed. (Huey instructed us that as a civilian caught in a firefight you should walk away, since running makes you look like "part of the action"—advice I thankfully have never had occasion to use.) I could not understand the driver's calmness and Huey's friends' attitude about the fighting.

Up until then, for me, war was an absolute. Being in a war zone meant dying, and there was no connection in my mind between a war zone and daily life. But in Beirut I began to learn that war is relative, that most people in a war zone survive, that war is hell but also life goes on. In Beirut in 1980, if war took place a block away, you went on with your day. If war came onto *your* block, well, then you went inside.

That night, out the hotel window, I saw outgoing artillery fire from some blocks away—not *our* block, though. A few minutes later incoming artillery set off big booms, but not close enough to break anything where we were. I realized that the incoming shells had landed pretty close to where the outgoing shells had come from. This made me feel safer because they seemed to know what they were shooting at and it was not me.

A five-year-old boy on his balcony was also not what the fighters were shooting at that day, but a stray bullet killed him. The day's fighting had killed five people in all. I saw it in the next day's newspaper. War took away this young child's life, with all the hopes and plans for the rest of it, and left a permanent gap in the fabric of his family and community.

For that five-year-old child, war was *not* relative; it was absolute. It does not matter whether he died among five that day or five thousand. It does not matter, for him, whether the street fighting in Beirut that day was a tiny fragment of a world awash in big wars, or the last skirmish on earth. (Similarly, the fact that deaths in Iraq hit a new low level in October 2008 did not matter for the family in Kirkuk that lost the last of its three sons, a seven year old killed by a stray grenade while playing soccer.)

But it does matter for us, the living. It matters for the *other* children around the world who would die and suffer if the world were awash in big wars, but would live peaceful lives if Beirut were the last skirmish on earth. Less of a bad thing is a good thing. Fewer and smaller wars are better than more and larger wars. They are better, not for one five-year-old in Beirut but for the world as a whole. I think that our brains naturally focus on human-interest stories such as the five-year-old and have a harder time with macro-scale assessments. But sensible policies depend on getting the big picture right.

The fighting that I drove into in Beirut that day marked the prelude to the Iran-Iraq War, which started five months later. (Many proxy battles played out in Beirut over the years.) The Iran-Iraq War would last eight years and kill more than half a million people. The Beirut clash lasted three days and killed thirty people. As terrible as each was, from a big-picture perspective the Iran-Iraq War was much worse than the Beirut battle.

So there is a scale from small to large, and this book is all about movement along that scale. At the high end of the war scale is global thermonuclear war, which has never occurred. A bit lower are world wars and lower still interstate wars and then smallish civil wars and terrorism. Peace also has gradations—the negative end of the war scale, if you will—from fragile cease-fire to stable cease-fire to formal peace agreement and transitional government to disarmament and democracy.

The Possibility of Progress

Can the world, step by step and with ups and downs, actually reduce the amount of war violence taking place? Can it move down the scale of war over time? Actually, this has been happening already for decades.

In the first half of the twentieth century, world wars killed *tens of millions* and left whole continents in ruins. In the second half of that century, during the Cold War, proxy wars killed *millions*, and the world feared a nuclear war that could have wiped out our species. Now, in the early twenty-first century, the worst wars, such as Iraq, kill *hundreds of thousands*. We fear terrorist attacks that could destroy a city, but not life on the planet. The fatalities still represent a large number and the impacts of wars are still catastrophic for those caught in them, but overall, war has diminished dramatically.

In the post–Cold War era that began in 1990, far fewer people have died in wars each year than during the Cold War. And within the post–Cold War era, the new century so far has seen fewer deaths per year from war violence than in the 1990s. More wars are ending than beginning, once ended they are less likely to restart, and the remaining wars are more localized than in the past.

1980 VERSUS 2011

Let us start with just one point of comparison to illustrate this dramatic change—the world situation around the time I visited Beirut in 1980, thirty years ago, compared to 2011. Javier Pérez de Cuéllar describes the state of the world when he became secretary-general of the United Nations (UN) in 1982: Iraq and Iran were in a "cruel war," Israel and the PLO were battling over Lebanon, the Soviet Union occupied and brutalized Afghanistan, U.S.-Soviet relations had hit a low, apartheid ruled in South Africa and postcolonial conflicts raged elsewhere in Africa. Central America had "social strife and insurgency. . . . And casting its ominous shadow over all was the mounting arsenal of nuclear weapons, bearing in them the threat to humanity's very survival." In the face of these wars and problems, the "Security Council had long been largely immobilized" by the Cold War standoff, since each superpower had a veto. In 1986 Pérez de Cuéllar "could not point to a single conflict that had been resolved during the previous five years as a result of the United Nations' efforts."

The Iran-Iraq War deserves note among these wars of the 1980s as one of the few cases in recent decades of *interstate war*, with regular armies (armed with tanks, missiles, and other heavy weapons) on both sides. Those wars generally cause more death and destruction than do the more common *civil wars*—including all of today's remaining wars—in which a government army on one side fights rebel militia groups (usually more lightly armed) on the other side.

The Iran-Iraq War was massively brutal and futile. Iran's ayatollahs sent teenagers by the thousands to their deaths, promising them paradise. Iraqis electrified swamps to kill Iranians wholesale. They used chemical weapons—the only such case in recent decades—and found them lethally effective. Both sides rained missiles on each other's cities. And in the end, hundreds of thousands of the deaths and a wasted decade later, the border was right where it had started, and both regimes were still in power, Saddam Hussein and Ayatollah Khomeini. Within a few years Saddam had invaded another of his neighbors, Kuwait.

How does that world of the 1980s compare to today's world? In Lebanon, the civil war finally ended in 1990. Hezbollah became a political party and won seats in parliament, although it also remained heavily armed and provoked a destructive war with Israel in 2006. In 2009, when pro-Western parties won elections, dealing a setback to Hezbollah and its allies, the losers did not turn to war. They turned to doing better in the next election and playing a key role in coalition politics in the government.

Similarly, in El Salvador the former rebel party won the presidency in 2009, some seventeen years after the end of the war there. In Nicaragua, since the war ended twenty years ago, power has twice changed hands peacefully through elections between the former rebels and former government. Elsewhere around the world, wars have ended and societies are enjoying the fruits of peace, albeit with the scars of war still aching. I will paint a more complete picture of this process in the coming chapters.

In fact, worldwide, wars today are measurably fewer and smaller than thirty years ago. By one measure, the number of people killed directly by war violence has decreased by 75 percent in that period. (Changes in indirect deaths from war, such as by epidemics, do not negate this trend, but I will postpone discussion of that complicated subject to Chapters 9 and 10.) *Interstate* wars have become very infrequent and relatively small. Wars between "great powers" have not occurred for more than fifty years. The number of *civil* wars is also shrinking, though less dramatically, as old ones end faster than new ones begin. This tremendous progress goes unheralded for the most part, as people's attention and media coverage gravitate toward the remaining trouble spots.

The overall peaceful trend since 1990 may be a harbinger of even greater peace, or just an interlude before new and more terrible wars. It may be robust or fragile. It may result from understandable causes or from an unknown confluence of events. But, for now, peace is increasing. Year by year, we are winning the war on war.

One explanation for the recent reductions in war that I will *not* propose is that people are peaceful by nature. Many theories and writings hold that our "true" peacefulness has been obscured by capitalism, the political opportunism of bad leaders, or some such interfering reason. This is clearly not the case. As Chapter 2 shows, the human species has been fighting since the get-go and our "true" nature includes the potential for lethal violence (as well as the capacity to avoid or overcome this potential). Over the centuries we have remained violent, and the first half of the twentieth century was a step backward from some progress that had been made. Mainly in the past hundred years the popular idea has grown that war is not the normal and expected state of the world but something to be avoided and reduced. In making these imperfect steps forward, we are not falling back on our true selves, but rather redefining ourselves and making new rules.

Another argument I do not make is that reductions in war are inevitable, irreversible, or part of an immutable trend. On the contrary, history tells us that the gains humanity makes in building peace are generally fragile, reversible, and require ongoing effort to sustain. Shortly before World War I, British journalist and activist Norman Angell published *The Great Illusion* to great public acclaim. He argued that economic interdependence, with wealth deriving not from territory but credit and commerce, had made war and conquest self-defeating and pointless. At that time, relative peace had prevailed for almost four decades since

1871—less peace than is sometimes claimed, as Chapter 2 will show, but still relative peace by historical standards. A really massive great-power war had not occurred in nearly a century. It was easy to think, in 1910, that war had withered away. Instead, the World Wars followed, even though they created the economic devastation in Europe that Angell had foreseen.

But does the failure of a hopeful lull in war a century ago mean that all lulls will end in disaster? Does a reversal of progress bar the possibility of later progress? This would be like saying that because the flying machines of the 1890s crashed, airplanes are impossible. Or that the failure of the Newton in the late 1990s meant that Apple could not build a tablet computer.

So, no, the culmination of today's hopeful trends in the permanent end of war is not inevitable, but neither is their reversal. We have good reason to worry, in a world of more and more powerful weapons, that a new outbreak of major war would be more devastating than ever. But at the same time we have good reason for hope, that such a disaster need not happen. World peace is not preordained and inevitable, but neither is a return to large-scale war.

THE INTERNATIONAL COMMUNITY

The reduction in war over several decades suggests that the international community is doing something right in trying to tame war. We are winning the "war on war," by which I mean the efforts of international peacekeepers, diplomats, peace movements, humanitarian aid agencies, and other international organizations in war-torn and postwar countries. Considering how few funds and resources they get, these international peace operations have succeeded remarkably well.

The "international community" consists primarily of national governments and the organizations they belong to, such as the UN, EU, NATO, and African Union. It also includes nongovernmental actors and individuals, and it draws strength from people's nascent identities as human beings, caring about others from different lands or tribes. But at heart the "community" is a club of governments, and they are none too idealistic or altruistic in their motivations. As we shall see, the mechanisms of the war on war operate creakily and inefficiently, as humanitarian ideals frequently bump up against cold national interests. Nonetheless, by participating in an international community, governments jointly achieve some mutually beneficial outcomes that could not be realized separately. The reduction of war worldwide is one of those outcomes.

The kinds of activities the book describes—such as peacekeeping, diplomacy, and humanitarian assistance—have the character of interventions in the sense that the international community comes in as foreigners to help make peace in war-torn countries. Of course, peace results from many influences, including local and national actions, and not just from the international community galloping around trying to put out fires. Nonetheless, as I hope to show, these international actions hold the central place in the process of building peace worldwide.

The UN lies at the heart of the "war on war." And that institution has many problems. Dictators from around the world gather to give long-winded speeches in the General Assembly, although not usually with a holster strapped on as Arafat had in 1974. Human-rights abusers led the UN's human rights commission. The oil-for-food program for Iraq was corrupt. Sex scandals have tarnished peacekeeping missions. The UN system is founded on the contradictory principles of universal human rights and paramount national sovereignty. The UN sometimes screws up spectacularly: For instance, in 1993, French UN peacekeepers providing secure transportation for Bosnian officials to reach the airport opened an armored vehicle with a vice president inside and allowed Serbian forces to shoot him dead. Some of the UN's problems are genuine failings that the UN struggles to correct over the years and decades. Others are mere theater. But they should not distract us from the tremendous good that the UN has accomplished, despite its problems, in reducing war since 1945.

Heated political rhetoric, such as calls from some "Tea Party" candidates in 2010 to withdraw the United States from the UN, sometimes gives the impression that Americans do not support the UN. But this is not true. In a 2007 public opinion survey, an overwhelming 79 percent of Americans favored "strengthening the UN" in general. Some 60 percent agreed that "when dealing with international problems, the United States should be willing to make decisions within the United Nations even if this means that the United States will sometimes have to go along with a policy that is not its first choice." In this survey, the U.S. public revealed a mature understanding of the benefits of the UN to the United States, despite its shortcomings, and the fact that they come at a certain cost in national sovereignty.

Why It Matters

Why does it matter if wars are diminishing or increasing? It matters because the question "Are things getting better or worse?" must be the starting point for making decisions about courses of action over time. If I have a disease and am trying a treatment, the first thing I want to know is whether the disease is getting better or worse. If better, I will figure out what I am doing that is working, refine and strengthen those approaches as I learn more, and see if I can sustain and complete the improvements seen already. If I am getting worse, though, I will more radically change course, abandoning existing approaches and looking for new ones. This is risky, because it might accelerate the disease rather than reverse it. But since things are getting worse I can see that what I have been doing has not worked.

A similar logic applies to other areas of life and society. Is the economy getting better or worse? Is crime getting better or worse? Are my child's grades in school getting better or worse? Yet, amazingly, few people think about the problem of war in our world that way. Is war getting better or worse? Many people seem to just assume war is getting worse, because we hear about such terrible crimes as the genocide in Darfur, the violent insurgency in Afghanistan, and the recurrent terrorism of al Qaeda around the world. But is it getting better or worse? If the world's wars are getting worse, then a radical change in strategy may be called for, but if wars are shrinking, then strengthening existing approaches such as diplomacy and peacekeeping would work better.

As an example of what happens if we get this "better or worse" question wrong when it comes to the world's wars, consider the argument of political psychologist James Blight and Robert McNamara, former World Bank president and U.S. defense secretary. They seek to apply the lessons of the bloody twentieth century to make the twenty-first more peaceful (good idea). But they start from the assumption that war is getting worse. Noting the high casualties of the two World Wars, they conclude that "in the twentieth century, war was a common occurrence, it was increasingly lethal, and its toll fell primarily on civilians." This idea that war was increasingly lethal over the past century is clearly wrong, however—certainly if you just compare the first half of the century with the second (as Chapter 2 will show).

Blight and McNamara project the level of warfare forward into the twenty-first century based on population growth, and suggest a "speculative" but "conservative" estimate of "at least 300 million" fatalities from war in the twenty-first century, of which perhaps 75 million would be military. That is to say, the new century would see an average of 3 million war deaths per year, with 750,000 of them military deaths. They acknowledge the tremendous uncertainties in war data and difficulties in projecting forward a hundred years, but note that "our projections . . . may well be *underestimates!*" (emphasis in original).

Based on these projections, Blight and McNamara call for major changes in the way the international community approaches the problem of war. Since what we have been doing is not working (war is getting worse), we need a new approach, in their view. They write, "Without significant reform of the UN Security Council, little can be done to stop communal killing around the world." This puts peace in line behind an intractable issue, Security Council reform. Recognizing these difficulties, Blight and McNamara say that if, prior to being reorganized, the Security Council cannot agree to a military invention to stop a war, then a "'coalition of the willing' should be assembled to approve the intervention and authorize it." (This was before such a coalition invaded Iraq.) Indeed, they say the UN Charter is "out of date and needs revising. . . ."

These radical suggestions would make sense if wars were becoming more numerous and lethal, just as it would make sense to try an experimental medicine for a cancer that had not responded well to conventional treatments. But for our world, today, the cancer of war *is* responding. The United Nations *is* succeeding, although it could work better with more support and resources. This stark difference in policy approaches illustrates why the question of "better or worse" affects actions and policies regarding wars.

More generally, political discourses driven by fears and worst-case scenarios, as today's discussions of war often are, promote dysfunctional policies such as very high military spending and aggressive military actions. Fear of war—a sense that war is pervasive and could get us at any moment—does not lead to the pursuit of peace, but rather to pessimism and policies likely to bring about the very thing we fear. The political dynamics leading up to the U.S. invasion of Iraq in 2003 illustrate this problem and its serious consequences.

Returning to the idea of a scale of war, we can look at changes through time along that scale, the same way your doctor would track changes in your cancer. The scale lets us ask whether things are getting better or worse. My main focus in this book is the period since 1945, but to make sense of that period we need to understand it both in its own terms and in the context of a deeper historical context. As we shall see, the big picture of war in the human experience shows how remarkable the recent period (a sustained low along the scale of war) has been.

2

THE LONG-TERM TREND

A Trip in a Time Machine, 2011 to Prehistoric Times

Imagine that we have a time machine to take us into the past. At stops along the way we can make a series of comparisons between time periods—are they more or less warlike?

- Past ten years compared with previous ten

- Past twenty years compared with previous twenty

- Past fifty years compared with previous fifty

- Past century compared with previous centuries

- Modern era (five hundred years) compared with medieval and ancient times

- Historical times compared with prehistoric humans

In this way, we can see the overall shifts in the intensity of warfare, up or down the scale of war discussed in Chapter 1, over the long sweep of human experience.

I. The Years since 1945

The period since the end of the extraordinary World Wars is the primary focus of this book. What is the character of these decades and how do they compare with earlier times?

THE TWENTY-FIRST CENTURY VERSUS THE 1990s

Get into the time machine, settle into the leather seat (time machines are expensive), and first scan back through the last ten years. Take a breath at the year 2000—hey, the Y2K bug did not destroy civilization!—and then scan through the previous ten years, the 1990s. Now compare these two scans. For the United States, the new century has been more war-prone—9/11, Iraq, and Afghanistan—than the peace and prosperity of the 1990s. But for the world as a whole, the opposite is true. To start with numbers, a data-set on battle-related deaths (which I will describe in Chapter 9) shows the world total dropping from about 100,000 deaths per year in the 1990s to just over 50,000 in the new century. Fifty thousand killed by war violence every year is outrageous, but only half as outrageous as 100,000 just a decade earlier.

Another measure—the number of serious wars going on in each decade—gives similar results. By one count, "in the mid-1990s there were eight extremely lethal conflicts: Sudan, Somalia, Rwanda, Burundi, Liberia, Angola, Bosnia, and Chechnya." By 2010, six of these eight had ended, with no appreciable fighting left. Only Somalia and Sudan had not arrived at some conflict termination whether by peace agreement or government victory. In the same time period, two similarly lethal conflicts began, in Iraq and Afghanistan. So, in the last fifteen years the world went from eight serious wars to four—excellent progress for such a short time!

In terms of numbers of people displaced by wars, the UNHCR's "population of concern"—refugees, internally displaced persons (IDPs), and stateless persons—fell by about a third from the early to late 1990s, then remained fairly constant from 1997 to 2008, at around 20 million. (The number of IDPs appeared to jump by 5 million suddenly in 2006, but this was entirely due to a change in methodology, and I do not include them.) In 2008, 1.1 million people were newly displaced, but at least 1.4 million were able to return home. So, on this dimension, progress is less impressive than numbers of wars and their lethality, but it is progress nonetheless.

Within the past decade, the decline in war deaths has slowed, as I will discuss later. Even so, improvements on other measures continue. A 2008 report from the Coalition to Stop the Use of Child Soldiers found that the number of armed conflicts where child soldiers were active dropped from twenty-seven to seventeen over four years. "This downward trend is more the result of conflicts ending than the impact of initiatives to end child soldier recruitment and use," the report said.

NGOs love to make indexes and my new favorite is the Global Peace Index. Using twenty-three indicators—ranging from military budgets to domestic crime rates, press freedom, corruption, sizes of armies, and numbers of displaced people—researchers from the *Economist* Intelligence Unit gave each country a score on how peaceful it was. The sponsoring NGO in Australia, Visions of Humanity, put the index on a world map, and you can see the map move through the last four years and see the temperature "cooling off," so to speak, as the world (especially Africa) edges a bit closer to peace. "Figures show that Africa has become the most improved region of the world for peacefulness over the last four years. The continent has experienced fewer conflicts, less military spending, and improved cross-border relations."

Even for the United States, the last few years show some encouraging signs. Brookings Institution researchers periodically make charts of progress in America's wars. The most recent chart compared April 2010 with April 2009 and 2008. In Iraq, the world's most expensive war of the decade, U.S. troop levels dropped from 150,000 to 95,000 (and in the following months, to 50,000). Monthly U.S. troop deaths dropped from fifty-two to eight. Iraqi security forces' monthly deaths dropped from 110 to 20, and civilian deaths from an estimated 1,000 to 250.

In Afghanistan, U.S. troops began a "surge" in numbers in those two years, and the violence increased accordingly while the situation had not really improved much. U.S. monthly deaths went from five to twenty, Afghan security forces from 110 to 120, and estimated civilian deaths from 136 to 150. (The civilian deaths in Afghanistan are still below Iraq's even with the latter down by three-quarters.) The number of Afghan children in school grew from 5.9 million to 6.5 million. The percent of Afghans saying their country is heading in the right direction grew from 50 to 60 percent, and the percent who support the government over the Taliban grew from 83 percent to 90. Those with a favorable view of the United States stayed steady at 40 percent. So it is not the case that Afghan got much worse as Iraq got better. Rather, Iraq improved and Afghanistan was a mix of improvement and deterioration in these past two years.

Sociologist Louis Kriesberg identifies eight "peace factors" that he sees underlying the decline in wars and violent conflicts since 1990: the end of the Cold War; the dominance of U.S. power; the economic benefits of globalization (which war would disrupt); spreading norms about peace and human rights; spreading democracy; the proliferation of NGOs; the increased participation of women in politics; and the growing field of conflict resolution. Despite the war in Iraq, the persistence of terrorism, and the rise in religious conflicts in recent years, Kriesberg sees the peace factors as enduring, though the world is not moving "inexorably toward peace."

Researchers at the U.S. Institute of Peace in 2005 listed a series of conflicts as "intractable," since they "continue to resist any kind of settlement or resolution." They included Israel-Palestine, Somalia, and Sudan, where "intractable" sounds like a good description. But in a majority of the cases, the five years since the publication of the book saw substantial progress toward settlement. In Sri Lanka military victory ended the war, and in Colombia a similar outcome seems possible. In the Balkans and Northern Ireland, shaky peace arrangements have become less shaky, and substantial violence has not resumed. In the African cases—Burundi, Ivory Coast, Democratic Republic of the Congo, Rwanda, Sierra Leone, and Uganda—UN missions have helped bring growing stability and made a return to war less likely (or, in the case of Congo and Uganda, increasingly limited the area of fighting). So even "intractable" conflicts are becoming tractable.

Thus, overall, while the United States moved up the scale of war intensity in the 2000s compared with the 1990s, the world as a whole went down the scale.

POST–COLD WAR ERA
COMPARED WITH THE COLD WAR

Now get back into the time machine, and put together everything you have seen about the post–Cold War era since 1990. We are going to compare that picture with what came before, during the Cold War.

The collapse of the Soviet Union and the transformation of superpower conflict into relative cooperation reverberated around the world and contributed greatly to the reduction of armed conflict. In terms of the twenty years before 1990 compared with the twenty years after, again using the battle-death data described later on, the annual average deaths was about 75,000 annually in 1990–2009 compared with about 215,000 annually in 1970–89.

Looking at the fatality totals by war instead of by year, it is immediately clear that the Cold War conflicts were simply much more lethal than the more recent wars. (All these fatality estimates are just for deaths by violence, not indirectly as by disease, but the Cold War conflicts had plenty of the latter as well.)

Vietnam	1.5 million
Chinese Civil War	1.2 million
Korea	1 million
Iran-Iraq	650,000
Afghan/Soviet	500,000
Afghan/post-Sov	90,000
Afghan/post-2001	20,000
Cambodia	370,000
Congo since 1996	150,000
Angola	140,000
Iraq	125,000
Uganda	120,000
Mozambique	140,000
Chechnya	90,000
Sri Lanka	75,000
Sudan/South	60,000
El Salvador	55,000
Ethiopia-Eritrea	50,000

Nuclear Fears

Beyond any statistics or casualty rates, the Cold War and post–Cold War eras have very different psychological characters. Younger readers who did not live through the late 1950s and early '60s might not easily understand the feeling of life under what felt like a real possibility of nuclear war. "The war" meant World War II, a fresh memory of an unbelievably violent trauma, so the idea of a war on the scale of nuclear war was not really "unthinkable," although there was something of a state of denial about it.

In 1957, the Soviets had launched the first satellite, and the same big missiles that could launch a satellite could also land a nuclear warhead on any American city. A "missile gap" motivated Washington to accelerate deployment of its own nuclear missiles, even though the "gap" later turned out to be nonexistent. Both sides armed up with thousands of missiles, and these hung over our heads like the proverbial Sword of Damocles dangling from a thread—a metaphor used by President Kennedy in addressing the UN in 1961.

In 1962, the Cuban Missile Crisis brought the superpowers close to nuclear war, closer than they realized at the time. American ships once harassed a Soviet submarine with small depth charges, not knowing that it was armed with nuclear torpedoes, which the captain nearly used. The good part of the crisis is that it scared the hell out of leaders on both sides and led to the more scripted rivalries that characterized the rest of the Cold War years.

The next year, a new Emergency Broadcast System began regularly interrupting radio shows with "This is a test. . . . This is only a test." On the wall of my sixth-grade classroom was a poster showing the meanings of different alert sirens that could sound in the event of a nuclear attack. I grew up on the Stanford campus, a small town, and on the old fire station in the center of campus was a siren that could sound the warning. They tested it Fridays at eleven, which I figured was when the Soviets would attack if a war started. One siren pattern meant get to shelter in the next thirty minutes—meaning a Soviet launch had occurred and the missiles would take half an hour to get here. Another siren indicated an all-clear, and another meant "duck and cover." This meant the missile had arrived and could detonate at any moment. We practiced in class putting our heads under the desks to be ready for a surprise attack. But even sixth-graders could see that it was a hopeless gesture.

So basically you had a generation of kids in those years growing up knowing that at any moment a siren could announce that—with zero to thirty minutes' warning—not only would they die but all their family, friends, community, and indeed possibly all of humanity would be destroyed, just like that. And there was nothing we could do about it. It was not just media hype either.

What is the reality of the nuclear arms race today? Are we making progress, stuck in place, or are things getting worse? The answer is crystal clear—things have dramatically improved since the end of the Cold War. Yes, the whole area of nuclear weapons needs greater attention and resources because of its paramount importance in the "war on terrorism." Nonetheless, in terms of sheer megatonnage, the world has seen substantial reduction in the post–Cold War era.

Nuclear weapons stockpiles, and the subset of deployed strategic nuclear weapons—those ready to hit the enemy homeland on a moment's notice—both climbed rapidly from the 1950s through the mid-1980s, peaking at a mind-boggling 30,000 to 40,000 total (and about 10,000 deployed) on each side. Since then the totals have fallen steadily—the biggest restraint being our ability to safely and affordably dismantle weapons—until by 2010 the United States had 5,000 and Russia fewer than 9,000, each with about 2,500 deployed. ¬

The combined total has fallen in just twenty-five years from 60,000 nuclear weapons to about 14,000. And this total represents 96 percent of the world's nuclear weapons—no other country's arsenal exceeds 300 weapons. The number of U.S. tactical nuclear weapons in Europe has dropped from more than 7,000 in 1971 to fewer than 200 today. In the mid-1980s, Germany had U.S. nuclear weapons stored at seventy-five locations. Today there is exactly one such site. The Soviet Union had about 500 nuclear weapons storage facilities, whereas Russia today has forty-eight. Those of us active in the movement against nuclear weapons in the early 1980s could hardly have dreamed of such a good outcome. And a new U.S.-Russian treaty signed in 2010 (and ratified by both sides within a year) will reduce these levels further in the coming seven years to 1,550 warheads each. This is still several times higher than makes sense, but impressive progress nonetheless. Overall, writes journalist Gregg Easterbrook, "historians will view nuclear arms reduction as such an incredible accomplishment that it will seem bizarre in retrospect so little attention was paid while it was happening."

The numbers I just quoted came from the *Bulletin of the Atomic Scientists*, a wonderful source of information. The *Bulletin* is also the creator of the famous "doomsday clock," which claims to track the rising and falling danger level for nuclear war over the years. In 1968 the clock was set to a dramatic "seven minutes to midnight" as the Vietnam War and other Cold War–era wars raged. Over the years the hands of the clock moved forward and back as tensions rose and fell. In 1988, they stood at six minutes to midnight. Given the progress on nuclear arms, one would expect the clock to be set back to at least eleven-thirty P.M. Yet in 2010 it stood at five minutes to midnight—worse than in 1968 or 1988! The best explanation for this would seem to be that the *Bulletin* needs alarmism to attract interest and donors.

Comparing the Cold War with the post–Cold War era on another metric, the number of refugees from wars is higher than during most of the Cold War, though lower than the peak near the end of the Cold War. According to the UN refugee agency (the High Commissioner for Refugees, or UNHCR), the total number of refugees seeking sanctuary across an international border rose from about 2 million in the early 1950s to about 10 million in the early 1980s and 18 million by 1992, then dropped below 12 million by the late 1990s, where it remains.

Despite these hopeful developments, military spending has not followed suit. In the 1990s, world military spending fell by about a third. But then, after 2001, U.S. military spending increased back to even higher levels than during the Cold War (although somewhat lower than the Cold War as a percent of the U.S. GDP). Europe reduced its spending, and Asia increased but from a smaller starting point. Thus, the United States now makes up half the world's total military spending. Overall, world military spending remains somewhat below levels in the Cold War, and this is even more true if spending is taken as a percent of world total GDP. However, military spending, and especially U.S. military spending, does not seem to have caught up with the reality of fewer and smaller wars in the post–Cold War era. In 2011, the U.S. defense secretary warned West Point cadets that "the Army will be increasingly challenged to justify the number, size, and cost of its heavy formations" in a world in which clashes of large armies have become unlikely. Of course he did not, perish the thought, propose a reduction in the $700 billion U.S. defense budget to help close the massive federal budget deficit.

Prophets of Doom

When the Cold War ended, it was not clear whether the new era would have more or less violence than before. Some writers foresaw a period of greater instability and violence. The University of Chicago political scientist John Mearsheimer famously predicted in 1990 that "the next decades in a Europe without the superpowers would . . . probably be substantially more prone to violence than the past forty-five years." We would soon miss the stability of the Cold War. Robert Kaplan foresaw a "coming anarchy" as ethnic and religious wars proliferated and globalization heightened inequality. Similarly, former national security advisor Zbigniew Brzezinski warned of "global turmoil" developing in the early 1990s.

These dire predictions did not come true, however. Instead, in the early post–Cold War era, "one after another of the ghastly and persistent civil wars came to an end." Even so, the idea of the post–Cold War era as an unleashing of violence, rather than its taming, has a hold on the popular imagination. Consider a recent volume of scholarly chapters on conflict management published by the U.S. Institute of Peace. Quite a few of the chapters mention that violence is decreasing. Yet, the book's foreword by the USIP's president says, "the world is no longer at peace, even a turbulent peace; the dogs of war are now rampant." Similarly, the volume editors begin the book by stating that hopes for "a new, more peaceful chapter in world history" have been "dashed." "Judging from its early years, the twenty-first century seems . . . no less dangerous or conflict prone than the century it succeeded." Only when previewing the chapters of the book do the editors notice a "surprising picture. . . . There is now compelling statistical evidence that the high-water mark of global conflicts came just as the Cold War was ending. Since then there has been a steady decline. . . ." In my view, this ability to hold two contradictory beliefs at once—the world is no less dangerous, and conflict has declined—reflects our confusion in thinking about war. ✓

COLD WAR AND AFTER
COMPARED WITH THE WORLD WARS

Now take it all in, the Cold War and the post–Cold War, everything since 1945. Step back into the time machine, and set the dial for the World Wars.

World War II killed something like five to ten million per year, depending whom you include—at least a hundred times higher than today's rate. Not only the scale but the indiscriminate nature of the violence was appalling. The Japanese rape of Nanking in 1937 resulted in the killing of "likely some 200,000 Chinese civilians and unarmed soldiers . . . and this was not an isolated case." Repeatedly Japanese soldiers massacred the inhabitants of towns and cities they captured, "executed suspected former nationalist soldiers, beat to death or buried alive those disobeying their orders or showing insufficient respect, and mistreated many others. Much of this killing was done in cold blood, and as thoughtlessly as one would swat a fly." The Japanese army also used biological warfare, such as the release of plague-infected flies to cause epidemics in the Chinese population. Nazi and Japanese bombing campaigns were "ruthless in their attacks on civilian targets. In China alone, the Japanese killed an estimated 560,000 Chinese civilians from the air. . . ."

British and American forces for their part "took aerial bombardment to new levels of deliberate civilian massacre." Using models of German and Japanese towns built in U.S. deserts to calculate outcomes from various mixes of bombs and wind patterns, the U.S. and British bombing campaigns created firestorms in cities, with intensely lethal fire and strong winds that sucked oxygen away from living creatures.

The raid on Hamburg in July 1943 fried and seared the bodies of a reported 45,000 adults and children whether in streets, buildings, or air-raid shelters. In Dresden a similar raid lasting fourteen hours inflicted the same torturous death on between 25,000 and 40,000 civilians. These fire-bombings were used against some fifty German cities and later, in 1945, on five Japanese cities including Tokyo, where 100,000 were killed in six hours.

The Tokyo raid used 279 bombers to drop 1,665 tons of incendiary bombs on urban areas containing 100,000 residents per square mile with almost all buildings constructed of paper and wood. The expansive fire reached eighteen hundred degrees Fahrenheit, boiling people who took refuge in rivers and canals, and making bomber crews wear oxygen masks to keep from vomiting as updrafts carried the "stench of burning flesh" up to their elevation of five thousand to ten thousand feet.

The firebombings were more efficient than previous methods, killing more people with fewer bombs and the loss of fewer bombers. Two months later, in a far more extensive campaign using incendiary bombs as the majority of tonnage dropped, the United States bombed sixty-four Japanese cities, nearly every Japanese city and town down to those with fewer than 50,000 residents. This campaign killed hundreds of thousands of civilians, wounded hundreds of thousands more, and left 8 million homeless. The atomic bombings of Hiroshima and Nagasaki later in 1945, which together killed about 200,000, differed in technology but not really in scale from the previous firebombings of Germany and Japan.

In the air war against Germany alone, 52,000 Americans died. The bombing campaign was very lethal for the bombers: "Of the 125,000 men and women who served in the British Bomber Command, about 56,000 were killed, about 28,000 injured, and 11,000 taken prisoner." The fire-bombings, the Nazi holocaust, Japanese atrocities in China, and a massive amount of conventional combat made World War II historically exceptional in the sheer scale of violence and its brutality.

Twenty-five years earlier, World War I saw a horrific level of violence. It was called simply the Great War. The battlefields were vast wastelands where artillery barrages had leveled every tree and soldiers lived underground in horrid conditions, only to periodically charge against enemy machine-gun fortifications while trying to survive chemical weapons attacks. At the battle of Passchendaele, in Belgium in 1917, for over three months the British used five tons of artillery for every yard of front line, then lost 400,000 men in a ground attack that failed. A British naval blockade against Germany "caused an estimated 800,000 deaths among German civilians as the result of hunger." In the end, something on the order of 10 million military and probably a like number of civilian deaths resulted directly from the war, not counting epidemics and other indirect war deaths. And worst of all, twenty years later they had to do it all again, only bigger.

In short, and with no doubt whatsoever, the comparison of the past fifty years with the previous fifty shows a dramatic decrease in warfare.

II. The "Bloodiest Century"?

One often hears that the twentieth century was the bloodiest, most war-torn century of all human history. Critics, however, say this claim "has no scientific basis." The twentieth century was bloody, all right. But was it the bloodiest ever? To answer this, we will need the time machine to take us back through previous centuries for comparison.

THE TWENTIETH CENTURY COMPARED WITH PREVIOUS CENTURIES

Before getting in, however, consider how wrongly framed the question is. The so-called twentieth century is an arbitrary span of time—a convenience. If we had five fingers instead of ten, and a century lasted fifty years, we would find 20A and 20B, the two fifty-year periods, so different that combining them would seem very strange. (Incidentally, China, like the world, experienced a particularly violent twentieth century, but again the violence was concentrated earlier in the century, with the last few decades dramatically more peaceful.) ↲

Yet many writers equate the extraordinary violence of the World Wars with the entire twentieth century. Historian Niall Ferguson defines an "era of truly global conflict" from 1904 to 1953. But then he calls it a Hundred Years' War and puts "twentieth century conflict" in the subtitle. The century and 1904–53 are not the same thing!

By one count, the twentieth century had 87 million war deaths (split 60–40 civilian to military), of which more than 85 percent were in the two World Wars. So what we are really talking about is a twin explosion of violence on an incredible scale, altogether consuming ten years over a span of thirty. Everything before, between, and after the World Wars was run-of-the-mill war, horrible as it is.

Nevertheless, let us go ahead and spread those ten years of extreme violence across the century, mix in the lesser wars, and average it all out—"the twentieth century." Now push the lever past 1900 and back into the nineteenth century.

The "Peaceful" Nineteenth Century

The nineteenth century is generally considered a time of relative tranquility, making the shattering of that peace by World War I especially heartbreaking. This conception of the nineteenth century has some problems, although I end up concluding that world violence was lower in the nineteenth than the twentieth overall, perhaps half as violent relative to the world's population.

One problem with the "peaceful nineteenth century" idea is that people often begin it in 1815, very conveniently right after the end of the biggest war ever known until then, the Napoleonic Wars, which consumed the first fifteen years of the century. Since data were harder to collect for war years, the major political science databases for studying war begin in 1816, making the past seem more peaceful than it was.

A second problem is that even in the period after 1815, major wars occurred, mostly outside of Europe. The Taiping Rebellion in China (1850–64) took millions of lives violently and perhaps tens of millions indirectly. On both sides "massacre . . . was general." In Anhui Province, 70 percent of the population apparently died during the war. When the rebels took Nanking in 1853, they reportedly killed 25,000 people, and when the empire recaptured the city the next year they killed 100,000, in three days. Ultimately, a million people may have been executed by imperial troops as they put down the rebellion. At the same time, a Muslim uprising resulted in 5 million deaths out of 8 million inhabitants of Yunnan Province. The suppression of the rebellion was capped with the slaughter of 20,000 men, women, and children.

In Latin America, in 1864–70, the war of Argentina, Brazil, and Uruguay against Paraguay devastated and depopulated Paraguay, killing hundreds of thousands of people. To the north, the U.S. Civil War in mid-century killed more Americans—600,000+ battlefield deaths—than did the two World Wars. The war was the first to use industrial technologies for weapons of massive killing, such as more powerful rifles and artillery. As one Confederate general put it, "It was not war—it was murder."

In the North, about a million men were under arms at the peak, representing about 5 percent of the population. This compares with nearly 4 percent of Prussia's population called into military service during the war with France in 1870–71. During the twentieth century, by comparison, in peacetime armed forces totaled "around 1 per cent of the population or less, in line with their historical levels of sustainability," but shot up to 13 percent during the World Wars. Similarly, military spending remained below about 5 percent of GDP in Western countries during the Cold War, as it had in peacetime in the eighteenth and nineteenth centuries, but rose in wartime to more than 15 percent, and as high as 50 percent in the World Wars. Thus, the character of the nineteenth century does not seem radically different from the twentieth.

Europeans themselves participated in massive war violence in colonial areas in the nineteenth century. For several years starting in 1899, Britain fought the Boer War to subdue white settlers in South Africa and secure control of a territory fabulously rich with diamonds and gold. The civilized British engaged in indiscriminate looting, and burned some thirty thousand farms, turning out the women and children into the cold without food. In the atmosphere of the war, "looting, burning, and devastation were regarded as acceptable weapons with which to defeat the enemy." Some of the farm-burning expeditions turned to systematic rape of Boer girls. As in today's counterinsurgency wars, conventions of warfare were widely disregarded, as when Boer guerrillas wore British uniforms and made it impossible to distinguish friend from foe. Atrocities on both sides followed from "the gradual erosion of even the most basic rules of conduct in war."

As the war dragged on, the British massed Boer families in concentration camps. The practice drew upon the experience of Spain in Cuba in 1896–97, where about 200,000 Cubans died in concentration camps set up by Spain to counter an insurrection. By the end of the Boer War, the British operated forty-six camps in which contagious diseases ran rampant. An estimated 28,000 women and (mostly) children would die in the camps. More than 100,000 black Africans were put in their own concentration camps under even worse conditions, and 20,000 died. A scorched-earth policy "successfully laid waste" to the region, denying sustenance to the guerrillas and civilians alike.

The size and extent of the Boer War in no way compare with the World Wars, but it illustrates that the world's leading great power during the most peaceful interlude carried on systematic atrocities against civilians in colonial areas. A few years later, in 1904, in nearby South West Africa (today's Namibia), Germany put down an indigenous rebellion by driving the population into the desert, killing 80 percent. Such atrocities were not uncommon throughout the colonial world in the nineteenth century. Indigenous societies themselves, and not just colonizers, used brutal methods. The slave-trading nineteenth-century Dahomey Kingdom in West Africa, for example, practiced slaughter, torture, and cannibalism as it conquered its neighbors and sold their people as slaves. ✐

Both the nineteenth and twentieth centuries saw warfare intentionally target civilians. Hugo Slim, an expert on humanitarian aid, calls the "lulls when certain wars were fought more cleanly . . . tiny exceptions in humanity's long and bloody history. . . ." All-out genocide may be "relatively rare in human history. Massacre is not." Civilians who survive a war face terrible suffering long afterward as a result of experiences as "refugees, wounded, orphaned, widowed, paupers, enforced prostitutes, or detainees." Such consequences may result unintentionally from military activity but often they are "deliberately intended and designed." Killing and causing the suffering of civilians can serve military goals such as displacing a hostile population from coveted land, or punishing a population for supporting insurgents. These motivations applied to nineteenth-century wars such as the Boer War, to twentieth century wars such as World War II, and to Darfur in 2004.

The Sixteenth to Eighteenth Centuries

Easing back in our time machine from the nineteenth century to the sixteenth, seventeenth, and eighteenth, we find the state of war not very different. Wars in those centuries were brutal, and "many conflicts . . . combine features of what we now think of as warfare and genocide. . . ." Some centuries were better, some worse.

The seventeenth was a bad one. The Thirty Years' War "was an unmitigated catastrophe." Never before in German history "had there been so universal a sense of irretrievable disaster, so widespread a consciousness of the horror of the period. . . ." The war reportedly reduced Germany's population by as much as a third, with as many as 8 million killed, 95 percent of them civilians. However, historians more recently estimate the population loss as closer to "about 15 to 20 per cent . . . ," which is small comfort. Direct deaths were far outweighed by deaths caused by famine and epidemics, especially "the bubonic plague, which broke out in many parts of central Europe during the war." (However, not all plague deaths were caused by the war.) Less spectacular diseases carried by troops and spread to civilians—such as typhus, influenza, and dysentery—caused large-scale loss of life.

"The mortality among the civilian population was certainly as great in proportion, if not greater, than among the armies." Cities and towns were severely depopulated, often by half or more, and the economy was utterly ruined from agriculture to trade. In the words of one of the generals, "I would not have believed a land could have been so despoiled had I not seen it with my own eyes." Other estimates of the destruction are somewhat smaller. Nonetheless, "those Germans who survived the war to its end knew that it had been an unprecedented catastrophe for the German people. . . ."

For the military forces, "losses in battle usually seem to have been heavy. . . . If the two sides were evenly matched . . . the slaughter on the field was terrible. If, on the other hand, the odds were uneven, the defeat of the smaller force would be followed by hot pursuit and perhaps greater slaughter: Many fugitive soldiers, and sometimes entire units, might be killed in cold blood either by their adversaries or by the local peasantry." Nor was much care available for the sick and wounded. Conditions for the local population were desperate, and "everywhere the records describe frequent brutality by soldiers. . . ."

As the Thirty Years' War raged in Europe, the Manchu (Qing) conquest of the Ming Dynasty in China caused a huge loss of life. China's population reportedly dropped by 20 million from 1600 to 1650. This represents one of the three steep drops in Chinese population—the others being the nearly 30 million loss from 1200 to 1300 (the Mongol conquest) and the 20 million drop from 1850 to 1875 (the Taiping Rebellion). In 1681, a rebellion in Kwangtung was followed by the execution of 700,000 rebels. Experts have puzzled over the real number of war deaths in the period. But historical population estimates make clear that claims of deaths in the tens of millions during this war period are credible.

The centuries after about 1500 were also notable for the intensity and brutality of colonial wars of conquest. To give one example, in 1603, the Spanish authorities in the Philippines ordered a massacre that killed more than 20,000 ethnic Chinese. In the Americas, the European wars of conquest proved extremely lethal to native populations. Especially notable were the collapse of the Aztec and Inca civilizations, "two of the largest empires known at the time." "Central Mexico's population fell from nearly 15 million in 1519 to 1.5 million a century later, and there was a similar demographic collapse of Andean America." In all, something like "20 million Indians died in the encounter" with Europe.

Some Native American deaths resulted from cruel violence, especially at the hands of the Spanish conquistadors. Contemporaneous observers stressed the brutal exploitation of the Amerindian population by the Spanish. For example, the Spanish commander at the Aztec capital in 1520 "ordered the slaughter of masses of unarmed religious celebrants in the temple. The carnage was terrible. . . . Spaniards fell on the packed throng, cutting off arms and legs and disemboweling their victims in a slaughter that continued until virtually everyone was dead."

More deaths came about indirectly through overwork and exploitation in mines and plantations. One eyewitness, Bartolomé de Las Casas, reported, "The newborns died soon, because their mothers, because of the hardship and hunger, had no milk in their breasts. For this reason, while I was in Cuba, 7,000 children died in three months." The greatest effect, however, was the devastation caused by diseases introduced by the Europeans.

THE MIDDLE AGES

Now push the lever in our time machine back to the Middle Ages, the age of chivalry, of knights and ladies, where stylized rules governed warfare under a code of honor. The reality was that warfare was frequent—in the fifteenth century "warfare of one kind or another was extremely prevalent"—and these wars were extremely brutal, far less "civilized" than today's. Michael Prestwich's study of English warfare in the Middle Ages notes that "war was savage, and codes of chivalry did little to soften its impact." Richard I was "one of the most apparently glamorous and chivalrous of medieval soldiers" but his concept of war involved "the ravaging of enemy territory."

A contemporaneous account of the sack of the city of Limoges in 1370 by Edward, Prince of Wales ("the Black Prince"), illustrates the limits of chivalry: "All ranks, ages, and sexes cast themselves on their knees before the prince, begging for mercy; but he was so inflamed with passion and revenge that he listened to none, but all were put to the sword, wherever they could be found." Prestwich notes that "it is not easy to reconcile head-hunting, the savage mutilation of the defeated, massacres, and the mistreatment of women with . . . knightly cultures." In particular, Edward I's campaigns contained "very little . . . that fits a chivalric model." Yet, "Limoges was not an exception atrocity." "Virtually all medieval siege commanders" committed atrocities. "The conventions of medieval siege warfare allowed free rein to a besieger when a town or stronghold was taken by storm." "Harsh action after a capture by storm . . . was accepted as a convention of war."

Another feature of medieval warfare was the large "scale of destruction of the property and lives of non-combatants. . . ." Contemporaries complained that warfare was becoming more uncivilized but in fact "the practice of waging war by destroying civilian property and slaying noncombatants was a constant theme" throughout the Middle Ages. "Henry of Anjou, in 1149, proceeded by 'pillaging all that came in his way and setting fire to houses and churches everywhere,' while the son of King Stephen of England, Eustace, responded by 'ordering his men to set fire immediately to the houses everywhere, to kill those who came in their way and commit indiscriminately every cruelty they could think of,'" in the words of one contemporary observer quoted by Prestwich. The atrocities of war were not committed just by common soldiers out of control. "Many of the horrors . . . were the responsibility of men of rank. Chivalry and atrocity were often proved to be close bedfellows."

In actual battles, "the sheer press of men and horses in the mêlée could create scenes of appalling horror." At the famous battle of Agincourt in 1415, "men clambered up on the bodies of their fallen comrades, only to fall themselves. Macabre heaps of suffocating men and corpses were formed, up to six feet in height." After the mêlée phase came the rout, during which "the bulk of casualties occurred." Soldiers drowned en masse if forced to cross a river during a retreat. Overall, "the evidence for the casualty rates in medieval battles is contradictory," but most estimates count thousands or tens of thousands of deaths in each major battle. Furthermore, improvements in armor did not lead to a decrease in casualties and the levels rose sharply with the Hundred Years' War— an estimated 40 percent casualties at two key battles. Indeed, the battle of Agincourt "was a slaughter on an astonishing scale." Also, "the execution of hostages and prisoners was a feature of medieval warfare. . . ."

Siege warfare saw the worst atrocities. For starters, "the principal siege weapon was starvation," and disease accompanied war everywhere—"typhus was called the 'war plague' because it occurred in every modern war up to the mid-1800s." Jim Bradbury's book on the medieval siege explains that when a town was besieged it could negotiate terms of surrender, which would at least usually be honored (and might include the survivors' fleeing, paying tribute to the victors, etc.). But if this did not occur and the town was taken by storm, it had no protection, and all manner of atrocity could be legally inflicted. As the medieval period progressed, "atrocities and ruthless behavior" only increased. "The common man, the infantry soldier, rarely benefited from any Christian mercy." After William the Conqueror took Alençon by storm in 1051, he "cut off the hands and feet of the offending garrison," which had insulted him during the siege.

Massacres and mutilations were by no means confined to the soldiers of a garrison, but freely inflicted on civilians. "At Ghent 1,200 were either raped or killed. When the French took Winchelsea, the women in the church were raped and killed. At Caen 2,000 were killed in the market. . . . At Roche-Darrien, Philip VI allowed the massacre of the citizens, though the garrison was given a safe conduct." Indeed, "rape was a constant factor in the sequel to capture by storm, and was perpetrated by all nations. . . ." ✓

The Crusades featured many massacres and atrocities. In the First Crusade in 1096, Christian crusaders on their way to the Holy Land paused in the Rhineland to massacre thousands of Jews. When they arrived in Jerusalem they massacred thousands of Jews and Muslims— men, women, and children. They "slaughtered until the streets ran with blood." When they took the town of Acre, "Moslem captives were taken out of the city and slaughtered" after a ransom for them was not paid on time. In the Fourth Crusade, a Christian army committed atrocities against a Christian city, Constantinople. Its conquest in 1204 led to "an orgy of massacre and pillage, . . . all by the book so far as medieval siege conventions are concerned, but a travesty of crusading ideals." And earlier, during the Albigensian Crusade, after the taking of Béziers by storm "all within were slaughtered" even though some were orthodox Catholics like the Crusaders.

War between groups that hated each other only increased the atrocities. When Turks reconquered Jerusalem in 1244, "many Christians were killed" despite a safe-conduct agreement in the surrender. Similar massacres in violation of agreements followed the Turks' capture of Safed in 1265 and of Acre in 1291. In 1453, the Ottoman Turks conquered Constantinople and unleashed "an orgy of looting" and massacre as part of a (Muslim and Christian) tradition of sacking cities for three days and then restoring order.

The Mongol Conquests

Outside Europe, "in all areas, massacres were equally common." The Mongol conquests in East and Central Asia in the thirteenth century took matters to extremes. In 1219–21, under Genghis Khan, the Mongols swept through Khorassan in Persia. After capturing Bokhara in 1219 they massacred 30,000 of its inhabitants, and followed the next year with the massacre of 30,000 at Samarkand, 50,000 in Kazvin, 70,000 in Nessa, and 70,000 in Sebzevar. Later they reportedly killed all the inhabitants of Rayy, a city of 3,000 mosques, and spent a week burning down Herat and killing its 1.6 million people when it rebelled after being let off easy (only its garrison of 12,000 killed) after its initial surrender.

When the Mongols captured the capital, Urgench (Gurganj), they massacred its unarmed inhabitants, reportedly 1.2 million to 1.7 million people, plus the cats and dogs. The heads of men, women, and children were piled into separate pyramids. Nishapur's inhabitants were "killed, the town razed and ploughed over." The Mongols killed another 700,000 to 1.3 million in Merv, where it took four days to evacuate the inhabitants and thirteen days to count the bodies after they were massacred. Merv had been "the pearl of Central Asia," with mosques, mansions, and ten libraries containing 150,000 books, "all sustained by cool water flowing through tunnels from a dam across the River. . . ." After its capture, "the place was ransacked, the buildings mined, the books burned. . . ."

Genghis Khan's biographer, John Man, writes that the 1.3 million reported killed at Merv, on top of the 1.2 million in Urgench, "sounds simply incredible" but "is a more than possible death toll for Merv. . . ." Indeed, he concludes that genocides such as the Nazi Holocaust or the Rwandan genocide cannot match what the Mongols did to Merv. Given the Mongols' attitudes and skills, "it is technically possible for them to have killed perhaps 3 million or more people in the two-year course of their invasion of the Muslim empire." But, Man notes, the stories of everyone getting killed often are followed by later episodes where there are more people (to get killed). "It is impossible to say" how many died. "There was no census, and all numbers are little more than guesses." Based on probable populations of the area, Man concludes that something on the order of one and a quarter million people may have been killed over the two years. "It was still one of the biggest mass killings in absolute terms in history; and in proportional terms, perhaps the biggest. . . ."

In China, the Mongols' scale of killing was no smaller. In 1226–33 Genghis Khan capped his career with the total extermination of an entire people, the Tanguts in China, who had failed to supply him horses and men for a war. "The Tanguts almost vanished from history, along with most of their records. . . . It is unlikely anyone will unearth an account of the carnage, because there was no-one left to write it." In China, a recorded population of 40 million dropped to about 10 million in just a few decades early in the thirteenth century. The conquest and rule of China in 1279–94, after Genghis Khan's death, brought the slaughter of nearly 20 million Chinese according to one Chinese writer—a number that may be considerably exaggerated but nonetheless indicates a vast scale of killing.

In its campaign to Europe, the army of Genghis Khan's grandson killed everyone at Bamian and massacred the inhabitants of "Riajan in 1237, Vlad in 1238 . . . [and] Kiev in 1240." When they reached Pest on the Danube River in 1241, the Mongols "stormed into the large Dominican monastery, killed the 10,000 people who had taken refuge there, and burned the building to the ground." In one victory in Russia, the Mongols counted the dead by cutting off the right ears—270,000 of them. "When the Mongols took Alamut [in 1256], they seem to have carried out a census of the population, as if for taxation purposes, but then put all to death." In 1258 when the caliph of Baghdad refused to surrender, the Mongols "captured the city, massacred 800,000 inhabitants, and razed the city. . . ."

A century and a half later, Tamerlane continued the Mongol conquests. According to the historian Arnold Toynbee, Tamerlane "razed Isfarain to the ground in 1381; piled 5,000 heads into minarets at Zirih in the same year; cast his Luri prisoners alive over precipices in 1386; massacred 100,000 prisoners in Delhi in 1398; buried alive 4,000 Christian soldiers of the garrison of Sivas after their capitulation in 1400; and built twenty towers of skulls in Syria in 1400 and 1401." Incidentally Uzbekistan has rehabilitated Tamerlane in recent years as a national hero.

The Mongols were not the only massacring army in the period. In the twelfth or thirteenth century, a sultan who invaded Bengal paid a reward for each of 180,000 Hindu heads cut off. In Central America, in 1487 the Aztecs inaugurated a new temple by slaughtering thousands of prisoners, although the conventional estimate of 80,000 in four days appears exaggerated. Still, "one conquistador wrote of a rack outside of Tenochtitlán with about 136,000 skulls," representing perhaps 1,500 each year for generations. ✓

The An Shi Rebellion in China, led by An Lushan in 756–63 A.D., supposedly killed more than 30 million, but this does not seem to hold up to scrutiny. The claim rests on censuses taken before and after the war showing, respectively, about 53 million and 20 million people. Historian Denis Twitchett's authoritative account of the period mentions the massacre of a garrison but not a massive depopulation. He warns that "we shall never get at the truth behind many of the events of the 740s and 750s—the materials simply do not exist." Historian C. A. Peterson notes bloody battles, such as one in which most of a 180,000-strong army was "annihilated." He indicates that "many of the war-affected areas . . . were partially depopulated," but apparently through large-scale migration rather than actual famine and death.

Pushing on back to the seventh century, Byzantium led an active military life "with 200,000 deaths claimed in its war against Persia . . . and another 200,000 in its war against the Arabs." And of course, as we move back through history, all these statistics on war deaths loom larger as a percent of the much smaller world population then.

In conclusion, Bradbury writes, "What to the modern mind are 'atrocities,' were a normal part of medieval war." Of course, most sieges did not end in storm but in a surrender on terms. "Having seen the normal consequences of being stormed: death, slavery, exile, loss of property, rape, torture, and almost any horror one could envisage, it is hardly surprising to find that far more medieval sieges were settled by agreement than allowed to go on to the bitter end." Then again, besieging armies often did not allow surrender on terms, since they "stood to lose all they might gain by loot from a storm attack." All in all, medieval warfare was not a model of civilized chivalry compared with today's barbarous warfare—quite the opposite.

ANCIENT WARFARE

Catch the time machine back to the ancient empires. They lived by war. In fact, for most of human history, writes Harvard psychologist Steven Pinker, "unexceptional features of life" included human sacrifice, slavery, conquest, genocide, assassination, rape as a spoil of war, and "homicide as the major form of conflict resolution." Pinker concludes that "violence has been in decline over long stretches of history, and today we are probably living in the most peaceful moment of our species' time on earth."

In 143 B.C., after conquering Carthage, the Romans burned the city to the ground, slaughtered 150,000 inhabitants out of a total of 200,000, and sold the rest into slavery. After several days of this slaughter, according to an eyewitness, troops brought in to clean up "shoved the dead and those still living into pits in the ground, using their axes and crowbars. . . . Human beings filled up the gullies. Some were thrown in head down, and their legs protruding from the ground writhed for a considerable while." When Athens, that wonderful democracy, defeated Melos during the Peloponnesian War in 415 B.C., it did what armies typically did—slaughtered all the men, raped the women, and took women and children as slaves.

From ancient times forward, "the raping of women seems always to have been a most terrible part of war. . . . Sexual enslavement was a norm in most raiding and warring societies." When Goths sacked Rome in 410 A.D., St. Augustine comforted the many rape victims, describing wartime rape as an "ancient and customary evil." Rape is not only a form of "loot" but a means of humiliating defeated enemy men who cannot protect their women. Nonetheless, "rape and sexual violence are not a feature of every war." Today, "rape is common but by no means universal and inevitable in war. . . . [It] seems to emerge most under certain conditions when it is ideological and deliberately humiliating, when military authorities see nothing wrong in it, or in loose sexual cultures in which predatory male behaviour . . . is already a peacetime norm."

In ancient times, as in later periods and still not infrequently today, looting was the norm in wartime. "Pillage has always been a core element of war. . . . Most pre-modern armies could not supply themselves and would not think to do so." Rome's invasion of North Africa in 256 B.C., for instance, "was a tale of torched villages, cattle raiding, and mass enslavement. . . . Roman soldiers were mainly paid . . . with the plunder from their campaigns." Furthermore, "in history, every army has plundered to some degree and often to extremes. Assyrians, Greeks, Persians, Muslims, Mongols, Crusaders, Nazis, and Communists all plundered cities and villages as they went about their wars." European museums are "filled with loot from early wars of colonial conquest."

In China, war took a vast toll in ancient times. Dynastic transitions were especially lethal. In the long transition from the Sui Dynasty to the Tang (618 A.D.) the population of 50 million dropped by two-thirds. The centuries of transition from the Eastern Han to the Three Kingdom period around 220 A.D. reduced population from an estimated 50 million to 7 million. And in 221–207 B.C., the Han Dynasty's replacement by the Qin reduced population from 20 million to 10 million.

The Assyrian Empire (1100–612 B.C.) was the most "ruthlessly militaristic [and] blatantly genocidal" of the ancient empires of Mesopotamia. One of its "most militarily successful and bloodthirsty warlords," Sennacherib (705–681 B.C.) said of the city of Babylon, "The city and its houses, from its foundation to its top, I destroyed. I devastated, I burnt with fire." "The principal business of the nation became war. . . . This was the first truly military society of history." Assyrian armies had almost 100,000 men, and "their exceptional cruelty and ferocity" supported a "calculated policy of terror. . . . It was not unusual for them to kill every man, woman, and child in captured cities."

Other Mesopotamian civilizations were also born at war. From 3000 to 2500 B.C., "Sumerian city-states were already at war and destroying one another, disputing territories, seizing each others' troops, and employing force to rob neighboring towns of their riches." And "there is every reason to believe that war dates back even further in Mesopotamia. Scenes depicted on Uruk 'cylinder seals'" from before 3000 B.C. show sovereigns "assisting in the cold-blooded execution of defeated prisoners."

War extended across the region and through the centuries in which early empires arose. From 3000 to 2000 B.C., the Eastern Mediterranean saw a "long succession of wars, invasions, and destruction." In the period before 1000 B.C., a "campaign was a huge raid, in which large regions were overrun, defeated armies slaughtered, cities destroyed, and entire peoples enslaved."

COMPARING MURKY BODY COUNTS

As is clear, the World Wars were not an abrupt reversal of centuries of peace so much as a sharp spike in the large-scale violence that went on throughout history. We could answer the question of whether the twentieth century was the bloodiest in history if we had estimates of historical war deaths. But putting numbers to the historical levels of war violence, in various times and places, turns out to be extremely difficult. Taking just recent centuries in Europe, some political scientists see a downward trend in war, others an upward trend, and others a series of ups and downs with no trend. The data get only murkier as one moves back through time and away from Europe.

Military historian Azar Gat, in a sweeping study of warfare, writes: "All in all, contrary to widespread assumptions, studies of war lethality, measured by military and civilian casualties, show no significant increase during the nineteenth and, indeed, the twentieth centuries in comparison to earlier historical periods, relative to population." Others have argued that war-related deaths in the twentieth century, relative to global population, were nearly triple those of the nineteenth and quadruple those of the seventeenth centuries.

One recent analysis studied 655 wars from 1816 to 2007 (each with 1,000+ battle deaths per year). Looking at the long sweep of time, and considering just the number of wars rather than their size, the researchers conclude that "there is no specific pattern evident in terms of an overarching decline or increase in the onset of wars. . . . There are peaks and valleys in the onsets of war but the pattern in the post-1945 era is not substantially different from patterns in the nineteenth century." It is true, they write, that "there has been a decline in wars over the past decade," but "the view from a longer historical period reveals that the number of war onsets rises and falls with great frequency." British sociologist and politician Evan Luard, writing before the Cold War ended, saw only increasing violence in his long-term study of war, except in Europe.

Various scholars have tried to compare numbers of war deaths over the centuries. All agree on one thing, that the entire enterprise is shaky. The problem is not so much the twentieth century, although estimates do vary depending on what one includes. A reasonable estimate is 110 million war deaths in the century, about two-thirds of them civilian, if you include war-induced famines and epidemics, and something closer to 60 million (two-thirds of them military) if you count only battle-related deaths. There were just over 4 billion total deaths in the century from all causes. Therefore direct war deaths made up about 1.5 percent of deaths worldwide in the twentieth century—or perhaps double that if you include indirect war deaths.

Corresponding guesses for the nineteenth century come in at about half the twentieth century level. For wars of the seventeenth to nineteenth centuries, the Russian sociologist Pitirim Sorokin (writing in the 1930s) estimated the war casualties (killed and wounded, military only) for nine European countries. Overall, he puts these at the equivalent of about 2 percent of all deaths for the seventeenth and eighteenth centuries and about half that for the nineteenth.

In the thirteenth century, the world's population was one-seventh that of the twentieth century, so the total number of deaths from all causes must have been something like 600 million (allowing for shorter life expectancy). If the Mongols indeed killed some 20 million in their conquests that century, this represents something like 3 percent of the world's deaths in the century, a figure that at least equals that of the twentieth century. But, the Mongol estimate being so rough, we really do not know whether the thirteenth or twentieth century was bloodiest.

In ancient Greek and Roman war, Sorokin finds overall casualty rates relative to population that "do not differ greatly" from those in Europe in recent centuries (before the twentieth). In Greece, the fourth century B.C. was the bloodiest. Casualties in ancient Greece (military killed and wounded) reached about 4 percent relative to population in that century, a level roughly equivalent to Europe in the seventeenth century (the Thirty Years' War). Rome reached 6 percent in the third century B.C. and 3 percent in the first century B.C. In other centuries, Greece and Rome ranged from well under 1 percent to below 3 percent. Sorokin considers these figures extremely rough. He calls the whole exercise a "'guessy' adventure."

I think that we can conclude from this guessy adventure that the twentieth century may indeed have been the bloodiest relative to population but is not really much different in character than earlier "bad" centuries. Historian Niall Ferguson concludes that the twentieth was "the bloodiest century in European history, in relative as well as absolute terms. It is less certain that the same can be said for Asia. . . ." Perhaps, he concedes, the century "was not so uniquely bloody. . . ."

III. Prehistoric War

Step back into the time machine and set the dial all the way back, to prehistoric times. Would you emerge to find a peaceful world, or a brutal world of incessant violence among groups of humans?

There are two ways to answer this, if you do not have an actual time machine—direct evidence dug up at archaeological sites and evidence from hunter-gatherer societies observed in modern times. Both show a "high fatality rate from warfare. . . . Twenty-five percent of deaths due to warfare [among adult men] may be a conservative estimate. Prehistoric warfare was common and deadly, and no time span or geographical region seems to have been immune." This is the conclusion of the foremost authority, Harvard archaeologist Stephen LeBlanc, and other experts agree.

MODERN-DAY PRESTATE SOCIETIES

Some decades ago many people believed that modern hunting–gathering societies were especially peaceful. Evidence has now shown conclusively that the opposite is true. One survey of thirty-one hunting–gathering societies found that twenty typically had warfare every year or two, and only three had "no or rare warfare."

Death rates from warfare in prestate societies seem to average around 15 percent of the population, or 25 percent of the men. "Time and time again, both archaeologically and historically, death rates due to warfare of 25 percent of the men over their adult lives, and perhaps 5 percent of the women in addition to many children, are recorded."

"Estimates of hunter-gatherers' mortality rates in fighting . . . are inherently tenuous, yet they tally remarkably with one another, even though they were formed wholly independently from each other. . . ." Azar Gat summarizes these mortality data: The Murngin of Arnhem Land, Australia, over twenty years, 30 percent of the men; the Tiwi over a decade, 10 percent of men; Blackfoot Plains Indians, 1805, 50 percent of men dead and in 1858, 33 percent. For primitive agriculturalists, the data resemble those for hunter-gatherers: The Yanamamo of Brazil, 15 percent of adults, 24 percent of males; the Waorani (Auca) of Ecuador over five generations, 60 percent of adult deaths; Highland Papua New Guinea, the Dani, 28 percent of men from all violence; the Enga, 35 percent; the Hewa, 0.8 percent of the population per year; the Goilala, 19 percent of the population killed over thirty-five years.

In searching for reasons why warfare was so common, LeBlanc discounts reasons such as revenge or prestige, and focuses on conflicts over scarce resources, "land, food, or even access to women for wives"—but most often food. In southern California, "direct skeletal evidence of violent deaths in the area surges from around 5 or 6 percent up to about 18 percent of all adults when there is also skeletal evidence of poor health."

DIGGING UP EVIDENCE

Archaeology in North America shows extensive evidence of violent deaths. At a site in Ohio, 22 percent of adult male skulls had wounds. In Illinois, 16 percent of people buried in a prehistoric cemetery site had died from violence. At a site in South Dakota, "almost 500 people of both sexes and all ages were killed and their village was burned. The inhabitants were mutilated before or after death"—all of this hundreds of years before Europeans arrived. "Sad to say, the act of massacring civilians is as ancient as war itself."

LeBlanc presents detailed evidence from archeology to contradict the "myth" that human beings used to be peaceful and have become more warlike through time. He rejects the French philosopher Jean-Jacques Rousseau's claim, in the 1750s, that human beings in their natural state were gentle "noble savages." Similarly, he challenges the "popular belief . . . that only after the development of 'civilization' or highly complex societies" did war begin to develop. In truth, "warfare was *quite* common in the past." Indeed, "the real history of warfare shows that it has declined over time. . . . There has been a decline in actual war deaths, on a per capita basis, as societies become complexly organized."

LeBlanc came slowly to this realization. After digs on three continents over thirty years, he came to "realize that wherever I have dug, regardless of the time period or place, I have discovered evidence of warfare. . . . I never chose to . . . excavate with the purpose of finding warfare. The evidence just turned out to be there. . . ." Other archaeologists were similarly slow to reach this conclusion. Paleontologist Lawrence Keeley writes that only after many years of excavating "skeletons with embedded projectile points" did he question his "acceptance of the traditional view that the native peoples of California had been exceptionally peaceful."

LeBlanc argues that tribal societies typically had, and have, quite frequent and brutal warfare. "Warfare among farmers organized as tribes is some of the most violent. . . ." In tribal warfare, "very rarely are men ever taken captive—except to be publicly killed later, often including torture." As tribes grow into chiefdoms, "the total deaths due to warfare actually decline," possibly by half. "The average commoner in a state-level society was far more likely to die of malnutrition or outright starvation than expire on the battlefield." LeBlanc argues that "though warfare may seem more terrible as a group's social and technological complexity develops, the opposite is actually true." Incidentally LeBlanc suggests that today's "warlords" represent "really chiefdom-level social organizations embedded in quasi states." Societies such as Rwanda, Somalia, Sudan, and Afghanistan contain "chiefdoms, and in some cases even tribal farmers, scooped up into a state but not really part of it."

At the state level, much effort goes into building fortifications and fleets, with all-out violence becoming yet more episodic and less constant. Whereas a tribal society might field 20 percent of its total population for battle, a large state army such as that of Egypt (30,000 men) was "minuscule" by comparison since it was drawn from a large society, and the "state-level armies of medieval Europe" of similar size fought for states with millions of citizens. "Certainly 25 percent of fighting-age men never died from warfare in state societies. . . . Even in the most violent epochs in Western Europe or Aztec Mexico, less than 5 percent of the population died from warfare. . . ."

Evidence from prehistoric sites excavated in Europe reinforce this picture. The population around Talheim, Germany, had been considered to be peaceful farmers in prehistoric times until a site excavated in the 1980s showed otherwise. Dating from around 5000 B.C., it was a "communal grave containing the remains of 34 individuals (18 adults and 16 children) all piled on top of one another and all having suffered a violent death. . . . These bodies were evidently thrown quickly and carelessly into a pit for disposal."

At another site, in Austria, a settlement from around 5000 B.C. held "67 bodies . . . all of which showed signs of a violent death. . . . 39 of the 40 skulls found were smashed and there are signs that multiple strikes and injuries were inflicted." Newer excavations near Mannheim, Germany, found skull fragments belonging to more than 300 individuals. "These skulls show definite signs of deliberate damage: the majority were smashed. . . . Many belonged to children." In all three of these European sites, the "communities were originally thought to have been calm, united, and fraternal. The new discoveries seem to suggest that they were, in fact, violent, barbaric, and brutal." Meanwhile, in France, evidence of arrow-inflicted injuries from the Neolithic age includes forty-four confirmed sites.

A grave site in Sudan dating from 12,000–10,000 B.C. contained at least 59 individuals, of which "a large proportion . . . were massacred" as evidenced by various blows, injuries, and embedded projectile points. The population represented there "suffered 'mass' violence affecting all age groups—young and elderly males, adult females, and children."

Rock paintings in caves in Spain dating from 10,000 to 5,000 B.C. "include several depictions of battle scenes," including groups of archers facing off and shooting each other with arrows. Similar artwork has survived in Australia, southern Africa, and the American plains. In Australia, "fighting scenes with the whole range of armaments are extensively depicted in Aboriginal rock art dating back at least 10,000 years."

These Australians, an estimated 300,000 people, pursued an extremely simple hunting-gathering way of life, and were so isolated until Europeans arrived in the late eighteenth century that they did not even have bows and arrows. But "warfare, with spear, club, stone knife, and wooden shield (unlike the others, clearly a specialized fighting rather than a hunting device) had been widespread. . . ."

Dating of fortifications at Jericho (6000 B.C.) and Catal Huyuk in Anatolia (7000 B.C.) show "that Neolithic men were waging organized warfare centuries before the invention of writing or the discovery of how to work metal." Going back further, to Neanderthals who lived more than thirty thousand years ago, "more than 5 percent of . . . burials show violence of one form or another. This is about as high a rate of evidence for violent deaths as is found for much more recent skeletal samples from around the world. Since many violent deaths do not leave skeletal evidence, one can surmise that Neandertal deaths from warfare were about the same as the 5 to 25 percent for more recent foragers. . . ."

THE QUESTION OF CAUSALITY

In sum, after centuries of ups and downs, never as bad as prehistoric times, war peaked in the World Wars. War has decreased since then and stands at perhaps an all-time low. I do not claim that the trend away from war is inevitable, irreversible, or even necessarily stable. That remains to be seen. Some deep-seated forces in human society still push toward the outbreak of new, large wars. Still, hope is an appropriate response to the world situation regarding war and peace.

But to what do we owe our good fortune? Several possible causes come to mind.

First is the notion that civilization has evolved over the long course of human history in a way that has gradually strengthened norms of behavior that discourage violence. Later in the book I will discuss evidence that changing norms have reduced barbarity in general, from torture and slavery to capital punishment, while building up an idea of human rights and the responsibility of governments to their people. As part of this process, war has gone from a standard and even attractive policy option to a last resort, at least in political rhetoric. One trouble with this explanation is that it would predict a gradual diminishing of war over the centuries, whereas instead we have found a long series of ups and downs culminating in the horrific World Wars.

A second explanation is that the invention of nuclear weapons made great wars impractical and gave political leaders pause when considering the use of force. Nuclear deterrence may in fact help to explain why World War III did not occur during the Cold War—certainly an important accomplishment. But nuclear weapons did not stop the superpowers from participating in destructive wars such as the American war in Vietnam and the Soviet one in Afghanistan. And nuclear weapons do nothing to help explain the most striking trend in the post-1945 world, the reduction of war from the Cold War era to the post–Cold War era even as the number of nuclear weapons fell dramatically.

Third, the theory that prosperity makes societies more peaceful does what nuclear weapons cannot, namely explain the reductions of war in recent decades when economic growth has lifted large swaths of humanity out of poverty and given people something to live for. The trouble here is that prosperity in Europe a hundred years ago did not dampen humanity's appetite for war. It just gave the European powers more resources to fight the World Wars with, and they threw every dime they had into the effort.

Fourth, the idea that democracies do not fight each other (discussed in Chapter 11) does help to explain the diminishing of interstate wars as more countries have become democratic. But it falls short in explaining why nondemocratic countries such as China have also followed the trend to less war (big-time in China's case), nor why civil wars are also becoming less virulent in recent years.

Fifth, the end of the Cold War certainly helps explain the big reductions in war violence after 1989. During the Cold War era, each superpower provided support to governments or rebels in proxy wars in Asia, Africa, and Latin America. As we shall see in Chapter 11, rebellions do not continue without sources of funding and weapons, be it from control of diamond mining, from sympathetic diaspora communities, or from foreign governments. Of these sources, support from outside governments, especially from superpowers, is by far the most important. It gives rebellions far more resources to fight on than would have been possible otherwise. The supply train from the Soviet Union to communist forces in Vietnam in the 1960s, or from America to anticommunist Islamists in Afghanistan in the 1980s, made those conflicts particularly deadly. Regardless of whether you blame the Soviet or American side for these proxy wars, the simple fact is that the superpowers' involvement in dozens of them around the world greatly increased the level of war violence during the Cold War years.

The end of the Cold War falls short as an explanation in several ways, though. It does not explain the decreasing levels of overall violence throughout the 1970s and '80s, well before the breakup of the Soviet Union. Nor does it explain the continuing decline in violence over the past twenty years, after the Cold War ended. Finally, we might ask whether the end of the Cold War itself reflected and constituted the declining war violence of our times, rather than seeing that event as an external shock to the system that caused violence to decline.

The kind of explanation we want would kick in mainly after 1945, and would accelerate after 1989. The UN system in general, and peacekeeping in particular, fit the bill in this regard. They are also the main big change in world politics that has characterized this era. Unlike prosperity or democracy, the *intent* of these developments was specifically to reduce war. And although we do not know exactly how much peacekeeping has contributed to peace, we do know that sending peacekeepers succeeds, on average, in reducing the chances of war breaking out again (as Chapter 5 will show).

In my view, the hopeful reductions in war over recent years and decades have multiple causes, not easily untangled. But the UN and peacekeeping are the central thread, and will be my main focus, though not the only one, in the chapters to come.

3

PALESTINE TO CONGO

The Invention of Peacekeeping, 1947–61

Step into the time machine, where we left it in prehistoric times, and push the lever full forward. The ups and downs of warfare over the centuries, with their drumbeat of atrocities, flash before us again. Then, the extraordinary violence of the World Wars explodes. Stop the time machine in 1945 and step out into the rubble.

This is the world the political leaders of the time faced: For all the progress in world civilization, massive and terrible wars had recurred. The attempts to solve the problem after the previous great war, in the League of Nations, had failed spectacularly. President Franklin Roosevelt was determined not only to win the war against Germany and Japan, but to "win the peace," as he put it, after the war ended. While World War II raged, Roosevelt put the State Department to work fashioning a new world organization that would correct the fatal problems of the League.

The new organization would need to have teeth, Roosevelt thought, and would need to give the great powers the main role. Those powers were the wartime allies—above all the United States, Britain, and the Soviet Union. They began working out Roosevelt's vision at the Tehran and Yalta summits and at a meeting with about fifty delegates in Washington, D.C., in 1944, just months after D-day and almost a year before the war's end. The Washington meeting needed a cool location to beat the summer heat, and borrowed a house in Georgetown with nice shady gardens, called Dumbarton Oaks, which the owners had recently given to Harvard University to house a museum and research center. The delegates, led by the U.S. secretary of state and the Soviet and British ambassadors to the United States, hashed out the nature and structure of the United Nations. Follow-up talks included China but not the Soviet Union. (Roosevelt insisted on giving China a place as a great power, despite Soviet reluctance.) Soon France was added, despite its postwar weakness. In 1945, in San Francisco, fifty countries signed the UN Charter to, as the preamble put it, "save succeeding generations from the scourge of war." Peacekeeping was not mentioned in the Charter; it would come later.

EARLY DAYS

The UN would not move to its permanent headquarters in Manhattan until 1952. Meanwhile it had several "shabby" temporary headquarters, including a college campus and a run-down hotel. By 1947, the Secretariat occupied a former gyroscope factory on Long Island, while the General Assembly met in a converted ice rink in Queens.

The job of actually running the UN fell not to the diplomats and heads of state who controlled it, but to a new group of pragmatic idealists—international civil servants. Scooped up from national diplomatic or political careers, they committed themselves to serving humanity as a whole. In this remarkable group, one remarkable man stood out. He was Ralph Bunche—African-American, professor, international civil servant, 1950 Nobel Peace Prize winner—and he would become "the founder, main architect, and director of UN peacekeeping operations."

Rising from a childhood of hardship and poverty, Bunche had earned a Ph.D. at Harvard, studying colonialism in Africa. In 1946, because of Bunche's expertise on colonialism, the State Department sent him to the UN to become the director of the Trusteeship Division. Trusteeship was a system in which the UN administered former colonial territories for years in preparation for independence. (The trusteeship process worked successfully, and went out of business in 1994 after the independence of the last trust territory.) Bunche's boss at the UN was from China, and *his* boss, the first UN secretary-general, was Trygve Lie from Norway. Bunche intended to help the UN get off the ground and set up mechanisms for trusteeship, then return to a professorship, according to Bunche's biographer and UN colleague, Brian Urquhart.

Instead, Bunche remained an international civil servant for the rest of his life. His race helped him at times win the confidence of postcolonial leaders suspicious of white Westerners and the United States. But being an American ruled out the possibility that Bunche could ever become secretary-general himself, since tradition barred from that position any citizen of the permanent five Security Council members (the United States, Britain, France, Russia, and China).

I. The Arab-Israeli Conflict, 1947–49

In 1947 the secretary-general put Bunche in charge of the UN Special Committee on Palestine (UNSCOP), which would investigate and make recommendations regarding the world's most explosive postcolonial situation, the end of the British Mandate (an earlier version of trusteeship) in Palestine. Bunche would organize the activities of, and draft the reports of, this committee, whose members ranged from "intelligent and earnest" to "rather a lightweight" to "a one-man sabotage team," in Bunche's words.

They were to visit Palestine and meet with representatives of all sides, but the Arab Higher Committee called for an Arab boycott of UNSCOP, while the Jewish side was severely divided. The official Jewish Agency favored partition of Palestine into a Jewish state and an Arab one, but Jewish terrorist groups—the Irgun and the Stern Gang—insisted on a Jewish state in all of mandate Palestine, which includes today's Israel, Palestine, and Jordan. At the heart of it all was the city of Jerusalem, where UNSCOP set up headquarters in the YMCA in 1947.

When UNSCOP first went to Jerusalem in 1947, Bunche wrote that the "British are everywhere and they all carry guns. As you go thru the streets you're constantly stopped by sentries. . . . Buildings are surrounded by barbed wire, pillboxes and road-blocks are abundant." Later, Bunche wrote of his arrival at Jerusalem's airport in 1948, "There was no paved strip then, just markers in the meadow, all the buildings had been destroyed." His plane "first swooped low over the field to drive the goats off and then bumped down. . . . What a mess of barbed wire and sandbag emplacements Jerusalem was. . . ."

Bunche wrote to a friend, "The longer we stay, the more confused all of us get. The only thing that seems clear to me after five weeks in Palestine is that the British have made a terrible mess of things here." The UN committee spent several weeks consulting, then retreated to Switzerland to write its report, which Bunche drafted. Palestine held prospects for success in the UN because the issue was not (yet) split along Cold War lines.

After Israel declared independence in 1948 and its Arab neighbors attacked, the Security Council quickly called for a cease-fire, and appointed a UN Mediator in Palestine, Count Folke Bernadotte from Sweden, to make it happen. The idea of a mediator "established the precedent of appointing a special representative of distinction and experience" to manage a conflict, an approach which is now standard in UN peacekeeping, most often under the title Special Representative of the Secretary-General (SRSG).

As the head of the Swedish Red Cross, Count Bernadotte wore a white uniform. When the UN chartered a DC-3 for his use as Mediator—a tool that few UN diplomats have had since then—he affixed both the UN and Red Cross insignias and had the plane painted white like his uniform. UN aircraft and vehicles have been white ever since. Bernadotte used his plane to dash around among the capitals negotiating agreements. Bunche wrote, "There has really never been anything like this. . . . We keep hopping from one place to another like mad in our plane and often on just a few moments' notice. As soon as we land anywhere we begin to confer and leave for some place else immediately the conference is over. I get practically no sleep and miss many meals." These efforts paid off with a truce, agreed June 9, 1948.

Bunche, because of his Palestine experience, was appointed Chief Representative of the Secretary-General in Palestine, to work with Bernadotte. Bunche was forty-four years old, and his appointment abruptly pulled him away from his wife and three children, not for the first time.

When his wife, Ruth, complained bitterly of his absence, Bunche wrote back, "We risk our lives out here almost everyday. We . . . stroll through sniper's territory—I stood last Saturday in Jerusalem on the spot where my friend Tom Wasson was killed."

On September 17, 1948, Bunche traveled from the island of Rhodes, which by then served as the headquarters of the Mediator mission, to Beirut, and then (borrowing Bernadotte's white plane) on to Haifa and finally Jerusalem. Because of a series of travel delays, Bunche was late in meeting up with Bernadotte, who went on ahead without him. Jewish extremists, members of the Stern Gang, blocked the road in front of Bernadotte's party, then went up to his car and shot him dead along with a French officer riding with him. "It just wasn't my time to go, I guess," Bunche wrote to Ruth. He had hoped to wrap up his work in Palestine quickly and get home to his family. Instead he took over from Bernadotte as Acting UN Mediator.

PEACEKEEPING 1.0

Bunche created a new enterprise to complement the mediation effort. The United Nations Truce Supervision Organization (UNTSO) was "the first UN peacekeeping operation, and there were no precedents for it. . . . Everything had to be improvised." Bunche "had not only to direct [UNTSO] but to elaborate the principles" for its work. As the first peace observer mission, it would create precedents for decades of later UN military observing.

The concept was to monitor the observance of a cease-fire and facilitate communications between the armed parties. Essentially, military observers would illuminate the murky interactions that go into upholding a cease-fire, providing accurate information and making sure the two sides could hear the other's version of events. Especially in the Palestine case, where playing to world public opinion and the international community was an important tool for each side, the prospect of bad publicity had deterrent value as well. If the international observers reported that your side started the shooting, it might reduce your negotiating power.

A first principle was to remain neutral. Bunche wrote in his plan for UNTSO that an observer "must be completely objective . . . and must maintain a thorough neutrality as regards political issues. . . ." Second, on Bunche's insistence, observers were unarmed, which did not come naturally to the military personnel participating in the operation. Bunche felt that carrying weapons would put the observers in greater danger, and that going unarmed would put the observers symbolically "above the conflict." Nonetheless, by September "six men, including the mediator, had been killed and seven wounded, and the observers, their vehicles, and their aircraft were frequently under fire."

Although identified with the blue UN flag, the UNTSO needed something extra to distinguish its flag from the Israeli flag of the same colors. Thus, the UNTSO painted its vehicles white, like Bernadotte's plane, with "UN" in large black letters. This has been the signature look of UN peacekeeping ever since.

Early UN peacekeeping missions, starting with the UNTSO, had one advantage that has diminished through the decades—they moved into action quickly. Today, it can take months to put together the troop contributions, the logistics, and the finances for a new peacekeeping operation. But the first UNTSO troops arrived in Jerusalem within two weeks of the Security Council's authorization of the mission in May 1948. After its quick start, however, the arrival of all sixty-three initial observers was "agonizingly slow." Bernadotte, who told the Security Council in mid-July that he needed 300 more observers to supervise the truce, became angry two weeks later when only 105 of them, and none of the 1,000 guards he wanted, had materialized.

The 1,000 armed UN guards had been requested by Bernadotte, over Bunche's reservations, to monitor Jerusalem. The first of these guards did not inspire confidence in the future of UN peacekeeping. "Sent to the area without indoctrination, training, or discipline," they misbehaved on their "first night on the town in Beirut" and were immediately sent back to New York. Later, Bunche would have to clean up "a smuggling ring that had developed among the temporary UN radio operators in Haifa."

Despite these problems, the UNTSO did effectively strengthen the truce between Israel and its Arab neighbors. Over the years, more wars would come, but little by little—starting from the 1948 truce—both Egypt and Jordan developed peace with Israel. It is a cold peace but a durable one. The UNTSO, like the Arab-Israeli conflict, has lasted for sixty years. It now has about 150 military observers supported by about 100 international civilian administrators and about 150 local civilian workers, on a budget of $66 million a year.

In his mediator role, Bunche spent nearly a year hammering out armistice agreements between Israel and its four Arab neighbors. This effort succeeded in 1949, and Bunche won the Nobel Peace Prize for it in 1950.

REDS IN THE UN?

Not everyone appreciated Bunche's work as much as the Nobel committee did, however. During the McCarthy era of the early 1950s, U.S. opponents of the UN whipped up the idea that communists ran the UN—this despite the very bad relations of the UN with the Soviet Union after the UN officially led the Korean War against the communists. (Communist China would not even become a UN member for twenty more years.) In late 1952, a federal grand jury accused "an overwhelmingly large group of disloyal U.S. citizens, many of whom are closely associated with the international communist movement," of infiltrating the UN. A Congressional committee claimed that UN officials participated in "a full-scale operation of subversive activities directed against the security of this nation."

President Truman, on his way out of office at the start of 1953, issued an executive order making all U.S. citizens working in international organizations subject to a loyalty investigation. An International Organizations Employees Loyalty Board was established. "This order was a serious blow to the Charter principle of Secretariat independence." Actually, the Soviet Union was no friend of this principle either. Soviet nationals at the UN took orders from Moscow and some used UN cover to spy on the United States. Years later, Secretary-General Pérez de Cuéllar noted that conservatives in the U.S. Congress "acted as if UN Headquarters served mainly as an outpost for the KGB" (the Soviet spy agency). And indeed while Pérez de Cuéllar "had no way of knowing which Soviet staff members were from the KGB, it was quite apparent that a number of them did not devote all of their time to Secretariat duties. . . . As a result, and to their understandable frustration, the Soviet nationals in my office were excluded from sensitive functions." By comparison U.S. citizens working at the UN showed more independence from their government. The development of a true international civil service, where members serve all nations rather than just their own, remains a work in progress.

By May 1954, the U.S. government had investigated more than 1,700 UN employees and held hearings on thirty-two of them, including Ralph Bunche. He was questioned and impugned for possible associations with possible communists years earlier. At the same time that Bunche was defending himself from these accusations, he was president of the American Political Science Association and a dinner guest at the White House. Bunche was officially cleared of all charges and suspicions, but right-wing opponents of the UN continued to resurrect them for years.

The UN's troubles in the United States were far from its worst problems in the early 1950s. You might think that its unpopularity with right-wing Americans would ensure its great popularity with the Soviet Union, but the opposite was true. After the 1949 Chinese revolution, the Soviets insisted that the new communist leadership of China replace the nationalists, holding out on the island of Taiwan, as China's representatives in the UN, including on the Security Council. When this did not occur, the Soviets unwisely boycotted the UN—a mistake they would not repeat again. With the Soviet Union absent, the UN took sides against North Korea when it attacked South Korea in 1950, creating the UN's "severest test of its five-year history. . . . The Organization was thus involved, by a freak of fate, in a collective military action directed entirely by a single great power," the United States. Meanwhile the Cold War brushed aside the concept of collective security in favor of new regional military alliances, notably NATO and the Warsaw Pact, that prepared for a potential new world war. When the first secretary-general's term ended, the Soviets blocked his renomination in punishment for his support of UN involvement in the Korean War.

MEET THE NEW BOSS

The great powers wanted the next UN secretary-general to be someone weak who "would concentrate mainly on the administrative problems and who would abstain from public statements on the political conduct" of the UN. "Such a careful and colourless official they thought to have found in Dag Hammarskjöld." He had grown up in Swedish political circles, the son of a prime minister, had studied economics and run a bank, among other technocratic jobs. He was an intellectual who followed developments in nuclear physics and wrote poems in a notebook he carried. He came across to many as a "reserved and cold member of the aristocracy. . . ." The outgoing secretary-general opposed the nomination because he thought Hammarskjöld would be "no more than a clerk."

In fact, Hammarskjöld would come to exemplify the ideal of an independent, activist secretary-general. President John F. Kennedy called him "the greatest statesman of our century." Journalist James Traub calls him "the standard against which all successive secretaries-general have been measured, and found wanting, for the very simple reason that the Security Council did not make the same mistake twice."

Hammarskjöld would be, after Bernadotte, the second Swede Bunche served, and the second one killed in the line of duty.

II. The Suez War, 1956

At first, Hammarskjöld kept Bunche off the Middle East, but in 1956, during another Arab-Israeli war, the secretary-general put Bunche back on the job. Israel had invaded Egypt, after guerrilla attacks on Israel from the Egyptian-controlled Gaza Strip. Two days later came a British-French invasion force to take control of the Suez Canal, which Egyptian president Nasser had recently nationalized. The crisis did not fit a typical Cold War pattern, since it split Britain and France from the United States. Israel had not yet developed close ties with the United States. Hammarskjöld "played a central role in getting the crisis under control. He was the leader in the effort to stop the fighting, to secure the withdrawal of the invading forces, and to provide the peacekeeping force."

Canadian diplomat Lester Pearson came to New York to address the General Assembly and proposed to Hammarskjöld an *armed* United Nations force authorized to use weapons in self-defense. He called it "a truly international peace and police force . . . large enough to keep these borders at peace while a political settlement is being worked out." Although doubtful of the idea at first, within days Hammarskjöld proposed such a force to the General Assembly, which backed the idea strongly. Britain and France, looking for a way out of what had been an ill-conceived intervention, had already said they would pull out of Egypt if a UN force went in. The Soviet Union considered such a force to violate the UN Charter, but did not oppose it because Egypt would benefit from it.

Authorization for the force came from the General Assembly, a "troubling" development given the Security Council's supposed role as sole holder of enforcement power in the UN. The whole operation "was done chiefly with the tolerance and not the leadership of the Great Powers, a disturbing sign for the future." Nonetheless, the proposal "was a masterpiece in a completely new field, the blueprint for a nonviolent, international military operation." Historian Paul Kennedy calls the creation of the force a "landmark event. . . . A new era had begun."

"Now, corporal, go and get me a force," Hammarskjöld instructed Bunche, teasing him with an imaginary low military rank. The new army would be called the United Nations Emergency Force (UNEF). Bunche and Hammarskjöld had already approached India, Norway, and Colombia about providing troops and, within two days, received additional offers from Sweden, Denmark, Finland, Czechoslovakia, Romania, and Ceylon (Sri Lanka). Bunche would say of the UNEF, "This is the most popular army in history, an army which everyone fights to get into." His first task was to turn away many disappointed ambassadors who offered troop contributions to the force but for one reason or another were not suitable as participants. Bunche and Hammarskjöld had already made a list of noncontroversial countries that might supply troops. Many contributing countries were part of the British Commonwealth; they found it easy to adapt to peacekeeping, having fought together as a coalition during the World Wars. The force did not include troops from the United States or the other permanent Security Council members. "The employment by the UN of armed troops instead of unarmed individual observers required new principles and rules, as well as command, staff, and logistical arrangements."

This was a profoundly new idea.

Many details stood between the concept and the implementation of UNEF. It was decided to dress peacekeepers in their national uniforms, rather than a UN uniform. (Bernadotte had given up his idea of "UN guards" in 1948, concluding that national uniforms would command more respect.) But some of the national uniforms were British-style, which was dangerous since the Egyptians were fighting the British. So as a common element, Bunche wanted to give them UN headgear, specifically a blue UN beret, which a sniper could easily identify (and, hopefully, *not* shoot at). However, not enough berets could be obtained in time to outfit the mission. So instead, UNEF bought war-surplus American helmet liners and spray-painted them blue, the UN color. Today, UN peacekeepers still use this signature look and peacekeepers are known widely as "blue helmets."

The UN established a United Nations Command for the new force, pulling in the chief of staff of UNTSO to run it. This was not the only way it could have happened. Hammarskjöld considered the alternative of charging "a country, or a group of countries, with the responsibility to provide independently for an international Force serving for the purposes determined by the United Nations." But Hammarskjöld preferred that a force be responsible directly to the UN, with its commander "fully independent of the policies of one nation. . . ."

The soldiers sent to the Suez Canal had ten days' supply of food with them. How would the UN feed them after that, with no logistics machinery of its own? The solution was to buy food sitting on board seventeen ships that Egypt had disabled in the Canal at the start of the war to impede British mobility. "Identity cards in four languages had to be formulated. . . . Tent stoves were another problem."

"The process of setting up UNEF took place in Bunche's conference room on the thirty-eighth floor [of the thirty-nine-story UN Secretariat Building in New York] and proceeded more or less round the clock. . . ." Brian Urquhart, who ran the working group there for Bunche, was the only one with actual military experience, having served in World War II. The planning included military representatives from the troop-providing countries and from the United States, which provided logistical support. The troop-providing countries—Norway, Canada, Brazil, Colombia, India, Pakistan, and Ceylon—also formed an advisory committee to assist the secretary-general.

Moving quickly was paramount, and Bunche was able to field the force within weeks. He pre-positioned the first troops in Italy, waiting for five days to move in quickly once Egypt gave approval. Bunche explained, "In this haste we wanted to demonstrate that the United Nations resolution was not an empty gesture, [and] to avoid the development of a vacuum in the area. . . ."

As an armed military force, UNEF (and every peacekeeping force since) has had to face the issue of national sovereignty. Israel would not allow UNEF to establish positions on its side of the border, and Egypt initially hesitated to let this international army operate on its territory. But eventually Egypt and the UN signed a status-of-forces agreement with such provisions as freedom of movement for the deployed peacekeepers, and holding the trials of peacekeepers in their home countries if accused of a crime in Egypt. The UN and Egypt also agreed, with Bunche's strong support, that peacekeepers would stop flying their national flags (as they had done at first), and fly only the UN flag.

And so the UN established the principle that any peacekeeping force needs the consent of the national government on whose territory it operates. A "holy trinity" of principles would govern traditional peacekeeping throughout the Cold War—"host state consent, impartiality, and minimum use of force."

The need for host state consent would later undermine UNEF when, in 1967, it had to comply with Egypt's demand to leave, and could not prevent a new all-out war with Israel. This pullout, although legally required, was later faulted by critics who said that Egypt's demand for UNEF to leave should not have been taken literally because it was intended for domestic political consumption. UNEF's withdrawal, they argued, showed "a lack of appreciation for the rules of political rhetoric in the Arab world."

In any case, UNEF successfully oversaw the end of the 1956 war. Its presence—4,100 troops at full strength—led directly to the French and British withdrawals, and it helped clear the disabled ships and get the Canal running. Israeli forces withdrew to the Armistice Line over the following six months.

UNEF was also the first UN mission to take on administrative tasks in a postwar society. After Israel withdrew from Gaza, UNEF moved in and ran the civil administration, although on a "purely temporary" basis. This foray into running a government would foreshadow major UN postwar missions decades later, such as in Cambodia, eastern Croatia, and East Timor. The Gaza operation succeeded, after a rocky start. On their first evening in Gaza, the international troops—lacking any knowledge of Arabic or Islam—heard the call to prayer from a minaret and took it for a call to civil disorder. They responded by spraying the minaret with machine-gun fire. After that, things settled down.

Bunche wrote, in a speech that Hammarskjöld delivered, that UNEF "in terms of potential effectiveness in performing its mission, must be rated as equivalent to a substantially larger military body." By 1958, according to Urquhart, "UNEF was generally recognized as a remarkable practical success as well as a triumph of innovative improvisation." To the peacekeepers themselves, Bunche wrote: "You are taking part in an experience that is new in history. . . . You are the front line of a moral force. . . . Your success can have a profound effect for good, not only in the present emergency, but on future prospects for building a world order. . . ."

Later, the UN would distinguish different phases and types of peace operations. "Peacemaking" would be diplomacy to achieve an agreement between warring parties, as Count Bernadotte had done in 1948. "Military observation" would be unarmed monitoring as UNTSO did. "Peacekeeping" would be armed intervention to make an agreement stick by giving belligerents confidence to stand down, as in UNEF. "Peace enforcement" would be the use of armed force to make a peace agreement stick, especially in the context of "spoilers" who seek to prolong the war. Finally, "peacebuilding" would refer to the many-sided ("multidimensional" or "complex") efforts to build stability in a country after war ends and prevent a return to fighting. Together this spectrum of efforts is known as "peace operations." At the time of UNEF, however, none of this conceptual apparatus was developed. Peacekeeping was whatever you came up with to keep a cease-fire from breaking down.

After UNEF, the UN did some military observing in Lebanon in 1958 (to see if Syria was sending arms and personnel to a rebel group). But for several years things were a bit quieter. The lull ended in 1960 when the Belgian Congo achieved its independence and fell into chaos.

III. Congo, 1960–61

By 1960, the year of Congo's independence from Belgium, the UN's days of meeting in a converted ice rink were more than a decade past. The ranks of experienced civil servants had grown. The dominant personality among them was Dag Hammarskjöld, who took a leading role personally in the Congo crisis of 1960–61 and died there in a plane crash.

If, as Ralph Bunche had observed, the British left Palestine a "terrible mess" when they departed in 1947, the Belgians had done far worse in the Congo. King Leopold II of Belgium had teamed up with the explorer Henry Morton Stanley in 1885 to colonize the Congo as a personal property of the king. Stanley used violence freely in making his way across the African interior, and wrote that "the savage only respects force. . . ." He founded a trading post that he named Leopoldville, which later became Congo's capital. The Congo has a vast interior and small coastline, because other European powers had stayed close to the coast and paid less attention to the interior, which was very hard for Europeans to reach because of disease. What the interior had, and the Belgians wanted, was mineral wealth of unprecedented quantity and quality—from gold and diamonds to tin and (later) uranium. Some 10,000 Belgian civil servants administered the huge territory, as large as Western Europe, with brutal efficiency.

A note on names may help avoid confusion. Across the Congo River from Leopoldville (now called Kinshasa) was Brazzaville, the capital of the *French* colony also called Congo. The French Congo is today the "Republic of Congo," while the Belgian Congo changed its name to Congo, then Zaire, then the Democratic Republic of the Congo, or DRC. Since the former French Congo plays no role in this book I will use "Congo" always to refer to the Belgian Congo/Zaire/DRC.

Leopold's personal rule lasted for twenty-three years, and resulted in the deaths of as many as 10 million Congolese, about half the population, through direct violence, overwork, famine, and European-introduced diseases. The territory, which Leopold called the Congo Free State, produced for him an estimated $1 billion (in today's dollars) in profits, primarily from raw materials exports. Body counts were verified to the white authorities by the presentation of baskets of severed hands, and torture was used freely on workers who did not meet quotas for rubber production.

In 1908, the Belgian government took control of the territory in the name of the state, in response to public opinion in Europe against the king's excessive violence. However, the violent exploitation continued. Murder, torture, and rape were used frequently in putting down the "savages" and keeping the minerals flowing. White Belgians held all positions of importance in the society, with the black population so underdeveloped that by the time of independence the number of Congolese with college degrees could fit in a living room—out of a population of more than 20 million.

In 1960, Belgium ended its rule abruptly and pulled out. Elections were held. The young, left-leaning Patrice Lumumba was chosen as prime minister, and independence day arrived the next month. The Belgian king gave an awful speech praising Leopold's work in the Congo, and went home. In the army, all the officers were white, and the soldiers, who were black, soon mutinied. This left a leaderless mass of armed soldiers attacking whites, who fled. The "mass exodus of Belgians included virtually all the administrators and technicians." This led to the "breakdown of essential services and all economic activity." The Belgian army came in, ostensibly to protect the remaining Belgians, and that prompted Lumumba to ask the UN to oppose an invasion.

Two weeks before independence, Hammarskjöld, already nervous, sent Ralph Bunche to Leopoldville to follow developments. A month later Bunche took charge of the newly authorized UN operation there. He lived through the dangerous days of the mutiny. Once he went to his hotel balcony to check out a commotion in the street below, and saw soldiers herding three Israeli diplomats and two British journalists along. "A soldier pointed his rifle at Bunche, who ducked back into his room just before the soldier fired." As in Palestine, Bunche felt that having a weapon would increase danger, and he asked his single armed guard to leave his gun behind when they traveled. When headquarters suggested he move across the river, out of the country, he declined, for fear of contributing to the panic among Westerners. The breakdown of order after independence was "more sudden and catastrophic than Hammarskjöld had foreseen," occurring with "lightning speed," and left Bunche and the UN at the center of a violent storm.

Two weeks after independence, the province of Katanga, with great mineral wealth and tens of thousands of white settlers, declared independence from Congo. The secessionist government was led by Africans but it was funded by white business interests and derived its power from Belgian troops and white mercenaries. The Belgian government frequently resisted the UN's efforts in Congo, and received at least partial support from Britain and the United States, as well as the backing of Western public opinion, which responded to a massively distorted propaganda campaign about the situation in Katanga.

Within days of Katanga's secession, the Security Council authorized a UN military force for the Congo. The concept was not radically different from what UNEF had been doing in the Sinai since 1956. The new force was called ONUC, the French initials for "United Nations in Congo." The UN sent an administrator from New York (Sture Linnér, another Swede), a military commander borrowed from the UNTSO in Jerusalem, and the head of UNICEF to organize food assistance.

Ralph Bunche felt that "swiftness in arrival is more important immediately than quantity." Hammarskjöld appealed for peacekeepers from African countries, and the first troops from Ethiopia, Ghana, Morocco, and Tunisia arrived in the Congo on American and Soviet transport aircraft "in a miraculously short time"—the first hitting the ground within twelve hours of the Security Council decision. Within four days the UN had 3,500 peacekeepers from four countries on the ground in Congo to "establish a UN presence in as many of the disturbed areas . . . as possible, if necessary even before the commander's headquarters staff was set up or logistical arrangements had been made." To reassure Europeans living in Congo, Hammarskjöld sent in two peacekeeping contingents from European countries neutral in the Cold War—Sweden and Ireland—in addition to those from African countries.

The hodgepodge of UN personnel in the Congo called themselves the Onusians, after the French acronym for the UN (ONU). The Onusians did not actually come from another planet, though they sometimes showed an embarrassing ignorance of local culture. Nor did they actually have their own nationality, although they often transcended their individual nationalities. But they were unique—a "heterogenous collection of human beings . . . Swedes, Indians, Irishmen, Canadians, Englishmen, Ethiopians, Frenchmen, Tunisians, Danes, Malayans . . . , all partly fused, under their blue caps, into something new—'Onusians.'" Like their counterparts in later UN missions, these foreigners brought tremendous idealism to their work but suffered from their unfamiliarity both with local conditions and with each other. In UNOC, the Africans and Europeans had divergent sympathies, and even the Swedes and Irish spoke different languages and saw things differently. As in later UN missions elsewhere, the foreigners most familiar with the country—in Congo, the Belgian former colonizers—could not be used as peacekeepers.

Because of the great speed necessary in the crisis, and the novelty of the mission, the force operated on "an entirely improvised basis." It was composed of "contingents of national armies that had never worked together before. They would be commanded and controlled by a commander they had never seen and by a staff that did not yet exist, in a situation about which there was virtually no reliable information at all." The ONUC mission was, in short, "quite unlike anything that had occurred before." And, as Linnér noted, even at its peak strength of 20,000 troops, the UN force had only one soldier for about forty square miles of territory in the vast country.

Not only was the Congo force larger than UNTSO or UNEF, but its mandate was more expansive. Bunche became the force commander until a Swedish military officer could arrive from UNTSO. Again everything had to be invented. A couple of weeks in, Bunche wrote to his wife, "I cannot begin to tell you how complicated and maddeningly frustrating our operation out here is. . . . It is like trying to give first aid to a wounded rattlesnake."

As an example of the improvisation required, and its potential for mistakes, on August 4 Bunche left Hammarskjöld in Leopoldville and went off to see the Katanga situation firsthand. "On the way to the airport it occurred to him that, having no UN base in Katanga, he would have to use Belgian channels to communicate with Hammarskjöld. . . ." To solve this potential problem, Bunche penciled a note to Hammarskjöld with a code: "Will report soonest" would mean UN peacekeepers could proceed into Katanga, whereas "Reporting fully" meant to delay the troops' deployment there. However, that evening, responding to a misleading statement by the Katanga secessionists, Bunche told the press he was "reporting fully" to Hammarskjöld, forgetting that this was a code word. (Since the secessionists were threatening to shoot down UN planes if they arrived, Bunche decided to delay the deployment anyway, so the confusion did no harm.) Incidentally, so out of touch with the outside world were the Katanga secessionists that one of their main leaders was surprised to find, when the African-American Bunche arrived, that he was clearly not Swedish like Hammarskjöld and Linnér.

TREASURE IN KATANGA

Hammarskjöld sent Irish diplomat Conor Cruise O'Brien to run the UN mission in Katanga. O'Brien wrote up his experiences afterward. The first thing in his book, before the introduction, is a set of maps, and the predominant features on the Katanga map are three copper mines, one cobalt mine, and one uranium mine, with a like number on the other side of the border with Northern Rhodesia (now Zambia), a British protectorate.

Tens of thousands of white Europeans lived on both sides of the border and controlled the extraction of minerals for profit. From Katanga, the Benguela Railroad carried the loot west, across neighboring Angola, to the Atlantic Ocean, for shipment to Europe and the world. So on the question of who would control Katanga, the stakes were high.

But commercial mining was not the whole story. Guess where the uranium came from that powered the atomic bomb dropped on Hiroshima? Tom Zoellner's recent history of uranium devotes its first fourteen pages to the Katanga uranium mine, called Shinkolobwe. In the 1930s and '40s it was by far the world's most important, richest, most accessible uranium deposit, with a purity "more than two hundred times that of most uranium deposits." Some parts showed a "freakishly high grade" of uranium. The deposit at Shinkolobwe was "a unique occurrence in the history of the planet, and stood as the best chance for the United States to gain a chokehold on world supply" during World War II. The U.S. military managed to secure access to the uranium, and keep it from the Nazis. "It is doubtful the Manhattan Project ever would have developed a bomb without Shinkolobwe," Zoellner concludes.

Control of Katanga by secessionist leaders backed by Belgian and other white mercenaries would ensure the continuing supply of uranium to the West. Control of Katanga by national Congolese leaders, who in 1960 were increasingly allied with the Soviet Union, would allow this vital resource to fall into communist hands instead. Thus, Katanga's uranium mine played a key role in the Cold War military posture of the United States and its NATO allies. (Belgium is a NATO member.)

Both the UN and leaders of African countries worked hard in the Congo conflict to keep out big-power politics. Ghana's president Kwame Nkrumah, a leader among newly independent African countries and one who sent peacekeepers to Congo in 1960, wrote at the time that "my policy has always been that at all costs Africa must not be involved in the Cold War." Ghana's goal in the Congo was "to prevent the direct intervention of any of the Great Powers in the African Continent." This was easier said than done.

WHICH SIDE ARE WE ON?

In the Katanga conflict, the UN basically took the side of the central government, working to remove the Belgian troops and the foreign mercenaries from Katanga. In this, the UN sided with the Afro-Asian bloc of countries that favored independence within colonial borders. Secessions could threaten many of those newly independent countries. Even today, the UN usually leans toward a central government, which is a UN member, rather than rebels and secessionists.

Hammarskjöld, however, was determined that the UN would not take sides or attempt to influence any internal political conflict in the country. This created a contradiction that plagued the mission for more than a year. In particular, the Soviet Union vehemently opposed the UN's policies and denounced Hammarskjöld as a lackey of imperialism because he would not use the UN's power to throw out foreigners and forcefully end the Katanga secession. Some European powers, on the other hand— with large investments in Katanga—opposed the UN because it went too far in supporting Congo's government and opposing the secession.

ONUC had to work with a Congolese national army that "did not take orders from anybody, did not know if and when it would get paid and by whom, or against whom it was fighting and why." The national government itself was similarly lacking: "Sometimes there was no government minister to discuss anything with, even in the key departments; or sometimes the opposite—there might be three or four heads of one and the same department who were bitter rivals with each other." Capping all these difficulties, the mission operated under Security Council guidance that perpetually fell short of clarity, as the permanent members papered over their serious differences with vague resolutions.

In August 1960, Hammarskjöld flew to Katanga and met with the secessionist leadership. He would not land until permission was granted for four other planes, carrying two companies of Swedish troops, to also land. He negotiated the UN's takeover of key strategic positions from Belgian troops, and the arrival the next day of more peacekeepers. "Hammarskjöld's personal intervention in Katanga was daring and unprecedented. By persistence and forceful diplomacy, he had obtained without fighting—which the UN troops were in no position to engage in anyway— the presence of the UN force all over Katanga, a move that only a week before was supposed to be resisted by armed force." Within weeks, the Belgian troops went home.

Unfortunately, Hammarskjöld's initial successes in the Congo did not resolve the crisis. The Congolese government suffered from internal splits and the Katanga situation remained frozen between secession and reintegration. The Soviet Union began sending direct aid to the national government led by the charismatic, leftist Lumumba. When government troops committed a massacre, Hammarskjöld had to confront an issue that has dogged the UN and the international community ever since but is nonetheless a relatively new problem for humanity—when do human rights violations justify foreign intervention in a country's sovereign affairs? "Prohibition against intervention in internal conflicts cannot be considered to apply to senseless slaughter of civilians or fighting arising from tribal hostilities," wrote Hammarskjöld. The Security Council authorized ONUC to use force in certain circumstances.

Congo's central government split between factions led by the president and prime minister, respectively, and things only got more complicated from there. Military officer Joseph Mobutu took power for a while in a coup (eventually he would seize power and hold it for decades), and Antoine Gizenga set up another self-declared national government operating out of the east of the country.

In September Soviet premier Nikita Khrushchev personally addressed the UN General Assembly and deplored the colonialists' "dirty work in the Congo" carried out "through the Secretary-General of the United Nations and his staff. . . ." Furious that the UN would not use its power to reintegrate Katanga and support Lumumba, Khrushchev demanded that Hammarskjöld resign and even that the role of secretary-general be scrapped in favor of a trio of officials. Hammarskjöld withstood withering criticism from all sides, determined not to give in to Cold War pressures. "From the extremities of East and West, and for the most part in the area between, there was a general attitude of carping criticism and defeatism with occasional flashes of ill-concealed glee at the trials and tribulations of ONUC."

By the time it adjourned in December of 1960, the General Assembly had not come to agreement on the Congo, and voted only at the last minute to continue ONUC's financing. Hammarskjöld became "even more isolated than before" as left-oriented African states withdrew troops from ONUC, former French colonies tried to form an alliance between the ousted Congolese president and Katanga's secessionists, and Western powers gave support to Mobutu's military government. "Hammarskjöld's independent position had alienated him to a large extent from all three groups, and yet the fact remained that his dogged maintenance of this independent position had allowed ONUC to prevent a lethal civil war between the factions in the Congo, supported by various outside powers." The 20,000 peacekeepers provided the only reliable security in the country, and the civilian UN administrators provided the only real public administration and financial management.

TROUBLE IN THE CONGO CLUB

Several levels of organization made up the UN mission. There was the New York headquarters. Then there was Leopoldville, capital of the Congo and location of the overall UN mission of which Katanga was a part. Finally, there was Elisabethville (now Lubumbashi), Congo's second largest city and capital of Katanga Province. The closer one got to the situation on the ground, the larger the problems were and the fewer the resources available to solve them.

The top UN advisors on the Congo called themselves the "Congo Club"—"highly informal, and perhaps rather eccentrically composed"— and it was they rather than the Security Council who advised the secretary-general on the Congo operation. As O'Brien describes it, the group held "business-like and civilized meetings. We all sit around a big table and go through the day's Congo telegrams, while refreshments are served."

Three Americans in the group were Hammarskjöld's closest advisors, most famously Ralph Bunche. Because the Soviet representatives in the UN Secretariat were assumed to be Soviet agents, Hammarskjöld did not rely on Eastern bloc nations in his inner circle. The Club also included two Indians, two Brits, and one Nigerian. The "most important" member of the Congo Club, because he knew the most, was American Heinz Wieschhoff, an anthropologist who had studied the Congo for four decades. The "American monopoly" of Hammarskjöld's inner circle was being "savagely denounced in the Soviet and Soviet-inspired press, and had caused considerable uneasiness among Afro-Asians" as a bloc in the UN General Assembly.

Back in the Congo, as Lumumba's government strengthened ties with the Soviet Union it turned against the UN and began provoking incidents. "UN employees were assiduously detained at checkpoints and generally harassed." At the Leopoldville airport, "Congolese soldiers forced their way aboard a UN transport plane and arrested fourteen Canadian soldiers, beating one of them unconscious." Meanwhile on the other side the Belgian government attacked Bunche for blaming Congo's problems on "Belgium's total failure to prepare the Congolese for independence."

The small apartment building that housed ONUC headquarters featured capricious elevators and an inadequate telephone system that worked in only two large rooms where the staff congregated. "Communications to other points in the Congo were still spasmodic at best. The only two sources of food were military rations and a Greek restaurant . . . on the ground floor. . . . The whole staff normally ate together and worked as it ate. Hammarskjöld vastly enjoyed these informal arrangements."

By fall of 1960 the Congo operation was "crisis-ridden." Lumumba had received help from the Soviet Union, but the military chief of staff, Joseph Mobutu, took power in a coup backed by the American CIA and kicked out the Soviets. The UN would not recognize the legitimacy of Mobutu's government.

Mobutu captured Lumumba and sent him to Katanga, where he was brutally murdered, an act carried out, perhaps personally, by Godefroid Munongo, Katanga's self-styled "interior minister." Munongo controlled the police, which was the province's armed force, and worked hand in hand with the white mercenaries. With his dark glasses and willingness to use violence, he was a force to be reckoned with.

Lumumba's murder became an international cause. The Soviet Union accused the UN of complicity, and especially criticized the American-dominated "Congo Club." The Soviets declared they would no longer deal with Hammarskjöld. India criticized Hammarskjöld for "passivity." Indonesia, Morocco, and Egypt withdrew their soldiers from ONUC in response to the murder. Indeed, the "worldwide uproar" over Lumumba's assassination led to a "well-organized . . . violent riot in the Security Council public gallery, where demonstrators battled with UN guards and hurled abuse at Hammarskjöld and Adlai Stevenson, the United States representative." Hammarskjöld became an "object of hatred" for the first time. When Bunche spoke out against the demonstrators, many of whom were African-Americans, he got "a flurry of angry letters from across the country accusing Bunche . . . of helping the white man to keep his hold on the Congo." Bunche even saw, outside the UN building, a black man with a sign reading Kill Bunche. When he asked the man who Bunche was, the man said, "I guess he's some joker in the UN."

"In the atmosphere of horror, disillusionment, and violence that followed Lumumba's death," the Security Council in February 1961 finally supported a stronger mandate for ONUC as Hammarskjöld had wanted. The force was authorized to disarm and send away the foreign mercenaries. However, the Council did not even recognize the past or present role of the secretary-general, apparently because mention of Hammarskjöld could trigger a Soviet veto (instead the Soviet Union and France abstained, allowing the resolution to pass). Worse, the resolution did not provide any new legal basis, any new troops, or any more funding for ONUC. Hammarskjöld described the resolution as "noble aims and no new means. . . ." To make matters worse, in April, undisciplined Congolese troops ambushed and massacred forty-four peacekeepers from Ghana.

By spring of 1961, "the problem of getting financial support for the Congo operation was becoming increasingly serious." Although the General Assembly had passed a budget, both the Soviet Union and France refused to contribute their shares. When the Assembly had to renew the budget again in late April, it was done again at the last possible minute, after midnight just before adjourning, and after a first attempt had failed. In the Secretariat overall, Hammarskjöld had to cut the budget severely and take on new tasks without increasing the size of the staff. Even when funding was available, the UN faced a tremendous challenge in finding skilled personnel to carry out its tasks.

TAKING CHARGE IN KATANGA

Hammarskjöld brought in Conor O'Brien to run the UN shop in Katanga and implement the new resolution. He had an Indian military contingent, a Swedish contingent, an Irish company, and a staff of about twenty. By September, he also unexpectedly had a refugee camp with 50,000 people to care for. Urquhart calls O'Brien's job an "impossible job."

Both the Katanga government (Munongo's police) and one of its main ethnic-based opponents (the Baluba) used massive atrocities in the conduct of war. "Torture, murder and mutilation moved in the path of the Baluba rebellion," reports O'Brien. On the other side, he saw from the air a scorched-earth corridor of villages burned by the Katanga government along the railroad line to ensure its smooth functioning in exporting minerals.

In late summer, the UN in Katanga carried out Operation Rumpunch to swiftly round up and repatriate hundreds of white foreign mercenaries. The operation went well, but was only "partially successful," since more than 100 mercenaries went missing. O'Brien argues that three things stopped the UN from finishing the job. First, Belgium promised to round up the rest but did not do so. Second, the UN's "oft-acknowledged lack of intelligence" made it hard to tell white mercenaries from white farmers. Third, "throughout large areas of Katanga . . . there were no UN forces at all."

As the Katanga UN office was planning a follow-up operation in September, Dag Hammarskjöld himself decided to come visit Congo and see if he could move forward a solution. The Katanga UN staff wanted to launch the operation either before or after Hammarskjöld's visit to avoid fighting while he was there. They decided on a quick strike before the visit—Operation Morthor (the Hindi word for "smash"). But this time it went badly.

The Indian and Swedish UN contingents, whose relationship was not "always entirely smooth and cordial," suffered a "linguistic factor" in that most spoke English only as a second language, which "could lead to serious factual misunderstanding." Some had little or no French, the local language. Beyond the linguistic issues, some political differences divided the two national contingents. The Indians, from a postcolonial third world country threatened by the very idea of secessionism, tended to oppose Katanga's government and support UN operations against it enthusiastically. The Swedish contingent, white Europeans, "sympathized, in various degrees, with the local Europeans." O'Brien emphasizes that "both groups of officers loyally executed the instructions they received, but they could not conceal from each other that they felt differently about their instructions." Urquhart describes the ONUC force as "poorly organized and lacking in leadership, political judgment, staff work, discipline, and forceful restraint that are particularly vital in UN operations." Its higher ranks were "bedeviled by national and personal rivalries and antipathies."

When the UN forces struck this time, the operation "went disastrously wrong and degenerated into a squalid battle. . . ." O'Brien found that there was "not a single UN soldier . . . to be seen in the neighborhood of the [Presidential] Palace," which he had assumed was blockaded.

O'Brien suggests that "the point about encirclement of the Palace got lost in the linguistic and other interstices between the two headquarters." Meanwhile the UN's effort to take over the post office and telephone exchange met with armed resistance and a battle ensued, with more resistance than the UN had expected. An Irish unit that went to a mining town where the UN did not already have a presence came under attack from a larger Katangese force, and eventually surrendered after running out of ammunition.

At the UN's military headquarters in Katanga, "civilians and Indian officers together, we were living on Indian box-rations and sleeping, crowded together, on the concrete floor of the basement" sheltering from mortar fire. Mostly the fighting was low-level, intended more for propaganda effect. "UN forces held their positions and unknown persons fired on these, rather at random, during the night." Most of the shooting appeared to come from local Europeans stiffened by mercenaries. Ultimately eleven UN troops and at least fifty Katanga police died in Operation Morthor.

The foreign press pounded the UN for its supposed aggressiveness in Katanga. And the United States, pushed by a pro-Katanga faction in the Senate, worried that the UN operation could lead to communist control in Congo.

MUDDLE IN THE MISSION

Where UNEF had to deal with the Israeli and Egyptian state military forces, UNOC had to deal with a toxic brew of great-power rivalry, local tribal conflicts, and the fresh trauma of seventy years of colonialism. O'Brien gives several examples of problems caused by inadequate resources for his mission. The UN was short of vehicles, had too few troops to cover Katanga, and the Indian troops with 1918-style rifles were outgunned by the mercenaries' modern Belgian rifles. Once, at ONUC headquarters in Congo's capital, a key document written by Hammarskjöld had to be presented to Lumumba, who spoke only French. The "complex and nuanced document" was in English, and "there were no professional translators in the ONUC headquarters. . . ."

Regarding a second problem, bureaucratic coordination, the UN staff answered to many masters and was pushed around by many political forces. The great powers passed Security Council resolutions (especially in February 1961) but then seemingly changed their minds and lobbied the secretary-general to change course. The Soviet Union constantly criticized ONUC, the Belgians actively undercut it, and the British appeared ambivalent at best.

The appointment of O'Brien himself illustrates how the UN must answer to sovereign nations pursuing their own interests. The Irish public's doubt about the UN delayed O'Brien's appointment by nearly three months. Ireland already contributed the commanding general of UN troops in the Congo and a battalion of troops. "A general election was due in Ireland that year and it was rumoured (incorrectly) that the opposition intended to use the slogan: 'The Best Irish Government the Congo Ever Had.'"

An Irish diplomat, however, was what Hammarskjöld needed, for the same reasons the battalion and the force commander were Irish. "Obviously he could not pick anyone from the Eastern bloc, which was then vehemently condemning his whole conduct of the Congo operation." But neither would a "committed Westerner" do, because of the West's ties to the foreign mercenaries and colonial interests in Katanga. And "there would be strong Western opposition to the choice of an Afro-Asian" because of presumed bias in favor of the central government in Congo over the Katanga secessionists. "The choice seemed to narrow to a European neutral and then . . . to Sweden or Ireland." Since a Swede already ran the overall UN mission in the Congo, and the secretary-general was Swedish, someone Irish was needed for Katanga. This method for selecting UN mission personnel in a key conflict area nicely illustrates the problems of an international civil service.

THE BITTER END

With military force having failed to end the conflict, Hammarskjöld turned to personal diplomacy. After arriving in the country, he threw himself into briefings and talks to find a way forward.

The worst day of the mission came on September 18, 1961—the day after the thirteenth anniversary of the assassination of Count Bernadotte in Palestine. Hammarskjöld was flying from the Congolese capital, where he had consulted with the government, to a town in British-ruled Northern Rhodesia, just across the border from Katanga. There he hoped to personally negotiate with Katanga's president a cease-fire with UN forces and an end to the secession. Hammarskjöld had wanted Ralph Bunche with him on the trip, and Bunche cut short a family vacation to return to New York and pack, but Hammarskjöld changed his mind and brought Wieschhoff, saying good-bye at the airport and leaving Bunche to take care of UN headquarters.

The plane, a propellor DC-6, carried fourteen people, including Hammarskjöld and Wieschhoff. It reached the airport in Northern Rhodesia, radioed in to the control tower, then disappeared on final approach. After several attempts to radio the plane, the airport personnel apparently just decided Hammarskjöld had changed his mind and decided to go somewhere else. They did not send out a search party, even when reports of explosion and fire reached them. When they went looking the next morning they went in the wrong direction from the plane, which was right where it should have been expected. By that time the plane had burned all night and its last survivor would die shortly after being found.

Researchers have put forward several attack or sabotage theories of the crash, but none holds up. The Katanga mercenaries—along with their employers, the foreign mining interests—had the *motive* to kill Hammarskjöld. His UN forces were the main element preventing Katanga from seceding. However, among other problems with such theories, Hammarskjöld had loaned his plane at the last minute to another diplomat to go to the same airport at almost the same time, so any assassination attempt would have hit the wrong plane. At the time, of course, before any investigations, suspicions ran high. O'Brien wrote in 1962, "In Elisabethville I do not think there was anyone who believed that his death was an accident."

ONUC continued its work after Hammarskjöld's death, although O'Brien was recalled the next month and replaced in Katanga by Urquhart, who was Bunche's assistant at that time. In November 1961, the Security Council voted a stronger resolution against the secession. Within weeks, UN forces battled Katangese mercenary-led forces for two weeks, with twenty-one UN soldiers killed and a "considerable" number on the other side. They would clash again a year later, but by 1963 Katanga was integrated into the Congo and ONUC began phasing out. The mission ended in 1964.

In all, ONUC had troop contributions from thirty countries, totaling about 20,000 military personnel at peak, supported by international civilian and locally recruited staff. It coped with three secessionist movements. ONUC suffered 245 military deaths and five of international civilian staff. The mission cost $400 million. It succeeded in holding Congo together. Unfortunately, after the UN left, Mobutu seized power again, with U.S. backing. He would continue the rapacious exploitation of Congo's wealth but now for his own personal fortune rather than King Leopold's. He ruled for more than thirty years, the country stayed desperately poor, and then war took the country over.

Considering the reign of Mobutu, clearly UNOC did not solve the Congo's problems or set it on a path to prosperity or democracy. However, the mission had several less dramatic successes. It held the country together, and in so doing perhaps discouraged violent secessionist wars in other postcolonial countries. It established principles for peacekeeping and helped the UN learn what worked and did not work. And the bravery of the peacekeepers on the ground prevented what could have been a very bloody civil war in the Congo, saving many lives.

As for UN peacekeeping, it would be quite a few years before the UN tried as large, strong, and multidimensional a force as ONUC. In 1964 the UN positioned peacekeepers along a cease-fire line in Cyprus, where they still are today. They also went to Lebanon and some other conflict areas. But the next big steps forward for peacekeeping had to wait until the Cold War was ending in 1989.

4

ANGOLA TO MOZAMBIQUE

Failures and Successes of the Early 1990s

The post–Cold War era started with great promise for peace. Although the end of the Cold War was a process, not an event, I remember it as one moment in 1989. I was in Berlin as part of a group of peace-oriented academics from East and West, and we had toured by bus around East Germany, then come across Checkpoint Charlie to West Berlin. The famous checkpoint was rapidly becoming obsolete, however, because a couple of weeks earlier the East Germans had punched out several large gaps in the wall and allowed people to cross back and forth freely after decades of forced confinement.

On December 14, we went to the Berlin Wall and saw young West Germans chipping away at it with sledgehammers. I reached down and scooped up two fragments with remnants of purple graffiti on them—one to keep and one for my colleague at the University of Southern California, Jim Rosenau, one of the few international relations professors to have foreseen transformational change in the international system.

Ten days earlier, presidents Mikhail Gorbachev and George H. W. Bush met on a boat in Malta, tossed about in stormy seas, to officially end the

Cold War after forty years. And with the end of the superpower standoff, the UN Security Council suddenly got a fresh wind, and started to operate as intended. Suddenly peacekeeping was not held hostage to opposing superpower interests in civil wars. A rapid expansion in peacekeeping followed. "The atmosphere at the UN during the early 1990s was positively triumphant," a moment of "sheer exhilaration." From 1948 to 1988, only thirteen peacekeeping operations had occurred, with five of these ongoing in 1989. Suddenly in 1991–93 some sixteen new missions began. However, the sudden upsurge in missions taxed a system that had not handled so many and such large missions before.

In January 1992, for the first time ever, a summit meeting of the leaders of all the members of the Security Council took place, and they called for a report on peacekeeping from Secretary-General Boutros-Ghali, which he wrote later that year. The report, "An Agenda for Peace," cast peacekeeping as a stage in managing conflict, following "preventive diplomacy" and "peacemaking" (trying to influence warring parties to come to peace agreements), and followed by "peacebuilding" which would rebuild societies decimated by war. The UN should also, according to the "Agenda," "address the deepest causes of conflict: economic despair, social injustice, and political oppression." Boutros-Ghali's reference to peacekeeping as "hitherto with the consent of all the parties concerned," implying that this might not be true in the future, hinted at problems to come in the early 1990s in places such as Somalia and Bosnia, where peacekeepers operated without consent.

In perhaps the most expansive call in the report, Boutros-Ghali proposed that member nations make military forces available to the UN on a permanent basis. Furthermore, in cases where warring parties had signed but broken cease-fire agreements, Boutros-Ghali proposed using heavily armed "peace-enforcement" units—available on call from member states—to force compliance by armed groups. Although the "Agenda for Peace" laid the conceptual groundwork for later developments in some areas, especially peacebuilding after wars end, the ambitious proposals for permanent UN forces and peace enforcement ran into serious opposition from the permanent Security Council members and never got off the ground.

I. Four Failures

By 1993–95, the UN had four fiascoes on its hands nearly at once, in Angola, Somalia, Rwanda, and Bosnia. These missions overlapped in time but their most disastrous moments, respectively, came in Angola in 1992, Somalia in 1993, Rwanda in 1994, and Bosnia in 1995, so I will discuss them in that order.

ANGOLA

The mission in Angola has the distinction of being one of the few where the UN's presence actually made things worse. The disastrous mission was actually the second of four UN missions in Angola in 1988–99. The civil war there had followed independence from Portugal in 1975, which had followed an armed struggle for independence, and had continued for decades as a Cold War battlefield. The left-leaning Angolan government was supported by the Soviet Union and Cuba, including at one point by 50,000 Cuban troops (who withdrew in 1988 near the end of the Cold War).

The most long-lasting and important of several rebel armies—UNITA, led by Jonas Savimbi—received support from the United States and apartheid South Africa. But earlier in the war, UNITA had advocated Maoism and received support from China, so clearly ideology was not the issue in Angola. The Cold War division awkwardly overlay an ethnic divide in the country, with the government and UNITA drawing support mainly from different regions with different ethnic populations. At yet another level, the war was, like Congo's, a struggle to control lucrative natural resources. UNITA sustained and enriched itself by exploiting abundant diamonds in areas it controlled, and the government funded its war effort with oil exports.

The war dragged on, killing 140,000 directly and perhaps twice that number indirectly, in a country of 11 million people, and displacing 3 million more before settling into a costly stalemate. Finally, in 1991, long efforts by a Portuguese mediator produced a peace agreement. A cease-fire took hold and elections were organized for 1992.

"The Security Council did not want to field another massive peace-keeping mission . . ." so it sent a small force of 500 military observers and 400 election monitors, a tiny force for a country of 9 million people with 200,000 troops to be demobilized. The mission was "underfunded and underpowered and thus quite incapable of demobilizing the rebels."

The incumbent president faced the rebel commander in a close presidential election, held with international supervision (which judged the election reasonably fair under the circumstances). But Savimbi declared it fraudulent when he lost the presidential race by nine points, and he returned to war, becoming a "spoiler" in the peace process. "The most vicious fighting of the war ensued. Upwards of 300,000 people were killed. . . ." Thus the UN mission "created a situation far worse than ever before during the war." The war raged on through the 1990s, as several more peace agreements came and went. It would be sixteen years until Angola's next election. Several times during the 1990s the Security Council imposed economic sanctions on UNITA, "the first occasions in history when a nongovernmental entity has come under UN sanctions." However, Savimbi was able to circumvent the sanctions well enough to sell diamonds and buy weapons.

What finally ended the war, after several more UN attempts to help, was military victory. The government crippled UNITA in an offensive in 1999, but Savimbi fought on guerrilla-style. I remember asking an expert on Angola, my colleague Jerry Bender at USC, what it would take to end the war there after all the decades of violence and devastation, the failed UN missions, and the sanctions. "A bullet to Savimbi's head," he replied without hesitation. As it turned out, he was dead right. In 2002 the Angolan government army caught up with Savimbi and put fifteen bullets into him in a final shootout—two to the head. Right away, the remaining rebels gave up the fight and resurrected the eight-year-old peace agreement. This time the UN sent a much larger and experienced force of 5,000 peacekeepers. The cease-fire lasted. The rebels demobilized and became the opposition party. Africa's longest war was over.

Recently, in 2008, Angola held legislative elections, the first since 1992. They did not rate much press. The opposition cried foul when the government won 80 percent, but African Union (AU) observers declared them fair, though European Union monitors criticized the government's unfair advantages such as control of the media. Despite these controversies, nobody talked about resuming the war. Angola still faces tremendous challenges. Two-thirds of its people live in poverty on less than two dollars a day, and corruption endures. The government is somewhat authoritarian and the economy relies far too much on oil export revenues. But the shooting has stopped. And that is the first step, for any war, toward prosperity, human rights, and social justice. Just a step—but almost always a necessary step. Angola's inflation rate, above 300 percent annually during the war, dropped to 12 percent in peacetime. China, thirsty for Angolan oil, has provided $7 billion in loans. A postwar reconstruction boom has begun putting the country back together again.

SOMALIA

In Somalia, the mission began as a successful U.S. military effort to secure humanitarian aid for a population in danger of starving. It followed years of peace talks—thirty-seven different efforts by one count—and it had both the support and attention of the Security Council and a decent budget of almost $2 billion over the years. In 1992 the first President Bush, a lame duck who had lost reelection, responded to public and media concerns about starvation in Somalia by sending a strong military force to ensure delivery of humanitarian aid. "The strategy . . . had no political basis or goals. The goal was merely to provide humanitarian support and exit the country within three months."

The nature of the mission morphed, however, and eventually both UN peacekeepers and U.S. military forces became engaged in hostilities against one of the major factions in the war. The UN mission chief in Somalia, who could negotiate with all the factions there, resigned after Boutros-Ghali got the Security Council to send 3,000 more troops without consulting him or the Somali parties. In response, one faction leader, Mohamed Aideed, who had trusted the mission chief, turned against the UN. Control of the mission reverted to the UN from the United States after three months but with continuing U.S. military involvement on the scene.

The UN force's "mandate . . . was deeply conflicted." The task of bargaining for a peace plan conflicted with the task of forcibly disarming fighters. "Troops were slow to arrive, as were funding, logistical support, and civil administrators. There were unclear chains of command, and poor inter-operability between the troops." The mission "experienced all aspects of organizational dysfunction." In one disastrous episode, as the UN tried to disarm Aideed's forces (while leaving his enemies armed), Aideed's forces killed twenty-four Pakistani peacekeepers. Then the United States sent in Army Rangers (not under UN command), who spent months raiding and harassing Aideed's militia.

When eighteen Americans were killed after their helicopter was shot down by Aideed's forces in 1993, and one of their bodies was dragged through the streets on live TV—the famous *Black Hawk Down* incident— the United States pulled out. The UN soon followed. Somalia's civil war has been raging ever since, and seventeen years later the conflict in Somalia is one of the worst in the world.

The experience of Somalia "played a particularly pivotal role in the perceptual transformation" that replaced a "tremendous burst of optimism for what the United Nations might accomplish" after the Cold War with a new pessimism and cynicism toward the UN. Thereafter, the "Somalia Syndrome" represented the prospect of getting bogged down in deadly local armed conflicts that one did not adequately understand.

Despite its political and military failings, however, the Somalia mission ended the starvation of Somalis, which had been taking 3,000 lives daily. This success, however, got a lot less attention than the eighteen American deaths. At any rate, the UN left Somalia a mess that persists to this day. And, worse, the "lessons" of Somalia were misapplied in Rwanda the next year with disastrous consequences.

RWANDA

In Rwanda in 1994, a small, inadequately funded UN mission (UNAMIR) proved totally ineffective in preventing or halting a genocide that killed more than half a million people.

Historian Paul Kennedy calls it "the lowest point in the UN's history."

Rwanda had been a German colony after 1890, a Belgian colony after World War I, and independent since 1962. The colonial powers had strengthened the position of the minority Tutsi group over the majority Hutus, and with independence the Hutus had taken power and expelled many Tutsis to neighboring Uganda. An authoritarian government had ruled since a coup in 1973, and had sponsored periodic massacres of Tutsis, while a Tutsi-led rebel movement, the Rwandan Patriotic Front (RPF) operated out of Uganda. The military government had "solid support" from France. The Rwandan government "was taken to be an honest and energetic administration [and] attracted substantial foreign assistance in the 1970s and 1980s." This prosperity was "superficial," though, and ended quickly in the late 1980s when the price of coffee, which made up three-quarters of Rwanda's exports, collapsed.

In the early 1990s the RPF rebels entered Rwanda and a civil war spread. For several years peace talks and agreements were on-and-off. In 1993 the RPF broke a cease-fire in response to government-instigated killings of Tutsis. The rebels gained ground, and threatened the government's hold on power. Under this pressure, the sides finished the Arusha Accords in August 1993. This comprehensive peace agreement was supposed to end the war and create a transitional government, with elections to follow.

UNAMIR was created in late 1993 to help carry out the agreement. When the UN went into Rwanda, conditions on the ground seemed favorable to success. There was a detailed peace agreement to end a civil war after several years, and both sides had requested the UN presence. The UN "wanted a successful peacekeeping operation to offset the failure in Somalia [and] believed that Rwanda promised such success. . . ."

But one problem was that the UN "wanted not just success, but success at low cost." Demands for economy, led by the United States, which paid nearly a third of the world's peacekeeping costs, resulted in a UN force one-third the recommended size. One UN military expert recommended 8,000 soldiers, the Canadian UN mission commander, General Roméo Dallaire, asked for 4,500, and the United States proposed 500. The final resolution set a level of 2,548. The mandate was also watered down so that the force could not realistically guarantee implementation of the Accords. "The overriding rule was to be the use of minimum force, [and] the force was lightly armed." (General Dallaire wrote rules of engagement, however, that gave the peacekeepers responsibility to stop crimes against humanity.) UNAMIR's budget was not approved until April 1994, two days before the genocide began. The Accords called for peacekeepers to arrive in a month, but they took four months. Thus, "the

Security Council failed to devote the resources necessary to ensure that the hard-won Accords were actually implemented."

"UNAMIR was forced to operate without adequate resources. From the very start, the operation found it difficult to obtain even basic supplies such as eating utensils and at one stage was unable to file situation reports because it ran out of paper. . . . Many of the peacekeeping troops that did arrive lacked not only training but also basic items such as boots." The peacekeepers' mandate was expansive, ranging from monitoring a cease-fire and integrating a new national army drawing on both sides to supervising police, human rights, refugees, land mine removal, humanitarian aid, and preparation for elections. Yet the resources provided did not match these aspirations.

Armored vehicles had been flown in from Mozambique in February but were so old they were completely unusable, and were eventually hauled to the gates of UN camps and used as bunkers. As the mission progressed, all the UN's vehicles "progressively broke down." In mid-April, after "much wrangling," the United States sent from Somalia on loan "six old, stripped-down (no guns, no radios, and no tools), early Cold War–era" armored personnel carriers. When a low-level officer at the Pentagon called UNAMIR to find out why as many as six vehicles were needed, he received a description of "our desperate logistics and our precarious situation. . . ." He replied, "Buddy, you'll get your APCs, good luck to you and God bless." Dallaire notes that "we got more and faster support from that one sergeant than from the rest of the United States government and armed forces combined."

Alison Des Forges wrote the definitive account of the Rwandan genocide, for Human Rights Watch. (After a lifetime of working for human rights, she died in a plane crash in 2009.) She describes the outbreak of the genocide thus: In an effort to keep their hold on power and destroy the peace agreement that threatened them, a group of Hutu politicians planned a campaign to exterminate their enemies that they believed "would restore the solidarity of the Hutu under their leadership and help them win the war, or at least improve their chances of negotiating a favorable peace. They seized control of the state and used its machinery to carry out the slaughter." These actions were not spontaneous. The perpetrators formed, armed, and trained militia groups. After they "concluded that firearms were too costly to distribute" to these groups, the leaders imported large numbers of machetes to arm their followers.

Three months before the genocide, Dallaire sent a telegram to UN headquarters warning that informants in the government had outlined the plans for genocide, including a plan to kill Belgian peacekeepers to provoke a Belgian withdrawal. The warning "was all but dismissed at UN headquarters." Boutros-Ghali did not even bring it to the Security Council's attention. Yet within months "everything that the [telegram] predicted came true and worse." In addition, "dozens of other signals" of the impending massacres were well known to foreign observers, and in January a CIA analyst even predicted that half a million people might die if violence restarted.

Dallaire in early 1994 "repeatedly requested a stronger mandate, more troops and more materiel." But "his superiors . . . directed him to observe the narrowest possible interpretation of his mandate." The warnings from the field of well-organized planning for genocide were replaced, in the UN Secretariat, by suggestions that chaotic, spontaneous violence had flared up from age-old ethnic hatreds.

On April 6, the Rwandan president was killed when his plane was shot down. The Burundian president was also on board and killed. Responsibility for this act has never been determined. The president's fellow Hutu leaders either instigated this crime or took advantage of it to put their plans into motion. But the RPF rebels may have shot down the plane to restart a war they thought they could win (and eventually did).

Immediately after the plane crash, Hutu ultranationalists in the government took control and unleashed a massive but systematic campaign of violence against their opponents. The genocide was carried out in waves over several months, beginning with killings by the military and then expanding to use armed civilians. Early phases targeted political leaders, Hutu opponents, and Tutsi men of potential fighting age. Later, Tutsi who had been spared, such as women, children, priests, and medical workers, were also exterminated. "Throughout the genocide, Tutsi women were often raped, tortured and mutilated before they were murdered. . . . Tens of thousands of women and girls were raped. . . ."

In the first days, the organizers distributed lists of targeted people to squads of killers who went door to door shooting them. Assailants also massacred large numbers of Tutsi just because they were Tutsi. At one church in a city, people had gathered for refuge (this strategy generally failed). A Hutu woman married to a Tutsi man was allowed to leave safely, and told that her eleven children could also leave with her. They were considered Tutsi based on their father's ethnicity. "When she stepped out of the door of the church, she saw eight of the eleven children struck down before her eyes. The youngest, a child of three years old, begged for his life after seeing his brothers and sisters slain. 'Please don't kill me,' he said. 'I'll never be Tutsi again.' He was killed." When killing infants, the perpetrators would remind themselves that the leaders of the enemy RPF had once been babies. Hutu who tried to save Tutsi children "had little success. . . ."

Many Catholic and Protestant clergy endorsed the government that was perpetrating the genocide, and refused to help the victims. A few clergy were even indicted later for war crimes, accused of inciting killers, delivering victims, or killing people themselves. Other clergy did defend the victims, however.

In all, "at least half a million persons were killed in the genocide, a loss that represented about three quarters of the Tutsi population of Rwanda." Des Forges reviews estimates of fatalities from several angles and comes up with this same figure, as does a recent Uppsala review. The figure of 800,000 put forward by one UN expert "included those who had died from causes other than the genocide." Yet today the 800,000 figure seems to have become the conventional wisdom, as though the more realistic figure of 500,000+ is not bad enough or somehow shows insufficient concern for the victims.

On a much smaller scale, the RPF rebel forces also "killed civilians in numerous summary executions and in massacres. They may have slaughtered tens of thousands."

The International Response

The day after the plane crash, the prime minister (a woman) and several other officials were murdered while under UN protection, and ten Belgian peacekeepers were "brutally massacred." Just as predicted, Belgium decided unilaterally to withdraw, crippling the UN operation. In the early hours of the genocide, Dallaire sent a message to UN headquarters saying, "Give me the means and I can do more," but he learned that "nobody in New York was interested in that." In addition to the Belgian peacekeepers killed on the first day, UNAMIR had suffered four wounded and "despite all our requests for resupply, even the field hospital's cupboards were bare. . . ." Dallaire had no air transport available so "in all likelihood any seriously wounded would die. . . . We had no medical safety net, and a lack of ammunition."

The contingent from Bangladesh had stopped following orders and "gone to ground inside their compounds in a state of fear." Their officers had requested guidance from back home and been told "not to endanger the troops by protecting Rwandans. . . ." Dallaire, as UN commander "could not fire any national officer over the rank of lieutenant colonel, and especially not a commanding officer, without permission from New York. . . ."

On the fifth day of the genocide, writes Dallaire, the Security Council and secretary-general's office "were obviously at a loss as to what to do. . . . What more could I possibly tell them that I hadn't already described in horrific detail? . . . There was a void of leadership in New York. We had sent a deluge of paper and received nothing in return; no supplies, no reinforcement, no decisions."

On April 12, "an experienced and well-equipped force of French, Belgian, and Italian troops rushed in to evacuate the foreigners, and then departed." During the evacuation, foreign forces made no effort to help resupply UNAMIR. "Running out of ammunition, gas, food, water, and other basic supplies, UNAMIR watched one cargo plane after another arrive empty and without provisions and leave with foreigners." Rwandan political leaders not involved in the genocide appealed in vain for foreigners to stay in order to limit the killing. Dallaire considers this "as the day the world moved from disinterest in Rwanda to the abandonment of Rwandans to their fate. . . . [The evacuation] was the signal for the génocidaires to move toward the apocalypse." The next day, the Security Council moved to withdraw or drastically scale back the Rwanda operation. They began questioning the basic concept of whether peacekeepers should try to protect civilians. As the genocide escalated, the Security Council voted to reduce the size of the mission from 2,500 to 270 troops (actually 450 stayed).

Dallaire later estimated that with 5,000 more peacekeepers he could have changed the outcome. The commander of the Belgian contingent believed that troops on the ground (including those sent to evacuate foreigners) "would have been strong enough to halt the violence." A se-nior French officer estimated that 2,000 to 2,500 "determined" soldiers could have stopped the killing in the early days. Nearly 2,000 capable foreign troops were already in the capital, with an additional 600 Gha-nians nearby, 800 Belgians in Kenya, 300 U.S. Marines next door in Bu-rundi, and hundreds more Marines off the coast. The serious government forces executing the genocide plan numbered only about 2,000. They would not have fought a foreign force that included French soldiers, their allies and former trainers. Nor would the RPF have opposed such an in-tervention. Dallaire believed that such an action "could easily have stopped the massacres. . . ." Dallaire said later that a peacekeeping "op-eration should begin with the objective and then consider how best to achieve it with minimal risk. Instead, our operations began with an eval-uation of risk and if there was risk, the objective was forgotten."

"The mission took actions to protect civilians, against headquarters' recommendations, but these attempts were subverted by France, Bel-gium, the United States, and Italy, which had all instructed their troops to evacuate only their own nationals." The United States considered jam-ming the radio broadcasts that were giving instructions for carrying out the killings, including names of persons to attack—but decided not to do so. The United States gave its officials written instructions to avoid the word *genocide*—which could have triggered a legal obligation to do some-thing, under the genocide treaty. The Security Council followed suit. President Clinton later apologized for his actions in allowing the genocide to happen.

The "one bright spot" for Dallaire, a Canadian, was that Canada prom-ised a dozen officers to replace the Belgians being withdrawn. "While others were abandoning Rwanda, Canada had taken the unique decision to reinforce the mission." Some humanitarians also stayed on. "The hos-pitals remained operational throughout the genocide, thanks to efforts by . . . the International Committee of the Red Cross," supported by Doc-tors Without Borders and an individual Canadian doctor. Dozens of med-ical workers were killed, and hundreds of Rwandans were "pulled out of ambulances and slaughtered on the spot."

On April 16, Dallaire received a request for help from the manager of the Mille Collines hotel, where more than 400 people were sheltered (the subject of the 2004 movie *Hotel Rwanda*). A small group of Tunisian peacekeepers "had done an excellent job in bluffing the militia and keeping the hotel safe, but the manager thought it only a matter of time before the militia assaulted the hotel. . . . I ordered Bangladeshi troops to reinforce the hotel but received a formal letter of protest from their commanding officer, stating the mission was too dangerous." On the other hand, Dallaire "can't say enough about the bravery of the Tunisians. They never shirked their duty and always displayed the highest standards of courage and discipline in the face of difficult and dangerous tasks." A captain from Senegal, Mbaye Diagne, "became virtually a legend among Rwandans for his bravery and inventiveness in saving people and in deterring soldiers who sought to enter the hotel Mille Collines at night to kill those whom he had saved during the day." He was killed when a mortar shell hit near a militia checkpoint he was passing.

Ultimately, the UN just pulled out and left the Rwandans to their fates. In one case, 2,000 Rwandan civilians had taken refuge in a Belgian UN base, with the genocide perpetrators outside waiting to attack. French troops evacuated the foreigners and then the UN peacekeepers "jumped into their jeeps and rapidly pulled out of the gate. Some of the Rwandans hurried to lie down in the road to block the departure, but they were too slow to stop the convoy. As some ran after the departing troops, shouting "Do not abandon us!" they were driven back by the UNAMIR soldiers firing over their heads. As the Belgian troops left, the militia and Rwandan soldiers rushed through one gate and the displaced began fleeing out another. . . . Most of the two thousand people were killed that afternoon, within hours of the departure of the peacekeepers." The next day, Belgium and the United States strongly argued for the Security Council to completely withdraw UNAMIR and thus abandon "30,000 unarmed civilians then in U.N. posts, just as the others had been deserted the day before."

When evacuating UN peacekeepers, the rule was laid down that no Rwandans, even on the UN staff, could be taken to safety. Some UN officers disregarded these orders. A Belgian lieutenant escorting fifty vehicles with foreigners and Rwandans to the airport stood his ground when a crowd armed with grenades began forcing Rwandans out of the cars. "He had to argue and bluff his way through several more situations," and took fire from a sniper, but delivered everyone safely to the airport. On the other hand, French troops later "were in a position to save Tutsi and others at risk with relatively little difficulty and yet they chose to save very few." And when UNAMIR at one point did fly a planeload of Rwandans out to Kenya, the Kenyan government refused them entry and they were flown back to Rwanda.

An important factor behind the failure in Rwanda was bad timing. The Security Council voted to create the Rwanda mission six months before the genocide, just two days after the deaths of the eighteen U.S. Army Rangers in Somalia. The United States had a "new disinterest in funding and fielding multidimensional peacekeeping operations in civil wars," and other Security Council members followed the U.S. lead.

A more traditional approach based on consent and impartiality resulted, unfortunately for Rwanda. Just three days before the genocide began, Boutros-Ghali said that "our whole philosophy is based on talk—negotiate—and then talk again. To use force is an expression of failure." The head of the Belgian contingent in UNAMIR learned that in the Rwandan language, the French acronym for UNAMIR was a word meaning "Your lips are moving, but they don't really say anything. And that's what we were from the beginning. After a few weeks the extremists knew we had no power."

Operation Turquoise

The sad ending of the sad story was a belated and wrong-headed military intervention by France, "Operation Turquoise." France had not expected trouble in Rwanda, did not act while the genocide was under way, but at the end—as the rebels were beating the genocide perpetrators—France rushed in to secure a "humanitarian" corridor, which actually sheltered the perpetrators and allowed them to escape into Zaire (Congo). In the end, despite France's intervention and the UN's cowardice, the RPF won a battlefield victory and ended the genocide. The spillover into Congo created a disaster there that led to the 1998–2003 war (see Chapter 6).

Operation Turquoise apparently aimed partly to prevent a victory by the RPF, which France had long helped the Rwandan government to fight. One French officer said later, "We were manipulated. We thought the Hutu were the good guys and the victims." France feared that a loss of power by the Hutu government "would be the first time that a regime loyal to France had been removed without prior French approval." Worse yet, the RPF was "largely English-speaking."

An international war-crimes tribunal for Rwanda was set up under the UN, following the example of the tribunal for the former Yugoslavia. The tribunals for Rwanda and Yugoslavia "share the same appeals chamber in order to assure a single body of legal precedent for both." Independent of the international tribunal, the Rwandan government itself tried people for participation in the genocide. In 1998 it executed twenty-two of them "in public stadiums in several towns." In 2008, fourteen years after the genocide, the UN tribunal convicted the man considered the mastermind of the genocide, and two codefendants. Found guilty of genocide, war crimes, and crimes against humanity, they were given life sentences. The trial lasted six years, heard 242 witnesses, and produced three hundred written decisions.

BOSNIA

Bosnia became the world's largest and most important peacekeeping mission in the early years of the post–Cold War era, so it was important to get it right. The whole world was watching. Unfortunately, the world watched the UN make a mess of it.

The war in Bosnia exemplified the "new" conflicts of the post–Cold War era. Yugoslavia, a multinational state populated by rival ethnic groups, had been created by the great powers after World War I and held together by a strongman after World War II. After his death and the fall of communism, Yugoslav politicians turned to ethnic nationalism as a new power base. The country disintegrated and one part with mixed ethnicity, Bosnia, found itself invaded by another, Serbia. The Serbian forces invented the term *ethnic cleansing* to describe their own territorial conquests, which terrorized, murdered, and displaced the "other" ethnic groups, especially the Muslim (or Bosniak) group in Bosnia. Many observers called it genocide. About 100,000 Bosnians died, and millions were displaced.

Many times in the war years of 1992–95, the worst case seemed imminent—that Serbian ultranationalists would overrun all of Bosnia, including its cosmopolitan capital city Sarajevo; that they would slaughter the inhabitants, sack the towns and cities, displace the survivors, and take the land for a Greater Serbia. Such an outcome could have ruined not only Bosnia, but the post–Cold War era itself, then still in its infancy. The new rules would be written in blood and played out in conquered territory. Only outside power could stop this—Bosnia did not even have an army of its own at the start of the war—and for three years the outside powers failed to do so.

The UN admitted Bosnia as an independent member state, but then did not help Bosnia restore its territorial integrity when attacked by its neighbor. "Once Bosnia was recognized by the UN . . . as an independent state, the moral objective of the institution derived directly from the Charter: to defend Bosnia's integrity. . . ." Instead, the Security Council passed an arms embargo against both sides, the well-armed Serbian forces whom the UN saw as the aggressors and the poorly armed Bosnians. Once again the UN tried to favor one side but be neutral. The League of Nations had put a similar arms embargo on the Fascists and Republicans during the Spanish Civil War in the 1930s.

The UN secretary-general, Boutros-Ghali, made "no secret of his distaste for the entire enterprise" of peacekeeping in Bosnia. At the end of 1992 he told the besieged residents of Sarajevo, civilians under shelling and sniper fire, "You have a situation that is better than ten other places in the world." He called Bosnian peacekeeping "a white man's war" that Westerners seemed more interested in than the conflicts in Africa. By some accounts, much that went wrong with peacekeeping in the early 1990s traces to the poor decisions of Boutros-Ghali.

Despite Boutros-Ghali's lack of enthusiasm, the UN sent a peacekeeping force into Bosnia with the explicit idea of protecting civilians from violence directed at them primarily from Serbian forces. It was called UNPROFOR, the UN "Protection Force." But it failed to protect the civilians. The peacekeepers were too few and too lightly armed to seriously take on the Serbian forces, so they depended on the consent of all parties, but meanwhile civilians kept being killed. The experience became known as "peacekeeping where there is no peace to keep."

When the UN turned to NATO to apply pressure on Serbian forces by air strikes, the Serbian forces simply took the UN peacekeepers hostage and handcuffed them to sensitive military installations to prevent Western military forces from bombing them. And the military arrangements for the UN and NATO in Bosnia were awkward at best. Each pinprick air strike required bureaucratic approvals, and a "dual key" arrangement gave both the UN and NATO veto power over them.

The Security Council declared "safe areas" comprising the main Bosnian towns either surrounded by or threatened by Serbian forces. But the UN did not protect these areas effectively when the stronger Serbian forces attacked them. The problems of the safe areas "are a classic example of organizational dysfunction and its potentially tragic results. . . . There was poor coordination between humanitarian and military divisions, between headquarters and the field, and between the UN mission and the local government." Boutros-Ghali presented the Security Council with a "heavy option" using 34,000 troops to actually protect the safe areas, or a "light option" with fewer troops. The Council chose "light" with fewer than 8,000 troops. Kofi Annan, in charge of peacekeeping, had trouble finding even that many troops. Journalist James Traub calls it "a decisive, and genuinely catastrophic, moment in the history of peacekeeping, and indeed of the UN itself."

One of the safe areas, the town of Srebrenica, had been besieged by Serbian forces and "protected" by a Dutch battalion under UN command. In July 1995, Serbian forces attacked and overran Srebrenica, including the military compound where the Dutch UN battalion and thousands of refugees sheltered. The Dutch did not put up a fight, fearing that resistance would provoke Serbian shelling of the compound and cause heavy casualties among the civilians there. The Serbian forces took UN vehicles and uniforms, and drove around making announcements to fleeing Bosnian Muslims that they should come out of hiding and the UN would protect them. Many did so, and were rounded up. The Serbian forces separated the men and boys from the women, sent the women away on buses, and massacred the men and boys, about 7,000 in all. The International Tribunal's indictment of Bosnian Serb leaders refers to "scenes of unimaginable savagery . . . scenes from hell, written on the darkest pages of human history."

At the same time that Srebrenica shocked the international community, Serbian forces were suffering military setbacks at the hands of Croatia, which had seceded from Yugoslavia and fought its own war with Serbian forces. The combination of circumstances opened the way for the United States to use air strikes against Bosnian Serb forces, and then bring in its toughest negotiator, Richard Holbrooke, to bang heads together until a peace agreement was reached. After a few months of cease-fire, Holbrooke assembled the parties at an air base near Dayton,

Ohio, to hash out a peace agreement. In Holbrooke's view, the belated but forceful U.S. actions in 1995 were "the most important test of American leadership since the end of the Cold War."

The negotiations on the Dayton Agreement came within a whisker of breaking up. With seven hundred reporters waiting outside the gates for a scheduled press conference, the leaders of Serbia, Croatia, and Bosnia finally bridged the last percentage point of difference in the division of land and put off the status of one key town for later arbitration. The Dayton Agreement was a hundred pages long, full of complexity and ambiguity—the roles of entities within entities, the powers of international diplomats, the rights of refugees, and so on. But the agreement held.

Entering in Strength

On December 31, 1995, a convoy of American tanks rumbled over a pontoon bridge across the raging Sava River and entered Bosnia. Behind them followed a large, heavily armed NATO mission that would enforce the Dayton Agreement. The bridge itself had not come easily. For days, army engineers battled flood waters, rain, snow, and mud to get the two-thousand-foot pontoon bridge in place. (The war had destroyed the real bridge there.) The logistical troops made so many supply runs from Hungary through Croatia to the bridge site—with the same bumpy route, the same lousy food, the same lack of rest, and the same grim weather—that they joked about living in the movie *Groundhog Day*. But they got the bridge up and the armor across. NATO fanned out to take up positions along the "zone of separation" agreed to in Dayton. The war in Bosnia was over.

When the American tanks crossed the Sava River, they did more than end a war. They marked a turning point in the fledgling post–Cold War era. Aggression, genocide, and brutal ethnic warfare would not spiral out of control. At some point the international community would intervene effectively. Since that day in late 1995, the UN's terrible failures of the early 1990s have not recurred. Many problems remain but the post–Cold War world order settled down considerably.

The intervention also proved a key point—go in strong. By committing a large force with tremendous firepower, NATO ensured its success. Despite fears of challenges from local armed groups, in the end NATO took zero battle casualties. NATO's 60,000 heavily armed troops with modern technology could overmatch any threat in short order.

Incidentally, not all U.S. military leaders were thrilled about using American capabilities to do peacekeeping in Bosnia and later in nearby Kosovo. Yet, after 2003, when the occupation of Iraq went all wrong, the officers with most success were those such as David Petraeus who had done peacekeeping in the former Yugoslavia and understood levels and types of military presence relative to population size. Thus, peacekeeping turned out to enhance U.S. military capabilities, not deplete them.

In 2005, ten years after the Dayton Agreement, "considerable progress had been made on multiple fronts." The 60,000 international troops sent in to enforce the agreement had been reduced to 7,000. Today, Bosnia remains unsettled. Ethnic tensions remain high. Many refugees still have not returned to their homes. But the war ended and has not restarted. Many of the highest-level perpetrators of abuses in the war, including the Serbian leader Slobodan Milosevic, were hauled before a war crimes tribunal in the Netherlands. Economic aid arrived. It may take decades more for Bosnia to recover, but war did not spiral out of control.

For the UN, which failed in Bosnia until the United States came to the rescue, the troubled missions of the early 1990s compounded each other. The aftermath was "the institutional equivalent of post-traumatic stress syndrome . . ." for UN peacekeeping. The gloomy mood, however, masked some hidden successes during the same period.

II. Four Successes

Lise Morjé Howard worked at the UN during the bad years of the early 1990s. The daily press briefing mostly concerned "disasters—in Bosnia, Somalia, Angola, and Rwanda." When she went to graduate school and "started examining the UN's record from the viewpoint of a social scientist," Howard "realized that there were numerous, unwritten stories of success." To find the sources of this success, Howard studied six very successful cases "where UN peacekeeping in civil wars worked." Four of these—Namibia, El Salvador, Cambodia, and Mozambique—took place in the same years as Somalia, Rwanda, and Bosnia in the early 1990s. In discussing these cases I draw primarily on Lise Howard's book.

NAMIBIA

The 1989 Namibia operation was the UN's first return to "complex peace operations—those having civil/political as well as military components"—since leaving the Congo in the early 1960s. Namibia redefined the role of the UN and pioneered new methods, notably in disarmament and reintegration of fighters. In Namibia, the UN mission "differed from all previous UN peacekeeping operations in that its primary means and purpose were political (in overseeing a democratic transition after decades of civil war and colonial rule), rather than military (where monitoring a cease-fire is the primary task)." The UN for the first time took over civilian police functions, established an information program to keep the population informed, and set up a "Contact Group" of western countries committed to helping with the process. The Namibia mission was the first of five—the others being in Cambodia, eastern Croatia, Kosovo, and East Timor—where the UN took over actual administration of a territory, "violating . . . sovereignty and democracy with the goals of establishing sovereignty and democracy."

Germany had colonized Namibia—then called South West Africa—in the 1880s, and had wiped out two tribes in a genocide when the tribes resisted German rule, in 1904–08. After World War I, South Africa—attracted, like Germany, to the area's diamonds and minerals—took control of the territory under a League of Nations mandate and, in the 1950s, refused to cede control to a UN Trusteeship, instead treating it as a province of South Africa. In 1966, armed conflict began between the South African government and the South West Africa People's Organization (SWAPO), which the UN recognized that year as the legitimate government of South West Africa although it did not control the territory. The war, intertwined with other armed conflicts in southern Africa, continued through the apartheid era in South Africa, but negotiations got going in 1978 and the UN Security Council became involved that year.

The peace operation finally began in 1989, but on the day it was to start, fighting broke out that lasted nine days and killed more than 300 people. Both sides broke the peace agreement, and the UN mission,

UNTAG (UN Transition Assistance Group), seemed to have "failed even before it began." One cause of this breakdown was the "budgetary and deployment delays that slowed the UN's arrival in Namibia." After the rough beginning, UNTAG deployed 4,500 troops, 1,500 police, and 2,000 civilians. The secretary-general's special representative was former Finnish president Martti Ahtisaari, who would later win the 2008 Nobel Peace Prize. As a high-ranking UN official, he spent the ten years of delays after his appointment for the Namibia mission in 1978 picking out the most talented international civil servants for service in Namibia when the time came. "Ahtisaari was also very conscious of the importance of recruiting women and maintaining a careful gender balance."

UNTAG quickly accomplished its main goals—educating the population about upcoming elections and the transition to independence; restricting military forces from both sides to their bases and disarming them; collecting South Africa's heavy weapons and returning them across the border to South Africa; integrating demobilized soldiers from pro– and anti–South Africa armed groups into the new national army; and helping the police force carry out its duties (a first for the UN, but now common).

South Africa tried to subvert the UN mission. UN spokesman Fred Eckhard recalls an incident in which the South Africans established a military camp right next to a UNTAG tent set up to repatriate SWAPO fighters. When a wounded SWAPO member came to the tent, the South Africans demanded to interrogate him. The British major in charge of the UN post said, "No way, he's our guy and you can't have access to him." When the South Africans raised their automatic weapons, he held his ground: "Over my dead body." So the South Africans said, "We'll be back in one hour and if you don't turn him over, we're taking him." The UN people on the scene could not reach the top UNTAG commanders, so they decided to hold the line. The major went outside and when the South Africans returned he drew a line in the dirt and said, "You cross that line and we'll shoot." The South Africans backed down and left. As a later observer notes, "despite the overwhelming force behind the South Africans, this UN official, with, in reality, no backup, demonstrated the courage and resolve to protect the wounded SWAPO member whom he knew would have been tortured by the South African troops had they gotten hold of him."

The UN refugee agency (UNHCR), working as an integral part of UNTAG, smoothly resettled more than 40,000 refugees who had fled the war (mostly to Angola and Zambia). Because the people did not trust the UN, resettlement was organized through the churches. The UNHCR budget, outside of that for UNTAG, had called for about a thousand dollars per person to cover repatriation and reintegration, but the budget was cut by about a third. Other UN agencies helped pick up the slack—the World Food Program with food, WHO with vaccines, FAO and UNICEF for seeds, and UNESCO for education. "All accounts attest to the remarkable cooperation" among the various UN agencies as well as the Namibian Council of Churches.

A tight timetable also governed the elections in November 1989, which were "the central purpose and primary goal" of the UN in Namibia. UNTAG set up two hundred offices around the country, partnering with churches and other groups to disseminate information. SWAPO won handily, but not with the two-thirds majority required to adopt a constitution. With the cooperation of the second-place party, a constitution was adopted in February 1990. The next month, Namibia celebrated its independence and installed the leader of SWAPO as its first president. "Namibia's independence is clearly one of the United Nations' greatest success stories."

EL SALVADOR

In El Salvador the UN came in after a long civil war that had started in 1980, pitting a rightist government against leftist guerrillas, each with a superpower patron. Talks began in 1989 as Soviet reforms deprived the guerrillas of support while the government absorbed steep cuts in U.S. military aid owing to human rights abuses. Both sides thus sought a solution to a war that neither could win, although fighting continued until they reached an agreement in 1992. Meanwhile the country had been devastated by a decade of war, a major earthquake in 1986, and a serious drop in the price of its major export, coffee, which accounted for half of El Salvador's economy.

During the early 1990s, in contrast to the previous decade, the external powers showed strong cohesion. The Security Council acted unanimously on El Salvador and supported the UN role in the peace process, but luckily was too absorbed with events elsewhere to micromanage the El Salvador mission.

The UN mission began in 1991 and, unlike missions elsewhere, played a key role *before* a cease-fire was established, emphasizing mediation. The "key figure" in this process was not the head of mission but the secretary-general's "personal representative" Álvaro de Soto. Like Secretary-General Javier Pérez de Cuéllar himself, de Soto was a Spanish-speaking Latin American, which strengthened ties between the field and headquarters in New York (as did the relative proximity and same time zone). After de Soto's mediation produced an agreement early in 1992, the UN set up military and police units with 800 international and local staff, and added 900 election observers for a few months before elections in 1994. After the elections, the UN wound down the mission.

Although the mission lacked resources it had a clear mandate, since the UN itself had negotiated the peace agreement. Primarily the UN was to verify compliance and assist with demobilization, reintegration, and election monitoring. But it also had "extremely broad powers to investigate . . . human rights abuses," with the issue of human rights becoming "the cornerstone of the operation." By 1993 the mission engaged in what it called "active verification," especially in the area of reducing human rights abuses, to make the most of its limited powers. Fortunately, de Soto personally had the trust of both sides, and used what he called "pressure through shame, cajoling, and persuasion" to get results.

A Truth Commission was established in 1991 with the consent of both sides, to establish the facts about human rights violations during the war. It had three international commissioners appointed by the UN secretary-general with the consent of the two warring parties. The commission took testimony from 7,000 people and received 22,000 complaints. Its report in 1993 "shocked the . . . government," as it named government and military officials as responsible for the assassination of the country's archbishop in 1980, the massacre of hundreds in 1981, and the murder of six Jesuit priests in 1989. It also found the guerrillas responsible for killing four U.S. Marines in 1985, but laid the great majority of serious violations on the government side. Although its recommendations— to fire those responsible and ban them from politics—were ignored, the commission resolved old debates and laid the groundwork for later changes such as the dismissal of high-ranking military officers.

The UN's police work suffered from a severe lack of funding and personnel as it "was not one of the favorite projects for donors." However, with only about 300 observers deployed—at least they had decent equipment, language skills, and professional background—the police division successfully oversaw creation of a new national police force that "became one of the most trusted institutions of El Salvador." Meanwhile the military division, which also had just over 300 observers, successfully oversaw demobilization of the military forces that had controlled the country. Despite many delays in this process, the cease-fire held. The UN, by the way, did not like to talk about "delays" in implementing various parts of the agreement, so it called them "recalendarizations."

The UN was not supposed to be involved in land reform, probably the most difficult aspect of the peace agreement. Guerrillas had given land to farmers in areas they controlled but owners wanted their land back after the war. Because the issue threatened the peace, the UN became active in resolving disputes and pushing land reform agreements forward. This illustrates the mission's ability to learn from, and adapt to, local conditions as they evolve—something that not all UN missions mastered.

Similarly, elections were not originally central to the UN mission, but when the government asked for help monitoring the 1994 elections the Security Council agreed, adding 900 people to the mission's tiny 36-member electoral division (supplemented by 3,000 non-UN international observers). The UN struggled with the government's Supreme Electoral Tribunal, which acted as virtually a wing of the ruling party, to get voters registered and allow campaigning by the opposition. Ultimately the ruling party won the presidency in a landslide and took almost half the legislature and most mayorships. The UN deemed the elections imperfect but "acceptable." Although the guerrillas did poorly in the election, they fulfilled central goals through the peace process, including removing the military's hold on society. They transformed from an armed group to a political party. In 2009, seventeen years after the peace agreement and nearly thirty years after the war began, the party of the former guerrillas won the presidency of El Salvador in national elections. Ballots ultimately got them what bullets could not.

CAMBODIA

In contrast to the modest mission in El Salvador, the UN in Cambodia employed nearly 90,000 people, half of them from outside the country, and cost about $2 billion. It produced "mixed results," but contributed to the end of the civil war, the return of hundreds of thousands of refugees, and the holding of elections (if not very democratic ones).

From 1970 to 1991 the Cambodia war killed an estimated 1 to 1.7 million people, mostly indirectly through famine and disease, with the high figure representing nearly one-quarter of the entire population. In 1975 the communist Khmer Rouge took power in Cambodia (which it renamed Kampuchea) and created disaster with its policies of killing elites and educated classes, abolishing money, and relocating populations from cities to the countryside, where many starved. Vietnam invaded and ended this reign of terror in 1978 but a long civil war ensued. The Vietnamese-backed government controlled most of the country and enjoyed Soviet backing, but the opposition had support from the United States and China as well as Cambodia's UN seat. By the late 1980s, the Soviet Union had embarked on reforms and China had begun its economic rise, making both lose interest in Cambodia.

Peace talks began in Indonesia in 1989, and in 1991 the four major factions signed the Paris Peace Accord, along with the UN and sixteen other countries, ranging from the permanent Security Council members to ASEAN and even Yugoslavia as the representative of the Non-Aligned Movement. The Accord gave the UN "broad authority" to oversee its implementation. Although the four factions agreed to this, and participated in a transitional government, the Khmer Rouge in particular stood to lose power and would become a "spoiler" as the process unfolded. The peace agreement in Cambodia presented great difficulties because of the large number of actors involved (four internal factions and various regional and global outside powers) and because the divisions among the parties did not follow ideological lines.

The mission lasted eighteen months in 1992–93. It had the familiar tasks of monitoring the cease-fire, demobilizing forces, holding elections, monitoring policing, assisting the return of refugees, and providing help with economic development and human rights. Because the Khmer Rouge had killed most of the people who could run a government, the UN mission was a "transitional authority" (UNTAC) that had "more power over the civil administration than ever before granted to a peacekeeping mission." Elections were considered central to the creation of a legitimate government, but rather than supervising them as in other missions the UN would actually organize and run them. Meanwhile it more or less ran the national government itself. The head of the UN mission had complete access to government administration and information, and could fire Cambodian civil servants and veto decisions of the transitional government that did not follow the peace agreement.

An immediate problem for the UN in Cambodia was a nine-month delay in deploying the mission. An advance mission deployed in the meantime "was in a state of organizational dysfunction throughout most of its existence. . . ." For example, during the long delay while awaiting deployment of UNTAC, the Khmer Rouge leader returned to the capital only to find an angry mob that looted and destroyed the group's new offices, forcing him to escape to Thailand. The Khmer Rouge, which had participated in the peace process before that point, lost confidence in the UN and two months later broke the cease-fire.

To run UNTAC, the largest and most complicated peace operation in UN history, Boutros-Ghali chose a career UN diplomat from Japan with "no prior experience in peacekeeping," apparently because the Indonesian president liked him and Japan had a growing interest in peacekeeping. The self-effacing diplomat managed to calm down Cambodian leaders, however, and over time took control of a disjointed UN operation. But even with its large size, the UN mission was dwarfed by its tasks. Civil administration depended on 200 international and 600 Cambodian staff, compared with 200,000 in the Cambodian government. The military division had 16,000 peacekeepers compared with 200,000 national troops and 250,000 militia members.

The military division was hampered by a severe lack of planning. When the mission's military commander went to New York to review plans for deployment he found no planning, no maps, and no speakers of the Cambodian language. This lack of planning and late arrival "inspired fear and insecurity" in the country's armed factions "who were, in essence, required by the accords to entrust the UN with their lives." After the UN broke its promise to provide security for the peace transition, the government broke its promises regarding the civil administration and the Khmer Rouge broke its promise to disarm. In turn, when the Khmer Rouge began to block the UN from its territory, the peacekeepers were in no way prepared to accomplish their tasks by force. In the end, "UNTAC was never able to fulfill any of the military division's original tasks." Meanwhile the police mission was even less successful.

In response to these problems, the UN redeployed the peacekeepers away from the cantonment and demobilization mission and toward support of the elections, which became the main focus. For the first time ever, the UN itself carried out the elections. The head of the election component of UNTAC had previously supervised the elections in Namibia and made detailed arrangements, including a twenty-six-volume operational plan. He set up 800 mobile, five-person voter registration teams and 8,000 seven-person polling teams. Another 460 UN volunteers staffed 200 district offices. During the elections, 1,000 international poll supervisors and 50,000 Cambodians worked the polls. The UN provided transportation and radio time to parties shut out by the government's monopoly on those resources. Hundreds of Cambodians and thirteen UNTAC staff were killed in the run-up to the elections, and UNTAC members were held as hostages four times.

The Khmer Rouge withdrew from the elections but the UN decided to go forward. (Boutros-Ghali decided the Khmer Rouge did not pose a serious threat and later said, "I felt I had no choice but to rely on my political intuition, which told me I was right.") Although it had not disarmed the factions, UNTAC used its military resources to protect the election process, and the elections came off smoothly. With a 90 percent turnout, Cambodians delivered an unexpected result that put the ruling party in second place behind another faction (neither having a majority). A somewhat unstable power-sharing government emerged, in which the Khmer Rouge had no representation, having boycotted the elections. The Khmer Rouge emerged weaker, and thousands of its troops defected to join the new national army.

UNTAC did not end political violence in Cambodia, but "dramatically reduced" it. After the UN left, Cambodia veered between democracy and authoritarianism for years. It remained a lawless, corrupt, and mostly very poor country, dependent on continuing international aid. Nonetheless, "while UNTAC was not able to cure many of Cambodia's ills, it undoubtedly helped to guide Cambodia's transition from war to peace."

The experience gained in Cambodia proved useful in a later mission that entailed civil administration of a territory after war, in eastern Croatia in 1996. It included a military component with 5,000 troops and a civilian side with 800 international personnel and more than 400 international police officers. The UN had NATO's robust military force nearby as backup if needed, which it was not. The operation's mandate to reintegrate the region of Croatia that Serbia had conquered during the war included demilitarizing armed groups, helping refugees go home, establishing property rights, setting up a police force, and holding elections. Secretary-General Boutros-Ghali did not favor a UN force in Croatia, and insisted that if sent it had to be large and ready to use force (which in fact it did when challenged). The UN Transitional Administrator used his power freely to fire staff members and take charge of problem areas. One problem area was police, with inadequate funding, weak support from the Croatian government, and loyalties on the force divided on ethnic lines. Also, the mission's funding was usually "slow to arrive." And the important issue of refugees was left mostly unresolved. Despite these problems the mission was generally considered a much-needed success for the UN.

El Salvador, Cambodia, and Croatia represented "paradigm-setting" cases of a new type of peacekeeping, "multidimensional operations" with police, civilian, and military components. These operations gave the UN expanded powers to monitor, and in some cases even take over, the functions of states emerging from civil wars. The UN carried out a wide array of tasks before, during, and after peace agreements. Usually some aspects succeeded and others failed, but the overall effect was positive.

MOZAMBIQUE

The UN mission in Mozambique (ONUMOZ) was perhaps the most successful of the missions in the early 1990s. It followed more than three decades of devastating war in the southern African country. Before the 1992 peace agreement, the country was a one-party state run by the leftist party, FRELIMO, that had led the anticolonial war against Portugal and governed since 1975. A right-wing party, RENAMO, had waged a guerrilla war against the government since 1977 with South Africa's support. Thus, Mozambique resembled nearby Angola, but without the diamonds and oil. By 1992, the ideological divide "had become obsolete" as FRELIMO gave up Marxism in 1989 and could barely control its hungry, unpaid troops who victimized civilians, while RENAMO became "more and more brutal" in repressing areas under its control, attacking humanitarian supply convoys, and at times massacring hundreds of civilians.

The peace negotiations were mediated neither by the UN nor by any external government—most of whom had either lost interest in Mozambique after the Cold War ended or suffered donor fatigue after years without progress there. Rather, mediation fell to a Catholic lay organization based in Rome, the Community of Sant'Egidio. This unusual arrangement began with a plea from the archbishop of a city in Mozambique for help with both poverty and government repression of the church. Sant'Egidio responded with three airplanes and two ships full of food, clothes, and other supplies. But the organization discovered that war "swallowed up" and "wiped out" such efforts. So, after failing to find institutional backing, it offered itself as mediator and hosted talks in Rome between the warring Mozambique factions—eleven sessions over twenty-seven months—that culminated in the peace agreement signed in Rome. Since the international community recognized the government of Mozambique as legitimate, the unofficial group Sant'Egidio was better able to provide RENAMO a place at the table. Over time, Italy took a leading role; it was Mozambique's largest trading partner and creditor, and host country for the peace talks.

Both sides asked the UN to help implement the agreement. Aware of its failures in trying to do too much with too few resources in Angola, the UN approved a much larger force, 6,000 peacekeepers with a budget of $1 billion. The peace agreement had specific and ambitious goals—a cease-fire, demobilization, humanitarian aid corridors, and holding elections. The government was eager for immediate action by the UN, but it took the UN three months to prepare an operational plan and nine months to deploy peacekeepers. This delay resulted largely from a lack of available peacekeepers, as the UN was deploying large missions to Bosnia, Somalia, and Cambodia at the same time, totaling 70,000 troops. RENAMO launched an offensive to gain territory before peacekeepers arrived, and meanwhile a drought threatened to trigger mass starvation.

"An overtaxed, divided, and pathologically over-regulated United Nations Secretariat nearly managed to destroy the momentum of the peace process. . . . Six months into the peacekeeping mission, there was nothing on the ground that even vaguely resembled the blueprint set out in the peace agreement." The search for a head of mission started late and was driven by nationality, given Italy's important role. A hasty and "somewhat random selection process fortunately led to outstanding results" in this case, as the Italian chosen turned out to be well suited to the job. Once the UN arrived, it successfully carried out its tasks and "the nearly moribund demobilization process took on new life, as Renamo felt protected against stabs in the back." The presence of peacekeepers "sent a message that there was no way back, and that continued violence was out of the question. Politics became the new game."

The UN mission operated with a high degree of autonomy, adapting to changing circumstances on the ground rather than following rigid directives from New York. Demobilization rather than elections was the focus of the UN mission. This was a long, drawn-out, but ultimately successful operation. The head of the UN mission traveled to the remote headquarters of RENAMO in the bush and impressed on its leader the need to supplement the rebels' "muscle" with "wisdom" and recruit young Mozambicans for the future rather than being perceived as mere bandits.

The mission head also "accurately assessed that money could play an important role in steering [RENAMO] toward cooperation," and established a "trust fund" that funneled $17 million to help the group transform into a political party (including almost $4 million to the leader personally in the year before the election to ensure his continuing control of the organization). "The Italian ambassador . . . repeatedly found essential money for things that auditors would not approve of, but that were crucial for keeping Renamo happy."

Another trust fund offered eighteen months' salary to individual soldiers as they reintegrated into civilian life, after two years of pay offered by the government. Initially the severance pay for demobilizing soldiers had been set so low that few took the offer, but the international community came up with funds to double the pay, and demobilization picked up steam. Eventually, 100,000 troops were demobilized, a few joining the new national army and most returning to civilian life. "Once demobilization was completed the game was essentially over, and the outcome of the peace process was no longer in doubt."

After the UN departed, Mozambique became a favorite of donor nations and its economy enjoyed strong growth. FRELIMO won the 1994 election and two later rounds, although the 1999 round was quite close.

No war-crimes tribunals or truth commissions were set up. Little reform of the police or judicial system took place. Nonetheless, the peace in Mozambique has lasted. This success illustrates a key point in peace operations—the single most important aspect is not elections, policing, or the justice system, but disarmament and demobilization. The central purpose of an outside armed presence is to provide security so that rebels can disarm without being stabbed in the back.

III. Comparing Failures and Successes

Why did four missions succeed when four others failed? Consider the two sets side by side—Namibia, El Salvador, Cambodia, and Mozambique with total population of about 30 million on the success side and Angola, Bosnia, Somalia, and Rwanda with about 29 million on the failure side. The two sets overlap geographically. Each took place in the same few years. "Lootable" natural resources—those that can provide ready income for rebels that control the territory where they are located—were a major factor only in Angola. The failure cases got twice the personnel and nearly three times the budget, relative to population, as the success cases, and incurred three times the fatalities. So what made the difference?

In looking at the two lists, the element that stands out in my mind is the "consent of the parties" to having the UN there carrying out its mandate. In each of the "failure" cases an armed faction, at least for a period of time, did not want the UN present and was willing to disrupt it, fight it, hold its peacekeepers hostage, or kill them. In Angola, it was Savimbi, who was simultaneously one of the two main presidential candidates in the 1992 UN-sponsored elections and the target of UN sanctions depriving him of revenue. In Bosnia, the UN saw the Serbian forces as the aggressor but expected its lightly armed peacekeepers to act as neutrals. In Somalia, the UN antagonized and fought Aideed's militia (which threw grenades at UN forces from within the ranks of women's street demonstrations). In Rwanda, Hutu extremists attacked and killed UN peacekeepers and slaughtered civilians sheltered there. By contrast, the rebels in Namibia, El Salvador, and Mozambique all had crimes to answer for but also genuine interests in seeing peace agreements carried out. The Khmer Rouge in Cambodia, with its bloody history and tendency to return to violence, fits this mold less well, but overall in these conflicts the parties wanted the UN there.

In addition to the consent of warring parties, Lise Howard emphasizes, the UN needs an ability to learn and adapt as it goes. Even when it starts out with consent, as in Angola and Rwanda, it can lose control later, whereas a daunting situation such as Namibia (with South African resistance) can turn out well with skillful UN leadership. Anthropologist Robert Rubinstein describes the cultural learning that must occur for peacekeeping to succeed. For instance, a colonel serving with the UN mission "knew nothing of the local culture when he arrived in Somalia. Needing to get to his post, he managed to get a ride in the back of a pickup truck with a small group of Somali men. He later learned that he was well regarded by local elders because his behavior and actions during that ride had conveyed an appropriate sense of respect. Their initial evaluation of him was transmitted from person to person . . . [and] facilitated his work for the rest of his stay." But he realized that, acting in ignorance of Somali culture, he could equally well have acted in a way that derailed his mission. If he had happened to ride in a truck with a different age or gender mix, the result could have been disastrous. Another cultural problem for UN peacekeepers is that in coordinating with IGOs and NGOs working the same territory, there is a mismatch of cultural expectations, such as different levels of centralization, precision, and resources, and different short- or long-term time horizons.

Peace missions also need to learn and adapt by meshing the cultures of their own personnel from various countries. This problem is magnified by the "cultural inversions" required in switching from traditional military work to peacekeeping—such as taking commands from foreign officers, having intensive interactions with civilians, using negotiation rather than force, and the use of officers and troops in nontraditional ways (e.g., an officer's having to scrub out a toilet). Military personnel must learn to do "things that they would not be able to do, or which would be unacceptable . . . during conventional military activity, . . . like placing one's body in the path of an oncoming tank." The inversion of ordinary tactics is illustrated by an ambush set by Canadian peacekeepers in Bosnia along a path newly cleared of mines, in which the peacekeepers "turned on bright lights pointed toward themselves" when an armed group approached.

ANALYSIS—DOES PEACEKEEPING WORK?

Taking lots of attempts to get to a successful outcome is not a failure. The peacekeeping missions of the 1990s encountered many problems but should ultimately be judged on their outcomes. Taking all the civil wars of the 1990s together, can we say whether sending peacekeepers made a cease-fire more likely to last? This was what political scientist Page Fortna set out to learn.

Fortna made a database of cease-fires in 1989–99 and compared cases where peacekeepers were deployed with those where "belligerents are left to their own devices." In the peacekeeping cases, she included both missions that had consent of all parties and "peace enforcement" missions that sometimes did not, and she included both UN and non-UN peacekeeping. In all, Fortna looked at ninety-four cease-fires in sixty civil wars.

The presence of peacekeepers reduced the risk of renewed war by somewhere between 55 and 85 percent. "The statistical evidence is overwhelming. In short, any way you slice the data, peacekeeping works." Quantitative studies by other researchers also "have reached a consensus, and it is an optimistic one." Although these studies find that peacekeeping is less effective in reaching a cease-fire in the first place than in making it last once reached, the success of the latter "has emerged as a strongly robust result in the quantitative literature." Thus, the answer to whether peacekeeping works is "a resounding yes."

Fortna identifies several pathways by which peacekeepers affect the calculations of combatants. Their presence changes incentives for peace and war; they reduce uncertainty about each side's intentions; they prevent and control accidental outbreaks of violence that could escalate; and they ensure the inclusion of all parties in the political process, preventing political abuses by those in power.

Despite these positive outcomes, peacekeepers are sent to only some of the conflicts where a tentative cease-fire has been established. Of the ninety-four cease-fires in 1989–99, peacekeepers were sent in thirty-six cases—thirteen enforcement missions, six multidimensional operations, ten traditional peacekeeping, and seven monitoring missions—while none were sent in fifty-eight cases. Some of these fifty-eight had success in maintaining cease-fires, but statistically they fell far behind the cases where peacekeepers were sent. The peacekeeping cases were not just the "easy" ones either. Overall, "peacekeepers tend to deploy to more difficult cases rather than to easier ones."

Economist Paul Collier, in a separate but parallel analysis, reaches a similar conclusion to Fortna's: "Somewhat to our surprise we got clear results: peacekeeping seems to work. Expenditure on peacekeeping strongly and significantly reduces the risk that a post-conflict situation will revert to civil war." Collier goes on to quantify the benefits of peacekeeping. Given the costs of wars, he estimates the benefits to be more than four times higher than the costs of peacekeeping. "Peacekeeping looks to be very good value."

Reversion to war after cease-fires occurred around half of the time in civil wars in the 1990s. So in the new century, "maintaining the post-conflict peace more effectively than in the past would be the single most effective way of reducing civil wars." One effective way to reduce the risk of reversion to violence is economic growth, according to Collier. The higher a country's income, and the faster its economic recovery after a war, the less likely is a new outbreak of fighting. Economic development and peacekeeping still need better integration, but "the coherence of the UN effort on the ground has markedly improved," according to one UN political affairs officer in 2003. I will return to the relationship between economic growth and civil wars in Chapter 11.

Political scientists Michael Doyle and Nicholas Sambanis built a dataset of "all peace processes after civil war from 1945 until the end of 1999." They, too, found that economic development greatly increased the probability of success, as did having a peace treaty and external peacekeepers. Thus, the statistical research on peacekeeping overwhelmingly supports its effectiveness.

Political scientist Roland Paris does not entirely share this view of peacekeeping successes. He looks at the fourteen major complex peacebuilding missions from 1989 to 1999, the same period Fortna analyzed. Paris holds these missions to a high standard: "If the test of 'successful' peacebuilding is simply whether large-scale conflict resumed . . . then most of the operations conducted in the 1990s were successful . . . ," he says. But using a standard of success of "sustainable" peace "that will endure long after the peacebuilders depart," then these successes fade because in their push for quick elections and market liberalization the missions often "inadvertently exacerbated societal tensions or reproduced conditions that historically fueled violence in these countries." For instance, in Nicaragua, El Salvador, and Guatemala, "there is in fact reason to doubt the success of peacebuilding efforts" because they did not adequately "address the underlying causes of conflict and establish the conditions for a stable and lasting peace." Paris lodges similar criticisms for Cambodia, Liberia, Bosnia, Croatia, Mozambique, and Sierra Leone.

Luckily, a decade has passed since the last of Paris's cases began, so we can evaluate results. Paris's fourteen cases are Namibia, Nicaragua, Angola, Cambodia, El Salvador, Mozambique, Liberia, Rwanda, Bosnia, Croatia, Guatemala, East Timor, Kosovo, and Sierra Leone. Today, in 2011, all of these countries are at peace (notwithstanding occasional gunfights in a few of them). In each case—except Namibia, which he calls a success—Paris criticizes the UN effort, particularly the focus on holding elections. But in each case, over the years, the country settled into a new phase of politics where the guns have gone silent, not just temporarily. The UN got the shooting to stop, did not solve all the underlying social injustices and grievances, and the shooting did not resume.

Especially telling is the case of Nicaragua. Paris blasts the results of the UN-sponsored elections that ousted the leftist Sandinista government. Deteriorating living conditions had driven up crime, with "armed bands roaming the countryside . . ." and youth gangs in the cities. Former fighters had not received promised land and resources. Assassinations, kidnappings, and armed takeovers had marred politics. "These developments cast doubt on the durability of peace in Nicaragua," especially because the poverty and inequality that fueled the original Sandinista rebellion had not been resolved. In short, "Nicaragua seems to be a recipe for renewed conflict, not lasting peace." After losing elections in 1996 and 2001, the Sandinistas would presumably lose faith in democracy and take up arms again to right these injustices.

They did not, though. They went back to elections and tried again. In 2006, two years after Paris's book went to print, the leader of the Sandinistas, Daniel Ortega—the revolutionary who had led the country during the civil war and lost power in the first elections afterward—was elected president on his fourth try, after sixteen years in the opposition. Nicaragua passed the hard test of stable peace—the peaceful, democratic transfer of power twice (first away from and then back to the Sandinistas).

To Paris's credit, his tone five years later better reflects these outcomes: "For all the shortcomings of liberal peacebuilding—and there have been many—most host countries would probably be much worse off if not for the assistance they received. The collapse of the peacebuilding project would be tantamount to abandoning tens of millions of people to lawlessness, predation, disease and fear. . . . The flaws of peacebuilding . . . need to be viewed against the backdrop of the larger record . . . [which] indicates that such missions have, on the whole, done considerably more good than harm."

Thus, the 1990s brought both heartbreaking failures as well as striking successes for peacekeeping. But overall, the odds of success in ending conflicts and preserving cease-fires increase with peacekeepers present. As we have seen, the lethality of war in the world also decreased substantially in that period. We cannot prove that peacekeeping caused the greater peace of the 1990s compared with the Cold War years, nor even that peacekeeping played the most important role in it. But the conclusions of Fortna, Collier, Doyle, and Sambanis show that peacekeeping did contribute to that outcome. Peacekeeping works. That message did not get through to the UN right away, however.

5

THE KOFI ANNAN REFORMS

Consolidation and Expansion, 1997–2006

After the problems of the early 1990s, which got more attention than the successes, UN peacekeeping went into a major decline and reassessment phase. Peacekeepers deployed worldwide dropped from about 80,000 to about 20,000. "Having gone from famine to feast in the mid-1990s, the United Nations had a bad case of institutional indigestion." Between 1995 and 1999 the UN "launched just two robust peace operations, in eastern Croatia and in Haiti," both relatively short-lived. In early 1999, "no one would have guessed that the Security Council would soon give the UN Secretariat another go at managing complex civil-military operations in dangerous and volatile, not-quite-postconflict settings." Yet this is just what happened. At the same time, UN peacekeeping went through a years-long process of assessment, drawing lessons, and adapting peacekeeping to changing conditions. These processes of consolidation, reform, and expansion in peacekeeping correspond roughly with the secretary-generalship in 1997–2006 of Kofi Annan (which, by the way, rhymes with *cannon*).

I. The Kofi Annan Story

Annan's years at the UN were a roller-coaster ride. He joined the UN in 1962 as a bright young civil servant from Ghana, and spent thirty years as a bureaucrat, moving from one agency to another, specializing in budgets and personnel, leaving the UN and returning to it. In 1987, at age forty-nine, he became assistant secretary-general in charge of personnel. Soon, the end of the Cold War allowed the Security Council to become active. Annan would later call it "thrilling . . . We were all excited."

With the rapid expansion of UN peacekeeping in the early 1990s, the undersecretary-general in charge of peacekeeping, Marrack Goulding, needed a deputy, and Annan applied for the job. He was appointed by the incoming secretary-general, Boutros-Ghali, with the general expectation that his personnel and budgeting skills would help run the office while Goulding would run the operations. But with operations proliferating around the world, and given Annan's African background, Goulding decided to split up the world and give Annan responsibility for peacekeeping in the Middle East and most of Africa. This division "led to difficulties," as Annan assumed he had full authority in his areas while Goulding assumed that he himself still had the final say on all peacekeeping.

Somalia was in Annan's region, and he favored sending peacekeepers there despite the divergence of that mission from traditional peacekeeping. Goulding did not agree, but Boutros-Ghali agreed with Annan and became what Goulding later called "a steamroller that would not be stopped." The U.S. ambassador later conceded that "we all had doubts. But we were working in an atmosphere of euphoria and that tended to hide some of the issues."

In February 1993, Boutros-Ghali took peacekeeping away from Goulding, whose traditional approach did not fit with the secretary-general's expansive views of the new possibilities of the era. He made Kofi Annan—who was surprised by the move—the new undersecretary-general in charge of peacekeeping. In that role, Annan "presided over the most spectacular rise in peacekeeping in UN history and over its most spectacular fall." He began six new operations in the first eight months. Peacekeeping staff in New York grew from dozens to hundreds of people. But the problems in Somalia "unleashed a mood of UN-bashing in the United States that would linger and then intensify throughout the rest of Annan's career." And the Bosnia mission "arous[ed] worldwide revulsion. . . ." In Bosnia, Annan set up the "dual key" system in which both the UN and NATO each had to approve any bombing missions. The arrangement was supposed to protect countries whose troops were on the ground as peacekeepers, but put Boutros-Ghali in the middle of a tug-of-war, with Americans pressing him to turn the key and Europeans resisting. Boutros-Ghali's decision to allow only small, symbolic air strikes made the UN look "toothless."

Annan's role in Bosnia was "far overshadowed by that of Boutros-Ghali, who liked to micromanage crucial issues." Boutros-Ghali personally held the "key" to authorize bombing, rather than turn it over to the UN force commander on the ground. After the 1995 Srebrenica massacre and a Croatian advance against Serbian forces, U.S. and European leaders agreed on the need for bombing. The U.S. ambassador to the UN (later secretary of state), Madeleine Albright, could not find Boutros-Ghali to get him to turn the key, so she called Annan, who told her Boutros-Ghali was traveling. Annan recounts the conversation: "When will he be available?" "When he arrives." "How can he be incommunicado for so long?" "He doesn't have a private plane. He flies commercial."

So after consulting with the UN commanders in Bosnia, Annan himself gave permission to turn the UN key, and the bombing began. His decisiveness made Annan extremely popular with Washington, and led to U.S. insistence a year later that Annan succeed Boutros-Ghali as secretary-general. U.S. negotiator Richard Holbrooke later said, "Kofi made a historic decision. Without that decision, we might never have gotten to the table." According to Holbrooke, Annan's "gutsy performance . . . in a sense . . . won [him] the job on that day." Meanwhile Boutros-Ghali removed Annan as head of peacekeeping and sent him to the former Yugoslavia as the special representative there, perhaps "shipping a rival as far away as possible."

In 1996, fourteen members of the Security Council voted to give Boutros-Ghali a second term. The United States voted no, using its veto to bar a second term. A weeks-long struggle ensued, with France vetoing the U.S. favorite, Annan, to show displeasure, while the United States and Britain vetoed anyone *but* Annan. Finally France agreed to support Annan if he promised to appoint a French citizen as head of peacekeeping. And that is how Kofi Annan became secretary-general and Bernard Miyet became undersecretary-general for peacekeeping. By the way, France got its money's worth from this maneuver, as Miyet was succeeded by another Frenchman in 2000 and yet another in 2008.

Annan became a famous and popular figure, even in the United States, where the UN had many opponents and few champions. Journalist James Traub describes him as "perhaps the most popular figure ever to occupy the office." Annan and Nelson Mandela, two gray-haired African men, were described as the "only two people with great moral stature in the world today." Annan and his tall Swedish wife, Nane, were a glamorous presence in New York social circles. To top it off, Annan won the Nobel Peace Prize in 2001. Before leaving to accept his prize in Norway, Annan even appeared on *Sesame Street* to resolve a conflict among Muppets.

After the September 11, 2001, attacks on the United States, Annan supported the U.S. position that under the UN Charter it could invoke the right of self-defense to attack al Qaeda and its Taliban hosts in Afghanistan. But Annan refused to support the U.S. invasion of Iraq in 2003, and even called it "illegal," although he did not "cry out and denounce the war in any dramatic way." Annan's support in Washington dropped precipitously and "Republicans clamored for his resignation." When the United States went to war without UN approval, to observers of the UN "it really did feel as if this sixty-year-old experiment in global governance had hiccuped, coughed, and died." But it got worse.

The international community wanted a UN presence in U.S.-occupied Iraq. To go in for four months and get the UN up and running in Iraq, Annan chose his trusted, uniquely qualified administrator, Sergio Vieira de Mello. He had run Kosovo and East Timor for the UN, worked on refugees and humanitarian affairs, and served as the top UN human rights official. The Iraq mission was a thankless task: The U.S. government generally distrusted the UN, which had not backed the war, and the growing Iraqi insurgency viewed the UN and other international organizations as infidel invaders. Moving among these opposing forces, neighboring countries, and the UN Security Council, Vieira de Mello had to reestablish the UN's importance in the world's most important security matter, and had to see to the humanitarian needs of the Iraqi people that had seemingly slipped between the cracks of the occupying power's military planning.

One day Iraqi insurgents drove a truck right up under Vieira de Mello's office and blew it up, collapsing much of the building. Vieira de Mello and more than twenty others were killed, and many wounded. It was "the worst day in the history of the United Nations," killing not only UN personnel but also "faith . . . that the UN stood apart from, and above, the violent conflicts in which it intervened." Annan suffered from "discouragement and melancholy." He said, "You send in some of your best people who are friends and they get killed for trying to sort out the aftermath of the war that you didn't support. . . . It was tough." "UN officials in New York walked around like zombies for a month. . . ." A follow-up bombing a month later led to the withdrawal of most of the UN mission.

Annan's (and the UN's) opponents in Washington also seized on problems with the UN "oil for food" program in Iraq, which had provided funds that were stolen by Saddam Hussein instead of being used for food, and that had been stained by corruption. Even Annan's own son in Switzerland played a minor role in the scandal. "The oil for food troubles were magnified and manipulated . . . to punish the secretary-general for his opposition to the war." Annan spent months in a depressed funk. He hung on through the end of his term in 2006, when the less charismatic Ban Ki-moon took over.

Actually, Annan did more than hang on. In those final years after 2003, the number of peacekeepers doubled from below 40,000 to more than 80,000. A new surge of peace operations in 2003–04 included Liberia, Ivory Coast, Burundi, Haiti, and southern Sudan. At the end of his term Annan left a UN back at the center of the fight to reduce war and bring stability to troubled regions.

Annan's tenure as secretary-general saw "an impressive handful of major achievements. First of all, he established the principle of the right of the international community to interfere when a government abuses its own people. . . . Annan also revived a weakened peacekeeping department and increased the deployment of troops to near-record levels. During his administration, the UN started seventeen new missions. . . . The UN's role as the main coordinator of international relief was solidified under Annan." He also organized a summit in 2000 that established the Millennium Development Goals for health and economic development. "Finally, Annan created an atmosphere of transparency and openness unique in UN history" and carried out extensive management and budgetary reforms in the organization.

II. New, Improved Peacekeeping

The Kofi Annan era saw not just an expansion of peacekeeping but an intensive effort to reform and adapt peacekeeping practices in the late 1990s.

THE PEACEKEEPING TOOLBOX

Various missions use different pieces of the peacekeeping toolbox, and can be grouped roughly along a spectrum from maximum to minimal use of force. At the maximal end is "peace enforcement," meaning the use of military force to compel parties to abide by terms of political agreements such as cease-fires or disarmament. Enforcement of sanctions, such as by preventing smuggling of weapons or conflict diamonds, also involves a high likelihood of the use of force. Slightly lower on the scale are the protection of delivery of humanitarian assistance. Then come supervision of cease-fires, assistance in maintaining law and order, and helping restore civil society such as by assisting political parties and citizen groups. Providing humanitarian assistance and offering "preventive" peacekeeping are lower still on the scale. And at the minimal end are traditional peacekeeping (neutral; force used only in self-defense) and finally unarmed conventional observer or monitoring missions.

Peacekeeping mandates are often described as either "Chapter VI" or "Chapter VII" mandates, referring to two sections of the UN Charter. Chapter VI calls for peaceful resolution of disputes. Chapter VII gives the UN enforcement powers, making decisions of the Security Council binding on members. It says that if nonviolent means do not suffice, the Council "may take such action by air, sea, or land forces as may be necessary to maintain or restore international peace and security." Thus, a peacekeeping mission with a "Chapter VII mandate," in which the Council authorizes the mission with reference to Chapter VII, is one where military force may well be used.

But while there are different types of peace operations, they do not fit neatly into "generations." Peace operations in the post–Cold War era are often seen as more complex and multidimensional than the "traditional" missions of earlier decades, focusing more on civil wars versus interstate wars and with more police and civilian components than before. But this is not entirely true. We have seen that the Congo mission in the early 1960s had many of the elements of today's complex operations.

In addition to peacekeeping, the Security Council also influences international security through diplomacy, moral persuasion, and nonmilitary forms of leverage. In the post–Cold War era, the UN has applied arms embargoes on at least eleven countries, put sanctions on specific exports (such as diamonds) in five, frozen financial assets of seven countries, withdrawn diplomatic relations twice, mandated travel bans (by not issuing visas) in eight countries, banned air travel to five, and applied comprehensive economic sanctions three times (Iraq, Yugoslavia, and Haiti).

THE BRAHIMI REPORT

In 1992 the Department of Peace Keeping Operations (DPKO) was created within a restructured Secretariat. "The UN began to develop a greater institutional capacity for peacekeeping by providing the DPKO with an Office of Planning and Support, . . . a Field Missions Procurement Section, a permanently staffed Situation Room, and a Lessons Learned Unit."

These developments in peacekeeping culminated in the so-called Brahimi Report in 2000, in which the Panel on United Nations Peace Operations reviewed UN peacekeeping and suggested reforms. The report became a touchstone for UN peacekeeping reform because it faced squarely some of the recurrent problems of missions since the days of Ralph Bunche, as well as the more recent multidimensional peace operations. The report highlighted the need for UN member states to "summon the political will" to support peacekeeping "politically, financially, and operationally." If the Security Council is divided, gives conflicting signals, or creates big mandates with inadequate resources, missions cannot succeed.

The report calls for robust military capabilities, with broad rules of engagement, to "project credible force" in complex peacebuilding environments where armed groups challenge the peace process. It also calls for the creation of rapid-deployment standby capabilities so that the UN can take advantage of "the first 6 to 12 weeks following a cease-fire or peace accord [which] are often the most critical ones for establishing both a stable peace and the credibility of a new operation. Opportunities lost during that period are hard to regain." A modest budget should be given to each mission head for "quick impact projects" to gain the population's confidence early on. Funding for disarmament and reintegration should come earlier in a mission. And the peacekeeping department headquarters in New York should be funded ($50 million a year) by the regular UN budget and not peacekeeping assessments, which are considered temporary and preclude permanent staffing of headquarters. In all, these reforms mean "bigger forces, better equipped and more costly."

Regarding headquarters staff, the Brahimi Report summed up the staff assigned to four complex peacekeeping operations established in 1999—Kosovo, Sierra Leone, East Timor, and Congo. With a combined budget of nearly $2 billion and fielding 28,000 military troops, 6,000 police officers, and 2,000 international civilians, these operations relied on combined headquarters support staff of 26 individuals. In any other military force in the world, this ratio of more than a thousand to one would be absurd. "No professional military would dream of operating this way." In 2000–01, $50 million in headquarters costs supported $2.6 billion in peacekeeping.

The secretary-general refined recommendations on deployment times in the Brahimi Report "to mean that 5,000 troops, half of them self-supporting, should be deployed to a traditional operation within thirty days of the issuance of a Security Council mandate, or that 5,000 troops should be deployed to a complex operation within ninety days."

Researchers have described a "golden hour" lasting a few weeks after the arrival of foreign forces. "Resistance is unorganized, spoilers unsure of their future." It is critical to have in place the needed components of the mission, military and civilian, during this period. Longtime UN leader Brian Urquhart emphasizes that speed of deployment matters more in responding to an emergency than planning, competent staff, or well-trained troops. "Because there is no standing UN peacekeeping force, each operation has to start from scratch and at the last minute. . . . In the early days, when governments were enthusiastic and not so aware of the difficulties ahead, we managed to deploy troops remarkably quickly." That ability has been lost, unfortunately.

Deployment now takes four to six months after the Security Council has adopted a mandate. Peacekeeping forces must be assembled from around the world, moved to where they are needed, and in many cases provided with basic equipment to operate. But experts on conflict argue that "if there is no visible and effective peacekeeper presence within six to twelve *weeks* of the signing of a peace accord, . . . then the peace may begin to unravel. . . . Would-be spoilers perceive a free lunch, while serious supporters of peace may lose heart."

Other major, recurring problems in complex peace operations include "muddled instructions" and confusing mandates that create a disconnect between the Security Council and the situation on the ground. "Under-resourcing has been a chronic problem for UN operations," especially when "powerful Security Council members refuse to support more than a fraction of what objective analysis suggests is needed to achieve a mission's objective." Unity in the ranks of peacekeepers also remains a problem, since "military forces will respond first and foremost to their national chains of command and act within the limits of their national doctrines and rules of engagement."

Post-Brahimi Changes

After the Brahimi Report, the UN doubled the staff of the DPKO in New York and "streamlined processes of procurement and logistics. . . ." However, little progress has been made on deployment speed and none on creating a standby UN force.

Following up on the Brahimi Report, a High-level Panel on Threats, Challenges, and Change reported in 2004 with similar ideas for the UN to adapt to the changing context. The panel, with 16 former government officials, laid the groundwork for an expansive report by Secretary-General Annan the next year and the ambitious World Summit in September 2005—"the largest ever gathering of presidents, prime ministers, and monarchs." Results of the meeting, however, fell short of the hopes of UN reform advocates, with *The New York Times* even editorializing that the "once-in-a-generation opportunity to reform and revive the United Nations has been squandered." At the summit, an "odd alliance" of the United States and developing countries supported the status quo by avoiding new policies authorizing humanitarian intervention or formal criteria for using force.

Many people emphasized Security Council reform as a key focus of UN reform in this period, and were seriously disappointed when the 2005 summit more or less killed off the idea for now. The idea was to "democ-ratize" the Council and make it better reflect the world, giving permanent places at the table to countries such as India and Japan, but without veto power. Given the past failings of the Council in responding to crises with clear mandates and adequate resources, the reform idea surely has merit. The problem has always come in the pesky little issue of exactly which countries would get these seats. Japan wants in but China has old issues with Japan. Brazil wants in but would this be fair to Mexico and Argen-tina? A Muslim country is a necessity but which one represents a diverse religious grouping that stretches from Morocco to Indonesia? As you add seat after seat to accommodate all these issues, the Security Council becomes unwieldy, perhaps even less able to respond effectively than today's Council. Reform would weaken the current power enjoyed by the Permanent Five, yet reform would require a change in the UN Charter that any of the five could veto.

We would not want to wait around for Security Council reform to hap-pen, if ever, before reforming and strengthening peacekeeping itself. The UN Charter did not create the Security Council to represent the people of the world, but rather to represent *military power*. Partly because of the founders' genius in giving China a seat, partly by luck, and partly because these things change slowly, today's Permanent Five members still repre-sent the world's military power very well indeed. They control two-thirds of world military spending: a third of the soldiers, half the warships, 85 percent of arms exports, and 99 percent of nuclear weapons. No other country fully fits the profile of a Permanent Five member. (Japan and Germany have large militaries but with restrictions rooted in World War II. India, Pakistan, and Israel have nuclear arsenals but lack either the capabilities or size of the great-power militaries.) So perhaps we should improve the Security Council by getting better consensus among the great powers, rather than by expanding the Council and changing its rules.

The UN created a Peacebuilding Commission (PBC) in 2005—the only major accomplishment of the World Summit—to help countries in post-war transitions. The PBC grew out of the High-Level Panel's observation that the UN lacked a "system explicitly designed to avoid State collapse and the slide to war or to assist countries in their transition from war to peace." Thirty-one member states sit on the commission, which works with a Peacebuilding Fund and a Peacebuilding Support Office in the Secretariat. It funds projects such as political reconciliation, democracy promotion, and police support. Across all four countries that the PBC initially took on—Sierra Leone, Burundi, the Central African Republic, and Guinea-Bissau—the total comes to less than $100 million, or just $4 per person per year in the four countries together. More countries, but not much more money, were added in 2009–10.

Peacebuilding thus has much smaller budgets than peacekeeping. One question is whether, in a country such as Sierra Leone that has made a swift and successful transition from war to peace (achieving both disarmament and democracy), the rapid decrease in UN spending from hundreds of millions to tens of millions per year will leave problems that could re-spark violence in the future. Local conflicts could be left unresolved. Militias might turn in most of their weapons, but perhaps many people kept a gun just in case—and who could blame them with lingering intergroup rivalries that have produced violence in the past? Even democratic elections, especially early in a transition process, can accentuate conflicts and retrigger war. Will the small peacebuilding budgets be enough to prevent this?

In 2007 the UN again restructured the peacekeeping apparatus, creating a Department of Field Support and other reforms to give better support to peacekeeping operations. The UN has also adopted a "zero tolerance" policy for sexual exploitation, including sex with children and prostitutes, for peacekeeping personnel. These reforms followed the 2005 Zeid Report by Jordan's ambassador to the UN, laying out recommended reforms.

THE UN BUREAUCRACY IS . . . BUREAUCRATIC

Since the beginning, and still today, the organizational weaknesses of the UN have created difficulties for peacekeeping. "It is amazing that large-scale UN peacekeeping, which after all started in 1956, remains on such shaky organizational ground."

We have seen how nationality and politics drive staffing decisions, such as sending Conor O'Brien to Katanga because the UN needed someone Irish. UN bureaucracy can be convoluted: The DPKO manual of peacekeeping principles includes a seven-page glossary of acronyms. The Brahimi Report notes large disparities in staff abilities and notes that "better performers are given unreasonable workloads to compensate for those who are less capable." Congo expert Séverine Autesserre reports that "all diplomatic and UN interviewees repeatedly mentioned the endless bureaucratic impediments that they faced . . . [and] complained that they spent too much valuable time filling out request forms, waiting for countless intermediaries to approve their requests, and attempting to comply with the numerous other UN standard operating procedures."

Although the UN and other international organizations generally champion liberal values such as democracy and transparency, they do not operate in that manner internally. Rather, they "are unabashedly undemocratic, and procedures for consent of the governed are very weak." Peacekeeping operations have an "inherently ad hoc, political nature . . . [with] disagreements about their ultimate purposes." And Security Council mandates are kept vague for political reasons. One observer noted of the Secretariat that "if a crisis erupts, nobody will start the day knowing how a decision will be reached. It's all ad hoc. A meeting will be called but without an agenda. They *never* have an agenda. Decisions aren't really taken, or someone is out to undermine them. No one is really confident that their voice will be heard."

Boundaries remain somewhat fluid (and sometimes competitive) between the peacekeeping department and the Department of Political Affairs (DPA). The DPA remained responsible for the mission in East Timor, which combined civilian and peacekeeping aspects, but the mission was transferred to DPKO in 2000 after a conflict with DPA over control. Currently the DPKO controls a mission in Afghanistan that is purely "political," without peacekeepers.

The UN's internal problems are perhaps overemphasized by those who find the UN an easy target. Pérez de Cuéllar complains that the Secretariat "frequently has been maligned as incompetent, overpaid, lazy, and even corrupt. None of this is true." The staff, drawn from 150+ countries, "represent highly disparate work cultures and management styles" but share "the impartiality that is the duty of an international civil servant." UN success, however, still depends on a few highly qualified, highly motivated individuals. The ideal Special Representative of the Secretary-General (SRSG) "must be able to 'walk on water, swim with the piranha fish, and fly with the angels.' These and the other qualities needed occur together only very rarely, and even when they do it may be discovered that it is the angels that have sharper teeth than the piranha."

DISARMAMENT, SECURITY, TRUTH

Peacebuilding has added new kinds of projects to the work of maintaining peace after a cease-fire. Elections, economic development, and humanitarian assistance are on the list. Three other areas deserve special mention—Disarmament, Demobilization, and Reintegration (DDR); Security Sector Reform (SSR); and Truth Commissions.

Disarmament, Demobilization, and Reintegration (DDR)

In the entire peacebuilding enterprise, DDR and above all disarmament hold an absolutely pivotal position. Until armed groups disarm there is an ever-present danger of war renewal. Getting them to disarm is a main reason for the presence of UN peacekeepers to guarantee security. One Swedish study, comparing ex-combatant communities that did and did not successfully demobilize, emphasizes the social networks among elites, midlevel commanders, and grassroots fighters as key to preventing a return to fighting. One issue in reintegrating combatants into their communities is that they may have knowledge of who denounced whom during the war, which could reopen conflicts in the community. A UN study emphasizes grassroots participation and criticizes existing DDR programs as too top-down.

In the past, "most DDR processes have run into funding problems at one stage or another. Delays are quite common." Assessed contributions by UN members for peace operations often fund DDR programs. Since the mid-1990s, multilateral trust funds managed by the UN Development Program or the World Bank, and using both World Bank and other donor funds, have become a major funding source for DDR. For example, in central Africa, a large-scale program works across countries and agencies to support demobilization and reintegration of 450,000 ex-combatants in Angola, Burundi, Central African Republic, Congo, the Congo Republic, Rwanda, and Uganda. The $400 million in funding, from the World Bank and other organizations, is managed by the World Bank. By 2006, about 40 percent of the target group had been simply demobilized, another 40 percent had received help with reinsertion, and the last 20 percent had gotten longer-term help with reintegration. Funding appears to be the big obstacle to more effective DDR programs.

Security Sector Reform (SSR)

Frequently, civil war violence fluidly crosses between the military and police spheres of responsibility. Armed police working for the government may play a key role in battling insurgencies, and may be a frequent target. They may also be part of the problem fueling the insurgency, if they use violence too brutally against a population. When civil wars end, armed groups may disband but the government's police force continues as an armed presence. Police and the entire judicial apparatus may be biased or oppressive toward a minority group or political party, especially with a recent war history. Wartime often worsens corruption in the justice system.

Thus, international civilian assistance seeks to help reform the security sector and strengthen the rule of law in postwar societies. For example, the European Union Police Mission in Bosnia and Herzegovina began in 2003, early in the war, and continued for years after the Dayton Agreement. It "monitored, advised and inspected" the Bosnian police forces with the aims of supporting police reforms, increasing accountability, and countering organized crime. In next-door Croatia, the UN rebuilt the police force in eastern Croatia to integrate Serbs and Croats, no easy task.

Courts, judges, and lawyers also receive assistance in SSR programs. War may have destroyed needed facilities such as prisons and courtrooms. Government funds may be unavailable for judicial reforms or for hiring needed personnel. Trained judges and lawyers may have fled the country or been killed. These practical issues come on top of the serious problems about bias, corruption, and ethnic dominance that may prevent even a well-functioning security sector from playing a positive role in rebuilding societies after war.

War-Crimes Tribunals

In many civil wars, serious war crimes have been committed by one or more parties. Different countries have dealt with these crimes by ignoring them, giving amnesty to the perpetrators as part of a political deal, creating fact-finding commissions, or bringing perpetrators to trial. The trials, where they occur, take place in several kinds of settings. National courts take up most of the load. Special international tribunals to hear war-crimes cases have been established in several important cases. And there is now an International Criminal Court that can occasionally try war criminals not dealt with in these other venues.

As we have seen, the atrocities committed in Rwanda in 1994 are still playing out in judicial cases in recent years, particularly in the special international tribunal set up for Rwanda. We also saw that in Mozambique no war-crimes tribunals occurred, nor indeed much SSR at all, yet the country put the war behind it.

Truth Commissions

Truth Commissions have been more numerous than war-crimes tribunals. Starting with Uganda in 1974 after the murderous reign of dictator Idi Amin, and then Bolivia and Argentina in the early 1980s, some twenty-seven countries operated Truth Commissions through 2002. In 2002, six were in business at once—in Peru, Panama, the former Yugoslavia, East Timor, Sierra Leone, and Ghana. A successful truth commission can help overcome postwar denial and help a society deal with psychological trauma.

The South African Truth and Reconciliation Commission (TRC) was among the most successful, and potentially a model for later commissions elsewhere. Established in 1995 after the end of apartheid, and headed by Desmond Tutu, the TRC had the power to grant amnesty to perpetrators of atrocities if it determined that the acts were politically motivated and that a full and truthful confession had been made. The TRC aimed for "restorative justice" rather than retribution. Whereas traditional trials focus on the criminals, with victims either ignored or brought in as witnesses, the TRC focused on the victims, spending 160 days of hearings just taking their stories.

The first day of these hearings, in April 1996, heard from the widow of an activist who had been assassinated by the apartheid regime eleven years earlier, when she was twenty years old with two young children. She sat in the hearing with two other women whose husbands had been killed the same day, and behind them sat victim-support counselors hired by the TRC. The widow described how her husband failed to come home, how the stack of newspapers she was to deliver to homes the next morning had a picture of his burned car, how she went to a neighbor's house for support. Her testimony led her to sway back and forth and wail with grief, at which point Tutu called a ten-minute break and then resumed by leading a popular antiapartheid hymn. A white journalist present later wrote that the widow's crying was "the signature tune, the definitive moment, the ultimate sound of what the process is about."

The TRC's work took six years. In the end, of more than 7,000 amnesty applications, about 1,200 were granted, 5,500 refused, and several hundred withdrawn. South Africa's experience with offering amnesties was more successful in moving the society forward than the experience of Rwanda at the same time, where a military victory by one side meant that there was no need to offer amnesties or seek reconciliation.

Truth commissions may bring closure to conflicts but may also stir up conflict. "Perpetrators' confessions unsettle listeners, who learn disturbing and lurid details of past authoritarian state violence, sometimes for the first time. . . . Conflict erupts over confessions as social actors dispute interpretations of what happened and compete for power over whose interpretations will shape the political agenda. . . ." Despite the hope that perpetrators' confessions will lead to reconciliation, often there are simply "irreconcilable differences between victims and perpetrators."

Although the South African TRC centered on confessions by perpetrators, "no other country has adopted the confessional model of reconciliation. Truth commissions elsewhere have provided amnesty without requiring confessions." Brazil gave a blanket amnesty; Chile's truth commission offered amnesty without confession; and Argentina had a "full array of truth commissions, trials, pardons and amnesty, and retrials. . . ." These three countries "tried, mainly unsuccessfully, to keep contentious issues off the public agenda in order to protect fragile political systems from polarizing debate. . . . Despite their failure to silence the past, these democracies have survived and flourished."

Political agreements to end wars may not adequately solve inequalities, address grievances, and punish atrocities. Security sector reform raises dilemmas. Justice and the rule of law are important, and conversely impunity for atrocities has bad consequences. However, ending a war may be as important, even if the rule of law is compromised. Victims may find such a peace unsatisfying. "What kind of peace do we have if the men who raped and killed women now sit in the government?" asked a Congolese woman at a U.S. workshop in 2003. The other women present, who came from a variety of war-ravaged societies around the world, agreed that "it was better to give blanket amnesties to end the war and tolerate the impunity than to watch the violence go on. On the other hand, they all agreed, ending impunity and bringing accountability for crimes committed during the war would [be] not only bringing justice but also helping to end the cycle of violence based on revenge and retribution. I will return to this issue of peace versus justice in Chapter 8.

COSTS AND COMPOSITION OF PEACE OPERATIONS

Within the UN, costs of peacekeeping missions are relatively straightforward, although the reimbursement of contributing countries remains subject to "ongoing haggling" among UN members. Overall, in 2003 the cost for worldwide peacekeeping by *industrialized* countries was nearly $150,000 per soldier, with the UN reimbursing less than $25,000 of that, whereas very poor countries such as Bangladesh had far lower costs, below the UN reimbursement.

Looking at just the UN costs and focusing on that "ongoing haggling," the peacekeeping budget is divided with almost half paid by the permanent members of the Security Council, about half by the developed countries, and just 2 percent paid by sixty developing countries and one-fiftieth of one percent of the budget coming from the poorest ninety-seven countries, which are a majority of UN members. Just as the famous bank robber Willie Sutton said he robbed banks because "that's where the money is," so the UN's peacekeeping efforts tap the richer countries because they have the money to pay the bills.

In terms of the size of peacekeeping missions—a major determinant of the cost—the number of troops is determined not so much by the objective needs as by what is authorized by a wary Security Council (or the equivalent body for a regional or multinational mission), and by what contributions actually materialize from troop-contributing countries. The process of rounding up enough peacekeeping troops is somewhat improvised and differs from one mission and organization to the next, with the UN most often drawing on neutral and distant countries whereas regional organizations more often make use of neighbors with interests in the conflict.

Troop Contributing Countries

Today's UN missions draw on troops from 60 percent of the world's countries. Of those, eighty-seven countries contributed at least 100 troops in a year in 2001–05. Historically, higher income countries were more likely than poorer ones to contribute troops, and democracies were three times as likely to contribute peacekeepers as were autocracies. But since 1970 the UN has relied increasingly on peacekeeping troops from poorer countries. Countries with GDP per capita below the world average supplied 50 percent of all peacekeepers in 1991–95, 65 percent in 1996–2000, and almost 90 percent in 2001–05.

In early 2011, the top fifteen contributing countries were Pakistan and Bangladesh with more than 10,000 troops each; India with almost 9,000; Nigeria (6,000); Egypt (5,000); Nepal, Jordan, Rwanda (4,000 each); Ghana (3,000); Uruguay, Senegal, Ethiopia, Brazil, South Africa, and China (more than 2,000 each). Thus, the four South Asian countries—Pakistan, Bangladesh, India, and Nepal—combined contributed almost 35,000 troops, a third of the world total.

Nepal is noteworthy on this list, having only recently emerged from its own civil war. As other countries have also discovered recently, one solution to the problem of demobilizing armed forces when a civil war ends is to send those battle-hardened troops out of the country, away from trouble, to keep the peace elsewhere. The government even gets paid for their services, unlike disarmament programs that require payments to former combatants.

South Asian countries have "both the capacity and competence to provide more soldiers to undertake the complex integrated missions" that the UN now operates. Historically the largest troop contributor in the world, India has sent more than 80,000 soldiers on forty-one missions. India also increases its troops' effectiveness by having individuals serve a year with the UN rather than the six months common for Western countries. "Indian armed forces take immense pride in this participation. It is seen both as the nation's commitment to international peace and as a showcase of its military proficiency."

India's archrival, Pakistan, is also "one of the UN's most reliable peacekeepers. . . . Indeed, rivalry and competition with India has been an important motivation for Pakistan in supporting UN peace operations." Surprisingly, for two countries that went to war several times during the decades of their UN participation, "there has been very good cooperation between Indian and Pakistani forces in the field (as well as with those from Bangladesh). Indian and Pakistani forces have served under each other's command. All manner of logistics and combat support tasks have been provided by one to the other, and these, too, have been very successful."

Bangladesh has specialized in peacekeeping for several reasons. It has a large army left over from a military government, but "no perception of a major external threat," and peacekeeping "helps keep the military engaged and profitably employed. . . ." Bangladesh, as a very poor country, especially needs the payments that the UN provides for peacekeepers. And as a poor, densely populated country it has a long-standing policy of exporting surplus labor. Finally, peacekeeping burnishes a positive image of the country in the eyes of donor countries on whose aid Bangladesh depends.

One country rarely represented in UN peacekeeping forces is the United States. American leaders assume, not unreasonably, that U.S. troops would become targets if they served in the relatively "soft" environment of UN peacekeeping. U.S. peacekeeping, such as in Bosnia after 1995, has worked best when authorized by the UN but run by NATO.

Originally, the UN was to coordinate military forces (to respond to aggression) through a Military Staff Committee, with officers from the great powers working together under the Security Council, using forces made available to the UN by member states. Mostly because of the Cold War, this committee was never used, although it still exists. Oddly, although the great powers refuse to use this apparatus, they also have repeatedly declined to abolish it. The committee is low-cost and might someday prove useful as I suggest in Chapter 12.

III. Regional Organizations in Peace Operations

In addition to the 100,000 or so UN peacekeepers now deployed worldwide, about 50,000 more peacekeepers serve with non-UN international peacekeeping missions. These non-UN peacekeepers play an important part in the overall picture.

THE ROLE OF REGIONAL ORGANIZATIONS

In aggregate, through 2006, the UN had organized sixty-eight peacekeeping missions, thirty-three regional organizations, and twenty-four multinational groups. But of the non-UN missions, more than a third were either approved or authorized by the Security Council. So the focus of peacekeeping remains on UN missions and mandates. "The two types of operations . . . thrive together, and overall appear to share burdens and (particularly during recent years) coordinate rather than compete."

In terms of success rates, UN and non-UN missions have similar outcomes. In each case, about one-fifth of the deployment-months in civil wars in 1948–2004 had ongoing war. For deployments in *interstate* wars, both types had much lower rates of ongoing war, below 2 percent of the months. This equivalence in outcomes does not necessarily mean that non-UN and UN missions are interchangeable or could be randomly chosen, since the international community may be selecting one or the other type based on which seems best suited to the circumstances.

Peacekeeping outside the framework of the UN is not new. The UN Charter proposes use of regional forces: "Nothing in the present Charter precludes the existence of regional arrangements or agencies for dealing with such matters relating to the maintenance of international peace and security as are appropriate for regional action." However, the actual use of regional organizations "was not explicitly decreed or even necessarily desired; rather it has come about in an improvised way and in response to specific regional situations."

In 1979, when Egypt and Israel made peace, they called for a UN peacekeeping force in the Sinai between them. However, as it became clear that Arab countries opposed the peace and that the Soviet Union would block UN participation, the two countries created, with the United States, a small, independent peacekeeping force, the Multinational Force and Observers. Still in business today, it has been one of the most durable and successful peace operations to date.

Some regional organizations can help the world respond to the need for more "robust" peacekeepers. Only one peace operation before the end of the Cold War, that in the Congo in 1961–64, was a "peace enforcement" mission. In 1990–2003, seventeen others were initiated. Only two of these were operated by the UN (Somalia 1993–95 and Sierra Leone), but seven others were mandated by the UN and their actual operation "subcontracted" to another organization. These other organizations were NATO (Bosnia), the European Union (Congo 2003), and various Multinational Forces patched together for each occasion (Somalia 1992–93, Rwanda, Haiti, Albania 1997, and East Timor).

The remaining eight peace enforcement operations were mandated and run *outside* the UN by other international organizations. NATO carried out one (Kosovo), the post-Soviet Commonwealth of Independent States (CIS) carried out one (Tajikistan), ECOWAS carried out three (Liberia, Sierra Leone 1997–99, and Guinea-Bissau), the Southern African Development Community ran two (Lesotho and Congo 1998–2002), and the International Mediation Committee delegated a multinational force to carry out one (Central African Republic). Incidentally, in this last case, the "mediation committee" was invented for the occasion. In terms of the lead states—providing the bulk of military forces for a mission—the United States played the lead role in five, France in three, Nigeria in two, and one each for Russia, Italy, Senegal/Guinea, South Africa, Zimbabwe, and Australia. Generally these lead states represented a capable military power located close to the scene of a conflict—Australia in East Timor, Russia in Tajikistan, Zimbabwe in Congo, and so forth.

Overall, "in the vast majority of [these] cases, international organisations effectively ceded immediate operational control over the interventions they mandated to a single nation-state." For example, the ECOWAS intervention in Liberia in 1990 was overwhelmingly an operation of Nigeria, which spent $5 billion and lost 500 lives there.

In sixteen other cases that had some aspects of peace enforcement—nine during the Cold War and seven since—an international organization gave a mandate to the operation in the majority of cases. While the UN may be less able to judge a conflict situation than the regional organization closest to it, nonetheless the UN is better able to confer legitimacy on an action. A lead state that cannot secure a UN mandate can turn to other international organizations such as NATO or the Southern African Development Community to legitimate its actions.

The four multidimensional peace operations that began in 1999 (Kosovo, Sierra Leone, Congo, and East Timor) and the four in 2003–04 (Liberia, Ivory Coast, Burundi, and Haiti) differed from those in the 1990s "in terms of one central, new, and general practice: non-UN, militarily robust, peace-enforcement troops often intervened to stop the fighting and enforce the peace, followed by (or in the midst of) more standard UN multidimensional peacekeeping missions." These outside militaries were: NATO (Kosovo), Britain (Sierra Leone), France/EU (Congo), an Australian-led multinational force (East Timor), the U.S. Marines (Liberia), France (Ivory Coast), and the United States (Haiti).

As the three Western UN Security Council members—France, Britain, and the United States—became more involved in peacekeeping in the 1990s, they developed new military doctrine that treated "peacekeeping and peace enforcement as waypoints on a single continuum that runs from non-use to maximum use of force." Peace operations and counterinsurgency operations have grown closer in nature, as seen in Afghanistan today where civil/political and military elements of counterinsurgency mix fluidly with humanitarian assistance, intertribal conflict resolution, and civil society capacity building, all under a UN mandate but with a large, heavily armed NATO force carrying it out.

In several cases, the UN has fielded its own peacekeepers but relied on robust "over the horizon" military forces of countries or regional organizations for backup. As we have seen, this support was important to the operation in Croatia, where NATO had strong forces next door in Bosnia, and it was to play an important role also in Sierra Leone (Britain) and Congo (France and the European Union), as we shall see in Chapter 6. In the Congo in 2006, the EU kept most of its forces next door in Gabon as an "on call force."

In 1999, the European Union launched its European Security and Defense Policy (ESDP), which attempts to coordinate European military actions taken outside of NATO, especially in humanitarian and peacekeeping tasks. The next year a European military staff and appropriate committees were established. The first major use of these new capabilities was in the Congo in 2003. With France in the lead, this action deployed more than 2,000 troops successfully, albeit from only five contributing EU countries. In 2004, the EU deployed 7,000 troops to Bosnia to take over from NATO there, continuing to use NATO assets in a "relatively unproblematic" transition. The 2,000 EU troops sent to the Congo in 2006 for the election there were the next major EU deployment. In responding to massive atrocities against civilians, the EU has "by far the greatest potential strengths" of any regional organization.

In 2001, the European Union made operational a long-planned Rapid Reaction Force that could potentially deploy 60,000 troops in sixty days and sustain them for a year. "In practice, however, this force has yet to undertake any serious peacekeeping," although EU forces have taken the lead in Macedonia and Kosovo since 2003.

In January 2000, a group of seven countries declared operational a UN Standby High Readiness Brigade (SHIRBRIG) with 4,000 troops. Participants are Denmark (the headquarters), Norway, Sweden, Poland, the Netherlands, Austria, and Canada. Deployments are supposed to take two to four weeks rather than months now. The unit sent a mission to Ethiopia and Eritrea in 2000–01 after the war there, and a mission to southern Sudan in 2005.

The European or American peace operations tend to be costly, although outside the UN costs "are not easy to calculate, as there is no standardized cost reporting . . . or central repository of such data." Operations undertaken by Western military forces are much more expensive than UN operations drawing on troops from poorer countries. In 1999, costs to deploy Western European NATO forces in Kosovo exceeded $125,000 per soldier per year, and for each American soldier, $200,000 per year. In Libya in 2011, a NATO-enforced no-fly zone cost more than $100 million just for the opening volley of cruise missiles.

Russia and the other members of the CIS, which loosely ties together most of the former Soviet republics, have run four major peacekeeping operations—in Moldova, Tajikistan, and two in Georgia. These latter two cannot be considered successes, since the status quo there broke down in 2008 with a brief but intense war between Russia and Georgia.

Other important regional organizations that have done peacekeeping include the African Union (AU) and its predecessor the Organization of African Unity, the Economic Community of West African States (ECOWAS), and others. Regional organizations vary greatly in their peacekeeping efforts, mostly because organizations such as the EU and AU differ so much in their resources and governance.

The Question of Legitimacy

One problem with "subcontracting" international missions to individual countries or regional organizations is that their national interests may take precedence, especially since the countries or organizations most likely to offer their services are those with greatest history or stakes in the conflict. This problem of national interest potentially undermines the legitimacy of interventions.

International organizations provide a very important role in conferring legitimacy on peace operations, in addition to their practical roles in organizing and funding such operations. Actions by a single country or a "coalition of the willing," as in the 2003 invasion of Iraq, have less international legitimacy than similar actions undertaken by NATO or the UN, as in the ongoing war in Afghanistan.

The UN stamp of approval confers "unique legitimacy"—as Kofi Annan said before the Iraq War proceeded without it in 2003. An "overwhelming consensus" has developed that the UN Security Council is the body best suited to authorize military actions. However, only national governments, not the UN or other international organizations, have the means to launch robust peace enforcement operations. International organizations, then, are needed not for their capabilities but for their legitimizing function. Nations conceive of themselves as members of an international community with rules, and care about the legitimacy of their actions "because they enjoy being seen as good 'club members' by other states."

Governance in Regional Organizations

Regional organizations have different internal governance than the UN. Without the approval of the Security Council, a UN peace operation cannot proceed. In regional organizations, the situation can be more ambiguous.

For instance, the intervention of ECOWAS in Liberia "was a watershed" as "the first peace enforcement operation launched by an African subregional organisation [and] . . . internationally recognised as a test case for regional conflict management." But when Nigeria sent troops to Liberia in 1990 under the ECOWAS banner, it violated ECOWAS rules that should have required all members' consensus for military action. Since two member states opposed the action, the Liberian request for assistance went to a Standing Mediation Committee that Nigeria had created within ECOWAS just months earlier, and where consensus did not apply. In the 1990s, Nigeria contributed between 62 and 86 percent of troops to the ECOWAS force.

Similarly, in 1998 Angola and Zimbabwe sent troops to the Congo under the banner of the Southern African Development Community (SADC), and saved the Kabila government there. In its efforts in the Congo, Zimbabwe "consistently sought to sideline South Africa," a fellow member of SADC, because the South African president, Nelson Mandela, opposed military action in the Congo.

AFRICAN ISSUES

African regional organizations have particular weaknesses in peacekeeping. In Africa, six different regional organizations have undertaken peacekeeping since 1979. The Organization of African Unity, predecessor of the AU, ran eleven operations, mostly small-scale. In French-speaking West Africa, a group of countries created an organization that sent military observers to monitor the border between Burkina Faso and Mali in 1986. ECOWAS sent five missions, including Sierra Leone (discussed in Chapter 6). The Southern African Development Community went into both the Congo and Lesotho in 1998. A group of states near the Sahara Desert sent a force to the Central African Republic in 2002, and later that year a different group of central African countries also deployed a force there. In 2006, an unsuccessful attempt to send peacekeepers to Somalia was made by the Intergovernmental Authority on Development (IGAD), a group of six eastern African countries.

AU forces in Somalia today remain "totally reliant on donor funding and on external technical support for mission planning and management." Despite obvious shortcomings, "the UN and the concerned international community . . . continue to authorize and promote new AU missions such as [in Somalia] with seemingly scant regard for the fact that Africa only began creating modest regional peace and security structures and capabilities during the past decade, while the vastly more capable UN has had nearly sixty years of experience in peacekeeping."

In recent years the African Union has set up five regional standby brigades available in principle for peace operations, each with several thousand troops along with hundreds of observers, police, and civilians. These include one from SADC in the south, one from ECOWAS in the west, and one from IGAD in the east, as well as central and northern African forces. As of 2011 these brigades are just getting off the ground. A planned sixth continental brigade at the AU headquarters in Ethiopia was scrapped, although it "may well have been the most useful tool in the box. . . ."

Thus, unfortunately, the region most in need of peacekeeping, Africa, has the least capacity to supply that demand. In Asia, also, obstacles to interstate cooperation have left the region without regional structures prepared for peacekeeping and conflict management.

Regional organizations may also lack basic capabilities needed for peacekeeping. For example, in 2002, ECOWAS committed to sending troops to Ivory Coast to support a cease-fire there, but "was hampered by funding constraints and stalled for more than two months." It eventually deployed with half the authorized force and "hopelessly insufficient resources." Early on, the operation "stalled . . . because of a lack of human, financial, and other resources." When the main body of the force deployed to the capital, "it had no vehicles and no place to work." The contingent from Benin was late to arrive in Ivory Coast because it had to wait for logistical support promised by Belgium but slow to materialize. A force of this type can also suffer discipline problems. By some accounts, West African peacekeepers with the ECOWAS mission in Liberia and Sierra Leone fathered thousands of children and spread HIV/AIDS and other sexually transmitted diseases.

The AU mission in Darfur, Sudan, "was never planned: it just happened," in the words of one expert on the conflict. The deployment "was put together in a rush because of political imperatives," and suffered from "a fundamental lack of capacity to set goals; integrate police, civilian, and military planning; sequence deployment; provide logistical support; and generally to develop the mission in a coherent way." Because of the AU's "severely limited . . . capacity," its impact has been "very limited."

The African Union's "interventions may be more acceptable to the host countries . . . [than a UN mission but] probably for the wrong reason"—not because of regional affinity but because an AU force is seen as weaker. And "troop contributions from adjoining states . . . [are] almost always a bad idea" because of the potential for de facto border adjustments. Neighboring states should be included in discussions, one report argues, but only in a third outer circle where the inner two consist of the major powers with troops and money at stake, and the major financial donors.

The United States, France, and Britain have each funded projects to help train and supply African countries for peacekeeping, but with little coordination among the three sponsors. A SADC peacekeeping training center located in Zimbabwe was financed by Denmark from 1997 to 2002 but became "moribund" after Zimbabwe's policies led Denmark and other Western countries to withdraw support. SADC countries agreed to fund the effort themselves, but "it is doubtful that any such contributions will materialize. . . ." Other peacekeeping training centers continue to operate, however, in Kenya, Mali, and Nigeria. And in Ghana, the Kofi Annan International Peacekeeping Training Centre, affiliated with ECOWAS but run by Ghana, has adequate funding from Western governments and provides courses on peacekeeping for African officers.

The first African Union peacekeeping mission was in Burundi in 2003, after a cease-fire agreement. The AU expected to cover the mission's $134 million budget with donations from Western countries, since it lacked adequate funds itself. But the West pledged only $50 million, and only $10 million of this, along with $12 million worth of in-kind contributions, actually materialized. Thus the AU mission could not fully implement the cease-fire agreements, nor get far with the DDR process. After a year the UN came in to take over responsibility in Burundi.

So subcontracting to a regional organization may work better if you get NATO's military capabilities than those of, say, the African Union. But, of course, those more robust capabilities cost a lot more.

The new mix of complex peace operations, UN reforms, and the use of regional organization to provide robust backup all came into play in the most recent wave of peacekeeping missions. These missions, from Sierra Leone to Congo, are the final piece of my peacekeeping story.

6

THE SIERRA LEONE MODEL
Multidimensional Peace Operations, 1998–2011

The fourteen UN peacekeeping missions worldwide in 2011 vary tremendously in size and mandate, but about two-thirds of all the money and troops in UN peacekeeping worldwide today go to five civil wars in Africa. These missions are in Liberia, Ivory Coast, Congo, southern Sudan, and western Sudan (Darfur).

These five African cases all follow more or less the same trajectory, but at different speeds and with different rates of success in staying on track. The trajectory starts with a cease-fire agreement, then a political agreement (power sharing and constitutional issues). A transitional government is formed, usually with rebel or other militia leaders occupying high positions of power such as controlling ministries or serving as vice president. Constitutional issues are resolved as a permanent government structure forms. At some point, elections take place. The UN oversees the return of displaced people to their homes, and the demobilization, disarmament, and reintegration of armed militias into either civilian life or the national army. Police are trained; corruption is reduced in the security sector. The international community may back the creation of either a war crimes tribunal or a truth commission, or both. Support is provided for civil society, human rights, gender issues, economic development, and other such areas. With political and military stability established, along with working democracy, peacekeepers can be withdrawn and a small civilian assistance mission left behind. That is the model.

I. The Mission in Sierra Leone

Sierra Leone is the sixth country on the list of five. It no longer appears on the list because the peacekeepers have gone home, mission accomplished. Economist Paul Collier calls it "a major success."

AN ESPECIALLY BRUTAL WAR

By the end of the 1990s, Kofi Annan estimated that the Security Council was spending 60 percent of its time dealing with Africa. And the most "immediately horrible" crisis there in 1999 was Sierra Leone. The war in Sierra Leone seems, at first glance, an unlikely place for a UN success story. The country had extreme poverty ($700 per person income per year on average), lootable resources (especially diamonds), and endemic corruption. And during the years of war, violence went completely out of control. All sides committed atrocities and used child soldiers. The most memorable aspects of the war were the rebels' widespread practice of cutting off civilians' limbs and the use of drugged children on killing sprees as shock troops.

Ishmael Beah was one of those children, fighting on the government side. Later he wrote a best-selling memoir about his experiences in the war. Journalists have questioned the truthfulness of some of his accounts, but the overall gist of Beah's experiences rings true and corresponds with accounts from other child soldiers in the war in Sierra Leone. Probably Beah served as a soldier for a shorter time than he claims, exaggerated some elements, and got some details wrong. Nonetheless, Beah gives us a picture of child soldiers' experiences in Sierra Leone.

Beah grew up with his parents and siblings in a village in the interior of Sierra Leone, near a valuable mining center. The war, when it started, seemed far away. When he was ten, however, war refugees began arriving at his village, some having walked hundreds of miles. The refugees told stories of killings and burnings, which Beah found hard to believe. His main information about war came from movies like *Rambo* and from BBC coverage of the war in next-door Liberia. In the refugees, he saw the traumatic effects of war—"The children of these families wouldn't look at us, and they jumped at" sudden noises.

In 1993, when Beah was twelve, his village was attacked by the rebels, who wanted control of the mining areas, while Beah was sixteen miles away at a town. People told him that "the attack had been too sudden, too chaotic; that everyone had fled in different directions in total confusion." "When we left home the day before, there had been no indication the rebels were anywhere near." Now, as it would turn out, Beah would not see his parents alive again. Later, Beah observes of being in a war that "things changed rapidly in a matter of seconds and no one had any control over anything."

The war that hit Beah so suddenly had begun a couple of years earlier, in 1991. Rebel forces calling themselves the Revolutionary United Front (RUF), led by Foday Sankoh, attacked the government from the Liberian border. Reportedly, Liberian president Charles Taylor, who wanted Sierra Leone's mineral wealth, backed the RUF—and he went on trial in 2008 in the international court in the Netherlands for crimes in Sierra Leone. The RUF attack destabilized Sierra Leone's politics. A coup overthrew the government the next year, and the military government continued to fight the RUF. In the period that Beah writes about, there was no UN in Sierra Leone, no negotiations, and no cease-fire.

The RUF used violence against civilians to terrorize and control the population in its territory. It serves as a prime example of the deliberate use of atrocities to amplify a small group's power by inciting fear in a large population. "The RUF signature atrocity of amputation left thousands of Sierra Leoneans graphically wounded for life. . . . Such signature wounds . . . are deliberately intended to spread an effect within society."

Beah, after seeing traumatic scenes of wounded survivors and bodies, ran away with friends. He describes long, difficult times trying to find food and staying on the move ahead of the war. His group of six teenaged boys found itself decidedly unwelcome in villages they came to. "People were terrified of boys our age. Some had heard rumors about young boys being forced by rebels to kill their families and burn their villages. These children now patrolled in special units, killing and maiming civilians. . . . This was one of the consequences of the civil war. People stopped trusting each other, and every stranger became an enemy."

After many ordeals, and after learning that his family (also refugees) had been killed in a massacre, Beah himself was inducted into the government army. He joined with a group of teenaged boys, and they were quickly swept into the nightmarish world of child soldiers. He became addicted to "white capsules" that "gave me a lot of energy," and he used cocaine mixed with gunpowder as well as marijuana. "After several doses of these drugs, all I felt was numbness to everything and so much energy that I couldn't sleep for weeks. We watched movies at night. War movies, *Rambo: First Blood*, *Rambo II*, *Commando*, and so on. . . . We all wanted to be like Rambo; we couldn't wait to implement his techniques."

"When we ran out of food, drugs, ammunition, and gasoline . . . we raided rebel camps, in towns, villages, and forests. We also attacked civilian villages to capture recruits and whatever else we could find." When sent out to fight, Beah reports, "the combination of these drugs gave us a lot of energy and made us fierce. . . . Killing had become as easy as drinking water." Beah describes a contest based on killing prisoners, and many graphic scenes of brutality.

"Sierra Leone has one of the world's worst records for recruiting children as soldiers," concluded a 2001 study. "Between 1992 and 1996, the period of the worst fighting between the Government forces and the Revolutionary United Front (RUF), an estimated 5,400 children were forced to fight on both sides." The study noted that "children are perceived to be the best fighters, obedient and easily manipulated." By another estimate, more than 15,000 children fought in Sierra Leone, making them a majority of the total combatants. The use of child soldiers is surprisingly common in wars around the world and, despite some isolated historical cases, a relatively new phenomenon. One researcher counts them as present in three-quarters of the world's armed conflicts. Child soldiers "did not need to be paid, and they followed orders better than adults. Many children were plied with drugs, forced to commit atrocities . . . and threatened with violent retribution against their families if they failed to fight." As one Chadian army commander said, "Child soldiers are ideal because they don't complain, they don't expect to be paid, and if you tell them to kill, they kill."

UNICEF, the UN agency concerned with the well-being of the world's children, became the lead agency in Sierra Leone on child protection in 1993, years before the peacekeepers arrived. And it was UNICEF in 1996 that abruptly plucked Beah, aged fifteen, from his military service under an arrangement made with both sides to demobilize some child soldiers. "A truck came to the village. Four men dressed in clean blue jeans and white T-shirts that said UNICEF on them in big blue letters jumped out. . . . The men were all too clean to have been in the war." After discussions with the UNICEF people, Beah's officer told fifteen boys to lay down their weapons and go with UNICEF. "Your work here is done."

The UNICEF staff were happy that they had liberated poor boys like these from a terrible ordeal. But for Beah and the others, the transition was traumatic. They were torn from their most important social relationship, with their unit, and suddenly isolated as well as disarmed. "The squad had been our family." And they did not understand why their work was done when they had been good soldiers and the war was still going on. In addition, they became crazed with withdrawal from their drug addictions. And "it was infuriating to be told what to do by civilians. . . . A few days earlier, we could have decided whether they would live or die."

Nonetheless, over some months Beah began to recover his life in a center run by UNICEF and NGOs such as the Catholic charity Children Associated with War (CAW). The international community was interested in the results of these programs. One afternoon at Beah's center, "visitors from the European Commission, the UN, UNICEF, and several NGOs arrived . . . in a convoy of cars." After a successful talent show, the center director called in Beah and said, "You and your friends really impressed those visitors. They know now that it is possible for you boys to be rehabilitated."

Agencies such as UNICEF and CAW working with demobilized child soldiers could have done much more with better funding. A *Washington Post* reporter noted in 2000 that "because of funding limitations, most children receive only thirty to ninety days of rehabilitation before they are forced to find jobs and fend for themselves." This created a particular problem in that the children, because of war crimes they had committed, were not always welcome back in their home communities, and might find jobs and fend for themselves by returning to violence. "All levels of society vigorously debated whether to treat child soldiers as victims or perpetrators. In many cases children played both roles."

Beah suffered flashbacks from war traumas. But he developed, and was chosen to represent Sierra Leone at a UN conference in New York. As he walked back from an interview for that position, "a convoy of cars, military vans, and Mercedes-Benzes festooned with national flags passed by. Their windows were tinted, so I couldn't see who rode in them."

It was, in fact, the new president of Sierra Leone in the car. In 1995, the UN had appointed a Special Envoy, an Ethiopian diplomat, to try to negotiate Sierra Leone's return to civilian rule (after the 1992 coup). Two regional organizations also participated in this process, the African Union (AU) and the Economic Community of West African States (ECOWAS), which had begun using Nigerian troops for peacekeeping in nearby Liberia in 1990. In 1996, elections took place, and Ahmed Tejan Kabbah—the man in the car with tinted glass—became president. The RUF did not participate in the elections, however, and the war continued.

Conflict Diamonds

"Conflict diamonds" played an important role in the war. By controlling diamond-producing territory, the RUF was able to export diamonds illegally through Liberia and fund its rebellion on the proceeds. The RUF revenues from diamonds in the 1990s may have been $25–$125 million per year. Over a number of years, first NGOs and then international organizations took up the issue of sanctioning this war-producing diamond trade. In 2000, the UN Security Council put an embargo on all imports of rough diamonds from Sierra Leone, then allowed only diamonds certified under a monitoring system (excluding RUF diamonds). Eventually certification procedures known as the Kimberley Process were developed to weed out conflict diamonds in other war zones as well.

Foreign Forces

Foreign armies and mercenaries also played important roles in the Sierra Leone war. Foreign mercenaries hired by the government of Sierra Leone were paid by foreign mining interests to attack the RUF rebels in the mid-1990s, including during the time Ishmael Beah was a child soldier. The foreigners were more effective and more professional than the national army Beah served in.

In 1995, when rebels advanced toward the capital, the military government brought in fifty-eight Gurkhas provided by a British security company to train its forces, but the Gurkhas' commander was killed. The government then hired the company Executive Outcomes to provide 150 to 200 armed foreign soldiers with helicopter support—a deal brokered by a mining company, with the mercenary firm paid out of mining profits once control was regained. "Just a month after their arrival, . . . [Executive Outcomes and the government army] drove the rebels away from the capital and caused hundreds of rebel deaths (and over 1,000 desertions)." They cleared rebels from diamond areas, then "moved on to destroy the [rebel] base." "Many reports indicate that citizens of Sierra Leone regarded [the Executive Outcomes] behavior as professional and were happy with its ability to put an end to the violence."

One visitor to Sierra Leone found that Executive Outcomes, although "far from a humanitarian agency, . . . appeared to be immensely popular in the areas they policed because they protected the people" from rebel atrocities. The group cost the government $35 million, about a third of the government's war costs, but "had EO not intervened, the RUF would have captured Freetown in 1995 and won the war."

In 1997, the government in exile, overthrown in a coup, turned to another foreign security company, Sandline, to train and equip a militia force and retake the capital with the cooperation of West African peacekeepers. A mining company "promised to underwrite the costs [$5 million] . . . in return for concessions from the restored government." The effort did not affect the outcome much but the government in exile did return to power. Sandline "probably . . . operated according to international norms more than did other forces in Sierra Leone," although it did not spread those norms to Sierra Leone fighters.

In addition to these various private foreign fighters, Sierra Leone hosted several official foreign military forces. The ECOWAS troops, UN peacekeepers, and the British military in turn came in to stabilize Sierra Leone. Of all these private and public forces, perhaps the most influential was the British military, which alone had both the legitimacy and the power to put down threats to security.

THE ABIDJAN ACCORD

With the UN Special Envoy's help, the government and RUF negotiated a peace agreement, the Abidjan Accord, in late 1996. "The RUF would be transformed into a political party, amnesty would be offered to all combatants, and a DDR program would be established. All foreign military forces and Executive Outcomes personnel would leave the country." The government and rebels would set up a joint monitoring group to oversee withdrawal of forces and disarmament.

Freeze that picture—what if the international community had been able to respond strongly, effectively, and with great speed to cement the peace agreement in place and maintain Sierra Leone's stability as it got back on its feet? The war could have ended then, in 1997, instead of 2001. Many lives would have been saved, and the eventual costs of intervention probably would have been lower.

This was not to be, however. The international community moved weakly and very slowly. "The timetable for implementing Abidjan was ambitious and optimistic, placing a great deal of faith in the warring parties' commitment to peace." But when a peacekeeping force is needed, first the Security Council must act—after sorting out the great-power politics. Then troop-contributing countries must be found and a budget agreed upon. Finally the multinational force must be patched together into something resembling a unified command in the field. One peacekeeping official likened it to hiring and equipping a fire brigade after the alarm comes in. "The fire breaks out, the aldermen on the Security Council agree it needs to be put out, and the fire chief is then sent out to hire firemen, rent fire trucks, find hoses of the right length, and look for sources of water to put into them."

While the international community dawdled, the rebels' "commitment to the peace process quickly became suspect. . . . Evidence surfaced that the RUF leader never intended to abide by the agreement and had decided to continue the armed struggle, using the accord to gain tactical advantage." Just months after the Abidjan Accord, the RUF and army joined forces in a coup against the elected government, which went into exile in Guinea. In 1997 the UN Security Council put an arms and oil embargo on the RUF/military regime in Sierra Leone. A new peace agreement was negotiated in late 1997, but the RUF did not implement it. A few months later an ECOWAS force, consisting mainly of Nigerian troops, intervened. It drove the RUF from the capital of Freetown, and restored President Kabbah to power. Ishmael Beah was back in Freetown when fighting overran it in 1998. But he moved to America, went to college, wrote his best-selling memoir, and became a public ambassador for UNICEF, speaking about child soldiers.

"ECOWAS was nearly totally dependent on Nigeria," which claimed that the operation cost it $1 million a day. The Nigerian dictator may have exaggerated that figure to allow diversion of funds, but nonetheless costs were substantial. Nigeria "received little assistance in its bid" to stabilize Sierra Leone. Inadequate resources hindered ECOWAS's military operations, as when "insufficient logistical support and insecure communications" contributed to the failure of its first offensive in 1997. In 1998 the ECOWAS military commander "argued that his troops lacked the appropriate equipment to undertake successful counterinsurgency operations. . . . Moreover, outside assistance for the force was slow in coming and not particularly generous." It was too weak to enforce sanctions and carry out an embargo against the rebels.

The UN put boots on the ground in Sierra Leone in 1998 when it sent a small force of 70 unarmed observers to document atrocities there, as a complement to ECOWAS. But that same year, when rebels retook most of the capital, the UN observers pulled out until ECOWAS once again secured the capital. Meanwhile a DDR program "quickly ran out of money and ceased" in late 1998 after disarming several thousand soldiers. "Indeed, the necessary implementation funds—estimated at $14 million—were never raised."

UNAMSIL

Finally, in 1999, the warring parties signed the Lomé Peace Accord, mandating a cease-fire and the formation of a government of national unity. That meant bringing the RUF, with its history of atrocities, right into the government. Did this mean that a group could shoot its way into power and receive the UN stamp of approval, perhaps showing "that butchery paid off"? On the other hand, if you did not bring a major rebel group into the transitional government, how could you end the war? The choice was to end the war. RUF leader Sankoh became vice president of the transitional government.

With this peace agreement reached, the UN sent a force of 6,000 armed peacekeepers, UNAMSIL, to encourage compliance with the agreement. The force would expand to 17,000 by 2001, with a $600 million budget. It also expanded its mandate and activities to include civil affairs, police, and administrative work. For instance, the UN operated a radio station starting in 2000 to provide reliable information to the public.

The UN "had a difficult time fielding the necessary force. . . . It proved equally difficult to find many of the additional support elements that the mission required." Although Nigeria had announced in 1999 that it was withdrawing its troops from Sierra Leone, the UN "was struggling to find troops and staff not only for UNAMSIL but also for other complex new missions in Kosovo, East Timor, and the Democratic Republic of the Congo." Thus the Sierra Leone UN mission's "resources were severely overstretched" in 2000. The operation also suffered from problems with logistical support, as most national contingents did not meet new UN requirements that "troop contributors be self-sustaining" in terms of equipment and supplies. Peacekeepers who were "rehatted" from ECOWAS to the UN mission "lacked not only logistics and communications assets but also basic military equipment." The commander, from India, relied heavily on his own contingent, because he was "asked to meet increasingly demanding challenges without proper resources." This increased tensions among the national contingents in the mission.

"Sierra Leone was probably the most dangerous environment into which UN peacekeepers had been introduced since Bosnia. . . . Sierra Leone had no army and no police. And despite the documents Foday Sankoh had signed, he and his ragtag followers had obviously not given up their hopes of taking the country by force." The rebels quickly disarmed first the Guinean and then the Zambian peacekeepers. "Annan feared that a fiasco was brewing."

The Lomé agreement, like its predecessors, came apart in 2000, when the RUF violated its terms. In May 2000, the rebels renounced the ceasefire, took hundreds of UN peacekeepers hostage, and stole their weapons. In this messed-up operation, a UN commander recalls that "there was a lack of everything." For instance, the front armored car in a column did not have a map, and the Zambian battalion that was taken hostage was not "prepared for combat operations" despite being sent into a "very dangerous operation." One UN worker recalls driving to UNAMSIL headquarters as rumors spread that the rebels were advancing on the capital. "It was one of the most surreal sights of my life. The place was in chaos— soldiers arguing, shouting, drinking, fistfights, an atmosphere of chaos." Journalist James Traub, who visited the country just before the hostage crisis, concluded that "the peacekeepers had proved unwilling or unable to speak the only language the rebels understood: the language of force. The most ambitious mission since Bosnia was looking like Bosnia redux."

Britain rode to the rescue with Operation Palliser. It sent a strong military force of 4,500 into Sierra Leone to evacuate foreign nationals and stabilize the country. "During a critical one-week period, when many were predicting the full collapse and withdrawal of UNAMSIL, . . . the British moved with incredible speed." A rogue militia took a British security patrol hostage—because the British decided not to fire on what their commander described as "children armed with AKs." The British rescued their comrades, killed at least twenty-five rebels, and captured their leader. The group, which had "terrorized civilians for months with near impunity, . . . ceased to be a cohesive fighting force thereafter."

This well-publicized incident "undermined the rebel movement's morale." The operation signaled to the rebel forces "that British troops could not be treated with the same degree of contempt as UN personnel. In this sense, [it] represented the crucial turning point where the combined government, UN and British forces gained the psychological upper hand over the rebels." During the hostage crisis, the government was able to arrest Sankoh, who would die in 2003 while awaiting trial. But the RUF fought on through 2001, and obstructed UN operations.

Britain's success showed that robust military forces from industrialized countries can successfully establish control in a chaotic environment such as Sierra Leone in 2000. Eventually, Britain worked on retooling Sierra Leone's national army, while UNAMSIL and other international organizations worked to retrain the police. Britain's commitment to Sierra Leone made a big difference in ending the war. British forces remained "over the horizon," ready to assist again if needed. "By not placing its troops under UN command, however," Britain showed that great powers "either did not trust and respect UN mission leadership or viewed affiliation with the United Nations as an avoidable drag on their decisions and field operations." If this *was* the British reasoning, given experiences in Sierra Leone up until then, who can blame them?

On the tenth anniversary of Operation Palliser, the commanding officer told BBC television that he had offered direct military support to the Sierra Leone government, which had been about to evacuate the capital, without getting approval from London. However, when British prime minister Tony Blair found out about it, he was happy to take on the mission, which seemingly could do a lot of good at a fairly low cost—as indeed turned out to be the case.

The peace agreement in May 2001 was the one that finally stuck. By that time the UN had 17,000 peacekeepers in the country. The next year, President Kabbah won elections in a landslide. As stability increased, the UN slowly drew down the number of peacekeepers, eventually withdrawing them at the end of 2005.

In 2002, a major sex scandal rocked the humanitarian aid community, as allegations were leveled against sixty-seven people, mostly local staff of aid groups but reportedly including some UN peacekeepers, for sexual abuse of women and girls in Sierra Leone refugee camps, including trading food for sex. However, researchers who investigated the claims found the sensational news reports "in significant ways untrue." An official UN investigation "was unable to substantiate any of the specific cases. . . . It found two [new] cases in which disciplinary action could be taken, but neither involved a UN or NGO staff person." Sadly, "the so-called sex scandal received more media attention than the widespread hunger." The researchers conclude that, contrary to news attention, "the real scandal in Sierra Leone was the general underfunding of all humanitarian efforts."

The Sierra Leone mission is a model not because it went smoothly but because it persisted, adapted, and (with British help) accomplished its tasks. The UN itself concluded in 2005 that UNAMSIL "may serve as a model for successful peacekeeping, as well as a prototype for the UN's new emphasis on peace-building." Its accomplishments over six years are impressive. The UN "helped organize Sierra Leone's first ever free and fair presidential and parliamentary elections by providing logistics and public information support." It enabled more than half a million displaced people to return home.

The UN successfully disarmed 75,000 combatants, including nearly 7,000 child soldiers such as Ishmael Beah. It collected 42,000 weapons and destroyed them. Reintegration proved difficult. After getting "small cash stipends" during a six-month training, the former fighters were sent out with a few tools to look for work. "Most have now joined the large pool of the unemployed and . . . former fighters roaming the streets will continue to be one of the Government's major challenges," as the UN put it in 2005 as the peacekeepers left. The entire reintegration program cost just $36 million, or less than $700 per participant. Economic aid also fell short. "Most aid agencies had trouble raising funds for Sierra Leone," which few people cared about, and "UN appeals . . . rarely met half of their target."

The UN had somewhat more success in police training and other aspects of Security Sector Reform. It recruited and trained 3,000 new police officers, expanding the force by about half, and built thirteen police stations, sixty-eight barracks, and five training centers. To counter corruption and ensure a legitimate flow of money to the government from the country's diamond exports, the UN helped the government establish a certification process for the diamonds. At the end of the UNAMSIL mission in 2005, a poll showed a strong majority of Sierra Leone citizens thought the peacekeepers had helped greatly and wished they would stay longer.

Historian Paul Kennedy calls Sierra Leone, along with the even more expansive East Timor mission, "initially disasters of the first order . . . ; huge numbers of innocents lost their lives, and the world community was slow to act. But both countries were eventually given resources, military and civilian, to quell the discords, protect the cease-fire, and restore the civil fabric. . . . Only by forcefully stopping banditry, warlordism, and ethnic cleansing could efforts begin to create, or re-create, a normal and democratic way of life."

At the end of 2005, the UN finished pulling out its peacekeepers in Sierra Leone, leaving behind a much smaller Integrated Office for Sierra Leone "to cement UNAMSIL's gains." With just 70 staff members in the capital, the UN office clearly lacks the reach of the peacekeeping mission deployed in strength across the country. Its budget also reflects this shrinkage, going from hundreds of millions annually for UNAMSIL to tens of millions for the Integrated Office programs. The UN's Peacebuilding Commission had approved, several years in, projects for Sierra Leone totaling $35 million. In addition, the IMF has recently completed a program of assistance to help the country stabilize its budget and reduce inflation. If these peacebuilding efforts prove successful and Sierra Leone continues its progress, the international community will have gotten a bargain.

II. Five Big African Missions and Beyond

The big five African peacekeeping missions today are following Sierra Leone's path. Imagine the postwar transition as a marathon, starting from a negotiated cease-fire and the arrival of peacekeepers. Sierra Leone is past the finish line, although clearly has far to go still in economic development and other areas. Liberia is farthest along and most successful. Next in line is Ivory Coast, more successful than not. Then follows the Congo, with its record of overall progress but persistent violence in some areas. Next, southern Sudan has had a mostly stable cease-fire for years and a successful referendum on independence in 2011 but there are still some attacks. Finally, back near the starting line of the Sierra Leone model, without even a durable cease-fire, is Darfur.

Liberia has the finish line in sight. The country survived a bloody civil war and—after fourteen rounds of negotiations that each produced quickly-broken superficial agreements—came out with a peace agreement, a transitional government, free elections, and a new government. Ellen Johnson-Sirleaf is the elected president (and the first elected woman head of state in Africa). The UN disarmed about 100,000 soldiers (completed in 2009) and so far has put two-thirds of them through reintegration programs. It helped hundreds of thousands of displaced people return home. It supports public projects to recover from the war, such as roads, lights, wells, and access to markets. Components of the multidimensional mission deal with police, disarmament, gender, human rights, economic recovery, civil affairs, HIV/AIDS, and other topics. Some 10,000 international personnel remain in 2011.

Next door in Ivory Coast, the UN is following a similar trajectory, though with detours. The UN force numbers 10,000 in 2011 and has a budget of half a billion dollars a year. It arrived in 2004, following a year-long political mission to support a peace agreement and absorbing much of an ECOWAS force that had provided, along with France, the first peacekeepers on the scene. The war had been fought over thorny issues of citizenship, immigration, and ancestry, but the first step was to put those issues off, divide the country in half along the front line, and stop the two sides from shooting at each other.

By 2007 a reporter found that "plenty of signs attest that the civil war that cleaved this country in two for half a decade is finally over." But a new deal between the main rivals—to disarm militias, issue identity cards, and hold elections—was shaky. The UN-occupied neutral zone splitting the country was dismantled and freedom of movement restored. But the disarmament of tens of thousands of rebel and pro-government militia soldiers began only in 2009. Rebel forces were supposed to demobilize two months before the elections, but this was delayed by a lack of money. France, which had supplied thousands of its own troops in Ivory Coast (outside UN command), reduced them to below a thousand but promised to support the UN with rapid reaction forces if needed. Overall, the secretary-general in mid-2009 called the security situation in Ivory Coast "generally stable."

The presidential elections, finally held in 2010 after five years of delay, tested that stability. The incumbent declared himself the winner and vowed to stay in office, but the UN and other credible observers gave the victory to the opposition leader whose base of support was in the former rebel areas. The incumbent received pleas, sanctions, and threats of force from neighboring countries, the African Union, the UN, prominent individuals, and Western powers. The opposition leader holed up in a hotel with his new cabinet, protected by the UN but without control of the country or its army. Over the subsequent months, government violence against political opponents increased, and by early 2011, fighting flared between the former rebel and government forces, breaking the long cease-fire. In a quick offensive backed by the UN and French troops, the new president took power and arrested the old one. The Ivory Coast fighting underscores the dangers of an incomplete transition and the holding of elections before the disarmament of warring parties has occurred. International actors must prepare for the possibility that electoral losers will not accept the results and may return to violence to resist them.

The large, important Congo mission receives attention later in this chapter, so, skipping ahead, the last two big African missions are in two regions of Sudan. In the south, a region separated by religious differences from the north, and rich with oil deposits, a secessionist war raged for decades, indirectly killed millions, and kept the population in dire poverty. Many boys were kidnapped and made into soldiers, while thousands of others, dubbed the Lost Boys by aid workers, trekked long distances to escape the fighting. With a cease-fire agreement, the UN put 10,000 peacekeepers on the ground to keep the lid on the conflict, which they did successfully for years. Periodically, local conflicts pop up—usually tribal disputes over cattle—and cause fighting or a massacre. Several hundred may die in such an incident, but such episodes are sporadic. In 2009 the Permanent Court of Arbitration, an international court in the

Netherlands, ruled on the disputed border between southern and northern Sudan, giving the best oil fields to the north but other coveted territory to the south. Both sides accepted the ruling. The two sides had sent the issue to the court after a 2008 battle in a disputed town threatened to escalate.

Under the peace plan, southern Sudan was to hold a referendum five years later about whether to secede from Sudan. That date arrived in January 2011, and as it approached, doubts grew about whether the UN could organize the vote and whether the central government would allow it to occur and, if so, would respect the widely expected vote to secede. Many observers worried that the civil war would resume. But instead, the referendum came off peacefully and the government accepted the vote, which overwhelmingly favored secession. Although low-level violence among different militias continued sporadically, the two sides began a mandated six-month process of working out the details of separation, and the world prepared to welcome South Sudan as the 193rd member of the UN. The surprisingly positive outcome of the peace process in South Sudan stands as a striking example of the world's slow-but-steady path away from war.

In Darfur, in western Sudan, the violence is less controlled, although much reduced from 2004. Despite several cease-fire agreements among the government and different rebel groups, there is no peace agreement that all groups have signed on to. Rebel groups took to violence after being left out of the peace agreement for southern Sudan. The government's response, especially in 2004, was to bring in a brutal militia, the Janjaweed, to exterminate or expel the population in areas of Darfur the government wants to control. The Janjaweed are North Africans and the populations they attack are black Africans (both are Muslim). In a typical raid, the Janjaweed attack a village on horseback with automatic rifles, while government helicopter gunships provide air support, and proceed to kill civilians wantonly—torturing, raping, looting, and burning every structure to the ground. The result has been both a humanitarian disaster, with more than 2 million people displaced from their homes and living in camps in desperate conditions, and also a disaster for international morality, as the world has failed to stop the first genocide of the new century despite a sustained public outcry in the West.

The UN has been in Darfur since 2007 but makes up only one side of a dual mission with the African Union (AU), which has even less money, people, and experience than the UN. In fact, "the AU had no experience fielding a peacekeeping force, and no funds with which to equip, transport, feed, or house them." Kofi Annan understood the "cynical game" played by Security Council members, "where everybody is coming to the African Union knowing full well they don't have the capacity, but at least your conscience is clear that someone is doing it. There's another cynical part of it, when you hear the Sudanese say, 'We'll accept these African troops,' knowing delay is in order."

In late 2007, three weeks before the hybrid mission was to begin, Secretary-General Ban Ki-moon had to beg for twenty-four helicopters— not fancy attack helicopters, just basic transport helicopters to get around the region. "Without the mobility and transportation, it will be extremely difficult for us to deploy our forces," he said. "We need on-the-ground capability, specifically helicopters. We're not getting them. Because of that, the entire mission is at risk." Ban wrote to the Security Council and asked leaders of countries throughout Europe, South America, and the Middle East, but reported, "I have not been able to get even one single helicopter commitment." In 2010 the mission finally received five tactical helicopters, not from the world's military powers but from Ethiopia, and was still appealing for eighteen utility helicopters to get around Sudan.

Despite the evolution and development of peacekeeping over the decades, Darfur illustrates the limits and backsliding that still hamper the effort. Here we have the top UN official in the world, responding to the most serious atrocity of the new century, personally begging, yet unable to secure a single helicopter for the mission. How many helicopters of its own does the UN have for such a purpose? None. Compared with 1960, when countries lined up to volunteer their troops and equipment to the UN, when Ralph Bunche could put 3,500 troops on the ground in the Congo in four days, we have indeed gone backward.

BEYOND THE AFRICAN FIVE

Although today's UN peacekeeping missions center on Africa, important missions are also ongoing in other regions. They include Lebanon, Haiti, and some smaller missions, as well as largely wound-down missions in Kosovo and East Timor.

Lebanon

In Lebanon a UN mission has gone through several tumultuous phases since 1978, when it arrived to keep tabs on Israel's withdrawal from Lebanon after a war. The mission's name, UNIFIL, stands for the UN Interim Force in Lebanon, but the "interim" has lasted more than thirty years. When Israeli forces invaded Lebanon in 1982 to kick out the PLO, they just went right past the UN peacekeepers. Nor did the peacekeepers stop tit-for-tat violence in the 1980s between the Islamist militia Hezbollah, lobbing rockets into northern Israel, and Israel, militarily occupying a strip of southern Lebanon. In 2000, Israel ended its eighteen-year occupation and Hezbollah claimed a victory. This phase of UNIFIL was "honestly meant but could do little. . . . The hapless international troops were insulted, disregarded, kidnapped, and shot at by all sides. . . ."

In 2006, Hezbollah attacks inside Israel sparked a new Israeli invasion that led to much damage in Lebanon. In response, the UN retooled UNIFIL with more backing from higher-capability European forces and an expanded mandate—to support the Lebanese army in deploying in Hezbollah territory, to prevent Hezbollah's rearmament (a failure), and to support humanitarian relief efforts. The mission has 12,000 peacekeepers on the ground in Lebanon, but is held hostage to domestic politics in both Israel and Lebanon.

Haiti

The UN arrived in Haiti, where it now has 9,000 peacekeepers, in 2004. It took over from an interim American-led operation and was the fifth UN mission responding to political violence in Haiti in less than twenty years. Most were small, short-lived, and not terribly effective. This mission, MINUSTAH, has already lasted longer and is larger than its predecessors. For decades, Haiti suffered under a dictator and emerged as the poorest country in the Americas. The dictatorship was followed by decades of political instability, violence, and poverty. The UN's multidimensional mission in Haiti today has less to do with separating armed parties than with supporting a society with a troubled history as it tries to get on track. The devastating earthquake in 2009 not only set the country back immeasurably but also killed almost a hundred UN peacekeepers, a record loss of life for a UN mission.

These seven world conflicts with the largest UN peacekeeping missions—the African Five, Lebanon, and Haiti—account for more than 90 percent of the UN's deployed peacekeepers and more than 85 percent of UN peacekeeping expenditures.

Smaller Missions

The UN also runs smaller, less visible missions. Six of today's missions have fewer than 1,200 personnel, and consist primarily of old-fashioned monitoring of cease-fires by unarmed or lightly armed forces. One of them, in fact, is the granddaddy mission discussed in Chapter 3, the UNTSO observer mission for Israel and its neighbors. It has operated continuously for more than sixty years and currently has 150 military observers on the ground. Another mission has monitored the Israeli-Syrian cease-fire in the Golan Heights since 1974. Another patrols the divide between the Greek and Turkish sides of Cyprus, frozen in place since 1964. And a fourth has observed the India-Pakistan cease-fire, lately quite stable, since 1949. Another mission has been marooned for nearly two decades in the deserts of Western Sahara, whose inhabitants were promised a UN-organized referendum but whose occupier, Morocco, does not want to hold one. Finally, the mission in Kosovo has wound down to a small administrative operation.

The most recently completed mission, in the Central African Republic and Chad since 2007, assisted the return of hundreds of thousands of refugees to their homes. It took over from a year-long joint EU-UN mission, with 3,300 European soldiers and 850 UN officers. The head of UN peacekeeping, Alain Le Roy, considers the operation a model, in which the EU can deploy quickly and robustly to stabilize a situation and then "the U.N., which takes much longer to get into gear, can take over." France, the former colonial power in Chad, contributed half the EU soldiers, 750 of the subsequent UN force, and meanwhile maintains more than 1,000 other troops in Chad to support the government.

Another recently ended mission had monitored the cease-fire between Georgia and its two secessionist provinces since 1993, shortly after the Soviet Union broke up. In 2008, the issue flared into war between Georgia and Russia, which inflicted a humiliating defeat on its much smaller neighbor. With the conflict now directly involving a permanent member of the UN Security Council, the 150 UN observers went home in 2009.

Not all monitoring missions are so unfortunate, though. At the same time as the UN's troubles in Rwanda and Bosnia, it undertook a mission in the Aouzou Strip. This was disputed territory between Libya and Chad that Libya had seized by force in 1973 and Chad had partially retaken by force in 1987. Thousands had died in the fighting. The two countries reached a negotiated settlement some years later and asked the UN to send monitors to verify its implementation by each side. The UN sent nine military observers, supported by six international civilian staff, from May to June 1994. The mission cost $64,000 and suffered no fatalities. A nice price for peace.

Kosovo and East Timor

Two additional missions, in Kosovo and East Timor, have wound down to relatively small scale, each now comprising fewer than 2,000 people. These territories suffered war as larger countries fought to retain sovereignty over them. East Timor won independence from Indonesia successfully, whereas Kosovo has declared its independence from Serbia but has not been recognized by the UN. In both cases a robust outside military force, not under UN command, provided security—NATO for Kosovo and Australia for East Timor—while the UN provided administrative assistance and other "multidimensional" services.

Wars ended, lives saved, and shattered societies rebuilt are the fruits of the UN's learning process and persistence in Africa and beyond.

III. The Congo Mission

The ultimate test of the UN's approach has played out over the past decade in the UN's largest and most expensive peace operation, in the Congo, with nearly 20,000 people and a budget of a billion dollars a year. After the UN left in 1964, the country went through waves of trouble, culminating in devastating wars from 1996 to 2003 and sporadic fighting ever since.

FROM ONE TO MULTIPLE DIMENSIONS

In 2006, as Charlotte Isaksson drove into Congo's capital from the airport, she did *not* think, *That was the airport where Dag Hammarskjöld took off on his last doomed flight forty-five years ago.* Rather she was struck by the sheer poverty of the people living along the road, the most abject she had seen. As a Swede, Isaksson knew all about Hammarskjöld, but she had more pressing matters on her mind.

Isaksson, deployed with the Swedish armed forces, belonged to a military force of 2,300 from twenty-one EU countries and Turkey. Known as EUFOR RD CONGO, they came to beef up the 17,000 UN peacekeepers already deployed in a mission known as MONUC (from the French initials for Mission of the UN in Congo).

Congo was about to hold its first democratic election in forty years and it needed all the help it could get. The Carter Center, run by former President Jimmy Carter, was there to monitor the election and declare it free and fair (which it did). Humanitarian aid agencies such as Doctors Without Borders were there, as well, though not for the elections. The EU had two other missions in the Congo in 2006, one for security sector reform and one for police training. Peacekeeping had come a long way in forty-five years since ONUC. Many international agencies and missions worked together to try to keep the peace in the Congo, especially during the election period.

Isaksson had a background in artillery, but she was not there to work with big guns. She was the first Gender Advisor on an international peacekeeping mission. She was there to advise the EU force commander and train the troops regarding gender issues such as sexual violence, the needs of women refugees, and the operational effectiveness of mixed-sex military units. These issues had gained prominence following several sex scandals involving international peacekeepers. In 2000 the UN Security Council had passed Resolution 1325 on including women and paying attention to gender in peacekeeping and development missions.

Isaksson's work in the Congo illustrates the *multidimensional* nature of today's Congo mission in comparison with that of Dag Hammarskjöld in 1961. First of all, in contrast to ONUC's narrow focus then on military and diplomatic actions, the international community's work in the Congo in 2006 ranged from cease-fire monitoring and police training to helping disarm militias, organizing elections, and providing economic and administrative assistance. Isaksson's work on gender represented one strand in this multidimensional fabric. Second, many more international organizations participated in 2006 than in 1961. Isaksson did not even work for the UN but for the EU.

To see how MONUC, and Charlotte Isaksson, got to the Congo, we need to go back and pick up the story after ONUC left in the 1960s. The UN had succeeded in holding together Congo as a country, putting down Katanga's foreign-backed secessionist rebellion, and moving from several "governments" at once to a single recognized government in control of the whole country. Unfortunately, that government turned into a dictatorship that put the country on a path to destruction.

THE ROAD TO AFRICA'S FIRST WORLD WAR

Joseph Mobutu took power in a coup in 1965, and held power for thirty-two years. After consolidating his hold on government, putting down some mutinies, he renamed everything from colonial names to African names in 1971. The country became Zaire, Leopoldville became Kinshasa, and Mobutu changed his own name to Mobutu Sese Seko. A few years later, Mobutu adopted a more aggressive anticolonial stance by nationalizing foreign-owned industries and kicking out foreign investors.

Actually, *nationalizing* is the wrong term for this expropriation. Mobutu's government was often described as a *kleptocracy*, meaning government by those who steal from the public for personal enrichment. The money that Mobutu piled up in his foreign bank accounts was legendary. At the end, Transparency International, an NGO that works to reduce corruption, cited estimates of $4 billion in Swiss banks and added, "President Mobutu is widely regarded as having systematically looted his country for the past 30 years." Indeed, Mobutu , with an estimated wealth of $5 billion, hit #3 on Transparency's all-time list of corrupt leaders from 1984 to 2004 (after Indonesia's Suharto and the Philippines' Marcos). In this tradition of kleptocracy, Mobutu followed what the Congo had known under King Leopold and Belgian rule. Mobutu did, however, deliver what the West wanted most from him—keeping the Congo and its strategic natural resources out of the hands of communists.

In 1977, Mobutu invited back the foreign investors he had kicked out three years earlier, but the investors for some reason seemed leery of returning. (Foreign troops from Belgium, France, and Morocco did, however, help Mobutu put down a rebellion in Katanga in 1977, as they would do again with looting troops in 1991.) The economy deteriorated. The GDP per capita went from the extremely low $380 in 1960 to an even lower $224 in 1990. (By the time the Europeans arrived for the 2006 elections, the GDP would be down further, to a pathetic $139 per person per year.) Multiply those extremely low incomes, falling over decades, by a country of tens of millions of people.

Poverty kills. For twenty-five years, up until the mid-1970s, Congo's death rate relative to the population size improved along with that for sub-Saharan Africa as a whole. But then, shortly after Mobutu's nationalizations and as copper prices dropped, the death rate flattened out and started to get worse, while sub-Saharan Africa continued to improve. Congo not only did not develop economically; it went backward for long periods. As the World Bank puts it, "By the 1990s the country's economy was near complete collapse due to economic mismanagement, corruption, and political instability."

Mobutu fell into ill health in the 1990s, and began to compromise by including opposition politicians in his governments—always retaining ultimate power over the instruments of violence, though. Laurent-Désiré Kabila for decades had nursed a rebellion in the east of the country, near Rwanda and across Lake Tanganyika from Tanzania. Kabila had even had the assistance of the famous Cuban communist guerrilla Ché Guevara and a hundred of his men, back in 1965, raising the banner of the murdered leftist prime minister Lumumba and fighting the corrupt, Western-backed government. (Ché considered Kabila a terrible leader and the operation a failure.) Kabila had also gained notoriety in 1975 for kidnapping several Stanford students working with Jane Goodall in the Gombe chimpanzee reserve in Tanzania, and taking them as hostages back to the eastern Congo until a ransom was paid.

Over time Kabila built up considerable power and wealth in the section of eastern Congo under his control. The event that precipitated his rise to national power, however, took place across the border in Rwanda in 1994. As Chapter 4 discussed, Hutu extremists committed a genocide of Tutsis and their sympathizers, but lost power and fled into eastern Congo. There, the genocide perpetrators mixed with civilian refugees and violently dominated the refugee camps. "Rwanda faced persistent attacks from this force, beginning sporadically in late 1994 and intensifying throughout the following year." Mobutu generally supported these unsavory Rwandans in the eastern Congo.

The new Rwandan government wanted to fight the Hutu genocide perpetrators sheltering in Congo, but Mobutu blocked it. Kabila, already supported by Rwanda's government, was willing to fight them. Rwanda stepped up its support of Kabila as a tool against Mobutu. Kabila captured most of the east in less than a year, then marched on the capital and seized control, with himself as the new president, in 1997. He renamed the country once again: The country that had already been the Kongo Empire, the Congo Free State, the Belgian Congo, the Republic of Congo, and Zaire was now the Democratic Republic of the Congo.

Alas, Kabila brought no stability to the country. He fell out with his former backers, Rwanda and Uganda—expelling Rwandan forces from eastern Congo in mid-1998—and those countries in turn sponsored new rebel militias against him, which "made dramatic military gains in the first week of the rebellion." After only a year in power, he had to call in military forces from three nearby allies, Zimbabwe, Namibia, and Angola, to stop a rebel drive on the capital backed by Rwanda and Uganda. (Sudan and Chad also backed the government while Burundi backed the rebels.) The country thus divided in pieces with various foreign military forces on its territory. Rwandan-backed rebels split with Uganda-backed ones, each holding on to mineral-rich territories near their borders. Meanwhile a new rebellion in the northwest of the country added to its troubles.

This war that began in 1998 (following smaller fighting that began in 1996) killed hundreds of thousands violently, and many more through war-induced epidemics and malnutrition. "By the end of 1998, what many called 'Africa's first world war,' with as many as nine foreign countries intervening, had engulfed the Congo."

In thinking about why the war was so deadly, several possible reasons stand out. First, as a rule, wars between regular armies with heavy weapons tend to do more damage and kill more people than wars fought with irregular forces. With the government's and five foreign armies on Congo's territory, a lot of firepower was used. Second, wars in desperately poor countries push a lot of people over the edge. War and poverty become a self-reinforcing cycle. Third, civil wars sustain themselves at more lethal levels for longer periods to the extent that rebels have access to material support either from a foreign backer or from control of natural resources in rebel-held territory—both true here.

THE TRADE IN LOOTABLE RESOURCES

Certainly one big motivation for neighboring countries' military interventions in the Congo was that familiar factor in armed conflict, lootable natural resources. A military force that controls an area where valuable resources such as diamonds or copper are concentrated can make easy money and in turn amplify its own power. One new twist in the 1990s since the conflict of 1960–61 was the importance of the mineral coltan in cell phones and other electronic devices. Abundant supplies of coltan in eastern Congo, mined without much equipment or technology, empowered armed groups that fought to control the deposits and illegally export the coltan.

To "exploit resources from eastern Congo and control the lucrative coltan and diamond markets, Rwanda pursued a policy of direct rule. It created a Congo Desk, to oversee its commercial and military operations in the neighboring country, which was distinct from [Rwanda's] official national treasury and thus beyond the scrutiny of international financial institutions." The budget, "based entirely on the exploitation of Congo's resources, was as much as $320 million for 1999, or 20 percent of Rwanda's [GDP]."

Uganda pursued a less centralized but equally exploitive policy in the Congo, taking coltan, diamonds, and gold. These minerals extracted from the Congo under control of Uganda's army "contributed to Uganda's impressive economic growth in the 1990s." Uganda's extraction of minerals in the Ituri region heightened local ethnic conflicts there with disastrous effects. Direct clashes between Rwandan and Ugandan forces in 1999 and 2000 centered on the diamond market in the town of Kisangani in eastern Congo. "Economic motives paralleled or even trumped security considerations as reasons for [Rwanda and Uganda] to keep a hand in the Congo." Even after the two countries withdrew most of their military forces in 2002–03, "elites connected to these governments continued to exploit the Congo's resources through covert and private means, inciting ethnic violence and sponsoring and arming militias."

When Laurent Kabila still controlled only a small part of the country, his rebel militia "negotiated lucrative resource deals" with foreign investors. "So aggressive was the swarm of mining corporations into rebel-held territories that in some ways it seemed like a replay of the wealth grab in the late nineteenth century when the Congo came under the control of Belgian colonialism." When Kabila's forces gained the upper hand in 1997, the U.S. mining company American Mineral Fields signed a nearly $900 million contract with the rebels for copper, cobalt, and zinc deposits. The next year when Kabila's government nearly fell to a Rwandan army, "the cash-strapped government relied on the country's resources to purchase weapons and secure allied support." The government set up "joint ventures with foreign firms in return for up-front payments."

Congo's government used minerals not only for cash but to secure crucial military support from its regional allies. It granted concessions, including "offshore oil wells to Angola, a share of a diamond mine . . . to Namibia, and mining, forestry, and agricultural rights to Zimbabwe." The Zimbabwean military even set up a company to pay for its presence in the Congo through timber, diamond, and manganese operations. In a 1998 deal between Kabila's government and that of Zimbabwe, the military intervention of Zimbabwe in the Congo was designated as "self-financing" through a vast timber concession (80 million acres), a 37.5 percent share in Congo's state mining company, and "ventures in other industries including electricity, agriculture, and civil aviation." The main beneficiaries were private individuals who were "cronies" of the Zimbabwean leader. "UN investigators determined that Zimbabwean and Congolese elites illegally transferred $5 billion of mining assets from the Congolese state to private companies from 1999 to 2002," an amount equivalent to Congo's entire GDP for 2000. The UN commissioned a report in 2002 on the illegal exploitation of Congo's minerals, but could do little to stop it.

As recently as late 2008, a reporter in eastern Congo described renegade armed groups using military force to control tin mining operations worth tens of millions of dollars a year. In many parts of the Congo, "life is slowly returning to normal. . . . But here on Congo's eastern edge, the war never really ended. The unfinished battles over the Rwandan genocide play out on Congolese soil among armed groups fueled by lucrative mines like [the tin mine] and by other mines controlled by the Hutu militias that carried out the genocide."

Not only mineral wealth but sheer size created problems for governing the Congo. In a country this size, with such poor infrastructure, governing the eastern provinces from the western capital has proven chronically difficult. The ethnic groups there span the border with Rwanda and other countries. Indeed, the Congo contains more than two hundred ethnic groups, seven hundred local languages or dialects, and several religions—Roman Catholic (the majority), animist, and others. The borders of the Congo represent what King Leopold could put together on maps, given what territories had already been taken by other European colonizers. The very shape of today's Democratic Republic of the Congo is based on the history of trade in lootable resources. Meanwhile the poverty remains crippling, with the infant mortality rate more than ten times that of the United States. What this means is that governing the Congo from Kinshasa, or coming in as the UN to help the government do so, in a country with desperate needs and little money, seems almost impossible.

FROM WAR TO PEACE

Ending the war in the Congo has been a slow process. It is not as though one day the war ended, the shooting stopped, and the UN arrived to keep the peace. In 1998, nearly two dozen peace initiatives came and went. Regional defense ministers met in Ethiopia in September 1998. Thirty-four African leaders came to a summit in France in November 1998. And the Organization of African Unity held a conference on the problem in Burkina Faso in December 1998.

In July 1999, the Lusaka Cease-Fire Agreement was signed by the Congo, Angola, Zimbabwe, Namibia, Rwanda, and Uganda. Kabila agreed to sign because he was under "enormous military pressure" from Rwanda and Uganda. Reversing his previous position, he allowed those countries to keep forces in the country until the arrival of a UN force. That force, MONUC, would arrive the next year with 5,500 troops. The cease-fire was shaky, however, and fighting continued though 2000.

Structurally, the agreement called for not only a cease-fire and UN peacekeepers but the creation of a Joint Military Commission on which representatives of the warring parties were joined by observers from neutral African nations. However, the commission "was paralyzed by its lack of financial resources."

"The Lusaka signatories thrust upon the United Nations, which had little direct involvement in the peace talks, a burden that it was not prepared to accept: namely, full responsibility for implementing and enforcing the peace agreement." Expansive tasks for the UN were adopted at Lusaka despite warnings from the U.S. and EU observers there that the Security Council would almost certainly refuse to base its mandate on Chapter VII (i.e., allow the mission to use military force). One senior UN representative noted that the agreement "called for UN forces. They didn't know what they were writing."

In contrast to the UN mission in the 1960s, this time "the Security Council lacked strategic interest in the Congo. This translated into the authorization of a peacekeeping force with a far too modest observation mandate [and] inadequate resources. . . ." Thus, the Lusaka cease-fire agreement "as an African solution to the Congo War . . . was impressive; yet it also represented abdication of responsibility by the signatories for the critical process of implementation, . . . pawning it off on an unprepared and reluctant United Nations." The UN in turn linked the size and speed of deployment of a UN force to the behavior of the parties, passing the buck back to the warring parties; but the latter "faced almost no consequences for continuing to prosecute the war and loot the Congo of its riches." Furthermore, "it was practically impossible to implement [Lusaka] within the artificial timetables specified. . . . The parties incurred few costs for transgressing or obstructing it because it lacked an enforcement mechanism. . . . Within months, the agreement was rendered nearly irrelevant."

The UN was hardly in a strong position to act effectively to end the fighting in the Congo. It was all very well to declare January 2000 the month of Africa, and invite the countries involved in Congo to meet with the Security Council. But the UN had just fielded a mission in Sierra Leone in 1999, and was preoccupied with running Kosovo and East Timor. The prospect of paying for a big UN mission in a country as large and poor as the Congo was also daunting, a problem worsened by the fact that with Congo's roads nearly all impassable the UN would have to rely heavily on expensive air transport. A 1999 UN study "estimated that a successful and credible peacekeeping force in the Congo would require upwards of 100,000 troops," and after Lusaka the secretary-general warned that a Congo mission would "have to be large and expensive."

For years the UN held down the size of MONUC, and its effectiveness, in order to reduce costs. The first phase, after Lusaka, was limited to 90 military personnel. In 2000, "serious logistical deficiencies" (as Kofi Annan put it), including shortages of troops, armored vehicles, and communications gear, forced a delay in the peacekeepers' deployment. Republicans in the U.S. Congress froze the disbursement of $41 million in U.S. funds allocated to support MONUC. In its first years, "MONUC found itself in a vicious cycle: the worse the fighting became, . . . the greater the need for an expanded peacekeeping force, but the more the Security Council resisted strengthening the mandate or enlarging the force, concerned (in part) about throwing money at an apparently intractable problem."

The U.S. administration favored a narrowly constructed peacekeeping mission for Congo—no more than 5,000 troops and only after the parties respected a cease-fire—but the U.S. Congress resisted even this. This "minimalist and incremental approach proposed by the United States" frustrated African countries. They wanted a much more robust approach, but lacked resources to carry one out themselves. In sum, "the war in the Congo was too gruesome and devastating for the West to ignore, but too difficult and too low a priority to address seriously." In 2000, *The Washington Post* correctly predicted that the UN force would be too small to facilitate peace but "too big to escape the blame when, say, civilians are massacred in the vicinity of blue helmets."

The situation changed abruptly in January 2001 with the assassination of Kabila, reportedly in a failed coup attempt. His son, Joseph Kabila, replaced him and decided on a policy of peace. The next month the younger Kabila negotiated an agreement with Rwanda and Uganda, and forces began to pull back. This was not a quick process; Rwanda and Uganda kept 10,000 to 20,000 troops in the country in 2002, as well as arming and funding local militias, as they exploited lucrative minerals. (Meanwhile, the killing of Angola's rebel leader in 2002 and the collapse of the rebel movement there removed a key incentive for keeping Angolan troops in the Congo.)

Nonetheless, although the process was slow and the UN mission underfunded, substantial progress occurred in 2001 and 2002. By late 2001, with fewer than 2,500 military personnel, MONUC had overseen the disengagement of hostile forces under the cease-fire, with 95 out of 96 positions verified. (Determining who is where plays a key role in maintaining a cease-fire.) MONUC then focused on disarmament, and shifted its attention from the cease-fire line to the violent eastern provinces. The DDR program remained stalled for months, but in mid-2002 the Congo government signed "breakthrough" agreements with Rwanda and Uganda to dismantle rebel groups based in Congo while those countries withdrew their own forces. In response, the UN expanded its size to 8,700 personnel, although MONUC's mandate "once again proved inadequate to the task, as violence in the [east] continued to thwart voluntary disarmament."

In Kisangani in May 2002, soldiers of a Rwandan-backed rebel faction mutinied, seized the radio station, and broadcast anti-Rwanda statements. Loyalists from the faction "brutally suppressed the mutineers, brought in reinforcements, and orchestrated a campaign of rape, looting, and systematic reprisal killings against civilians and military. . . . MONUC, which had around 1,000 peacekeepers . . . in the city, refused to intervene militarily. . . ."

Beyond these specific incidents, "the sheer scale of the task [was] enormous. . . . The Congo was still host to a kaleidoscope of well-armed, sizable, and potentially hostile militias, Congolese and foreign, totaling 30,000 to 50,000 fighters." These included 15,000 to 20,000 from the Rwandan Hutu genocide perpetrators. A more decentralized set of local Congolese militias, the Mai Mai, allied with various governments, had 20,000 to 30,000 fighters. Sorting out the conflicts and interests of these various groups required "microlevel mediation efforts between armed factions" by MONUC.

At the end of 2002, after a number of failed attempts over the preceding months, all the major Congolese parties signed a power-sharing agreement. The Congo formed a transitional government with four vice presidents that included various militia leaders. The transitional government took office in mid-2003, by which time all the foreign armies had left the country (except when they returned on incursions occasionally in the subsequent years). Unfortunately, the departure of foreign armies left a security vacuum partly filled by smaller, splinter militias that were not participants in the peace process. Serious human rights violations resulted.

In the spring of 2003, "particularly gruesome ethnic violence" hit the Ituri district, which the UN had identified two years earlier as "highly explosive." Uganda justified its military presence there as needed to keep peace between rival ethnic groups, but in fact "its paramount motive was economic," as the district was "rich in gold, diamond, cobalt, timber, and oil reserves, and Uganda stoked ethnic tensions in the region to ensure control of these lucrative resources." The UN, for its part, "scrambled to send peacekeepers to Bunia," the capital of the Ituri district, but although the Security Council had authorized an increase to 8,700 troops four months earlier, "only 4,700 had deployed . . . and no extra troops were available. Critically, a brigade from South Africa" that could have responded appropriately "had been delayed by logistical difficulties and thus was not available to MONUC for deployment in Ituri." MONUC had only 700 guards to attempt to stabilize a region the size of Sierra Leone and fill a security vacuum left by the departure of 7,000 Ugandan troops. "The disconnect between the international diplomatic pressure to force the Ugandan forces out of Ituri and MONUC's limited capacity to replace them was extraordinary. . . ." After the Ugandan forces pulled out, "unchecked militias ravaged Bunia," with control passing back and forth between the rival ethnic groups and hundreds killed.

The UN turned to a European Union force, led by France, for help with enforcement. This Operation Artemis, 1,500 strong, got its funding from the EU, mostly France, rather than the UN. But it was authorized by the UN, under a Chapter VII mandate with the right to use all necessary means to carry out its mission. The force had "helicopter gunships, heavy armor, and the ability to call on fighter aircraft operating from French bases in Chad." The intervention was to last three months, with the Security Council strengthening MONUC to fill the gap afterward. MONUC now had authority to use all necessary means to protect civilians in the worst-hit areas of the east.

"The Ituri crisis finally forced the Security Council to concede that MONUC's mandate and capabilities, relatively static since February 2000, were wholly incommensurate with the changing conditions on the ground." The UN appointed a new head of mission and beefed up the mandate, including invoking Chapter VII. A year after the Ituri crisis, however, a new outbreak of "horrific violence" occurred in the Bukavu area, "caused by power struggles between ex-rebel and government commanders within the new, ostensibly integrated, Congolese army." The UN responded with "more troops and a tougher mandate," but still "far fewer troops than the secretary-general had sought." The Security Council added such tasks as inspecting cargo and confiscating arms, protecting officials of the government, assisting returning refugees, and contributing to disarmament and demobilization programs for combatants. The mandate was further expanded in 2008, but each time with no more than modest increases in the resources provided to MONUC.

The UN force was drawn more directly into fighting in 2004 and, worse, its "rapid expansion contributed to disciplinary failures . . . including a sexual abuse scandal in 2004 . . ."—"the worst instances of sexual exploitation and abuse by peacekeepers to have surfaced in recent years." And the "core, unresolved problem" remained in 2005, as it would in 2011—the presence of thousands of Rwandan Hutu rebels "preying on local populations and provoking cross-border conflict with Rwanda. . . ."

During the Bukavu crisis, the main peacekeepers were from Uruguay and most "were not professional soldiers: they had signed up for peacekeeping duties and received hasty training." When crunch time came, the Uruguayan commander phoned home to his capital and, with his government's OK, "refused to implement the order—an act of gross insubordination in a normal military setting." The peacekeepers surrendered the airport and the rebels "poured into Bukavu, where they engaged in a four-day orgy of rape, pillage, and murder."

In the west of the country, however, things looked better. The government organized elections for 2006, which would be Congo's first free elections since Mobutu seized power in 1965. In the years leading up to the 2006 elections, MONUC peacekeepers helped enforce a shaky cease-fire and protect civilians.

The UN and its various helper organizations such as the EU did in fact pull off elections in 2006, deemed free and fair by observers. Incumbent president Joseph Kabila was elected after a runoff against his main rival, the militia leader Jean-Pierre Bemba. A photo taken afterward shows Bemba surrounded by many microphones and cameras on all sides. He was the man of the hour. If he went back to war, as Angola's Savimbi had done after losing elections in 1992, his region of the Congo could be overcome by violence. If he stayed at peace the political process could develop. He decided against war, although denouncing the election results and refusing to attend Kabila's inauguration.

Bemba left the Congo in 2007 when some fighting erupted between his forces and the government's. Then, unexpectedly, he was arrested while in Belgium in 2008 and sent to the International Criminal Court (ICC) in the Netherlands on a secret ICC arrest warrant. He is being tried for war crimes committed during operations in neighboring Central African Republic. This created the awkward situation in which the leader of the Congo's main opposition party was in a foreign jail. The ICC also holds three other Congolese suspects, none as high-level as Bemba.

Trouble continued intermittently in the eastern Congo, but the situation slowly improved, with many cease-fires and sporadic demobilization of armed groups and returns of refugees home. The UN learned from Operation Artemis: "Disciplined soldiers equipped with helicopter gunships and armored personnel carriers, or sometimes just with guns they were willing to use, had taken the fight to the bad guys, demonstrating that robust peacekeeping could accomplish a great deal that timid peacekeeping could not."

In 2008, an offensive by a militia in eastern Congo threatened that progress. A Rwandan-backed Tutsi militia leader, Laurent Nkunda, seized territory and was poised to attack the important town of Goma (headquarters of aid efforts in eastern Congo). The national army of the Congo fled in panic, looting and attacking civilians as it went. The UN sent attack helicopters against Nkunda's forces, but without stopping them. Thousands of civilians fled the fighting, some overwhelming aid centers and others hiding out with no food or water. The fighting hindered the work of humanitarian organizations and halted aid shipments.

Civilians threw rocks at the UN peacekeepers who had failed to protect them from the new violence. In one case rebels went through a village and massacred 150 people while the 100 peacekeepers stationed less than a mile away had no idea anything was amiss. The peacekeepers were "short of equipment and men . . . [and had] a mix of poor communication and staffing, inadequate equipment, intelligence breakdowns, and spectacularly bad luck." The company of Indian peacekeepers was missing a translator (English-French) for two weeks. The commander, "unable to speak to most of the population and with almost no intelligence capabilities, . . . groped his way through a fog of rumor, speculation, and misinformation." And the force of 100 peacekeepers with three armored vehicles was no match for the rebels. The UN aborted patrols if fired upon. "Making matters worse, the peacekeepers' armored vehicles are largely unable to handle the muddy terrain of the neighborhoods hit hardest by the violence."

In the middle of it all the commander of UN peacekeepers in the Congo resigned abruptly, after just seven weeks on the job. Observers wondered if Nkunda's well-trained army, 10,000 strong, would march to the capital and take over the whole country. But Nkunda decided not to attack Goma, much less Kinshasa. He agreed to a cease-fire instead.

Almost as soon as the shooting stopped, the gears shifted from reverse to forward. Aid flows resumed. People started going home. The economy, such as it was, resumed. In the following weeks, fighting stopped and started as cease-fires took hold and fell apart—not an uncommon thing in this kind of war. Each time fighting started, the gears shifted into reverse; each time it stopped, the gears shifted into forward. Thus, whatever other changes are desirable in a postwar society, a durable cease-fire is step one. Stopping the shooting is a prerequisite for almost anything good you could hope to have happen in a society.

The leaders of Congo and Rwanda sat down and worked out an understanding. Rwanda would get rid of Nkunda—who indeed was soon arrested when he crossed into Rwanda—and the Congo would let Rwanda's army come in to fight the remnant of the genocide perpetrators who had used eastern Congo as a base since 1994. Part of Nkunda's group joined forces with Congo's army. This agreement shows that even in a civil war seemingly dominated by nonstate armed groups, the relationships between states (Congo and Rwanda) still have tremendous effect.

THE PERSISTENCE OF LOCAL FIGHTING

The good news is that Congo, Rwanda, and the UN are all on the same side, on one issue anyway, fighting to defeat the genocide perpetrators, who call themselves the Democratic Forces for the Liberation of Rwanda (FDLR). With the UN's support, some thousands of these fighters had returned to Rwanda (which has set up programs to reintegrate them in what is now a peaceful and fairly successful society). MONUC reports helping somewhat over a thousand people repatriate in 2008. But about 6,000 remained in early 2009 when the Congolese and Rwandan governments collaborated in a new military offensive. Again civilians suffered abuse from all sides.

The bad news is that this fighting continued in the eastern Congo in 2009, with almost a hundred thousand newly displaced people as a result, adding to a million displaced since 2006 in the area. The UN went up in its attack helicopters again, and shifted its resources to eastern Congo to eliminate the FDLR "spoilers" who destabilized the country. This easier-said-than-done job has been a "disaster for the civilians, who are now being attacked from all sides," according to Human Rights Watch. The NGO Oxfam, which provides assistance to 800,000 Congolese affected by the conflict, criticized the UN for supporting an offensive in which Congolese army and rebels alike committed war crimes and in which the government army was "the main perpetrator of sexual violence." Oxfam surveyed affected communities and concluded the offensive had made people less safe, not more, and that most feared both sides. "The peacekeeping force should withhold support from the operation if abuses continue or go unpunished. . . ."

The widespread use of rape as a weapon of war by both sides in eastern Congo has generated an international outcry, but continues (albeit at lower levels than in 1998–2003, as discussed in Chapter 10). In 2009, U.S. secretary of state Hillary Clinton visited the area to highlight the situation there.

One other group has spoiled the peace in eastern Congo in recent years. The Lord's Resistance Army (LRA) has operated near the border with Uganda, where it originated. The LRA, with many forcibly conscripted child soldiers, is a cult that regularly commits atrocities against civilians in its path. In 2008, Congo and Uganda, with active advice and help from the United States, planned an offensive against the LRA from Uganda. They attacked from three sides but unintentionally left an escape route for the LRA into the Congo, where LRA members proceeded to go on a murderous rampage against villages—killing, raping, and looting. In 2010, the LRA's leader and core fighters were pursued across the Central African Republic (CAR), where they fled from eastern Congo. They continued a moving spree of killing, rape, and kidnapping in the CAR, and experts worried in late 2010 that they could enter and destabilize the southern Sudan region in early 2011 as the region held a referendum on independence. (The LRA had received financial support in the past from Sudan's central government.) This did not happen, but in early 2011 the LRA was on the attack again against civilians in eastern Congo.

At the end of 2008, the Security Council mandated MONUC to shift emphasis from western Congo to the east near Rwanda and Uganda, where violent flare-ups continued, and seek to build a rapid reaction capability to respond and protect civilians—areas of glaring UN failure there in the recent past. From the perspective of eastern Congo, the UN has failed to come through as needed—failed to end the violence, failed to expel the genocide perpetrators who have destabilized eastern Congo for fifteen years, failed to protect the civilian population from vicious armed attacks, failed to get those displaced by conflict back home.

Séverine Autesserre knows the story of these failures well. Starting in 2001, she left France and went to eastern Congo as a volunteer with Doctors Without Borders, a large NGO that operates in the most difficult wartime environments—sometimes after all the larger aid groups have departed because of high risk. (It won the 1999 Nobel Peace Prize.) Later, she returned as a doctoral student to research the UN in the eastern Congo. Autesserre got a different view of the Congo than did Charlotte Isaksson. Autesserre had no large military organization behind her, and while Isaksson was deployed in the west, Autesserre was in the east.

Among her criticisms of the UN, Autesserre points to an international peacebuilding culture—translated into procedures and routines in the UN and other institutions—that is not attuned to local conditions. She mentions several stories that illustrate the feelings of disappointment and anger toward the UN among the local population. In one instance, a young boy in a large town ran to the UN compound seeking help as his neighbor was being attacked by an armed militia and was about to be raped. But the UN soldier there, from Uruguay, did not speak French or Swahili, and did not understand the boy. Finally the soldier thought he understood, went inside, and came back with a pack of cookies for the boy. In another story, perhaps apocryphal, a UN bureaucrat is transferred from East Timor to the Congo, and when preparing his report takes entire sections from previous reports on East Timor and does a global search-and-replace to put "Congo" where "East Timor" had been (but he misses some). UN staff in this view tend to adopt the same template for action anywhere in the world, ignoring local conditions.

Autesserre talked with an old man in eastern Congo who recalled the arrival of the UN, the humanitarian NGOs, and the diplomats in the mid-1990s. "We called them 'the humanoids,'" he told her, "full of ideals, of vigor, . . . but they come from another planet. They are completely disoriented." Inheritors of the culture of the "Onusians" in 1961 described by

Conor O'Brien in Chapter 3, the international organizations observed by Autesserre "have their own world, with its own rituals, its own beliefs, . . . in brief, its own culture."

Autesserre's central criticism of this culture is that it fails to address *local* conflicts, which lie at the heart of many of the world's civil wars. In places like eastern Congo, *some* of the problems can be solved using a top-down approach. For example, in the 2008 fighting, the agreement reached between the governments of Congo and Rwanda quickly solved the problem of Nkunda. But a durable peace proves elusive as long as local conflicts produce violent clashes. "Throughout the eastern Congo, bottom-up rivalries played a decisive role in sustaining local, national, and regional violence after the conflict officially ended [in 2003]. These agendas pitted villagers, traditional chiefs, community chiefs, or ethnic leaders against one another over the distribution of land, the exploitation of local mining sites, the appointment to local administrative and traditional positions of authority, the collection of local taxes, and the relative social status of specific groups and individuals." Furthermore, local armed groups "were not unitary actors." For instance, the Mai Mai militias had no unified command structure and "fought on all sides of the war."

IF YOUR CHILD DIES . . .

Recall the idea mentioned in Chapter 1: If your child is killed in an isolated battle, in local fighting, it is every bit as bad as your child's being killed in a major war that kills a million people and is fueled by superpower interests. Similarly, if you live in certain places in eastern Congo, things did not really improve with the arrival of the UN in 2000, the end of the war in 2003, or the elections in 2006. But elsewhere in the Congo things did improve dramatically. Overall, when the UN arrived ten years ago there were at least a half-dozen regular armies and various nonstate armed groups actively fighting each other. Now, in 2011, the country has one regular army—though it has big problems—belonging to its pretty-democratically-elected government, and some rebel militias in the east. Several Congolese militia leaders are on trial in the Netherlands for war crimes. Programs for police training, security sector reform, demobilization of rebels, return of refugees, and economic development are all actively in motion, although too slowly and ineffectively for the desperate needs of the country.

The UN has done good things, but has failed to do other good things. When Autesserre asked UN officials why they were not addressing local violence, they "usually mentioned their lack of human and financial resources. . . . They repeatedly emphasized that the peacekeeping operation was clearly too small to cover the immense Congolese territory or even the unstable eastern provinces." (Autesserre herself does not buy this argument, and focuses on the need to understand that local conflicts matter.) What would make the international community more successful and speed up its progress in the Congo? The answer is simply more resources—more personnel and money.

Just as in 1961 the UN tried to do a lot with too few resources, so, too, has MONUC tried to undertake a daunting mandate with inadequate resources. An instructive comparison can be made with U.S. forces in Iraq in 2003, which proved too small to maintain control despite having five times the number of soldiers as MONUC, with vastly better equipment, for a country with half the population of the Congo. Autesserre reports that "UN, diplomatic, and non-governmental staff members constantly enumerated the obstacles that they met in their daily work. They deplored the presence of spoilers, the continued involvement of Rwanda and Uganda, the national and foreign interests in the looting of natural resources, the collapsed state, the unceasing security problems that rendered many areas inaccessible . . . and the tremendous logistical hurdles."

Autesserre reports that "almost all of the [MONUC] officials . . . I interviewed, in both the Congo and New York, at the bottom and at the top of the hierarchy, deplored a lack of financial resources." The $1 billion annual budget of MONUC sounds less impressive in the context of a vast war-ravaged country with 66 million people and almost no income. The UN's budget in the Congo comes to about $15 per year for each person in the country. Adding the other sources of support for Congo's postwar transition, Autesserre estimates the cost at $39 per person, which she calls "trifling" compared with other missions such as El Salvador ($79), Kosovo ($240), and East Timor ($278). The flow of humanitarian aid came to about $3 per person in 2004, compared with $89 for Darfur. The peak number of UN peacekeepers in the Congo, during the 2006 elections, came to 33 peacekeepers per 100,000 inhabitants, compared with over 100 in Burundi and 500 in Liberia. Autesserre concludes that "it would have made sense to devote additional resources" to the Congo. By the way, the costs of the UN mission in the Congo get divided among UN members, and the American share costs the average American about one dollar per year. One dollar.

In addition to the money problems, MONUC's multinational nature created major challenges. Autesserre heard repeatedly from "diplomatic and UN interviewees" of the "endless bureaucratic impediments they faced." MONUC's staff and military contingents in many cases remained loyal to their national governments. Some "reportedly consulted with their capitals before deciding whether they would obey the orders of their UN Force Commanders," a problem that the UN itself blamed for its inadequate response to attacks in Bukavu in 2004. The UN mission also suffered from many personal conflicts among its diverse participants.

As with ONUC in 1961, language barriers impeded MONUC's work. Congolese speak mainly French, Swahili, and local languages, but MONUC was officially an English-speaking mission. Thus, "many staff members, including those within the top management," could not speak "any of the languages widely used in the Congo." Some of those who did speak one of the languages of the Congo did not know English. In general the international community had poor intelligence and faulty assessments of the situation. For example, Autesserre attended a meeting in 2004 at which "everyone concluded that the province [South Kivu in eastern Congo] was relatively calm. . . . All present agreed that the city of Bukavu, where the meeting took place, was once again stable and uneventful. A few hours later, large-scale fighting broke out in Bukavu and quickly spread to the entire province. . . ."

Soldiers themselves were not only inadequate in number; Congolese and foreigners alike "considered many battalions incompetent, cowardly, and unmotivated." As for the civilian staff, some of it "lacked competence, training, capability, experience, or motivation to fulfill their tasks." All of this helped make the UN unpopular among the population, according to Autesserre. The "final blow" came with the "major sexual exploitation scandal" in MONUC in 2005.

And yet, despite all these problems, the UN has done a lot of good in many parts of the Congo—perhaps not some places in the east yet, but much of the country. The wars of 1996–2003 have not resumed on a large scale. Many civil wars restart, sometimes more violently than ever, as Angola's did after UN-sponsored elections in 1992 and Sri Lanka's did in 2006. Congo's did not. Some fighting continues sporadically in the east, but the UN counts among its accomplishments "the pacification of the vast majority of the territory . . ." and the organization of the first democratic elections since independence. Like Autesserre, economist Paul Collier, after strongly criticizing MONUC's performance, nonetheless concludes that "the presence of peacekeepers has averted a catastrophe" in the Congo.

In addition, the UN and other international organizations clearly played a key role in creating a new Congolese democracy. And international humanitarian aid, which helped nineteen million Congolese in 2008, has begun to improve public health, albeit from a terrible starting point. Polio vaccinations reached 10 million children. A UN health survey in 2010 put the death rate for children under age five at 16 percent, very high but still down by a quarter from the 21 percent who did not make it to age five in 2001.

In 2010 the Security Council converted the Congo mission to a "stabilization force." MONUC became MONUSCO. This was a step in the direction of winding down the UN force and giving Congo's problems back to the government, which proposed ending the UN mission in fifteen months. The Council "noted that substantial progress had been made since the deployment of the mission in 1999. . . ." But it was going slow on drawing down the force.

REVISITING THE SIERRA LEONE MODEL

Congo has all the issues and problems found in the other African peacekeeping missions, and is perhaps unusual just for being the largest and for having so many issues at once. Some countries at war are extremely poor, some have violent ethnic divisions, some have lootable resources, some see extensive rapes, some have foreign armies on their soil, and so forth. Congo seems to have it all.

In thinking about the UN missions in Sierra Leone and the Congo, why has the road to peace taken so much longer in the Congo? Why did Sierra Leone have more success? One reason, surely, is that the missions of similar scale (nearly 20,000 peacekeepers in each) addressed countries of dissimilar scale. Sierra Leone has 6 million people. The Congo has more than 60 million. So relative to population size the Sierra Leone mission had ten times the resources to work with and—surprise—it worked better. From the perspective of the Congo mission, we should recognize the successes of the UN in reducing the horrors of war, considering the low cost and small size of the mission relative to the country. With more resources, even more good could have been accomplished.

7

THE UNARMY

Nonmilitary Forces Supporting Peace

When my friend Jerry Bender used to visit Angola during the war there, he would stop near the airport to buy a few flats of eggs with American dollars at a local street market before proceeding into Luanda, the capital city. In those days, in Angola, eggs had tangible value, whereas the printed currency had none. The war and the government's misguided economic policies had destroyed the money economy, despite the funds pumped into each side by exports of oil and diamonds, respectively. Much of the population lived in dire poverty, with disease and malnutrition rampant. Most people relied on what they called "schemes," involving barter, connections, corruption, and ingenuity, to get by. In those days, eggs could get you around Luanda a lot better than money could.

During decades of civil war in Angola, the Cold War superpowers backed opposing factions. Jerry Bender, an International Relations professor at USC in Los Angeles, shuttled back and forth to Angola, talking alternately to the Angolan government officials, UNITA rebels, U.S. oil company executives, and foreign policy experts in the U.S. Congress and administration—all of whom he knew personally. Because of his gregarious, free-wheeling manner, his great sense of humor, and his unruly hair, he became known as a "licensed lunatic" (his words) who threatened no one and could talk with everyone. Along with many other people inside and outside Angola, Jerry tried persistently to end the civil war, just as many thousands of people around the world have worked to end other wars. Mediators, peacekeepers, diplomats, NGO staffs and volunteers, citizen diplomats, businesspeople, peace activists—all have put a tremendous effort into ending the world's wars. And, more often than is generally recognized, they have succeeded.

The CIA officer who ran the secret Angola operation supporting UNITA during the Cold War (who then resigned and spilled the beans to Congress) recalled that "the professor who stopped the war, my war in Angola, was . . . young Professor Jerry Bender . . ." Bender saw what the CIA was doing in Angola and called his senator to alert him that the CIA was lying to Congress (which indeed it was). The Senate passed an amendment that cut off funding for the Angola war.

Jerry's licensed-lunatic theory was put to the test when he went to Angola as an election monitor during a cease-fire in 1992. With three other Americans he was sent to a somewhat remote polling station in UNITA-controlled territory. When the group came in and introduced themselves, the UNITA commander in charge became agitated and pointed at Jerry. "Bender! Bender! Sit down." All the soldiers in the room cocked their guns at the ready, and the other Americans edged away from Jerry. "Why do you spread lies? On the BBC on [such and such a date] you said . . ." and he listed off points Jerry had made on a BBC interview years earlier, and went on to quote things Jerry had said on a dozen different BBC and Voice of America interviews over the years. This might suggest that all politics is global, and it's on BBC, but the point of the story is that he did not shoot Jerry. Electoral politics, not violence, was the game at that time. The rebel commander finished dressing Jerry down verbally, then gave him a hug and said, "Let's go out and dance with the UNITA girls." And they did.

Jerry Bender is a member of a vast but disorganized mass of people and organizations working for peace around the world. I call it the Unarmy because it is an unarmed force working in an unmilitary fashion to accomplish some of the same goals as peacekeepers.

The Unarmy includes many components, ranging from lone individuals to civilians working with peacekeeping missions, in NGOs, or for governments. "NGOs, independent experts, consultants, and committed citizens . . ." have become "an integral part of today's United Nations." In this chapter I will focus on three wings of the Unarmy—diplomacy, humanitarian assistance, and women's peace groups. (Peace movements get their own chapter next.)

I. Diplomacy: Credibility, Not Impartiality

A key component of the world's efforts to reduce war is unarmed diplomacy, carried out by governments, international organizations, and non-governmental groups and individuals. Long before peacekeepers arrive at a conflict scene, these diplomats must have mediated, negotiated, communicated, and cajoled to get to even a fragile cease-fire agreement, much less a durable settlement.

One of the UN's most dedicated diplomats, the self-described "man without a gun," was the Italian Giandomenico Picco. Picco worked for Pérez de Cuéllar, "probably the most underestimated secretary-general of all" by one account, who used the thaw in U.S.-Soviet relations in the late 1980s to empower the Security Council and end the Iran-Iraq War.

As a UN political officer sent to the Cyprus conflict in the late 1970s, Picco learned "the manual labor of mediation" using the "hand tools of diplomacy." He found that "it was essential to develop personal relationships with the individuals involved on both sides. . . . I learned how to personalize every matter, which frankly isn't all that hard for an Italian." Over time, he also learned that "impartiality is not a useful concept. . . . What both sides want from a mediator is not impartiality but credibility—the ability to deliver the goods." In Cyprus, Picco had to arrange complex deals with reciprocal gestures and concessions. But over the years, Picco concluded that reciprocity alone was not the main element of finding a solution—"there are a right and wrong in most matters, . . . and not an inevitable middle ground that sacrifices principle."

Cyprus also taught Picco the difference between mediation and providing "good offices" for negotiations. "A full-fledged mediator usually has a mandate and the independence to make his own proposals regardless of the positions of the parties. A good officer . . . can only encourage the two parties to stretch their positions until they touch." The UN secretary-general was generally seen as a good officer, to emphasize his "limited ability to negotiate and the circumscribed scope of his initiatives." But his representatives, such as Picco, tried to "stretch the confining rubber band as far as possible without snapping it." In Afghan negotiations in the 1980s, the UN negotiator was charged with launching talks based on four simple points, but "what began as four lines became four lines with an additional paragraph attached to each. Over the years, the paragraphs became a set of articles, then a more complete text, and eventually each item became an individual legal instrument that represented a long chapter of the entire agreement." Those negotiations lasted eight years and culminated in a peace treaty signed in Geneva in 1988.

One limit of UN diplomacy is that only member-state governments, and not rebel groups, are recognized as legitimate actors. We have seen this problem in Mozambique, where it took an Italian religious community to talk with the rebels. In working on the Afghanistan problem in the 1980s, Picco had to deal only with the Soviet-backed government there, and let the government of Pakistan "speak for itself and the Afghan mujahideen it supported." Thus, civil wars and domestic conflicts tended, especially in the Cold War era, to be approached at the international level as proxies for national governments, when in fact the causes of conflicts might be localized and the substate actors independent.

Incidentally, one skill Picco developed in Afghanistan was how to seem interested in boring talks. In Picco's meetings with the Afghan president, the latter always rehashed the same story about Pakistani aggression and "by the third telling, I found myself nodding off." Because Picco was the note-taker for the meetings, and could not "remain idle lest the principals think their words are being ignored . . . I had developed a system of fake writing, jiggling my pen up and down on the pad so that the result looked like an EKG."

Pérez de Cuéllar had taken over as secretary-general in 1982 and, by the late 1980s, had helped end the Iran-Iraq War and get the Soviet Union out of Afghanistan. Picco, working closely with him, was trying to "reinvent the office of secretary-general." The UN head "had become a real player in international affairs without using the instruments of a state, which are mainly money and weapons." Rather, the secretary-general's power was based on proposing his own ideas based on what was right, and remaining free of the vested interests that states always have. This reinvention of the office "involved a cultural shift of no small magnitude at the United Nations," especially in venturing into "peacemaking"—the active negotiation of agreements to end conflicts. "Many governments thought it blasphemous" and a threat to state sovereignty, but in fact the idea dated back to Ralph Bunche.

Peacemaking was viewed by many, nonetheless, as a new concept and, by its enemies, as "Picco's concept." Picco avoided opposition by working with "a very small group of people and, in some cases, in great secrecy." Picco realized that "peacemaking could not be agreed upon as a concept and then implemented; it had to be the other way around. . . . Deeds more than words were its currency." In 1989, Secretary-General Pérez de Cuéllar received authority to open political offices in conflict areas around the world to support diplomacy. They even gained diplomatic status equivalent to embassies in one case. But when Boutros-Ghali took over, he shut down the three offices, known in the UN as "the Picco offices." Finally, in another turnaround, in 1992 the first summit of Security Council members adopted a declaration that included peacemaking among the functions of the secretary-general, giving Picco victory in his effort to gain acceptance of this concept.

During the last years of the Cold War, in the late 1980s, Picco and others working under Pérez de Cuéllar, quietly negotiated progress in conflicts in Namibia, Western Sahara, and El Salvador—"working in small teams or alone, avoiding publicity that would only embarrass our clients and harden their positions." The goal of these negotiators was "to come up with win-win solutions, except in cases where nations had blatantly violated international law."

The reform-minded Soviet leader Gorbachev transformed the Soviet attitude toward the UN— which had been seen with some suspicion ever since the Korean War and vilified during the Congo crisis in the early 1960s. Now, Gorbachev declared, "the UN will become part of our foreign policy." Furthermore, in the Iran-Iraq War (1980–88), the two superpowers found themselves on the same side (against the new Islamic Republic of Iran). Pérez de Cuéllar got the five permanent members of the Security Council together for the first time to push for an end to the Iran-Iraq War. He also hoped, in vain as it turned out, to use the momentum to do the same for the Israel-Palestine conflict. But he began hosting "unity lunches" of the foreign ministers from the "Perm Five," and they gave him a new "long leash" to negotiate on his own.

The secretary-general thus gained a new independence, and Iran in particular saw him "as a presence separate and apart from the Security Council" (which was composed of Iran's enemies). "Indeed, in a world of nations they saw as almost uniformly hostile to their interests, the Iranians considered Pérez de Cuéllar the one official anywhere who was willing to listen to their position." Picco then became deeply involved in the negotiations to end the Iran-Iraq War, although the UN bureaucracy was "not particularly enthralled with the new peacemaking role that the secretary-general was trying to create."

Picco found that negotiating styles differed drastically for Iraq and Iran. "In general, countries with a monolithic and very authoritarian structure maintain the same position in negotiations, immutable for a long period of time. Then, one day, they advocate a different position with the same bottom-line vehemence. . . . The other side rarely sees it coming. . . . This was the Iraqi style" under Saddam Hussein. By contrast, the Iranians at first appeared "reasonable, flexible, understanding, and ready to adjust their position," but in reality proved reluctant to change position and sometimes reopened "what everyone thought was settled ground. They may be intellectually stimulating, but they're a bear to pin down."

To help pin the Iranians down after they neither accepted nor rejected the Security Council's resolution in 1987, Pérez de Cuéllar took the "unprecedented" step of writing down, on his own, fourteen pages of details about how the resolution would be implemented. "Whether this exceeded his authority is an open question, but it was plainly the shortest route to the end of this long, bloody war," and in fact the Security Council supported him in the year-long negotiation that followed.

Picco had to push both sides hard, but especially the Iraqis who, opposite to the Iranians, considered the Security Council their friend and the secretary-general a "partisan villain." Parties in a negotiation accuse mediators of bias, Picco argues, to pressure them and see how they stand up. "Any intermediary who tries to relieve the psychological pressure by yielding . . . should find another job." Picco notes that "90 percent of diplomacy is a question of who blinks first. . . ." A more real pressure was that of time. As the war continued despite the UN's efforts, Picco worried that "diplomatic efforts can be sustained for only so long before they fizzle out or blow up." As negotiations neared their conclusion, Picco realized that "this was the first time since the days of Ralph Bunche, forty years earlier, that the United Nations would actually be playing a major role in ending a massive conflict."

The talks came down to the wire, and a Security Council meeting scheduled for eleven A.M. was delayed because the Saudis—a crucial intermediary who never spoke publicly about their role—had not gotten Iraq to agree on the final terms of a cease-fire. But just after one P.M., with the Security Council "waiting restlessly downstairs," the phone rang. The Saudi king, on the other end, said "I would like to be the first to congratulate you, Mr. Secretary-General. You have just brought the Iran-Iraq war to an end." A minute later the Iraqis called to confirm the deal.

Picco hoped that Iran would feel it "owed us one" for helping end the war with Iraq, and would respond by helping free Western hostages held by Iranian-allied militants in Lebanon. The basis for the hostage negotiations was a declaration by the new U.S. president Bush that assistance in freeing the hostages would "be long remembered. Goodwill begets goodwill." In the end, after the hostages were released, the United States gave nothing to Iran in return and Picco had to scurry out of Tehran before radical elements took out their anger on him. Meanwhile Picco was working on several other issues. In a three-week period in early 1989 he traveled to fifteen different cities. Later, in thirty-six hours Picco flew from New York to London to Damascus to Cyprus and back to Damascus, only to be awakened at midnight by a phone call telling him that "there are some complications. . . ."

The "toughest part" of negotiating on behalf of the secretary-general, such as in the hostage negotiations, was that unlike governments, "the secretary-general had no money or weapons to trade." Picco also had to travel and conduct diplomacy in dangerous neighborhoods with rudimentary equipment and security. For instance, he had to carry documents from Syria into Israel in a small UN jeep, across a hostile border that nobody else had crossed at night since the 1967 war. Later he had to meet shady characters in back streets of Beirut, Lebanon, who would drive him at high speed, blindfolded in the backseat, then shoved from car to car, to meet leaders of militant groups holding hostages. After negotiating during the night, Picco would sleep a few hours in the morning, then fly by UN helicopter to the Israeli border (thanks to the Italian helicopter unit in UNIFIL) and cross over to negotiate the release of Lebanese prisoners held by Israel, "my body running on pure adrenaline in lieu of sleep." After many repetitions of these routines, he was driven by the militants to a jeep with one of the hostages, Jackie Mann, in the back. Picco got in and said, "Mr. Mann, I'm Gianni Picco from the United Nations, and I'm here to tell you that you are now going to be freed."

One time, a hostage had supposedly been kidnapped by a Palestinian militant group in Lebanon with ties to Libya, so Picco was asked to go to Libya to arrange a deal. A Libyan envoy in Syria told Picco that Libya could not send a Libyan plane in time, "and suggested I rent a plane, with the cost to be paid by his government. I quickly agreed. . . ." The plane rental cost $50,000, Picco spent less than a day in Libya, did not get to see the Libyan leader, and "incidentally, the Libyans never paid for the plane rental. The bill had to be picked up by the United Nations. It turned out to be the largest single cash expense we incurred in freeing the hostages. . . ."

The whole hostage mission cost less than $100,000 over four years, not counting twelve helicopter flights across Lebanon that Italy covered. The U.S. share would have been $25,000, "but all the expenses were charged to a little fund for peace that an elderly American lady had donated to the secretary-general some fifteen years earlier." So the hostage operation cost the Americans nothing.

The arrival of the new secretary-general, Boutros-Ghali, severely hampered Picco's work, both because of new bureaucratic requirements and because the secretary-general personally involved himself in delicate diplomacy with a lack of skill.

Picco left the UN convinced that "over and over again, the human factor is at the basis of crises and the individual at the source of solutions." Reform of an institution such as the UN should leave "enough room for an individual to maneuver in a world of unforeseen events. The Charter . . . gave the secretary-general that kind of wiggle room."

Another source of wiggle room within the Secretariat can be found in the quiet diplomacy of the UN Development Program's Resident Representatives who live in most of the world's countries and are closely aware of local conditions and problems. Most often the "Res Reps" serve in a role similar to an ambassador, coordinating UN activity in the country, and often they become the Special Representatives of the secretary-general in countries with more intensive UN missions. Because local leaders know the Res Rep and consider him or her to be neutral, opportunities arise to resolve conflicts and head off violence.

In Madagascar in 2002, when two men claimed to have won a presidential election, the Res Rep, a Malian named Adama Guindo, worked with the government, churches, opposition groups, and foreign powers to resolve the crisis. He personally brought the two to talks in Senegal, where they formed a unity government pending a recount. When the recount favored the opposition leader, Guindo defused a military confrontation and, within two months, got the incumbent president to cede power and leave the country.

WHEN THE TIME IS RIPE

Many of the world's remaining armed conflicts have been going on for a decade or more. These conflicts are harder for diplomacy to resolve because they "have been entrenched in the social fabric and the parties have learned how to block peace efforts." But William Zartman, an experienced negotiator and scholar, argues that conflicts can be effectively settled when both parties have reached a "hurting stalemate" and have given up on winning easily, and at the same time a "way out" is available as a joint solution for which the parties can aim. At this point a conflict is "ripe for resolution." Thus, in negotiating peace, timing is key.

In particular, when bad rulers in collapsed or collapsing states have created disasters, Zartman argues, timely intervention could have prevented the problem in most cases. "Specific actions identified and discussed at the time could have been taken that would have gone far to prevent the enormously costly catastrophes that eventually occurred." But instead, opportunities to end conflicts have too often been allowed to slip away.

Having reached the point of a mutually hurting stalemate, "the parties to conflict confront an immediate difficulty. Having publicly fully committed themselves to victory . . . the parties could not very well sue for a cease-fire without harming their reputations with their own people." Political scientist Fred Iklé, in his classic *Every War Must End*, emphasizes that ending wars depends on domestic politics as a war drags on and exacts costs. Leaders who make peace can be labeled "traitors" who betrayed the cause that supporters have died for. Yet this kind of compromise is the most common route to peace. Often, "the military hero of an earlier day is the man who can best conclude a 'peace of betrayal,'" because he is less vulnerable to charges of treason.

Thus, continuing to fight means saving face but suffering further losses, whereas stopping means stemming losses but losing credibility. In this context, the powerful external actor, the UN, solves the dilemma by letting parties reframe their decision to stop fighting as a response to the international community and thus a responsible action.

In some cases, a "ripe" moment does not fully materialize. Instead there is "a soft stalemate that is stable and self-serving," so that the parties themselves do not fully see the growing dangers and are not eager to solve the conflict. In these situations third-party intervention is needed, even more than in hard stalemates. In either case, conflicting parties tend to distrust outside intervention—"a mediator is always regarded as a meddler to some extent. . . ." In a civil war, "external intervention favors the weaker party, . . . and it suggests that the sovereign state is not able to handle its own internal affairs." Nonetheless, "conflicting and collapsing parties need help out of their predicament."

PERSISTENT, UNCOMFORTABLE MEDIATION

Mediation is "a form of third-party intervention in a conflict" that, unlike peacekeeping or military assistance, does not involve the use of force or aim to help one side win. The third party enters the negotiations to help the parties find a solution that they could not find by themselves. Since "mediators often meet initial rejection from the conflict parties," they must be persistent. And since agreements often fall apart, mediators must remain engaged long-term: "Early satisfaction with superficial results and premature disengagement by the mediator is one of the most frequent causes of failure in peacemaking."

Mediation often requires multiple attempts before a durable agreement emerges. An authority on mediation, Jacob Bercovitch, examined eighteen serious conflicts, resistant to settlement, in 1945–95, that produced seventy-five serious military clashes. In these conflicts, 382 mediation attempts were made—more than twenty per conflict on average. The mediator was a representative of an international organization in about a quarter of the attempts, of a large government in another quarter, and the leader of an international organization in almost another quarter, with the remaining cases scattered among different types of mediator. In half the cases mediation was unsuccessful, and in another 10 percent it was turned down by the parties, while 24 percent of the attempts resulted in partial agreements and only 5 percent in full settlements.

Incidentally, pressure on negotiating parties can take various forms. When Ralph Bunche mediated Israeli-Egyptian talks in 1949 on the island of Rhodes, he turned poor accommodations to advantage. "The physical arrangements in Rhodes—even the appalling food—were, on the whole, advantageous to the mediation effort. . . . Rhodes presented no incentives for dallying or staying a moment longer than was necessary. A determined mediator could use these conditions as an additional element of pressure." By contrast, South African mediators in Congolese negotiations in 2002 made the mistake of hosting talks at a luxury resort, much more comfortable than back home, and negotiations dragged on for seven weeks.

In the post–Cold War era, "the United Nations remained the preeminent international actor in the pursuit of peace, but its efforts were part of an extraordinary growth in conflict prevention, mediation, peacekeeping, and peace-building undertaken by other multilateral institutions, regional and subregional organizations, individual states, nongovernmental organizations (NGOs), and private peacemakers," writes NYU conflict researcher Teresa Whitfield. As other researchers have noted, conflict resolution began making a difference in the 1980s in places such as South Africa, and the new kinds of conflicts that predominated in the post–Cold War era were "exactly the type of conflict that had preoccupied the conflict resolution thinkers for many years."

Advocates of conflict resolution emphasize timing, in that a "narrowing of political space" accompanies escalation of violence and a "widening" of that space occurs with de-escalation. In the narrow middle, conflict "containment" may be the most that can be accomplished, whereas earlier or later in the process more transformative outcomes may be possible. A wide range of conflict resolution techniques, from fact-finding to special envoys to truth commissions and many more

possibilities, are appropriate to different stages of conflict. Conflict resolution processes can also operate on several "tracks" at once. "Track
One" consists of official negotiations with top leaders and international
organizations and governments. "Track Two" involves midlevel leaders,
international NGOs, churches, academics, and similar unofficial channels. "Track Three" consists of grassroots peace efforts in the conflict
area. Many Track Two efforts over the years have addressed various
conflicts with mixed success—the Israeli-Palestinian conflict would have
been long since solved if Track Two were a surefire solution.

The Folke Bernadotte Academy, named for the UN Middle East mediator assassinated in 1948, is "a Swedish government agency dedicated to
improving the quality and effectiveness of international conflict and crisis management, with a particular focus on peace operations." It recruits
and trains civilians for international peace operations, operating from its
facility on a small island in the Swedish countryside. The academy runs
workshops and training sessions such as "conflict prevention," civil-
military coordination in EU peace operations, and a course on personal
security issues for people deployed in a conflict area.

NGOs oriented to conflict resolution can "monitor conflicts and provide
warning and insights into a particular conflict. In certain situations they
can pave the way for mediation and sometimes undertake mediation
themselves. . . . NGOs may carry out education and training for conflict
resolution . . . help to establish a free press and . . . provide technical assistance on democratic arrangements that reduce the likelihood of
violence. . . ." For example, in Russia and Eastern Europe since 1991, the
Project on Ethnic Relations has conducted mediation with leaders on both
sides of long-standing ethnic conflicts, such as between Serbian and Alba-
nian communities in Kosovo. Another NGO, Search for Common Ground,
seeks to diminish risks of violence on several continents, especially in the
Middle East. In promoting the understanding of differences and chances to
act on commonalities, the group uses tools ranging from radio and television shows to shuttle diplomacy, training workshops, sports, and song. Yet
another NGO focuses on education and training to promote human dignity
and reduce humiliation, which the group sees as a key driver of conflicts.

In 2000–03, a small, newly created Swiss NGO played a critical role in
mediating negotiations between the government of Indonesia and the
secessionist movement in Aceh Province. The success of this effort ended

a fifteen-year war. The fact that this NGO had no history or resources to speak of actually may have helped the Indonesian government select it to facilitate the negotiations. "In a period of just under three years, a nonofficial organization from Geneva managed to put an obscure and forgotten conflict on the international map and to broker a peace agreement." The cease-fire quickly broke down in 2003. But after the devastating tsunami at the end of 2004 renewed both sides' interest in peace, they turned to another NGO, a Finnish group headed by the former president Martti Ahtisaari, to host talks in early 2005. The peace agreement that resulted, broader than that in 2003, has lasted ever since. Ahtisaari won the 2008 Nobel Prize for his work in Aceh and for a lifetime of diplomacy.

The trouble with NGOs as mediators, writes Whitfield, is that unlike states "they have no political power or economic resources and thus bring neither leverage to a negotiation nor the promise of resources to peacebuilding."

GROUPS OF FRIENDS

Outside of the formal decisions of the Security Council, a "plethora of *ad hoc* groupings of states gathering outside the Council's chambers" work to resolve international conflicts. Some of these informal groupings go by the name "Friends of the Secretary-General" and others—less tied to the UN and more self-selected—by the name "Contact Group." Being *ad hoc* groupings, put together for the occasion, they are free from some of the limitations of the Security Council with its great-power politics, its mandates, and its complex relationship with the Secretariat. They have "developed as a critical element of an incipient system of post–Cold War global security governance."

These informal arrangements date to the early years of the UN and have greatly expanded in recent years. In the 1990s, they helped end wars in Cambodia, Angola, Haiti, Western Sahara, Guatemala, Suriname, Bosnia, Georgia, Afghanistan, Tajikistan, Sierra Leone, Central African Republic, Kosovo, East Timor, Guinea-Bissau, and Congo. Since 2000 the list continues with Ethiopia/Eritrea, Sudan, Somalia, Liberia, Iraq, the Rwanda/Burundi/Congo area, and Uganda. The total number of these groupings grew from fewer than five in 1990 to more than thirty in 2005.

The first to operate under the label of "Group of Friends of the

Secretary-General" took form in the El Salvador war. Unlike the earlier Western Contact Group for Namibia, which operated outside the UN framework, the El Salvador "friends" worked in conjunction with the UN's efforts, and served to enhance the voice of the secretary-general, mostly because these countries could bring to bear capabilities that the secretary-general himself lacked. For example, the Friends provided security to guerrilla leaders and raised funds for peace-related programs. The El Salvador friends were Spain, Mexico, Venezuela, and Colombia, eventually joined by the United States. Their role was "important," writes Oxford researcher Jochen Prantl, but "largely unrecognized. . . . And what they had done was difficult to quantify, as befits the quiet labor of diplomacy that attends a complex mediation. . . ."

In recent cases, sometimes several informal groups operate side-by-side in a single conflict. What one cannot accomplish perhaps another can get done. In the Kosovo war in 1999, these included a group known as the Troika (individual diplomats from the United States, Russia, and the European Union), another called the Quint (the five most powerful NATO members), and the Group of 8 (G8, a general group of the big industrialized economies). Negotiations involving the G8 and Troika failed to solve the problem, and NATO undertook a military intervention outside the UN, without Security Council approval. After the UN returned, Kofi Annan created a larger group of countries called Friends of Kosovo.

Some wars are more likely than others to result in the formation of a "friends" or similar group. They seem to be most likely in wars that are neither at the top nor the bottom of the great powers' agendas, but of middle interest, and neither in the most devastating nor the most trivial wars in the world. Belonging to a "friends" group may offer participating countries who are not great powers a chance to have influence and "to maintain a front-row seat in the diplomatic process without any hard undertaking to commit resources, troops, or diplomatic muscle to the effort." A group's composition is usually "directly related to the interests of its members." Critics of the groups include "elected members of the [Security] Council . . . concerned with the usurpation of their authority. . . ."

THE WORLD COURT

One branch of the UN that gets little attention despite some spectacular successes in preventing wars is the World Court (formally, the International Court of Justice). Its fifteen judges, including one from each permanent Security Council member, meet in The Hague, Netherlands, to hear cases brought by states, not individuals. Almost all the world's countries have signed the treaty creating the Court, although only a third have signed the optional clause promising to follow the Court's rulings. (The United States withdrew from that clause in 1986 when Nicaragua sued it over the CIA's mining of a Nicaraguan harbor during the "Contra War.")

In 2002, the World Court awarded control of a disputed oil-rich peninsula to Cameroon, and the much stronger party, Nigeria, pulled its troops out in 2006. This dispute, fueled by a combustible mix of oil and border-crossing ethnic conflicts, had the potential for a serious interstate war. The reason that successes such as this one do not get more attention is precisely that they were successful—there was no war.

Kofi Annan has suggested providing modest financial and technical expertise to poor countries to allow them to use the World Court to resolve disputes. The Court has recently played a central role in some explosive border disputes, notably between Eritrea and Ethiopia, so Annan's idea could yet prove to be very productive at fairly low cost.

II. Humanitarian Assistance

Humanitarianism makes up another "wing" of the Unarmy. It is a large-scale enterprise. In less than a decade, 1997 to 2005, the overall international humanitarian system including the UN, international Red Cross, and NGOs grew by 77 percent in personnel, with fastest growth in the NGO sector. A "plethora of NGOs" works on humanitarian action in war zones, side by side with the UN but sometimes with a "lack of concerted action." Other actors are involved too—"states, for-profit disaster firms, other businesses, and various foundations. . . ." Aid levels have also increased dramatically, from about $2 billion in 1990 to $6 billion in 2000 and over $10 billion in 2005.

Some of the most important humanitarian actions in war zones, however, result from the actions of individuals—sometimes working with NGOs and sometimes freelance. One of the greatest was Fred Cuny. I remember his appearance on TV news after a terrible market shelling in

Sarajevo, in which he pointed to the sky where NATO jets flew over, and asked why they were just flying around instead of doing something to stop the atrocities on the ground. Cuny was the anti-NATO in this case—unarmed, tiny, underfunded, but there on the ground doing good work every day for the Bosnians. Not so tiny actually, Cuny was a six-foot-four-inch optimistic Texan and an ingenious engineer. With a couple of million dollars, he designed and built a water purification system that served more than 100,000 people under siege in Sarajevo. He designed the pieces to fit in twelve C-130 transport plane loads, each of which could unload in under seven minutes because the airport was usually under fire.

Cuny got started, along with many of the old veterans of international humanitarianism, during the war in Biafra, Nigeria, in 1968. It was the first time that images of starving children proliferated in the mass media, leading to "the first great international response to humanitarian disaster." Cuny later noted that Biafra was still the "yardstick" by which performance in humanitarian crises was measured. "It's the defining moment," during which strategies such as supplementary feeding were first developed.

It did not go smoothly at first, though. When Cuny arrived in 1969 he told the Nigerian interior minister, "I'm from Texas and I'm here to study your war and tell you what you can do when it's over to get humanitarian aid in." The minister took Cuny's passport and ripped out the Nigerian visa. "We don't want anything to do with these damned Biafrans and all you Americans and others that are helping them. I want you out of here in twenty-four hours," he said. Cuny left the country and returned on the Biafran side to help feed people.

After Biafra, Cuny went on to help get aid to people in need in countries around the world. He became a leading figure in humanitarianism. After his success in Sarajevo in 1994, before the war there had ended Cuny was off to Chechnya to help its people during a particularly traumatic war between secessionist rebels and the Russian government. Chechnya was one of the most dangerous places on earth to be a humanitarian or journalist. Cuny was reported missing in 1995, and months later, after intensive investigation, he was declared dead although his body was never found. Rumors and theories swirled about who killed him and why, but the only sure truth is that Fred Cuny was never seen again, and the world is poorer for it.

Cuny's fate is becoming more common. In 2008, 122 humanitarian aid workers were killed and 138 more "kidnapped or seriously injured in violent attacks. This toll is the highest of the twelve years that our study has tracked these incidents," wrote researchers at NYU. Not only have numbers risen steadily since around 2001, but even relative to the number of aid workers active in the world the number has risen. However, the chances of a given aid worker in the field experiencing one of these crimes in a given year is still below one in a thousand. The most dangerous countries were Sudan, Afghanistan, and Somalia, and they accounted for all the increase in recent years. "As security worsens, aid operations are often scaled back or withdrawn, affecting both the quality and quantity of assistance beneficiaries receive."

ISSUES FOR HUMANITARIANISM

British humanitarian aid worker Conor Foley uses his experiences to criticize recent trends in humanitarian aid in war zones. Human rights NGOs have come together with humanitarian groups that traditionally restricted themselves to temporarily helping people without getting into politics. The result of this merger, Foley says, was a "political humanitarianism" that advocated for military intervention during humanitarian crises in the 1990s, culminating in the NATO intervention in Kosovo in 1999.

Foley criticizes humanitarian organizations that have worked with military forces, as in Afghanistan. The government or rebels can give or withhold access to aid depending on various communities' cooperation with the war effort. Foley argues that only the traditional principles of neutrality, impartiality, and independence that have defined humanitarianism in the past can "potentially fit all the situations in which humanitarians work. . . . The shift away from these principles in recent years has caused more problems than it has solved." Foley finds humanitarian interventions "at best a necessary evil," and at worst something comparable to the "rush of missionaries, teachers, and doctors who followed the soldiers of European armies" in colonizing Africa in the late nineteenth century.

Recently the lines dividing military from humanitarian operations have blurred. Insurgents began targeting all foreign groups, often finding

NGOs and the UN to be "softer" targets than military forces. At the same time, military forces in counterinsurgency operations have integrated humanitarian aspects in their efforts to "win hearts and minds." In some ways traditional humanitarian agencies and military organizations are today "jockeying for position in conflicts around the world," write researchers Ian Smillie and Larry Minear.

One dilemma for humanitarian aid from Biafra to Bosnia and beyond has been that the assistance may sustain rebel groups and prolong the war, leading to more suffering. In 2010, international food aid in Somalia was found to be going partly to the Islamic militant groups fighting the government. In Bosnia, "UN humanitarian aid . . . had undoubtedly kept many people alive, but it had also sustained the war which had killed many others." In some cases, UN convoys carrying desperately needed aid to UN-designated "safe areas" in Bosnia had to supply diesel fuel to the besieging Serbian forces in exchange for passage to the safe areas. By one estimate, between 35 and 70 percent of relief assistance to Bosnia was captured by the combatants.

In Sierra Leone, after a coup during the war, Britain suspended desperately needed humanitarian aid because of concerns it would be diverted from its intended purpose. Some NGOs felt the aid suspension, along with an embargo on fuel and arms, had political purposes, to pressure Sierra Leone for a political solution, but a British minister called this an "absolute lie." Nonetheless, the situation on the ground "deteriorated rapidly" as most NGOs pulled out of the country and the government-in-exile urged others to follow.

"When politics intrudes on humanitarian action, the higher the level of the policy maker, the higher the political quotient in the humanitarian equation. Human need looks more compelling on its own terms from the front lines than from donor capitals." Nonetheless, Reagan-era American aid to Ethiopia, and Clinton-era aid to North Korea, reflected genuine humanitarian concern rather than political calculation.

The combination of humanitarian and political concerns results in different "tiers" of emergencies, where the top tier of "high-profile political crises such as Bosnia, Kosovo, Afghanistan, and Iraq" get most attention and funding. "Second-class emergencies" are the more traditional big humanitarian crises such as Sudan or Mozambique, with genuine need but lacking strategic political value. They receive less funding but are not entirely ignored either. The "third-class emergencies" are the "forgotten" cases and also the majority of cases. After the top ten recipient countries receive half the world's humanitarian aid, a hundred others share the other half, according to Smillie and Minear.

Another issue is that bureaucratic budgeting at the global level, especially by UNHCR, does not necessarily reflect the quickly changing realities on the ground, as when UNHCR budgeted for 2,000 Liberian refugees in Sierra Leone in 2002 but found instead more than 50,000 needing help.

Humanitarian organizations are reforming in response to such problems. After Rwanda, where aid was delivered to genocide perpetrators who controlled refugee camps across the border, humanitarians asked hard questions. Reforms included new codes of conduct, better coordination of efforts across groups, and accountability in budgets. The business "remains messy and imperfect," though. "There is at present no humanitarian regime—that is, no set of standards, enforcement sanctions, and accountabilities . . . ," write Smillie and Minear. Activities reflect a mix of the needs of people in distress and "what humanitarian agencies think the political traffic will bear and what they think donors will provide. . . ."

Relations between NGOs and host governments do not always go smoothly. In Sierra Leone, the government did not always appreciate the help of NGOs that, understandably, preferred to deal directly with the population where possible rather than working through the government. However, legally, the obligation to help citizens resides with their governments. After the number of NGOs in the country grew from about thirty to ninety from 1996 to 2002, the "mutual antipathy between NGOs and government" became "open hostility." The government complained that international NGOs resisted coordination and openness, and consumed scarce resources such as vehicles. "When they get into trouble, they come running to us. Otherwise they simply ignore us," complained a senior government official. The NGOs were exempt from import tariffs, which were a key source of government revenue.

Of the ninety NGOs in Sierra Leone, about twenty were large "brand-name" groups such as Save the Children and Lutheran World Relief, and others were less familiar to Sierra Leone officials but fairly well known in the humanitarian community, such as the British group Marie Stopes Society. About fifteen others were "less well known"—an NGO with three medical ships, a French group helping land mine victims. Dozens of others, however, were "mom and pop" NGOs that might raise money for a single hospital or water system in Sierra Leone, and did not want the distraction of dealing with government red tape. The relief effort in Sierra Leone did have problems. But "often missing from the long catalog of problems, misperceptions, false starts, and mistakes is the tremendous dedication that most humanitarian agencies and workers applied to their work in Sierra Leone."

The transition from short-term emergency aid to long-term development assistance is a perennial problem in humanitarian aid. The director of a major international agency complains that the World Food Program "doesn't care about relationships, and they will often get you started and then shift the money elsewhere. . . . The UN is the most difficult donor to manage." In Sierra Leone, aid agencies were ready to move to "recovery" in late 2002 but had available only donor funds earmarked for "emergency" purposes. The head of one UN agency in the country said, "Recovery appeals don't work. They send a signal to the emergency departments of donor agencies that they can begin to phase out, and the development departments don't pick up the slack because recovery isn't seen as development." A USAID official agreed: "Humanitarian agencies are not here to do poverty alleviation. Nobody is interested in development in Sierra Leone. Development simply isn't on CNN."

"Unlike membership dues in the United Nations and contributions for peacekeeping, all humanitarian resources are completely voluntary . . . ," note Smillie and Minear. Yet the world raises about $10 billion a year in this way, about the same as UN dues and peacekeeping assessments combined.

A special place in the humanitarian system is reserved in international law for the International Committee of the Red Cross (ICRC), a Swiss-based group independent of the national Red Cross or Red Crescent societies in different countries. The ICRC historically put priority on working to facilitate the well-being of prisoners of war, as well as care of wounded soldiers and other issues of international humanitarian law. The ICRC operates independently and follows strict neutrality in war zones. In 2009 it had a budget of about $1 billion, with about 2,000 Swiss and expatriate personnel and 10,000 local staff in the eighty countries where it operated. The ICRC visited nearly half a million detainees in

2009, and supported more than 500 hospitals and health facilities that treated about a million people, notably in thirty-three first-aid posts established near combat zones. Governments contribute about 80 percent of the ICRC's funds. In these operational aspects, the ICRC resembles other humanitarian agencies such as Doctors Without Borders and the UN refugee agency. But unlike most nongovernmental organizations, the ICRC also conducts diplomacy, such as getting governments to comply with treaties they signed. And it promotes norms regarding war-affected populations, such as asserting the illegitimacy of land mines.

III. Women and Peace

Sanam Anderlini, a pioneer in women's peace activism, notes that what was a "bandwagon of women in peace and security" a decade ago "is now a full-fledged convoy on a bumpy road." She ties the rise of recent women's peace activism both to the changing nature of war—especially the blurring of lines between military and civilian spheres—and to the UN-sponsored conference on women held in Beijing in 1995. The Beijing conference brought together women peacemakers from the civil wars of the early 1990s in places such as Bosnia, Rwanda, and Northern Ireland. The women were often motivated to take action after losing children to war. After Beijing, "local, national, and international women's activism in peacemaking and security-related issues grew exponentially, with regional and international networks taking shape."

At the five-year follow-up conference to Beijing, in 2000, NGOs appealed for a Security Council resolution on women and war. They worked with governments holding temporary seats on the Council—Bangladesh, Jamaica, Canada, and Namibia—and shepherded Resolution 1325 to passage later in 2000. Under that resolution, all UN peace operations are supposed to take gender into account in terms of women's participation as peacekeepers, women's involvement in peace processes, and attention to the protection of women and girls in conflict areas. Implementation of 1325 has been uneven, but the overall effect positive. A new resolution in 2009 reaffirmed the goals of 1325 and emphasized women's roles in peacebuilding. Yet, of the 80,000 military peacekeepers deployed in early

2008, fewer than 2 percent were women. This reflects the composition of national military forces in contributing countries.

In Sri Lanka (where, incidentally, women made up about a third of the rebel Tamil Tiger combatants), about a hundred women formed Women for Peace at the start of the war and collected ten thousand signatures across the country, calling for the war's end. In Israel, Women in Black dressed in black and stood in protests against the occupation of Palestine starting in 1988. Women in Serbia and Palestine emulated this tactic. In 1995–96, when the genocide in Rwanda threatened to repeat itself in next-door Burundi, women's groups launched radio shows, workshops, and female-run mediations. Reportedly, violence was lower in communities where such women were active.

In Liberia, a schoolteacher speaking on a radio show called for a mass meeting and 400 women showed up, starting a women's initiative that was critical to Liberia's progress toward peace. "They ran workshops in which members of opposing parties were forced to partner with each other to complete simple tasks. . . . They kept their public support through demonstrations. They were the first sector of society to speak up to the fighters." Ellen Johnson-Sirleaf, the president of Liberia, credits these women's efforts with ending the civil war in her country—they "sat in the rain and sun promoting peace, advocating reconciliation and the end to the war." She also argues that if women ran the world, "it would be a better, safer and more productive world," with no wars. (This is a long-standing argument that has never been put to the test.)

However, more often than not women's peace activism is "not enough" to end wars, as it "comes too late," notes Anderlini. Women's peace groups generally do not plan for worst-case scenarios, and have trouble responding effectively when their hopes for peace are overwhelmed by an outbreak of violence. Most women's peace efforts begin small and remain below-the-radar, with either local grassroots groups eventually seeking help from NGOs, or sometimes NGOs identifying and supporting potential women leaders to take action. One recurrent problem faced by women's groups is that international donors and organizations "that could be their natural allies are often ignorant of their existence." A UN official realized that "we keep focusing on bringing organized groups to the table, but women are organized in a different way so they do not appear in the picture. They are not invited to the table." In 2006 in Nepal, for example, there were no women in the multiparty peace negotiations, although women's organizations had helped catalyze the talks.

In the Niger Delta region in the south of Nigeria, where a low-level violent conflict has run for decades—poor local communities want more money and less environmental damage from the massive oil drilling there—women in 2002 took a new tack. They staged a nonviolent sit-in against Chevron/Texaco to push for the same demands that men had been seeking with guns. Chevron/Texaco opened a dialogue with the women and agreed to adopt a "different philosophy," in the words of one company executive, to "do more with communities" by funding schools, clinics, water, and electricity, and giving microcredit to women. The conflict in this region diminished in 2009, with a government amnesty and a reduction in rebel attacks, although the final outcome is not yet clear. No doubt the women's nonviolent actions contributed to the progress that the Niger Delta has made.

Women also played a vital role in South Africa's peaceful transition from apartheid to democracy in the early 1990s. One in four peace monitors sent out under the National Peace Accord was a woman—included in each monitoring group because they were found to "bring the temperature down." A UN official in Alexandria Township, where rival black groups were prone to violence, found that a local group, Women for Peace, made the local peace efforts effective. "With men it was war all the time. . . . the women were keen to get peaceful resolution. . . . [It] helped to get men to buy in. . . . Sometimes I would hear them [the men] talking among themselves . . . saying 'we need to show respect for our mothers.' "

Women as actors in conflict-torn communities, especially as mothers of fighters, can be more effective than men at cooling tempers and getting men's cooperation in a peace process. In Papua New Guinea, one UN worker observed "women being able to disarm a drunk or rowdy man or group of men, whereas a police or outsider would have enflamed the situation." In Cambodia, a 2004 report on disarmament concluded that "in most cases involving weapons, women managed to do a better job than men. . . . Some women were so brave that they dared confront people even when threatened with weapons. The braveness even shocked armed men as they had usually considered women as the weaker sex. And as a result, those armed men turned their disputes in a compromising way." Yet these "community-based women, working informally or within small organizations, receive little support and rarely a penny of the millions pledged by donor governments" for DDR programs.

Gender awareness can also improve conflict early-warning and prevention. "Deterioration . . . in the status of men or women can be the earliest signs of conflict trends that might lead to violence." For example, Islamic radicalization in a society may begin with repressive actions toward women's freedom and then lead to violence against the government or foreigners. Secretary of State Hillary Clinton finds an "absolute link" between the oppression of women and U.S. national security. Groups that threaten U.S. security "are making a stand against modernity, and that is most evident in their treatment of women." In Rwanda prior to the genocide, a popular tract portrayed Tutsi women as temptresses who steal away Hutu men while staying loyal only to the Tutsi group.

Another gendered aspect of conflict prevention is the potential for women to see conflict coming, if only the relevant officials or peacekeepers would ask them. In Sierra Leone, "women watched as arms were shipped in overnight along the river," and wanted to warn peacekeepers but had no access to them. Conversely, the emergence of more violent concepts of masculinity may predict war, as when unemployed young men in Serbia "were readily recruited by hypernationalists into 'soccer teams' and indoctrinated with ethnic hatred," later morphing into the "militias and armed gangs that terrorized the region as the war spread."

After a war, women have until recently found themselves sidelined in disarmament programs, because combatants were assumed to be men. Women kidnapped by rebel organizations and forced to fight have often been left on their own to try to reintegrate after the war. In Sierra Leone, for example, ownership of an AK-47 automatic rifle was required to participate in the DDR program, but women fighters had often shared a gun or had their gun taken at the end of the war by a commander who gave it to a man so he could receive the DDR benefits. At the outset of the DDR program, the Sierra Leone government estimated that 12 percent of combatants were women, but by the end of the program only 7 percent of the fighters registered with the program were women. Of the roughly 12,000 girls (under age eighteen) in the armed groups, fewer than half a percent participated in the DDR program.

Recent initiatives to include women in DDR programs have focused on the women's rights to be included, but Anderlini argues that an additional benefit of these initiatives is to improve the overall outcome of the DDR process. For example, although DDR has usually focused on young men as the greatest threat of becoming "spoilers" who will not disarm, in some traditional societies women who have joined rebel organizations "as a means of exiting traditional life are often more reluctant to lay down their weapons than male fighters." This was the case in Sri Lanka, Nepal, and Congo. One woman former combatant in the Congo said, "We used to protect ourselves by weapons. Now there is no one to protect us." Also, in their roles as support for fighters (cooks, porters, medics, wives or sex slaves), women and girls are essential for the operation of rebel groups, which therefore may be more hesitant to release them to civilian life than their male comrades. By targeting women and girls for DDR programs, international organizations could pull away the infrastructure that would allow armed groups to threaten the peace process.

In transitional justice after wars, as in early warning and DDR, women again can play a key role. In the war-crimes tribunal for the former Yugoslavia, investigators found that women "literally saw things that men could not," as when men but not women were blindfolded in concentration camps, and therefore proved useful as witnesses. In the Yugoslavia tribunal, the participation of women also led to the first prosecution based entirely on sexual violence as a war crime.

UN Secretary-General Dag Hammarskjöld was ahead of his time in 1960 when he told a top UN official that when acting in a UN capacity he should "first of all acquaint myself with the *position of women* in the country" and favor countries that allowed women to freely develop their capabilities.

Although recent attention to women in war has had positive effects, it also can cause a distorted view in which male victims of war, the majority of those killed and injured, become invisible. Hillary Clinton was wrong when she declared in 1998, "Women have always been the primary victims of war. Women lose their husbands, their fathers, their sons in combat. . . ." It is safe to say that the "primary victim" is the one killed, not the one left in mourning, although certainly both are victims.

Incidentally, one often hears that the majority of refugees (or other civilian war victims) are "women and children." This is misleading, since a strong majority of any *population* is women (half the adults) and all the children. Almost half the refugee population of concern are children under eighteen, and half of those are boys. Women and *girls* make up 49 percent of the population of concern according to the UNHCR, and this shows there is no real gender imbalance in the makeup of refugee populations. Nor are women and girls disproportionately targeted in wars—quite the contrary. As Nicholas Kristof notes, the population of South Kivu, in the Congo, "is 55 percent female because so many men have been executed." To say that resources and protection should go to females at the expense of males in refugee populations is very odd considering that the males are at demonstrably higher risk. On the other hand, if NGOs find they can raise more money overall to help war victims by pandering to gender misconceptions held by donors, this is not entirely bad.

Given the diversity of initiatives to stop fighting, clearly much of humanity shares a deep seated desire for peace that manifests in whatever way it can. In each of these three wings of the Unarmy (and they are not the only ones), individuals and organizations from NGOs to governments are working hard every day around the world in very different ways for what amounts to the same goal. Others are seeking that goal by another route, one closer to home. They belong to peace movements seeking to change the government policies that create and sustain wars.

8

PEACE MOVEMENTS
If You Want Peace, Work for Peace

I have lived through four waves of peace activism in the United States. The first, when I was young, was the small but vocal movement to "ban the bomb," to stop atmospheric nuclear testing, and to negotiate agreements with the Soviet Union to rein in a spiraling arms race. The second came along with the Vietnam War. Third was the nuclear freeze movement in the early 1980s to stop the nuclear arms race. The fourth wave was the effort to stop the United States from invading Iraq in 2003.

As many others have noted, Vietnam was the defining event of my generation. I went to my first big antiwar march in San Francisco—tens of thousands of people streaming through the streets. We thought the government would have to end the war right then and there, so overwhelming was the outpouring of sentiment. But it ground on year after year. Because of the draft, the war cut deeply into the personal lives of my generation. A lottery began just before I turned eighteen and I drew a high number, meaning I would not be drafted. I did visit a draft board at age eighteen, however, to get arrested as part of a nonviolent civil disobedience organized at Stanford and carried out across the Bay Area.

I. The Question of Peace and Justice

In those days I thought we needed a social revolution in order to end wars like the Vietnam War. I did not like the violence condoned by the Marxist analyses prevalent at the time, and knew those theories got the story wrong, but I did accept the idea that wars are caused by injustice. This is why I worked with the Black Panther Party (as a teacher in a free child-care center) to try to bring about social justice. Only a decade later did I conclude that war is an important problem in itself and not just a derivative of injustice. Then I went to graduate school in political science to study war in order to directly address the problem of ending it.

A VISIT TO NEBRASKA

The question of whether to treat war as a primary issue to address in its own right or a secondary issue to be solved by tackling other problems—inequality, exploitation, sexism, etc.—has long bedeviled the American and European peace movements. The two sides are nicely represented on one ten-mile stretch of Interstate 80 in Nebraska.

At the eastern end of this stretch lies Lincoln, home to the University of Nebraska and to Nebraskans for Peace (NFP), a group with branches and contacts around the state. This outpost of the peace movement is especially oriented to social justice. Indeed its motto is "There is no peace without justice." In 2008, the group honored as "Peacemakers of the Year" a civil rights leader and an environmentalist legislator, neither with much connection to antiwar activism. One of two keynote speakers at its 2010 conference spoke on U.S. hate groups and immigration. (The group continues to engage in traditional antiwar protests as well.)

The group's description of its own history notes a difference of opinion in the group soon after its founding in 1970. "Some discussants wanted NFP to focus on Vietnam alone; others said that Vietnam was only the symptom of deeper ills and that the range of these ills blocking peace and justice needed tackling, the position that [a predecessor group] had held for some time. The 'peace-and-justice' position prevailed. . . ." Thus the top items on the NFP website in 2009 concerned health care reform and the economic recession. The group also opposes "NAFTA and other globalization efforts that have helped to destroy stability and decent standards of living for millions of people."

The assertions about globalization are dubious. In the era of globalization, more than a billion people have risen out of poverty in China and India. Health care indicators such as child mortality rates have improved substantially around the world. A billion people remain left behind in extreme poverty, but their number has shrunk as a percent of the world's population. It is true that the economic collapse of 2008–09 had dire consequences in poor countries, but the world economy did not die. On balance, NAFTA itself has neither driven lots of people into poverty nor lifted them out of poverty. So if you are asking people to oppose globalization as a condition of joining your peace movement, you may lose a lot of potential supporters of plain old peace.

Then, too, the Nebraska group's insistence that "there is no peace without justice" actually is not true. You might say there *should not* be peace without justice, or that peace without justice is less durable or less valuable than with justice. But, in fact, many parts of the world are at peace without justice. China, to take an important example, has not fought a military battle in decades, yet its authoritarian rulers punish dissent and abuse citizens' human rights. Corruption is a serious problem, and issues such as Tibet also fail the justice test. Similarly, in most of South America justice has not arrived, yet a durable peace prevails.

Finally, "There is no peace without justice" is a worrisome slogan. How far removed is it from the position that breaking the peace is acceptable in the course of fighting injustice? ("I will deny you peace until you give me justice.") Does this endorse violent revolutionaries, suicide bombers, and others who destroy peace in the name of fighting injustice? Those groups are, in this century, part of the problem, not the solution, in ending and preventing wars. Anyway, we know this is not what Nebraskans for Peace means to convey, since they favor nonviolence. But the problem shows how the emphasis on justice muddies the waters for no good reason.

The focus on justice, unfortunately, has come to dominate today's American peace movement from coast to coast. For instance, in Palo Alto, California, where I grew up, the old Palo Alto Peace Center changed its name to the Peninsula Peace and Justice Center in the early 1990s. And in western Massachusetts where I live now, the famous Traprock Peace Center—which opened in 1979 and focused on nonviolence, disarmament, and militarism—recently changed its name to the Traprock Center for Peace and Justice. Similarly the Peace Development Fund, also in western Massachusetts, has the words "Through Justice" plastered on top of its logo. It funds grants to "projects that recognize that peace will never be sustained unless it is based on justice. . . ." The group defines "peace as just not the absence of war or militarism, but as the presence of equitable relationships among people, nations, and the environment." Theirs is thus a long road to peace.

Now from Lincoln, Nebraska, head out of town, west on I-80. About ten miles down the road, get off at an exit marked by a tall "GAS/CAMP" freeway sign. Across from the gas camp (boarded up) is an abandoned two-story house, forlorn in the endless Nebraska prairie, with rainbow colors painted across the front and a handwritten inscription at the top, "PRAIRIE PEACE PARK." The park opened in 1994 after organizers raised funds, bought a house with twenty-seven acres next to I-80, and obtained exhibits such as a thirty-two-thousand-piece sculpture representing U.S. nuclear weapons. Among the more than seventy exhibits eventually developed were an eighty-foot-long ceramic children's World Peace Mural and a thirteen-step Path of Hope depicting "violent practices that had been believed to be part of human nature, but were now being eliminated." In 1994, the park opened with 1,500 people in attendance including actor Ed Asner, singer Raffi, and Nebraska's senator James Exon. It closed in 2005. The ceramic mosaic and a twelve-foot-diameter globe sculpture remain on the site, while the other exhibits were donated to camps and churches, with the thirty-two-thousand-nuke sculpture going to a peace farm in Texas. (With the U.S. stockpile down to five thousand the sculpture is now a historic relic.)

Other than an exhibit about challenges facing small farmers in Nebraska, the Peace Park focused on antiwar issues rather than justice broadly conceived. The trouble is that with ups and downs in the peace movement over the years, and especially the dwindling interest in the nuclear weapons problem, the major project could not sustain itself. By contrast, the justice-oriented peace groups, by forging alliances with labor, civil rights, environmental, and other "progressive" groups, could better weather the downturns between antiwar upsurges. The Prairie

Peace Park was a peace center too far—a project too ambitious for a remote location. So the justice approach, although strategically wrongheaded, may be tactically superior. Even so, I doubt its long-term efficacy.

A third approach to peace comes from spiritually oriented peace centers, often able to sustain themselves within churches or other "faith communities." Yet these groups seem to gravitate to the individual and local levels and do not engage much with the work of ending wars in the larger world. The Florida Center for Peace connects to Jesus through the Virgin Mary. At the Center of Peace in Boise, Idaho, the executive director trained at the International Metaphysical Ministries. The Peace Center in Chicago offers sacred dance, yoga, twelve-step support, and pet blessings, as well as Gandhi T-shirts at the Peace Center Store.

Between the "work for justice" peace activists, the antinuclear movement, and the inner spiritual peace approach, what is largely missing is a peace movement speaking up for the UN, for peacekeeping, for the multidimensional efforts of international, national, and private organizations to stop wars and keep the peace.

So the peace movement all across America, organized and motivated for peace, puts its efforts into helping the homeless, pressing for immigration reform, supporting health care reform—and none of these efforts are ending the world's wars. And then out there in the eastern Congo is a soldier from Bangladesh with a blue UN helmet, trying to stop the violence of a society torn apart by decades of war after decades of colonialism. And this soldier does not have enough comrades, enough equipment, enough political support, to do half of what he or she could do with adequate resources. But back in the United States the peace movement is doing very little to push the United States to support peacekeeping, to empower the UN, to get that soldier in the Congo what he or she needs to succeed. Thus, my modest proposal for peace activists is, "If you want peace, work for peace." Support what is working now in ending wars and spreading peace.

THEORIES OF PEACE AND JUSTICE

The substantive theories about how injustice leads to war actually do not hold up very well. One big problem is that people have different views about what justice means. The saying "If you want peace, work for justice" originated not with a socialist or hippie but with a pope. In 1972, Paul VI argued that a "peace that is not the result of true respect for man is not true Peace." His definition of peace itself included justice: "Where . . . forms of Justice have been injured or crushed—be they national, social, cultural, or economic—could we be sure that the Peace resulting from such a tyrannical process is true Peace? That it is a stable Peace? Or, even if it be stable, that it is a just and human Peace?" The pope's idea of justice was expansive. He wrote, "Is not an integral part of justice the duty of enabling every country to promote its own development in the framework of cooperation free from any intention or calculated aim of domination, whether economic or political?" Therefore, the pope argued, "if you want Peace, work for Justice."

So to have "true" peace, in this view, we need to end international economic and political domination, ensure cultural and economic justice within societies, and have universal respect for our fellow human beings. My reaction is that we will be waiting a long time for peace! More problematic still is the 1999 extension of this approach by Pope John Paul II to include his call to oppose abortion: "America: if you want peace, work for justice, if you want justice, defend life!" Whatever its merits, this is probably not the kind of justice that leftist groups have in mind when they repeat the slogan.

Those leftist ideas of justice, however, themselves hold little promise as avenues to peace. Three common targets in these approaches are big corporations, oil companies, and globalization. These supposed causes of war are all red herrings that distract the peace movement at best and discredit it with the public at worst. Corporations as a whole are not pro-war; most of them make money best in a peaceful world with free trade. War is a risk factor, and risk is bad for business. *Certain* corporations profit from war, but they do not have as much power as the major large corporations taken as a whole. Blackwater or Boeing certainly try to influence U.S. war decisions but they do not dictate them. Others such as retailers and the travel industry also lobby, and they make more money on peace than war.

When oil prices go up, as they did after the Iraq War began in 2003, oil companies make more profit, but big industrial and transportation companies (consumers of oil) make less profit. Exxon made record megaprofits while airlines went bust. Since the Bush family had oil ties, presumably they did what was good for oil companies by starting the Iraq War. But wait a minute: Does that mean the U.S. leaders deliberately botched the war to drive up oil prices, so that oil companies would profit? No, the theory on the left was that the United States went into Iraq for cheap oil, not expensive oil. Cheap oil would be good for the American economy and would help the powers-that-be stay in power in Washington. But cheap oil would be bad for oil companies, lowering their profits. So do not blame oil companies for the war.

As for globalization, it has coincided with a period of diminishing war in the world. That makes it an unlikely candidate on which to blame the world's wars. In the era of globalization before the crash of 2008–09, and again as world economic growth recovers, incomes have risen substantially in poor countries, notably India and China. Health and education indicators have improved considerably as well. So it is hard to argue that globalization indirectly causes wars by increasing poverty.

The confusion of the present-day peace movement was on full display at the Group of 20 (G20) summit meeting in Pittsburgh in September 2009. A local peace center sponsored a protest march and some activists protested the U.S. presence in Afghanistan and Israeli occupation of Palestinian land, but calls for peace were submerged under a bewildering wave of protests of dubious connection to peace. "Protesters with Iraq Veterans Against the War, wearing fatigues, marched alongside Tibetans chiming cymbals, chanting denunciations of China. . . . Others held up signs like 'We Say No To Corporate Greed.' . . . One group held aloft . . . a giant replica of a dove made of white fabric. . . . A sign . . . said 'Capitalism Kills.' . . . Before long, singers from the Raging Grannies and workers from the United Steelworkers of America took the stage to talk about the need for jobs." If the peace movement's message was to end the Afghanistan war, that message got a bit lost.

II. A Brief History

The peace-justice problem has a long history in the European and American peace movements. Quakers (Friends) played the central role in American peace activism at the outset in the seventeenth century. Under persecution in England, they adopted "an ambiguous pacifist posture" as one element in an evolving way of life illuminated by the light of Christ's teaching.

In 1681, almost a century before American independence, William Penn founded Pennsylvania on a huge tract of land, as a "holy experiment" in Quaker living. It was part business venture, part haven for persecuted Quakers, and part model Christian community. Penn's framework, "rooted in the vision that peace depended on justice," provided for broad representation in government, religious toleration, and accommodation toward the native Americans.

A century later, the idea of world peace appealed to the leaders of the American independence movement. Thomas Paine declared, *"Our plan is for peace for ever.* We are tired of contention with Britain, and can see no real end to it but in a final separation. . . . For the sake of introducing an endless and uninterrupted peace, do we bear the evils and burdens of the present day." Thus, not for the last time in American history, violence today was undertaken in service of peace tomorrow. However, this contradiction did not serve the cause of independence: "Paradoxically, the antimilitarism that shaped early American nationalism nearly undercut the country's main means of nation making—the Continental Army. . . . The Continental Congress was notoriously tightfisted in funding the army, and enlistments were erratic and brief." Attempts at conscription "provoked major outbreaks of antidraft violence."

Conversely, patriotic fervor caused a backlash against Quakers who "respected the sect's traditional injunctions against the bearing of arms or the payment of soldier-substitutes. . . . Inflamed local patriots executed two unresisting Friends in Pennsylvania. . . . One North Carolina Quaker received forty lashes for his refusal to shoulder a musket, while countless draft-age Friends were arrested and jailed throughout the rebel colonies for their objection to military service."

NINETEENTH CENTURY MOVEMENTS

After independence, the peace movement quickly reached a peak in the unpopular War of 1812, which provoked "vehement and widespread" opposition. The declaration of war barely passed Congress, and the "War Department could never man the army to more than half its authorized strength." When Congress did declare war, the governor of Massachusetts, Caleb Strong, "called for a public fast of atonement . . . ," and in 1814 Harvard University "awarded five honorary degrees to leading antiwar critics. . . ." By late 1814, the Massachusetts governor considered seceding from the Union because of the war, but peace arrived before anything came of it.

After the War of 1812, "peace societies" began to spring up in America. In 1815, merchants, clergy, and philanthropists formed the New York Peace Society and, two weeks later, the Massachusetts Peace Society, without the two groups' awareness of each other's existence! They were quickly followed by societies in Rhode Island and Ohio, then in London and Paris. Soon fifty peace societies had appeared, from Maine to Philadelphia to Ohio. Historian Charles DeBenedetti calls the formation of these Christian private volunteer societies the invention of the "modern nonsectarian peace movement." These patriotic Protestants saw "war as a moral evil that God and progress intended to destroy through the free will of enlightened men."

In 1828, the peace societies joined in a national organization, the American Peace Society (APS). Incidentally, "women constituted a sizable minority—at times the majority—of the APS's audience" but the male leadership showed little interest in them. Among the main groups, only the Massachusetts Peace Society even allowed women members.

The poet Alfred Tennyson in 1835 wrote "Locksley Hall," a long poem that at one point envisions a world at peace: "Till the war-drum throbb'd no longer, and the battle-flags were furl'd / In the Parliament of man, the Federation of the world. / There the common sense of most shall hold a fretful realm in awe, / And the kindly earth shall slumber, lapt in universal law." Tennyson's image "influenced many people in the English-speaking world, especially those who urged the end of mass warfare and the creation of international organizations to resolve disputes peacefully."

The years of the APS saw substantial progress in working with European counterparts to promote international law and organization—ideas that would eventually culminate in today's UN. New England sea captain William Ladd, who had a religious conversion after the War of 1812 that brought him into full-time peace activism and eventually the presidency of the APS, published a collection of plans for a "Congress of Nations" in 1840. He envisioned a congress representing "the most civilized, enlightened, and Christian nations" to create international laws and work for peace. In addition, an international court would arbitrate cases brought to it voluntarily by conflicting parties. The idea of arbitration as an alternative to war, especially the idea of getting countries to agree in advance to submit disputes to arbitration, gained much support in the mid-nineteenth century. In 1843, an international peace congress in London brought together activists from the United States and European countries. It supported Ladd's plan for an international congress, as well as arbitration and the promotion of free trade. A similar conference followed in 1848 in Brussels (after organizers gave up on Paris, consumed by street fighting that year as urban uprisings swept across Europe).

The peace-justice issue came to a head with the antislavery movement and tore the movement apart in the years before the Civil War. The APS meeting in 1846 "approved resolutions requiring the Society to remain apart from 'extraneous' reforms like abolition and open to all Christian peace seekers, 'whatever their views respecting defensive war.'" Elihu Burritt, a blacksmith and popular lecturer, and his allies quit their leadership positions in the APS. "With their withdrawal, the organized peace movement lay broken in three parts. Revolutionary nonresistants . . . rejected all physical force and opposed any kind of coercion. Moderate pacifists like Burritt upheld 'the strict inviolability of human life,' but accepted the coercive function of orderly government. And conservatives opposed the custom of international war as being contrary to Christianity, though sometimes necessary for defensive purposes."

Burritt went on in 1846 to found the League of Universal Brotherhood, whose members took a vow to work to abolish war. It immediately attracted 30,000 supporters in England and 25,000 in the United States, but lost direction and fizzled out in about a decade. In England, meanwhile, the peace movement "destroyed itself while rallying to the government cause" in 1853 during the Crimean War.

In America, even radical pacifists began moderating their positions in light of the rising violence leading up to the Civil War. One declared in 1854 that activists had "to choose between two evils, and all that we can do is to take the *least*, and baptize liberty in blood, if it must be so." The next year, a Kansas man who had been to prison for refusing to bear arms, took up the gun against "pro-slavery Missourians [who] are demons from the bottomless pit and may be shot with impunity." Indeed, after 1850 "most peace reformers tolerated or welcomed antislavery violence. . . ." The divisions over slavery "split and eventually shattered the peace movement." After the Civil War, the APS collapsed altogether.

David Cortright, a longtime leader of today's American peace movement, describes how the tension between peace and justice played out in the movement on both sides of the Atlantic in the nineteenth century. Napoleonic-era German philosopher Immanuel Kant's theories of peace "did not address questions of social equality. Socialists and feminists brought these issues to the fore [in mid-century] and broadened the peace agenda to include problems of economic injustice and patriarchy."

The peace-justice issue developed in the late nineteenth century as "two distinct schools of thought and separate organizations" in the peace movement in Europe. One group, formed in Paris in 1867, followed the leading peace activist of the time, the French economist Frédéric Passy, who later won the Nobel Peace Prize. This group "considered peace the preeminent concern and necessary requirement for national liberation and all other social progress." Passy opposed the "democratic revolutionaries" of his time "who prioritized the struggle for social justice."

In the other corner, a group founded in Geneva the same year became "the largest and most influential continental peace organization of the nineteenth century." Its agenda "prefigured the concern for social justice and human rights that was to become the hallmark of peace activism in the twentieth century." At the group's meeting in 1869, Victor Hugo declared that "the first condition of peace is liberation. For this liberation, a revolution is needed . . . and perhaps, alas, a war which shall be the last one." (Hugo was ahead of his time, as the "war to end all wars" was forty-five years in the future.)

Cortright traces the peace-through-justice approach to a merger of socialism, which holds that "an end to economic exploitation and imperialism is necessary for genuine peace," with pacifism. Yet this merger seems contradictory. Socialists have rarely altered their own goals or strategies to seek common ground with peace advocates. In fact, when the justice-oriented peace activists met in Geneva in 1867, Karl Marx urged socialists to stay away, and they refused to join the group. At the First International meeting the next year, the socialists declared that peace groups had no reason to exist. If they wanted to end war, they should join the socialists in making revolution to wipe away the real causes of war. Marx considered pacifism to be "bourgeois sentimental-ism." Trotsky denounced efforts for disarmament (since they would leave capitalism intact) as more dangerous than all the world's explosives, and declared that "the masses of people are poisoned in peacetime by the fumes of pacifism." Socialists completely rejected, and still reject, the view of peace advocates such as Passy that "class divisions are not rel-evant to the question of peace" and that the "best way to achieve justice and economic equality" is to end militarism and war.

In the late nineteenth century a new wave of American peace activism gathered steam. The movement grew in parallel with the women's suf-frage movement but initially without much overlap: "Women assembled a wide range of independent reform organizations in the last third of the nineteenth century. But their peace efforts were weak and shallow." Con-versely, a national conference on arbitration in 1896 excluded women from participation.

THE ERA OF THE WORLD WARS

The peace efforts before World War I focused on practical proposals such as international arbitration, and drew on support from business leaders, notably Andrew Carnegie. The new APS leader declared that war could not be "settled by singing." This generation of peace activists believed in the "global extension of Anglo-American racial supremacy," which would spread democracy and freedom. However, the American flirtation with empire at the time led also to popular organizing against imperialism, such as the formation of the American Anti-Imperialist League in 1899. The U.S. war in the Philippines in 1899–1902 bolstered this case, as it killed hundreds of thousands (directly and indirectly, 7,000 of them American troops) and cost hundreds of millions of dollars.

Americans also drew strength from the movement gathering steam in Europe. Hundreds of thousands of Danes and Brits signed petitions in support of a peace conference in The Hague in 1899 sponsored by the czar of Russia, whose "militaristic and autocratic policies" had earned the scorn of peace activists until then. The press declared the effort meaningless but the peace movement made the most of it to press its cause. A second Hague conference was held in 1907, with the focus of both conferences being on international arbitration. The term *pacifism* was coined in 1901 at a peace congress in Scotland, but its meaning was debated (and still is). The movement reached a peak of support and influence right before World War I, culminating in the construction of a Palace of Peace in The Hague, Netherlands, in 1913. Nearly 200 peace societies operated in dozens of countries. However, this peace activism in Britain and some other European countries did not take root in Germany, where a small peace movement before World War I struggled against a militaristic culture shared by elites and the public.

In the United States, meanwhile, after the Philippines war the peace movement experienced "a growth spurt unequaled in the history of the peace reform." Some forty-five new groups formed in 1901–14. Carnegie used his wealth to support several new and existing groups, and used his prominent position to speak out frequently about the virtues of peace. A group of lawyers centered on Secretary of State Elihu Root promoted international law, beyond just arbitration, as an alternative to war. In 1906, they formed the American Society of International Law, still active today. Root's role in creating a Central American Court of Justice helped win him the Nobel Peace Prize in 1913. In 1907, more than 1,200 delegates—including cabinet members, senators, and Supreme Court justices—held a four-day conference in New York on arbitration and peace, organized by Carnegie and underwritten by wealthy backers such as John D. Rockefeller. The creation of the World Peace Foundation and of the Carnegie Endowment for International Peace followed in 1910. That same year, William James published his influential essay "The Moral Equivalent of War," arguing that positive functions played by war in social and individual life (e.g., sacrifice; heroism) could be accomplished in other ways. (He referred to peace efforts as "the war against war"—a phrase used in 1912 as the motto for two Socialist Congresses in Europe.)

Social reformer Jane Addams took up the peace cause in 1898 after the Spanish-American War, and used "her influence as the best-known and most respected woman in the country" to advocate pacifism and the redirection of war resources and sentiments into democracy and social reform. She remained largely distant from the organized peace movement, if only because the latter did not welcome women in leadership. Addams felt that the empowerment of women would promote peace. In 1915, as World War I raged, she organized a women's peace conference in The Hague, where participants founded the Women's Peace Party—active today as the Women's International League for Peace and Freedom. Addams remained resolute in opposing World War I and war in general, despite a high personal price she eventually paid for this position.

Jane Addams was very much the exception in her opposition to World War I. Just as had happened in England during the Crimean War, most peace movement supporters rallied to their governments' sides under the pressure of the war. The "peace movement collapsed and fractured." Before the war, the women's suffrage movement had seen the peace movement as a natural ally. When women got the vote, they would vote for peace, people assumed. But when the United States entered the war, suffrage leaders—except Addams—changed course abruptly and supported women's wholehearted participation in the war, including in traditionally masculine occupations such as factory work. In part, the victory of women in gaining the vote in 1920 grew directly from their contributions to the nation's war effort in 1917–18.

Americans who, like Addams, did not support World War I found themselves punished by the government for their stance. In 1917, President Woodrow Wilson and Congress instituted compulsory registration for conscription for men aged eighteen to thirty-five. The Espionage Act punished anyone who made "false statements" about the war, caused disloyalty to the military, or impeded conscription. This "Espionage Act" never caught a German spy, but effectively silenced the antiwar movement. About a hundred socialists and labor leaders were sent to federal prison, and publications that criticized the war were banned from the mail. Socialist Party leader Eugene Debs received a ten-year jail sentence for giving an antiwar speech. Meanwhile mob attacks on Americans of German or Scandinavian background brought the White Fright to anyone whose loyalty might be suspect. Dozens were hanged or burned to death. Thousands of conscientious objectors (COs) were confined to army camps, some subject to "beatings and abuse," although the government allowed the American Friends Service Committee (AFSC) to organize young Quakers in "war relief and reconstruction" instead of combat.

World War I was "the turning point" in American views about peace. After the war ended, peace "seemed more necessary than ever before. Yet it also became more remote. The modern peace movement arose after 1915 to resolve this paradox." After World War I, an "extraordinarily active peace movement" revived as the public realized the insanity of warfare on a massive industrial scale. Two wings of the movement emerged—one focused on "liberal internationalism," which favored international institutions, law, and similar mechanisms for bringing about cooperation among nations, and the other focused on pacifism and transnational connections that would promote common values among individuals across borders. The first of these aligned in theory with Wilson's efforts to promote a League of Nations and other international institutions, but the movement "provided little help" for Wilson in selling this program to Americans. Philosopher John Dewey and others of like mind opposed Wilson's reforms and wanted instead to outlaw war altogether and set up a world court independent of the control of the League (which was controlled by governments). The peace leadership turned down Wilson's "personal request for help in his campaign" for the League. The pacifist wing of the movement "had even less use for Wilson's work," attacking the punitive nature of the Versailles Treaty and opposing involvement in Europe's politics.

In the end, "peace advocates watched helplessly and with a sense of foreboding" as the U.S. Senate voted down the League. Just as today's conservative politicians attack the UN for supposedly infringing on U.S. sovereignty, "the senators who rejected the League did not wish to see U.S. sovereignty compromised by membership in an international organization." And just as today's peace activists seem little interested in the UN, many peace activists in the 1920s and '30s "were skeptical of the collective security concept and doubtful that a League dominated by the major imperial powers" would effectively oppose aggression (which, in fact, it failed to do in the 1930s in Manchuria and Spain). The progressive wing of the U.S. peace movement supported the League through the 1930s—as an organization that they hoped could "create a more equitable international political and economic order." But the embedding of the League in an unjust treaty, Versailles, alienated both progressives and conservatives in the movement.

Indeed, President Wilson was far more popular in Europe than at home. After the war he was "hailed as a hero for justice and peace" across Europe, and in Paris "an unprecedented crowd of two million cheered 'Wilson, the Just.' . . . Wilson came to embody the hopes of people throughout the world for an end to war. . . . He strode across the stage of history as a savior to deliver humankind from the scourge of war."

H. G. Wells wrote that Wilson "ceased to be a common statesman; he became a Messiah." By contrast, the political leaders of the European powers steadfastly opposed Wilson's radical plans, and insisted in particular on holding on to their colonies.

After Wilson failed to get the League of Nations ratified in the U.S. Senate, the peace movement lobbied the Warren Harding Administration for disarmament. The resulting 1922 Washington Conference, mandating naval arms reductions, "signaled the finest achievement of positive citizen peace action in the interwar period." Leading intellectuals called for individual resistance to military service, notably Albert Einstein's proposal that if just two percent of those conscripted to fight refused, the government would not dare jail them. In 1935, 150,000 protesters on 130 college campuses opposed the rising threat of a new war. The same year, in Britain, a private referendum, the Peace Ballot, drew nearly 12 million participants (more than a third of the adult population) and showed strong support for arms reductions, participation in the League, and collective security even involving military response to aggression. The movement drew new strength from its successes, and women now played a central role. New groups formed, including the War Resisters League, led by women, which gathered nearly 20,000 pledges to refuse to support any war. The peace activists planned to respond to the next war with a general strike. It did not work out that way, of course.

With the focus on inequality during the Great Depression, the peace movement went through a "significant conceptual evolution" in the interwar years, with a "shift toward greater recognition of social justice as a requirement for peace. . . ." The "economic roots of war" received great attention in this period. I recall researching my Ph.D. dissertation, which concerned economic aspects of war, and finding relatively scant material available on the subject until one day I dropped in at Stanford's Hoover Institution and found piles of works on the topic from the 1930s. During the Cold War, this view of war as having economic roots became suspect in the United States as communist-type thinking, but in the 1930s it was still popular.

Old issues again split the movement in the years leading up to World War II, as in the years before the Civil War. Internationalists wanted to support anti-Nazi forces, while pacifists supported U.S. neutrality. Most peace advocates in the late 1930s did not favor absolute pacifism but a forceful response to fascist aggression, including economic sanctions and even military force. With the attack on Pearl Harbor and America mobilized in support of the war, peace activism again withered.

During World War II, Leavenworth federal prison held about 30 Japanese-American draft resisters from the Heart Mountain internment camp in Wyoming. The camp housed more than 10,000 Japanese-Americans forcibly removed from their homes on the West Coast. In 1944, the government instituted the draft for the camp's young men, and 88 served time in federal prison after participating in an organized nonviolent resistance to this draft.

THE COLD WAR ERA

During the Cold War years, the pressures for patriotism and toughness against communism held back peace work. "The outbreak of the Korean War in June 1950 demonstrated most fully the humiliating weakness of the peace movement. . . . One-time pacifists . . . backed the U.S. intervention, while internationalists . . . approved the combined U.S.-UN action as a vindication of the principle of collective security." Human rights activists and dissidents in the communist countries for their part came to distrust the very word "peace" owing to "the Kremlin's propagandistic manipulation of the term. . . ."

Eventually, however, a new peace movement arose from the ashes. Central to this movement were atomic scientists who, although patriotic, were deeply troubled by the lethal potential of the nuclear weapons they had created—and which many of them had witnessed exploding. The social scientists who created the field of peace research in the 1950s also contributed to the revival. A combination of scientists and pacifists organized the group SANE in 1957 to oppose the nuclear arms race. That year, 11,000 scientists, including 2,000 Americans, signed an appeal against testing nuclear weapons in the atmosphere, an effort that succeeded in 1963. These early Cold War–era peace groups always had to fight off attacks that they were influenced by, or even front groups for, communists. In SANE, such attacks led to a ban on working with communists, which in turn led a group of pacifists to quit SANE. One response to the Cold War red scares in the peace movement came from the women who organized Women Strike for Peace in 1961. They cultivated an image of themselves as harmless housewives who just wanted to protect their children from nuclear war.

Nuclear weapons were not the only reason for an emerging concern with disarmament in twentieth-century peace movements, supplanting the nineteenth-century focus on arbitration. Generally, weapons had become much more destructive, and peace activists felt that "large military establishments and excessive levels of weaponry increase the tendency of governments to use military force. . . ." Profiteering by weapons makers during World War I supported the view among many peace advocates that "merchants of death" promoted war in order to profit from it, an idea already coming into prominence before World War I. In the 1920s the League of Nations confirmed that weapons makers had contributed to war scares and arms races, and in 1934 the U.S. Senate's "Nye Committee" held widely publicized hearings into the influence of the munitions industry, at a time when the Great Depression had already turned public opinion against industry. This idea of blaming munitions makers for war has evolved over time into a present-day theme that "capitalism" is a source of war.

During the early Cold War years, when the American peace movement was at low ebb, the country that America conquered, occupied, and remade—Japan—embarked on an experiment in renouncing war, a policy with "no precedent in history." The Japanese policy against war as an instrument of policy was originally imposed by the United States, but gained broad support among Japanese citizens. An active peace movement in Japan kept the government from abandoning the antiwar policy, and particularly from developing nuclear weapons, even when American governments changed position and urged a stronger military posture on Japan as a way to support U.S. military actions and counter Chinese and Soviet power.

Another peace effort grew in the 1950s, the movement for world federalism. In 1947, Americans by nearly two to one favored turning the UN into an actual world government. By 1949, world federalists had organized 46,000 members in 720 chapters in the United States, with similar organizations in 17 other countries. However, the movement "peaked in 1949" before the Korean War and the Cold War turned U.S. opinion against the idea of world government.

Vietnam

"The Vietnam antiwar movement was the largest, most sustained, and most powerful peace campaign in human history." The 1969 Mobilization brought out 350,000 people in San Francisco and 500,000 in Washington, "the greatest outpouring of mass protest that the country had ever known." However, the antiwar movement could not convert this high level of protest energy into effective action to change U.S. policy. Activists were, as Cortright recalls, "frustrated and disillusioned at their seeming inability to halt the carnage."

Internally, the movement "was plagued by divisiveness." On the one hand, student radicals in the "new left," along with traditional pacifist groups, sought to "make explicit connections between ending cold war militarism and promoting domestic justice and democracy." They "adopted adventurist and mindlessly confrontational tactics that turned off potential supporters," as Cortright puts it. On the other hand, "old left" groups, notably Trotskyists, relied entirely on legal, mass demonstrations but in support of a socialist revolution that never stood a chance of taking root in America. And on the third hand, more mainstream liberal groups such as SANE called for de-escalation and negotiation but had a hard time getting their message heard amid the noise of the leftists. Cortright argues that "in the end each element of the movement made a contribution toward ending the war," but my memory corresponds more closely with DeBenedetti's claim that radical elements undermined the movement's effectiveness. I was out there with the young student radicals who wanted a revolution in America, but we were wrong. We might have saved a lot of Vietnamese and Americans lives by focusing more narrowly on ending the war.

As the years went by and frustration mounted, the "new left" came to dominate the movement, at least in the public's perception. In 1971, in Washington, D.C., 12,000 people were arrested, "the largest mass jailing in U.S. history," and an aura of "lawlessness and anarchy" developed around the movement. A poll that year showed that 70 percent of Americans opposed the war, but most also opposed the antiwar demonstrators.

Against the Nuclear Arms Race

Another wave of activism against nuclear war accompanied the "second Cold War" of the Reagan Administration, which increased military spending and readiness while talking about nuclear war as a viable military option if needed. In 1981, 70 percent of Americans—and even more

Europeans—said they considered nuclear war a real possibility, a big increase from the 1970s.

Randy Forsberg's eloquent call to freeze the nuclear arms race (stop building and deploying nuclear weapons as a first step) galvanized a huge upsurge in the peace movement, responding to these fears with a practical policy that everyone could understand. In 1980, dozens of towns in western Massachusetts passed nonbinding referenda supporting the freeze. Many other towns and cities followed suit. From town meetings in New England to the far-reaching 1983 statement of the U.S. Catholic bishops, millions of Americans joined in. "The nuclear weapons freeze movement swept through the United States in the 1980s like the proverbial prairie fire." In 1982, Forsberg spoke at the largest political demonstration ever held in America up to that time, a million-strong march and rally in Central Park, New York. In Western Europe, protests in 1983 brought out 3 million people against the nuclear arms race—"the largest mobilization of peace sentiment in human history up to that time."

Later in 1983, ABC television broadcast a graphic two-hour movie, *The Day After*, depicting a nuclear war from the perspective of Lawrence, Kansas. (With the city's support, ABC turned downtown Lawrence into a postapocalyptic scene by knocking out storefront windows, importing burned cars, and hiring thousands of local students to shave their heads and stop washing to mimic radiation sickness.) A hundred million Americans watched the movie, the second half of which ran without commercial breaks because no sponsor would run an ad after the nuclear attack scene. ABC operated a toll-free hotline during and after the show for alarmed viewers. Because of the peace movement's work in dragging nuclear policy out of the think tanks and into the streets, millions of Americans were thinking about the unthinkable and not liking it.

The freeze movement did not achieve its policy aims in the short term, but it did dampen the bellicose policies of the Reagan Administration, encourage Soviet reforms, and set the stage for the 1985 Geneva summit between Reagan and Gorbachev that began to change the direction of the superpower rivalry.

THE POST–COLD WAR ERA

After the Cold War ended, brutal aggression and genocide in places such as Bosnia and Rwanda confronted the movement with the choice of supporting U.S. military intervention—contrary to most activists' instincts—or deciding to "stand aside when innocent populations are murdered wantonly and a minimum application of force could stop the killing. . . ." The dilemma resembled, in milder form, the problem of responding to the rise of fascism in the 1930s. In 1999, the hundredth anniversary of the Hague peace conference organized by the Russian czar, thousands of peace activists gathered in The Hague for another peace conference. However, by the time the conference got under way NATO had begun an air war against Serbia to force its withdrawal from Kosovo, where the Muslim population had suffered brutal repression at the hands of the Serbian government. Delegates to the Hague conference were split, some supporting the logic of justice by which NATO action liberated Kosovars from oppression, and others supporting the logic of peace by which NATO had violated international law by using force without authorization from the UN Security Council.

Iraq

Before the Iraq War in 2003, "an estimated 10 million people demonstrated against the . . . war in hundreds of cities across the globe," an effort that Cortright (who helped lead it) calls "the largest, most intensive mobilization of antiwar sentiment in history." Yet, as with Vietnam, the war dragged on year after year with the political leadership seemingly oblivious to the peace movement. Old issues reemerged with the Iraq War. The peace movement relied for support on "the global justice movement," such as labor unions and civil rights groups. Tactically this helped increase numbers quickly and organize impressive demonstrations against the war. However, the argument against the war became muddled, once again, with antiwar views predicated on "connections between the U.S.-led war and Western-oriented globalization, recognizing, as one activist leader put it, that 'militarization is just the other arm of the corporate agenda.' "

This "corporate agenda" idea did not help in changing U.S. policy in Iraq, nor does it make much sense. Very large, greedy corporations lost huge amounts of money as a result of the Iraq War. It drove up world oil prices and arguably led directly to the bankruptcy of General Motors. It enriched oil companies only because it failed to obtain the "cheap oil" that leftists claimed it was after. These theories faced, and failed, a hard test when a progressive Democrat, Barack Obama, replaced the corporate-leaning George W. Bush. Obama continued, indeed escalated, the U.S. war effort in Afghanistan, to the surprise and dismay of the peace movement, despite there being few corporate interests, globalization connections, or oil there.

In sum, the peace movement, after more than a century of debate about working for justice versus working directly for peace, has come down on the wrong side of the question. Meanwhile, as activists have chased after distracting or implausible goals, they have lessened the movement's contribution to the work that is actually making a big difference in spreading peace—the UN, peacekeeping, humanitarian aid in war zones, and similar efforts described in the previous chapters. That is the bad news.

III. The Growing Desirability of Peace

The good news is that over the long term, peace movements have contributed greatly to the emergence of new norms that delegitimize war and promote the value of peace.

At the time of the European treaties of 1713–15, war "was not yet regarded as an evil. . . ." In the eighteenth century, among political leaders "there was no hint of pacifism, much less the idea that war was some sort of social ill . . . that could be eliminated through reason and international institutional devices. Quite the contrary." And in the nineteenth century, right up to World War I, most Europeans saw war as inevitable, as beneficial to the winners, something "to be welcomed, not avoided . . . , a philosophical and moral good." Indeed, "War had become sufficiently popular that most of the constraints against the use of force had effectively been eroded."

After World War I, these attitudes shifted completely and have never been the same. The senseless slaughter swung public opinion in the West against the idea of war as a good in itself. People endured the Second World War but did not glorify it. Since then, "attitudes have shifted dramatically. . . . Few states have renounced the potential use of force, but clearly today it is seen among millions as an exceptional, if not pathological, form of behavior."

Political scientist Martha Finnemore describes the evolution of international norms concerning military interventions. "States used to intervene militarily in other states for reasons and in ways that they no longer do." For example, military interventions used to be an acceptable way to collect debts owed by other countries, but this is no longer the case. These changes over the centuries, she argues, result not so much from changing technologies or power relationships, but changing "state understandings about the purposes to which they can and should use force." These understandings changed in part because of the rise of international law and "the increased presence of lawyers at international conferences and treaty negotiations." Also, over the centuries, the concept of who "qualifies as human" and deserves intervention has expanded, from just European Christians in the nineteenth century to all human beings by the end of the twentieth.

Finnemore finds a "clear trend" in "the steady erosion of force's normative value in international politics. In the seventeenth century, war was glorious and honorable. States actively sought it out not only as a means to wealth and power but as an end in itself. . . . Over the last three centuries, however, war has become less legitimate. . . ." In 1918, "war was still officially deemed legitimate if it aimed at national self-determination. By 1928, however, sixty-five states . . . declar[ed] self-defence the only legitimate reason for war."

Parallel trends accompany the changing norms regarding the use of force through the large sweep of history, as political scientist Neta Crawford shows. Slavery used to be near-universal. "Aristotle declared it to be an inevitable feature of human society. Today it has virtually disappeared. . . ." Two hundred years ago, supporters and opponents of slavery faced off in British public discourse, and the opponents, harnessing religious ideas, "denormalized, delegitimized, and proclaimed . . . slavery against Britain's national interests and identity." Later, decolonization in the twentieth century was accomplished peacefully in most cases—"war was the exception"—by appeal to norms of humanity and colonizers' identities. This, too, marked a change from the possibilities in the nineteenth century.

Human sacrifice was also widely practiced in earlier days, but has all but vanished. Cannibalism was widespread in the world but norms have evolved that make it now unacceptable. Violent street riots "were a frequent occurrence in earlier times, a normal part of social life." Dueling, once common, has also completely gone out of fashion.

Norms against the use of force continue to strengthen in recent decades. Military coups have decreased—in Latin America they dropped from one or two per year on average in the 1950s to 1970s down to one or two per decade by the 1990s. Terrorism in Europe, notably in Northern Ireland and Spain, peaked in the 1970s and has since declined drastically. Terrorism in Latin America ended by the mid-1990s except in Colombia.

A fine example of the power of changing norms—and a big victory for the peace movement—is the International Campaign to Ban Landmines. In the early 1990s, the campaign took form as an outgrowth of humanitarian and political NGOs working on war-induced disabilities (especially amputations). The head of the Vietnam Veterans of America Foundation was shocked to find, on a visit to Cambodia, the large number of civilian victims of land mines left behind after the war. He hired a humanitarian aid worker from Vermont, Jody Williams, who had worked with civilian war victims in El Salvador, to organize a coalition of NGOs to end land mine use. She coordinated a very informal worldwide coalition of nongovernmental groups working on land mines, a coalition that had no central headquarters or bank account. Drawing in governments of small and middle powers, the campaign began negotiating the text of a treaty, working outside the normal diplomatic frameworks, the UN, and the great powers.

After a year of intensive negotiation centered in Ottawa, Canada, spurred by a challenge from Canada's foreign minister to move quickly, the Mine Ban Treaty was signed in 1997 by 122 countries. The campaign won the Nobel Peace Prize that year. The process of reaching a treaty differed greatly from the usual treaty negotiations, in terms of participants (NGOs, civil society, UN agencies, and governments together), speed, and decision-making process (voting, instead of the usual consensus method).

The Mine Ban Treaty entered into force as the required number of countries ratified it, and now has 156 nations on board. Of those, 85 have completed the destruction of their land mine stockpiles. However, several dozen countries have *not* joined the treaty, and these include the United States, China, and Russia as well as quite a few important regional actors such as Israel, Iran, Pakistan, India, Vietnam, and both Koreas.

The great power of the treaty, however, seems to be in changing norms, delegitimizing mines, and causing most of the nonparticipants to go along with the treaty's provisions in practice. In fact, only Burma and Russia still actively use land mines. So, the campaign represents a great example of the power of grassroots, bottom-up organizing, bypassing official channels and great powers, to bring about real, tangible change in international security matters. Land mines are just one slice of the much bigger problem of war, but the effort shows that peace activism can at least occasionally march straight into the halls of power and bring about real changes.

Political scientist John Mueller attributes the changing patterns of war violence to shifts in attitudes and cultures. He does not buy several alternative explanations of decreasing war—the existence of nuclear weapons, economic development (since industrialization in 1750–1900 did not make war unfashionable), the rising costs of war, democracy, trade, and international institutions. The "remnants of war" consist mostly of civil wars, most of which "are more nearly opportunistic predation waged by packs—often remarkably small ones—of criminals, bandits, and thugs. . . ." Thus in Mueller's view "the best solution to . . . civil warfare lies in the development of effective domestic governments . . ." rather than international policing.

Attitudes about violence changed at different times in different places, according to political scientist James Payne. "In English-speaking lands, a shift occurred in the last half of the nineteenth century. Elites became uneasy about massacres that soldiers and mobs carried out." For example, the massacres of 130 Cheyenne at Sand Creek, Colorado, in 1864—just as the norm was beginning to shift—led to investigations by the army and Congress, although nobody was punished for it. But a "consensus against genocide did not emerge in the West until after World War II." In "underdeveloped countries . . . the evolution against the use of force is far behind that of the developed regions. . . ."

Restraints on killing civilians are relatively recent. Only after "the widespread civilian atrocities and genocide of the Second World War" did a treaty on the protection of civilians take effect—the Fourth Geneva Convention of 1949. (Previous Geneva Conventions dealt with military prisoners and wounded.)

Norms against violent civil disturbances similarly changed at different times in different places. In England, France, Germany, and Ireland, dozens of full-scale riots took place each year in the early nineteenth century, but the number dropped dramatically after about 1850. In the United States, this change occurred somewhat later, after the mid-1920s. Racial violence in the United States also diminished: In the South after the Civil War, thousands were killed yearly, whereas race riots around the time of World War I and in the 1960s claimed only dozens of lives at a time. Since 1990, only one major such incident has occurred, in Los Angeles in 1992, with fifty-three deaths.

In the most recent example of the power of peaceful norms, nonviolent revolutions swept authoritarian governments from power in Tunisia and Egypt in 2011. The young protesters, relying on technologies such as cell phone cameras and social networking websites, followed strategies based on previous experiences of nonviolent movements in other countries. In the face of violent repression and provocations from the government, large crowds marched through Cairo streets chanting, "Peaceful, peaceful." They won over the population, the international community, and eventually the military, forcing out a dictator and beginning on a path toward democracy. In Libya, the brutal violence of the government convinced protesters to turn to arms, and a small but bloody civil war ensued in early 2011. Nonetheless, the success of peaceful revolution in Egypt, the largest Arab country, with eighty million people, was historic and a sign of a world changing for the better.

It is hard to say whether changing norms themselves should be seen as a driving force behind changes in amounts of warfare, as Mueller sees it, or whether something else drives both the increasing peace and the norms about violence. There is only one world history and many causal elements at play. The causes of war turn out to be the effects of war as well, and the same holds for peace. Specifically, sustained peace changes norms, and norms can sustain peace. Unfortunately for political scientists, life as we know it is not a good experimental design!

9

ASSESSING PROGRESS

Is Peace Increasing since 1945?

I mentioned in passing that the field of "peace research" contributed to sustaining the idea of peace during the paranoid days of the early Cold War. Peace researchers had a novel idea, that science—data, measurement, and statistics in particular—could supplement activism by developing solid knowledge about the conditions for peace to develop. In this chapter, I will explore how their methods can help us confirm and better understand the progress in reducing war that I first laid out in Chapter 2. The results of peacekeeping and the other efforts since 1945 that previous chapters have described can be assessed by measuring war through time to see if it is increasing, decreasing, or staying the same.

I. The Body Count

First consider the importance of measuring war fatalities and the results of that exercise. Later in the chapter I will discuss other ways to measure wars.

COUNTING IS THE FIRST STEP IN CHANGING

Counting things—measuring, data collection, data analysis—can be a form of activism. My friend Randy Forsberg, who authored the 1980 nuclear freeze proposal, did a lot of both.

The last time I saw her, Randy lay on a hospice bed near the end of an amazing life. Actually her mere presence there in 2007, dying of cancer, was a triumph. When I'd first met Randy twenty-five years earlier, she had just survived cancer and Legionnaires' disease at the same time. Randy was tough.

In those days, the mid-1980s, Randy was a star, a MacArthur Fellow (the so-called "genius award"), and foundations gave her money to press forward with her work. The institute she founded and directed measured and analyzed both weapons and arms control agreements. In later years, the foundations moved on to new trendy topics and Randy scrimped and sacrificed to keep her institute afloat. But she never gave up.

When I went to see her in the hospice with my friend Neta Crawford, another professor of international relations and a former worker at Randy's institute, Randy looked up when we came in. "Oh, Neta, Joshua, I'm glad you're here." And then she launched into a list of where each project stood. "The data on aircraft are in pretty good shape, but ships are missing the last three years," and so forth. The arms control annual had found a new editor but her class at City College still needed a new professor. What she cared about was that the work continue, including the work she uniquely had done in counting and measuring things concerning war, military forces, and arms control treaties.

Randy believed in empirical data. You might expect that her institute in Cambridge, Massachusetts, would be filled with young idealists organizing peace activists to rise up and change the government's policies, or lobbying government officials to do so. And they did that. But more often you would find young idealists entering data and writing reports about the world's military forces and arms control agreements. Randy compiled the definitive listing of arms treaties in near-real time and sold it to agencies such as the CIA. She assembled the World Weapons Database, "bean counting," as they used to call it in the defense program at MIT where Randy had studied. When I wanted to know, for my college textbook, how many tanks and warships each of the great powers possessed, I got the answer from Randy's database. I still sometimes tease Neta Crawford about her first book, published while at Randy's institute—a thick volume listing all Soviet military aircraft by type and capabilities, enticingly titled *Soviet Military Aircraft.*

If you want to change the ways military forces get used in today's world, Randy thought, you have to understand who has them, what types, with what capabilities, and how they are using them to achieve certain political ends. Thus, counting is the first step in changing.

Randy shared this fondness for counting with the Stockholm International Peace Research Institute (SIPRI), in Sweden, where she originally worked as a typist. She thought the stuff she was typing looked very interesting! SIPRI, then as now, compiles data and writes reports about the status and trends for armed conflicts around the world. For example, if I want data on military expenditures in the world's countries, I find them in the *SIPRI Yearbook.*

Randy worked her way up from typist to doing research at SIPRI, then entered MIT to get a Ph.D. in political science, working in the defense studies program. She finished her course work but postponed writing a dissertation—for more than a decade, as it turned out—to start her institute, create the nuclear freeze proposal, and collect her own data as SIPRI did. Decades later she returned to MIT, wrote a dissertation about the end of war, earned her Ph.D., and accepted a position as a professor in an endowed chair at City College of New York, which took in her institute and library collection. Her students loved her. But in a year she was gone.

Randy was one of the few people who would speak openly about the end of war, which was almost a taboo subject. She thought war could end the way cannibalism, once widespread in human society, had ended. She believed that the route to ending war was a step-by-step program leading away from the justified uses of armed force. She thought that controlling U.S. and other great-power interventions would reduce the use of force, and that international norms of behavior could gradually make the use of force anachronistic. Democracy and citizen activism could push this process forward. Randy did not directly measure conflicts and fighting to assess progress. But a group of researchers not far from her starting point in Stockholm have done just that.

A WAR MONITORING SYSTEM

Imagine that we had a global observation satellite monitoring war fatalities worldwide. A spot of light would appear on a world map whenever someone died from an act of violence in a war. We could look at this map and see people dying in wars every day in Iraq and Afghanistan, and flashes of light somewhat less often from other wars. Over time, we could see increases or decreases in the total numbers killed each year.

As it happens, we do have such a system, but it's not a satellite. It's a group of Swedes. To find them, take the train from Stockholm about an hour north to the famous university town of Uppsala (where Dag Hammarskjöld once studied). There, find a small building off an old square in a very old university. Up a little staircase and down a narrow corridor, about twenty young researchers work under supervision of Professor Peter Wallensteen and project leader Lotta Harbom. They run the Conflict Data Project, and they are the world's experts on counting wars.

The Uppsala researchers scour journalists' accounts from around the world, sometimes visiting conflict areas themselves, to seek out all sources of information reporting wars and war fatalities, and amass the information into a database of the world's armed conflicts. Since 2003 their primary source for updating armed conflicts has been scanning of the Factiva electronic news database based on twenty-eight thousand news sources in two hundred countries. When a filter identifies a story as possibly a war report, one of the researchers reads it and puts the relevant information in the database.

The most important measure the Swedes report is "battle-related deaths." This measure includes both military and civilians killed by war actions such as shelling, shooting, car bombs, or air strikes—and also acts of terrorism. But it includes only violent deaths, not those indirectly caused by war. (And it excludes one-sided violence such as genocide that does not involve fighting by both sides.) The indirect deaths may greatly outnumber direct deaths, or sometimes vice versa, but overall they tend to move together in the same direction. Thus if battle-related deaths rise or fall worldwide, indirect deaths probably follow the same trend.

The Swedish researchers define an armed conflict as a "contested incompatibility" concerning either territory or control of government. The conflict must involve the use of force by at least one national government's military forces and one or more other military force, and must cause at least twenty-five battle-related deaths each year.

The Uppsala researchers also have begun estimating deaths in "non-state" armed conflicts where neither side is a government, but these are only a tenth the size of conflicts involving a government, and declined by two-thirds in lethality from 2002 to 2006. The researchers also measure "one-sided violence" in which a reciprocal threat of force is not a factor, as when a state kills unarmed members of an ethnic group. These are separate from, and smaller than, the battle deaths.

The Swedish researchers have compiled detailed battle-death data only for the post–Cold War era. Before that, they simply classify armed conflicts in terms of three levels of fatality—under twenty-five deaths in a year, between twenty-five and 999, and over 1,000. This is of limited use in gauging trends through time. Fortunately, researchers at the Peace Research Institute, Oslo (PRIO) in Norway have estimated for each armed conflict since 1945 a low, high, and "best" estimate of battle fatalities. These data—the best estimate where available or the midpoint of low and high if not—are the numbers I will use here. Various counting methods based on the Uppsala/PRIO conflict list produce somewhat different estimates, but all agree on the general trends over the past sixty years and also over the more recent years.

The battle-death data can be criticized for underestimating or excluding certain deaths, such as indirect war deaths caused by epidemics, but as long as the researchers are consistent from year to year in applying their methods—and they are—the PRIO battle-death data are especially good for measuring trends through time. In terms of absolute levels of war deaths, the data are conservative because they count only documented and direct war deaths and therefore do not show the full effects of wars, which kill in many ways over many years (famines, diseases, and suicides, as well as violent deaths that never get recorded).

ISSUES IN COUNTING DEATHS

Counting war deaths does present challenges. First of all, everyone who has worked with war data will tell you that the fatality estimates are not reliable, especially on the civilian side and especially as we move back in time. Wars kill many people in remote places who are buried without being counted by anyone. We are forced to make guesses and sometimes to rely on sources such as Micheal Clodfelter's reference book, which does not cite specific sources for the numbers given. (Despite being written by someone without academic training or affiliation, his guesses seem reasonable as far as I can tell.) So a kind of murky fog envelops the field of war fatalities, getting thicker as one moves either back through time or out into poorer areas of the world. Looking just at the period since 1945 the fog is not too thick to obscure the overall trends, although data for any particular war may be suspect.

There is also, let's face it, historical baggage attached to the idea of a "body count." During the Vietnam War, U.S. commanders used it to create a false sense of control in a counterinsurgency war that did not go well. But are we better off with the U.S. military's approach in Iraq, avoiding "body counts" and refusing to estimate enemy or civilian fatalities in the war? This just seems to replace misrepresentation with denial. In my opinion, we do the dead no dishonor by counting them—quite the contrary. I wish we could count and name every individual, the way the moving Vietnam Memorial does for the U.S. war dead, for instance.

COUNTING NUMBERS OF WARS

Other ways to measure ups and downs in war are not as good as battle deaths. In particular, people often count the *number* of wars in progress year to year. (By "war" I mean what Uppsala calls "armed conflicts.") One major problem with this approach is that it equates big and small wars. And because the world has a lot more small wars than big ones, it overstates the importance of small ones. Furthermore, this measure is too sensitive at the small end of the spectrum of wars, because when a war ends and kills fewer than twenty-five people in a year it drops off the list but if there is a tiny flare-up in fighting that kills twenty-five people—for instance, one bomb in a market—the war goes back on the list and the count of wars in the world goes up by one. A war that rages all year long and kills tens of thousands of people would count the same as this one incident.

The number of wars you count also depends a lot on how you count them. For instance, are the wars in Afghanistan and Pakistan one war, two wars, or a bunch of little wars? Similarly, in Darfur, Sudan, and neighboring Chad and Central African Republic a number of armed groups fight each other and the various governments; is it one war or a handful? The Uppsala researchers do a careful job of counting each armed group, but if, for example, an armed group splits into two factions it looks like the world has an additional war. For all these reasons battle deaths are a preferable indicator because they combine the number and size of wars worldwide and are comparable from year to year.

INDIRECT DEATHS

Indirect deaths are those caused indirectly by a war, such as when war refugees suffer higher rates of death from disease or malnutrition. For example, if war disrupts agriculture in a poor country, displacing people from their land, and they go on to starve to death, are those not war deaths just as much as if bullets had killed them? Famine and disease "are often the greatest killers of civilians" in wartime. "War and hunger go hand in glove with devastating effect and have always done. Sudden flight so often means destitution and a complete loss of livelihood and access to food." In a "sad paradox," the actions people take to stay alive in a war zone, such as fleeing their homes, "can in fact prove deadly." And sometimes starvation of civilians is a deliberate tactic in war rather than a mere by-product, as when policies of blockade or scorched earth seek to deny sustenance to an enemy army.

Indirect deaths are thus important, but they have a big problem. They depend on a counterfactual, that is, an alternative history of what might have been if war had not occurred. Yet we cannot rerun history with a different scenario to compare the death rates. (Chapter 10 shows how doing so to estimate indirect war deaths in Congo went wrong.) Without the war, presumably, certain people would not have been uprooted and the cholera rate would not have increased, for example, so a certain number of people would have lived, instead of dying of cholera.

However, war's social effects are complex and not all are negative. For instance, by displacing masses of people into refugee camps, war makes them available for vaccinations and other health interventions perhaps not yet available in the countryside as a whole. In Angola, war isolated the country from its neighbors, keeping Angola's HIV infection rate below that of other countries in Southern Africa. Do we "credit" the lives thus saved, those who would have died of AIDS except for the war, on a balance sheet? Do we debit the lives lost because war held back economic growth and kept a country in poverty? The estimation of indirect deaths then becomes an economic estimate of how much war deepened or prolonged poverty, a very hard thing to calculate. We simply do not have a counterfactual world in which the war did not happen, and historically some countries at war, like some at peace, overcome poverty while others remain stuck.

The bottom line is that war has major social effects, mostly negative ones on balance, but we cannot readily quantify them into lives lost. Indirect deaths *matter* as much as direct ones. It's just that indirect deaths are much harder to count.

Battle deaths turn out to move usually in the same direction as indirect deaths. If fighting breaks out and armies start shooting their way through territory, both direct and indirect deaths increase. Indirect deaths result from "the scope and intensity of fighting (for which combat deaths are the best measure), the numbers of people displaced, the pre-existing levels of nutrition and access to health care, and the timeliness, degree, and efficacy of humanitarian intervention. Since war numbers, combat deaths per conflict, and the numbers of people displaced have all declined in the past fifteen years, while funding for humanitarian assistance has more than doubled over the same period, we have every reason to expect that indirect deaths should have declined as well." Furthermore, contrary to claims that "new wars" are more brutal, with more atrocities than in the past, the Uppsala researchers used data on civilian casualties over several decades to show that no such trend exists.

So if we look just at direct deaths we can meaningfully track ups and downs in war. They are not, of course, a complete reckoning. Calculating all the costs including criminal violence, disease, trauma, sexual violence, loss of property, environmental damage, and other sources "quickly defies straightforward accounting."

WHAT THE DATA SHOW

The PRIO battle-death data show that although war fatalities have gone up and down over the years since World War II ended, the overall trend is clearly downward. In particular, war deaths in the post–Cold War era were well below the Cold War average. During the Cold War (1946–89), most battle deaths resulted from interstate wars, between two or more regular state armies, especially Korea, Vietnam, and the Iran-Iraq War. Wars between regular armies, each side with heavy weapons, kill large numbers of people.

In the post–Cold War era, however, interstate wars have become rare. In 1989–95, only five of the ninety-six conflicts counted by the Uppsala group were "clear-cut interstate armed conflicts. . . ." Nonetheless, interstate war was "not extinct," since most of the years in the period saw at least one interstate war under way. Since 1995, however, interstate wars have decreased further, with none at all in 2004 to 2007. In 2008 this streak was broken by a border dispute between Eritrea and Djibouti. However, this may be an exception that proves the rule, as it involved four days of skirmishes on a disputed border that killed few people. A BBC report put the word *war* in quotation marks in its headline.

A more serious war, although a short one, between Georgia and Russia in 2008, was not classified as an interstate war by the Uppsala researchers because technically it was between Georgia and its breakaway republic, which Russia was merely supporting. This makes it an "internationalized civil war"—one with foreign troops fighting on the side of either a government or opposition forces. This form of civil war has sputtered along in the post–Cold War era with typically four or five in progress. Usually, however, the outside army fights on the government's side. In this case, with Russia supporting the secessionists, two regular state armies clashed, a rare occurrence in recent years. Even in this case the violence was limited in scope (part of Georgia), duration (five days), and mortality (about 500).

From the mid-1970s through the 1980s, civil wars grew in intensity. Postcolonial wars in newly independent countries accounted for much of this wave. Cold War rivalries fueled opposing sides in some civil wars, which dragged on and took a terrible toll on their societies, as in Angola and Central America, for instance. In the post–Cold War era, these civil wars gradually diminished as well. New conflicts emerged in places where the fall of communism led to turmoil, such as in the former Yugoslavia, but these, too, gradually decreased, and fewer new wars broke out. Old wars ended faster than new ones broke out.

The trend does not move uniformly in one direction. For instance, large reductions in armed violence briefly followed both Korea and

Vietnam but did not last. In particular, a lull almost comparable to today's, but shorter-lived, followed the end of the Korean War and the death
of Stalin, in 1953. (This reminds us there is no guarantee that today's lull
will last.) But overall the direction is down, especially in the post–Cold
War period:

1946–49	417,000 battle-related deaths/year
1950–54	266,000
1955–59	44,000
1960–64	118,000
1965–69	181,000
1970–74	293,000
1975–79	125,000
1980–84	230,000
1985–89	211,000
1990–94	109,000
1995–99	83,000
2000–04	55,000
2005–08	53,000

Total since 1945: Approximately 10.5 million battle deaths

The battle-deaths data begin in 1946, just *after* the bloodletting of the
World Wars (higher than the entire 10 million since then). Thus, if extended back a few years earlier, the data would show an even more dramatic downward trend. Nothing remotely as bad as World War II has
happened since.

Finally, as I mentioned in Chapter 2, looking just at the early years of
the twenty-first century, war fatalities have dropped again compared to
the 1990s. In the past few years, the trend has flattened out, with the
numbers of wars and deaths remaining fairly steady, even rising modestly with the Iraq War, but still at a low level overall compared with
earlier periods. That decline occurred as world population grew by more
than one-quarter during the two decades of the post–Cold War era.

WHY WE DO NOT BELIEVE IT

The battle-deaths data caused a small ripple of interest in the media
around 2005, led by an article in *The New Republic* and an op-ed in *The*

Washington Post. These articles joined earlier ones noting the evidence of "a steady downward trend in conflicts since the early 1990s." People did not contradict or criticize these articles, but they mostly ignored them.

Peace researcher Andrew Mack tries to explain why the decline in conflict does not seem to get through to the public. First, people get their information from the media, which plays up the drama of violence much more than the quieter successes of peace. Second, the mandate of humanitarian and human-rights NGOs is to draw attention to problems, creating the impression of rampant violence, yet no NGOs have a mandate to report good news. Third, there are no official statistics on wars and casualties, so international organizations and governments "have had no way of determining whether things are getting better or worse. . . . The dearth of official statistics on security issues stands in stark contrast to the vast amount of government data (on development, health, education, etc.) that track progress . . . toward meeting the 2015 Millennium Development Goals. . . ."

The headlines and news stories from particular wars cannot be trusted to show trends, because of what social scientists call "selection bias." This means that we study something by looking more at one of the outcomes we are studying than at another. War reporting suffers from such a bias. Whenever a war breaks out, the world's journalists flock there to tell us of its horrors. From the perspective of that time and place, war is an unmitigated disaster. And as globalization shrinks the world, making information more and more accessible to us from distant locations, journalists expose us to the horrors of war more completely and more directly than ever before.

Peace researcher Kenneth Boulding suggested decades ago that although news reports are "biased toward reporting the worst," a consoling thought is that this means the catastrophes such as wars are "relatively scarce" and thus newsworthy. "Good things are not reported simply because they are common and dull. When a newspaper reports only good news, that is the time to get really worried, for this will suggest that the bad news is too commonplace to be reported."

What you see on TV and read about in newspapers is not representative of the world, but of the extremes. Small wars and big ones all look the same when they are plastered all over your TV screen or newspaper page in up-close gory detail. As such, the picture does not change much even if the *average* situation changes, because the extremes still look as bad. If, for example, the number of people killed in wars declined from 1 million in a certain time period to 100,000, over several generations, "reporters are still able to find plenty of images of violence, for . . . 100,000 people are still dying." Thus, "the public will never suspect this change" to a dramatically more peaceful world. Indeed, as more reporters with better technology cover the world's extremes more completely, violence will seem to be increasing. Selection bias is a serious problem. It is hard to make rational policies based on large numbers since we are drawn to the few dramatic cases. It is, on the contrary, easy to presume that war is inescapable.

Editors, for their part, play up the horrors of war because dramatic conflicts bring in readers and capture our attention. In the news business, they say, "If it bleeds, it leads." This is not a fault of journalists. It is their job to bring to our attention what is out of the ordinary (i.e., news). But who has the job of putting those events in a larger perspective, aggregating the many conflicts around the world to tell us how we're doing overall? That is the job of peace researchers such as those in Uppsala and Oslo, and professors of international relations such as myself.

Another reason for people's misperception that war is getting worse is psychological. If we expect the worst, we harden ourselves against the horrors and traumas of war, which are still with us even at reduced magnitudes. If by contrast we hope that wars will end and peace will spread, this leaves us vulnerable to disappointment. Journalist Gregg Easterbrook, in *The Progress Paradox*, explores psychological processes that lead people to feel worse despite objective improvements in their circumstances. "Despite what evening-news carnage suggests, armed conflicts and combat deaths worldwide are in a cycle of decline. Global democracy is rising, military dictatorship and communism are on the run. Each year the number of nuclear warheads in the world declines. . . . In the last decade, almost everything in international affairs has gone spectacularly well." (Yes, this was written before the setback of the Iraq War and its broad reverberations, but in retrospect the Iraq War alone does not negate the long-term trends Easterbrook refers to.)

Political scientist James Payne notes a similar tendency with regard to the decrease of all types of violence over the length of human history. Payne writes that based on the historical record, "we live in a much more

peaceful world than has ever existed. . . . But, for most people, the observation seems to be wrong—and not merely wrong, but irresponsibly
wrong and irritatingly wrong. Swayed by a number of fallacies and distor-
tions, they are convinced that, compared to the past, we live in particularly vicious, bloody times."

Payne identifies another potent reason to miss a downward trend over
time, "chronological bias." This refers to the problem of having more information about recent events than long-past events. We have a "tendency to assume that events of the present are larger, more important,
or more shocking than events of the past." For example, a TV viewer who
sees a story about a murder in Yorkshire, England, might say, "What is
the world coming to?" but in fact the murder rate in Yorkshire in 1348 was
seventy times the rate today. We just know much more about today's
murders.

This chronological bias occurs not just because records and memories are lost over the years, but also because improvements in technology allow us to collect more and more information from around the world
as the decades go by. Today, it is unlikely that a sizable battle could occur
anywhere in the world without some information about it coming to the
attention of researchers studying wars, such as those in Sweden. But if
those same researchers look at wars from thirty or forty years ago, much
less two hundred or two thousand years ago, the same cannot be said.

Payne takes to task the main compilers of war statistics in political
science—Quincy Wright, Lewis Frye Richardson, David Singer—for forgetting about chronological bias. Richardson first notes hundreds of
nineteenth-century Chinese wars of which he is aware but for which he
has no casualty data. But later Richardson forgets these omitted wars,
some of which, according to Payne, were "stupendous bloodlettings that
cost millions of lives," and says his data show no upward or downward
trend. Payne argues that with the inclusion of the omitted deaths earlier
in time, the actual trend would be downward. Similarly, sociologist Evan
Luard excludes from his grand survey of war all past wars in Asia and
Africa, since they are probably not proper wars and information is "in
any case inadequate to provide a proper record or basis for comparison."
But then in his conclusion Luard declares that wars in these places are
more costly now than in the past. He "assumes that the modern events
he knows about are larger and more frightening than past events of which

he is not aware." Chapter 2 described these actual trends; the point here is the importance of chronological bias.

Harvard psychologist Steven Pinker adds that we miss long-term declines in violence because "the decline of violent behavior has been parallelled by a decline in attitudes that tolerate or glorify violence. . . . From a contemporary vantage point, we see [today's atrocities, mild by historical standards] as signs of how low our behavior can sink, not of how high our standards have risen."

Payne also notes that various groups have vested interests in portraying the world as more violent than it really is. Journalists want to increase readership and viewership. Military organizations tend to play up threats to promote higher military spending. Morally concerned people and organizations "emphasize the wrong in order to attract attention and support. There is but a small degree of difference between emphasizing a wrong and exaggerating it, and this fine line is routinely crossed in just about every campaign of reform the world has ever seen." An observer who points out that violence is declining "seems to lack moral concern" and seems "insensitive, implying that the wars and genocides . . . weren't all that bad and that we shouldn't worry about a repetition. . . ." And thus "peace organizations obey the same imperative: if they report that the world is getting more peaceful, they make their mission seem less necessary, and donations to them will slack off." As journalist Gregg Easterbrook puts it, "Most contemporary fund-raising turns on high-decibel assertions that everything's going to hell. It is not. . . ." Steven Pinker adds, "No one ever attracted followers and donations by announcing that things keep getting better."

In addition, people have trouble thinking realistically about war trends because war is so traumatic and horrible. Psychological trauma interferes with the ability to measure and compare information accurately. Traumatic memories are frozen in isolated snapshots that do not connect with the metrics of daily life. After a society goes through war, often people just put on blinders and move forward without dealing with the painful memories of the war. After we have blotted out past memories it is hard to compare today's difficulties with those past times.

Finally, of course, the generation that experiences a terrible war remembers it more clearly than subsequent generations, so our "social memory" of war fades, as historian Arnold Toynbee noted.

In addition to these reasons to deny that peace is spreading, people confuse present events with the danger of future events. War is not diminishing because some big war might be about to start or restart, they reason. For example, India and Pakistan remain nuclear-armed enemies, and a war between them could kill ten million people. Or recent wars such as in southern Sudan could restart if present cease-fires collapse. Or Iraq could fall apart when U.S. forces pull out.

But we should not confuse *possible* future events with today's realities. Many terrible things *may* happen, and I cannot repeat enough that the current hopeful trend may reverse in the future. (I think our actions now can affect the chances of such a reversal.) But to *assume* that the worst will happen, that potentials for bad outcomes will always be realized, does not make sense in light of past history. The countries that have not had wars for decades might have them again, but that does not mean they definitely will. The trend toward fewer and smaller wars in the world might reverse tomorrow, but it might continue until no active war fighting is taking place anywhere. The point is not to predict which will occur, and certainly not to assume one or the other, but to figure out what we can do to increase the odds for one outcome and decrease those for the other. Meanwhile we should distinguish what is true today from what might or might not happen tomorrow.

Some people find it immoral to recognize humanity's progress toward peace, even if true, because that would lessen people's horror about war. But is progress a reason to stop trying? It should be obvious there is still much to do, and past successes should encourage us to carry on.

II. The War Data Network

In addition to the Swedish and Norwegian peace researchers, other scholars in several disciplines and countries have studied recent trends in war. The remainder of this chapter discusses their perspectives on the issue.

THE VANCOUVER GROUP

A group of researchers in Vancouver, Canada, compiled the *Human Security Report 2005*, which popularized and publicized the Swedish/Norwegian data, and has added to the data on several dimensions over the subsequent years. They point to an array of evidence that peace is increasing: International arms transfers dropped by about half from 1987 to 2000. The number of international crises peaked in 1981 and declined by about three-quarters by 2000. Instances of genocide and "politicide" (armed attacks on entire groups for their political views) also fell, from ten in 1989 to two in 2000. Coups d'état in sub-Saharan Africa peaked in the 1980s and are down by about a third since then. Worldwide, coups fell from about twelve a year during most of the Cold War to about six a year since 2000 (most in Africa). And in the 1990s about half of negotiated settlements broke down with a renewal of violence, but in 2000–05 only two of seventeen (12 percent) broke down. Preventive initiatives were "decidedly unsuccessful" in the 1990s, since there was a "huge increase in conflict onsets" (though an even larger increase in conflict terminations). Since 2000 the number of conflict onsets has dropped sharply, which could indicate (among other explanations) better results for conflict prevention.

One area where things did not improve from the 1990s to the 2000s was *one-sided violence*, that is, campaigns by governments that intentionally target civilians with armed force. Although still below Cold War levels, the number of such campaigns actually grew modestly from the 1990s to the 2000s. Deaths from one-sided violence are very hard to estimate, but seem to have decreased since the Rwandan genocide of 1994. The last campaign of one-sided violence to kill more than 1,000 people was in Darfur, Sudan, in 2004.

The number of terrorist attacks decreased, from about 650 in 1987 to just over 200 in 2003, although total casualties from them increased. Since 2003, the Vancouver group concludes, data seeming to show an increase in terrorism actually reflect a change in counting methods. Insurgent attacks on civilians in Iraq were counted as terrorist attacks, and made up 80 percent of the world total, but similar acts against civilians in other wars such as Sudan were counted not as terrorism but as war crimes. Taking out the Iraq War from the terrorism totals, the data show a decrease of fatalities by 40 percent since 2001. And as the Iraq War began winding down around 2007, even the official data with Iraq included showed a sharp drop in terrorism.

The Vancouver group attributes the positive trends in war in recent years to several factors, including the spread of democracy, but most importantly the upsurge in international actions to manage and reduce conflicts, including peacekeeping.

THE MARYLAND GROUP

Researchers at the University of Maryland have emphasized the problem of persistent civil war in their reports for the Washington policy community, *Peace and Conflict*. In 2000 the Maryland researchers highlighted the downward trend in war. Based on data developed at Maryland, they documented a sharp decrease in the number of conflicts worldwide, after a decades-long increase during the Cold War. The "Highlights" page at the front of the report begins, ". . . a world more peaceful than at any time in the past century." The report scores countries on their peacebuilding capacities and identifies thirty-three "at serious risk of armed conflict and political instability for the foreseeable future." (Also listed are a half-dozen "surprising successes" and fifteen to twenty countries in "risky transitions.") The challenge, say the report's authors, "is to sustain these positive trends . . . [which] can easily reverse."

A decade later, the trends have indeed continued, despite setbacks in the Iraq and Afghanistan wars and some relatively minor slippage in the past few years. The thirty-three at-risk countries identified by the Maryland group in 2000 showed modest progress. Almost half, fourteen countries, were not involved in an armed conflict in 2000 and still were not in 2008 (Tajikistan, Kyrgyzstan, Cambodia, Egypt, Nigeria, Guinea-Bissau, Cameroon, Lesotho, Congo-Brazzaville, Tanzania, Burkina Faso, Comoros, Kenya, and Zambia). Several of these have seen some instability and political violence in recent years for sure, but usually of short duration. Another ten of the at-risk countries were already at war in 2000 and remained so in 2008 (Afghanistan, Pakistan, Algeria, Iran, Burundi, Congo-DRC, Ethiopia, Sudan, Eritrea, and Chad). All but Afghanistan diminished in intensity by 2008, however. Another six countries were at war in 2000 but at peace by 2008 (Rwanda, Angola, Sierra Leone, Uganda, Liberia, and Guinea). Some of these were major wars that together had killed millions of people indirectly, though mostly before 2000. Finally, three at-risk countries that were at peace in 2000 were involved in armed conflict in 2008 (Georgia, Somalia, and Niger), but none of these were of high intensity. Beyond these thirty-three at-risk cases, the Uppsala data show an overall slight decrease in the worldwide number of countries with armed conflicts, from twenty-eight in 2000 to twenty-six in 2008.

Yet, the otherwise excellent 2008 update of *Peace and Conflict* did not celebrate this progress—extending the most peaceful period in history from ten to almost twenty years—but instead focused on a slight uptick in the number of wars after 2005 and declared that the hopeful trends had "begun to reverse." These researchers are honest and competent social scientists (I know them personally). The problem, I think, runs deeper than one or another's misjudgment: We all focus on bad news or things to worry about. The Washington policy establishment, the Maryland researchers, and their research donors all would tend to see a minor uptick as a worrisome reversal. Nobody wants to leave us open to a nasty surprise, to declare peace in our time only to find it anything but. Why we think that way is one subject explored by Harvard psychologist Steven Pinker. He argues that "we estimate the probability of an event from how easy it is to recall examples. Scenes of carnage are more likely" to be remembered.

REVERSAL, OR CONSOLIDATION?

Recently, both the Maryland and Uppsala researchers have warned that the decrease in war had halted, or reversed, in the mid-2000s. The Uppsala researchers wrote in 2007 that "although the number of conflicts remains relatively low compared to the peak of fifty-two in 1991 and 1992, the continuous decline seen in the 1990s now seems to have ceased. This makes it questionable how successful the international community has actually been in solving conflict. . . ." At the same time, the Maryland group similarly pointed to the reversal of the trend to fewer wars. However, this "reversal"—especially if we look at battle deaths rather than numbers of wars—might be better characterized as a flattening out at a low level. Obviously, wars and fatalities can never go below zero, which is where they would end up if the downward trend continued from over 200,000 battle deaths in the 1980s to under 100,000 in the 1990s. This flattening out of battle deaths around 50,000 in the new century seems to me more of a consolidation than a reversal of the downward trend.

The Maryland group also argued that more *countries* were at war recently, but this is a worse measure than counting numbers of wars. The increase in countries at war resulted from multinational forces' drawing on a larger number of allies, particularly NATO in Afghanistan. This multinationalization of military operations is part of the trend toward peace, moving in the direction of peacekeeping, and not an indication of growing war in the world.

Although a consolidation is more comforting than a reversal, there is nonetheless a real cause for concern in the flattening out of the decline. Most of the decrease in war over recent decades resulted from the ending of large wars, especially interstate wars. But the number and size of civil wars showed a much less impressive trend. In other words, the problem of civil wars may remain in some fundamental way unsolved, despite our success in taming big wars. I will return to these ongoing civil wars in Chapter 11.

Despite all these complexities and some ups and downs, the year 2010 was probably the most peaceful, in terms of battle deaths relative to population, in the history of the world. The relatively minor upsurge in 2008 and 2009, mainly in Sri Lanka, Pakistan, and Afghanistan, ended with the government victory in Sri Lanka and less fighting in Pakistan. No new wars of consequence meanwhile began.

SUPPORT YOUR LOCAL PEACE RESEARCHERS

Peace researchers—such as Randy Forsberg and the groups in Uppsala, Oslo, Maryland, and Vancouver—are an international interdisciplinary community, once estimated to contain about 20 percent each of sociologists and political scientists, 10 percent psychologists, and the rest "educators, physicists, biologists, economists, philosophers, historians, theologians, lawyers, military scientists, and anthropologists."

Compared to the vast efforts going into tracking world finances or world health, the resources devoted to peace research are tiny. The Swedes in Uppsala occupy one suite of offices. The Vancouver group has offices on one part of one floor of a downtown high-rise where Simon Fraser University has a campus. The Maryland group's office suite is in the basement of a university building. The biggest of the peace research institutes, PRIO in Oslo, has its own little building with a lobby, conference rooms, a library, and offices on three floors. They edit the *Journal of Peace Research* there. The researchers eat lunch together at a long table in the cafeteria of the larger Norwegian Red Cross next door.

These laudable efforts to understand peace and count armed conflicts are underfunded, understaffed, and underappreciated, considering that they represent the most important attempt to understand perhaps the most important problem in the world. Peace research pioneer Kenneth Boulding wrote in 1978 that "peace research is a minuscule operation . . . [with] only a few hundred people" engaged in it. "It has frequently been a discouraging and disheartening business, harder to finance I think than almost any other operation around a university." "The peace research movement has always operated on a shoestring and has always been starved for funds."

Political scientist Karl Deutsch, in a 1965 preface to the second edition of Quincy Wright's monumental *A Study of War*, noted the paltry resources then given to peace research: "Today millions of men and women in medical work and medical research carry on [a] struggle against death. But . . . in the entire world only a few hundred or thousand men and women are engaged in serious professional research on what causes war and on how war could be abolished." Nearly fifty years later, the situation is the same, except that medical research has made fabulous progress and receives vaster resources than ever.

Sociologist Pitirim Sorokin in 1937 pleaded that, although war data are low quality, they are better than nothing. Because war casualties are very difficult to estimate, "overcautious scholars prefer to pass the problem by as not lending itself to be studied satisfactorily." Yet he recommends we "go ahead and take these chances" and "try to be as careful and unbiased as possible in the study of the facts." Try to make the facts better and more complete than previous studies have, and do not "claim the privilege of infallibility or validity . . . but . . . simply say, 'Let us study the relevant facts as well as possible and then see what the results will be, without certainty as to whether they are accurate but with confidence that they are more reliable than purely inspirational theories or theories based upon only fragments of the existing data. . . .'"

I have a dream that someday the curse of poverty will lift from peace researchers, and that the hardworking scholars in the world's leading peace-research center will have their own cafeteria and not just their own table at the cafeteria next door.

EPIDEMIOLOGISTS WEIGH IN

Peace researchers have been joined by a new group of researchers in measuring war's impacts. They are epidemiologists, who study public health and the spread of disease. Several have tried to measure war deaths by sampling bits of the population, determining rates and causes of recent deaths, and then extrapolating the results to a whole country. This is what epidemiologists do generally in tracking epidemics and other public health problems. But it has turned out to be much harder for war deaths.

For example, in the recent war in Iraq, which took place under the glare of media attention and with the involvement of the world's leading information-savvy superpower, estimates of civilian casualties vary widely. The Iraq Body Count project added up confirmed cases that appeared in news articles, as a conservative (low) estimate, similar to the peace researchers' "battle-related fatalities," and came up with a number just over 100,000 as of 2010. But one epidemiological study showed far higher casualties. Published in *The Lancet*, the research was led by public health researcher Les Roberts (who also did an inflated Congo estimate two years earlier that I will discuss in Chapter 10). One study coauthored by Roberts estimated that by mid-2006 there had been 650,000 "excess Iraqi deaths as a consequence of the war." Critics of the Roberts study have argued convincingly that the sample method was biased.

If people have this much trouble agreeing on estimates of civilian casualties in Iraq, imagine how much harder it is for wars with less powerful participants, those with fewer journalists in attendance, or those that happened in bygone decades leaving incomplete historical traces. As one recent epidemiology conference concluded, "The science of casualty estimation requires far more development."

THE SEATTLE GROUP

Several epidemiologists at the University of Washington have tried to estimate worldwide violent (direct) war deaths from public health surveys, a problem they admit is "notoriously difficult." "The fundamental challenge in quantifying the health impacts of conflict is that health information systems, particularly civil registration systems that record the event and cause of death, often cease to function in populations affected by conflict." The group includes the prominent epidemiologist Christopher Murray, who coauthored an authoritative 1996 study on worldwide causes of mortality. Murray also coauthored, with Harvard political methodologist Gary King and others, a 2002 article using WHO mortality data to estimate worldwide war deaths at 310,000 in 2001, a far higher estimate than Uppsala's battle deaths.

The new Murray article analyzes data collected in the 2002–03 world health surveys, in which one member in each household reported on sibling deaths, including whether war injuries caused them. The survey included about 39,000 deaths in thirteen countries from 1955 to 2002, of which about 800 deaths were attributed to war violence. After an application of heavy-duty statistics—like "simulating 1,000 simultaneous draws from the variance-covariance matrix . . ."—they extrapolate the 800 war deaths to 5.4 million total for the thirteen countries during the period. It is more complicated than that, of course, but that is where they end up, though with a big "confidence interval," meaning they could be off by millions in either direction. This total, the researchers conclude, "suggests that war kills many more people than previously estimated"—about three times as many as the PRIO data for the same thirteen countries.

The magnitude of this claim came under criticism from other researchers. As the authors themselves admit, "as the survey was not specifically designed to measure war deaths, the absolute number . . . is small, leading to considerable uncertainty. . . ." PRIO's Nils Petter Gleditsch points to the case of Bosnia, where postwar investigation led to an accurate count of the actual war deaths (close to 100,000), yet the Seattle researchers estimated a much larger number (176,000) based on surveys. University of London economist Michael Spagat, along with Mack and others from Uppsala and Simon Fraser University, criticized the survey-based methodology on several grounds—sample bias, its comparison of apples and oranges, and its starting in 1955 right after a big war ended.

The Seattle group claims to find no downward trend in war deaths during the period, but this is entirely due to their unusual time frame that starts with a ten-year total for 1955–65, wedged in between Korea and Vietnam. After getting past this initialization problem, their estimates of violent war deaths per year during the four decades starting in 1965 decline from 205,000 to 129,000, 49,000, and 36,000, respectively. In comparing their survey-based estimates with the Uppsala data, the Washington researchers write, "Although the levels of deaths are different between the two sources, the time trends in war deaths are similar at the aggregate level."

THE PARADOX OF DECREASING MORTALITY IN WARTIME

Just as epidemiologists have crossed into peace-research territory by counting violent war deaths, the Vancouver group of peace researchers has recently returned the favor by looking at an epidemiological measure, overall mortality rates. The peace researchers discuss the paradox of mortality *declines* during wartime. They note that the "revolution in child survival" in the past thirty years has brought down mortality rates, especially under-age-five mortality, worldwide. This revolution, the result of campaigns by the World Health Organization and UNICEF, along with national governments, raised rates of vaccination of children in poor countries from 5 percent in 1974 to above 75 percent in 2006. One reason wars have less effect on mortality than in the past, say the Vancouver researchers, is that "immunization in peacetime saves lives in wartime." Similarly, breastfeeding advocacy has resulted in a rise in exclusive breastfeeding rates from 15 to 32 percent in sub-Saharan Africa—strengthening infants' immune systems and making them less vulnerable to two big killers of children in war, diarrheal diseases and respiratory infections.

Thanks to these efforts, recent data show a substantial drop in early childhood deaths globally owing to improved health care. The under-age-five mortality rate declined by more than a quarter from 1990 to 2009, as agencies from UNICEF to the Gates Foundation implemented cost-effective strategies such as promotion of breast-feeding, vaccination against measles, and distribution of antimalarial mosquito netting.

In countries at war, refugees and IDPs who leave their homes often end up in refugee camps where the UN and other international and local actors try to help them, albeit usually with inadequate resources. The average amount of humanitarian aid per displaced person rose from about $150 to $300 in 1990–2006. In some wars, the armed groups agree to "Days of Tranquility" to give immunization campaigns access to children in rebel territories. In Congo the immunization rate rose continually over the course of the conflict, from about 20 percent to 80 percent, according to the Vancouver researchers. The international help does not outweigh the rise in mortality that fighting causes locally. But the Vancouver group argues that wars are becoming smaller and more localized, so that the mortality rise from war in one area does not outweigh the falling mortality in the country as a whole.

Whether it be mortality rates, battle-related deaths, or combat aircraft, the ability to count things accurately provides a foundation for policies about war and peace. Now let us see how serious misconceptions about war trends can result from counting things badly.

10

THREE MYTHS
Finding the Truth When Conventional Wisdom Is Wrong

Some pieces of conventional wisdom, nearly universally accepted as true, are simply wrong. This chapter discusses three of them. All are cases where mistakes in using numbers led to wrong conclusions that make things seem worse than they actually are.

The first piece of conventional wisdom is that a century ago 90 percent of war deaths were military, but nowadays 90 percent are civilian. This turns out to be just an error made in preparing the UN's *Human Development Report 1994*. The error then propagated out until it was almost universally accepted. The truth is that military-civilian ratios show no particular trend through time, and remain somewhere around 50-50 overall (though varying greatly from war to war), as they have for centuries.

Second, the claim that 5.4 million people died as a result of the war in Congo since 1998 is way too high. One or two million would be much closer to the truth in my reading of the evidence, and is certainly bad enough. Congo's mortality rate was high before, during, and after the war, mainly because of the extreme poverty there. The war just made things worse.

Third, there is not an unabated epidemic of sexual violence in eastern Congo. There *was* an epidemic during the war in 1998–2003 but it diminished after 2003. In fact, overall, in the decade that the UN has been in the Congo, both mortality and sexual violence have decreased substantially.

These three myths play into a larger myth, that war is increasing, that war is out of control, that war is changing its character and becoming more brutal. None of these is true.

Before tackling these three myths in detail, consider an example of how easy it is for war-counting myths to take hold—the "Great 'War Figures' Hoax." A widely cited set of figures—3.6 billion people killed in 14,500 wars over the past 5,550 years—originated with newspaper columns written by Norman Cousins in 1953, which proposed the numbers as a purely "imaginary experiment" (a phrase included in his title). They illustrated what Cousins guessed might be found if it were possible to count wars and deaths over that long time period using an "electronic calculating device." Cousins's first sentence is "The following editorial is of course fanciful." Nonetheless the figures appeared as results obtained "with the aid of an electronic computer," in such publications as *Time* magazine and the *United States Naval Institute Proceedings*. Dutch researchers found that "there is no factual, empirical basis" for the numbers and they appear far too high.

I. Civilians Were 10 Percent of War Deaths But Now Are 90 Percent—Not

Now consider the three myths in detail. First: Conventional wisdom holds that war is becoming more savage and less civilized because a century ago wars killed almost entirely soldiers, far from civilian populations, but now wars kill almost entirely civilians. Specifically, in World War I war deaths were 90 percent military, but by the 1990s they were 90 percent civilian. Sometimes it's 85 percent or 95 percent rather than 90. Sometimes it's "a century ago" or "at the beginning of the twentieth century" rather than during World War I. But the basic outline remains the same.

A WIDESPREAD CLAIM

Many books about war repeat this claim, usually to highlight that war is getting worse over time. An award-winning book about peacekeeping has it on page 1. An authoritative book on civil wars puts it on page 4. The definitive World Bank report on civil wars has it on page 17. The Carnegie Commission on Preventing Deadly Conflict works it in by page 11.

These and other works put forward this statistic early in their books to establish with numbers that war is a worsening problem that urgently needs our attention. One political scientist sees the 90 percent statistic as "a grim indicator of the transformation of armed conflict" in the new, more brutal kinds of wars now prevalent. Another source calls it evidence of "a reversion to older types of warfare." The 1992 UNICEF report on the world's children uses the statistic to argue that a "'war on children' is a 20th century invention." A 2003 report on women and children in war, by the group Save the Children, uses the statistic to show that "war is not what it used to be. Its horrors are no longer experienced primarily by soldiers fighting on far-off battlefields."

Since so many people rely on it, this statistic must be true, right? Actually, both the World War I claim and the 1990s claim are mistakes. We can trace back the citations and see how it happened. Each citation leads to either the source of the data, a dead end, or a citation to an earlier source. When you trace back the chain of citations for these claims, the only ones that go anywhere lead to two books. First is the United Nations Development Program's (UNDP) *Human Development Report 1994*, which made the claim of 90-10 percent. Second is a 1991 book by a member of the Uppsala conflict data group, Christer Ahlström, where the UNDP got its information.

The UNDP's 1994 report is the key work that propagated the myth of the shifting 90-10 ratio for military-civilian war deaths. It says, "At the beginning of this century, around 90% of war casualties were military. Today, about 90% are civilian. . . ." Once the story had a UN stamp on it, other UN agencies picked it up. UNICEF's influential report *The State of the World's Children 1996* included a version in its section on "Children in War," citing the Ahlström book.

Also in 1996 the UN released a major report, "The Impact of Armed Conflict on Children," authored by a high-profile figure of great moral stature, Graça Machel. (She was former education minister and first lady of Mozambique, and the future spouse of Nelson Mandela.) Machel had been commissioned by the UN secretary-general to lead the two-year process culminating in the report, which was requested by the UN General Assembly in 1993 and presented to the General Assembly in 1996. In the report, Machel writes, "In recent decades, the proportion of war victims who are civilians has leaped dramatically from 5 per cent to over 90 per cent."

The UN put the claim in a press release for the report, and highlighted it the next year in its "cyberschoolbus" publication aimed at classroom use, putting it thus: "Civilian fatalities in wartime climbed from 5 percent at the turn of the century, to 15 percent during World War I. . . . These days, more than 90 percent of people who die in war are civilians. . . ." With the United Nations spreading the word to classrooms worldwide, the claim had legs.

WHERE IT CAME FROM

What did Ahlström actually say? In the course of a wide-ranging report, he mentions in passing that, in World War I, 14 percent of "victims" were civilians and 86 percent soldiers. This number is wrong, but the point for now is that Ahlström uses the word "victims" to mean only battle-related fatalities—civilian and military direct deaths inflicted by weapons in fighting. But later in the book, Ahlström uses the same word, "victims," differently to include deaths, injuries, and people "uprooted" by war (all refugees and internally displaced persons). The uprooted often outnumber the dead by about ten to one, so these two types of "victims" are not comparable at all. Including these larger totals, Ahlström concludes of the 1980s that "nine out of ten of all victims (dead and uprooted) are civilian." The publisher highlighted the "nine out of ten" statement on the back cover of the book but left out the explicit reference to "dead and uprooted"—thus, "Nine out of ten victims of war and armed conflict today are civilians." Ahlström says in each place what he means by "victims," but the UNDP missed it—an innocent mistake with big consequences.

The UNDP put the "nine out of ten" number together with Ahlström's earlier mention of World War I and the myth was born. Note that later references to "the 1990s" or "the end of the century" are wrong, since

Ahlström's data are all Cold War vintage and his book appeared in 1991. Also 14 percent of victims got rounded down to 10 (perhaps to mirror the 90-10 ratio claimed for the 1990s).

As for that 14 percent number for World War I, it was Ahlström's mistake. He took it from a book that lists the World War I casualty totals (in passing), but with a "+" sign after them to indicate that the civilian data are incomplete. That book in turn got the numbers from a short monograph published in London in 1968. One page, in this survey of all the wars of the twentieth century, lists World War I. The totals show 8.4 million direct deaths of soldiers and 1.3 million, flagged as "(estimate)," for civilians. But this "total" does not include Russia, Serbia, and Bulgaria—and Russia alone probably accounted for most of the civilian casualties of the war! This is why the careful author added the "+" sign when he reprinted the totals.

Even the incomplete 1.3 million estimate is of unknown origin since the chain of citations back from 1968 goes cold. A 1934 book in that citation chain reports, with no further citation, that "Kirby Page quotes an estimate by Professor Bogart: '. . . the loss of civilian life due directly to war equals, if indeed it does not exceed, that suffered by the armies in the field.'" The author calculates "on this basis" that 13 million civilians were killed in World War I, equaling military deaths.

So, although we know that something on the order of magnitude of 10 million soldiers died in World War I, we have no reliable data on civilian deaths. But the figure of 5 percent civilians "is far lower than the range cited by most historians." World War I did include horrendously bloody battles involving only soldiers. Men went over the top from their trenches to charge into machine guns. A few very large battles such as at Passchendaele, Belgium, killed more than 100,000 soldiers and far fewer civilians. However, in the same war, front lines moved through populated areas. The huge number of artillery shells fired in the war landed on many civilians in addition to many soldiers. Each side attempted to starve the other's civilian population through blockades. Although civilian direct deaths from war violence were probably lower than the historical average for wars, as a ratio to military ones, the civilian *indirect* deaths were high, especially if you include the 1918 influenza epidemic, which may have killed 20 million people worldwide. (Half of these, outside Europe, connect to the war very indirectly.)

A BETTER GUESS

The top expert on civilian casualties in Uppsala, Margareta Sollenberg, writes: "Hasty conclusions have sometimes led to 'truths' that have been proven to be unsubstantiated, such as that of the proportions of civilians and soldiers killed over time." When I asked her about civilian and military deaths over the past century, Sollenberg suggested that a typical ratio might be about 50-50, with no evident trend through time. Similarly, a book on civilians in war estimates that civilians were half of all war-related deaths over the past three centuries, and 50–62 percent in the twentieth century. And respected epidemiologists studying war deaths using world health surveys concluded that "for every military death there is at least one direct civilian death."

Another peace researcher, William Eckhardt, tabulated civilian war deaths as a percent of the total for each of the last five centuries. In the sixteenth to twentieth centuries, they were: 45, 50, 43, 50, and 58 percent, respectively. Comparing the period just since 1700 with the longer period since 1500, he finds 50 and 56 percent civilian deaths respectively. Elsewhere he concludes that "the civilian percent of war-related deaths was generally about 50%, although this figure varied from place to place and from time to time." Considering only wars with more than 100,000 deaths, "the percentage . . . remained 50%," and for wars above 1 million deaths, it was 48 percent. The consistency of this figure "suggests some stability over the centuries and around the world."

For the twentieth century itself—the period of the 90-10 claim—Eckhardt finds these percentages of civilian deaths decade by decade: 78 percent in the 1900s, 50 percent (the World War I decade), 50, 57, 60 (World War II), 55, 56, 67, and 74 percent. Clearly there were better and worse decades, but 78 percent of war deaths were civilian at the beginning of the century and 74 percent were by the 1980s. Most of the century's war deaths, by far, came in the two world wars, which saw 50–60 percent civilian deaths. These data completely contradict the idea of a dramatic trend toward higher civilian deaths relative to military ones over the past century. "The strange idea . . . that civilians only really began to suffer massively in war during the last century . . . is clearly wrong."

Some wars kill a lot more civilians than soldiers, while other wars show the opposite pattern. But this is not a trend through time. In the seventeenth century, many wars fought by mercenaries played out on set battlefields with little direct effect on civilians, whereas the Thirty Years' War (1618–48) killed perhaps 20 or even 30 percent of Germany's civilian population, far higher than even the worst wars of recent times. World War I hit civilians much harder than had the wars of the eighteenth and nineteenth centuries, but World War II hit them harder still. Nothing in the 1980s and 1990s, as horrible as those wars were, compares to the civilian casualties of World War II in magnitude.

PRIO researchers found that in African conflicts from the 1960s through 1980s, civilian deaths, including estimated indirect deaths, were relatively high compared with battle deaths (80–95 percent of the total; other researchers found 75–95 percent) but did not show any strong trend. These African civil wars are probably not typical of all recent wars, however. Another study found that direct combat accounted for about a third of the total years of healthy life lost because of wars, the rest being from indirect effects.

Recently the trend toward "smart" targeting has reduced civilian deaths relative to military ones. "Smart bombs . . . in both wars against Iraq, the NATO bombing of Kosovo, and the U.S.-led invasion of Afghanistan have massively reduced civilian death and suffering." The increasing use of armed drones by U.S. forces against Taliban and al Qaeda targets in Pakistan, which increased substantially in 2009, also has produced a much lower ratio of civilian to military deaths. Where an army previously would have blasted its way in to the militants' hideouts, killing and displacing civilians by the tens of thousands as it went, and then ultimately reducing whole towns and villages to rubble with inaccurate artillery and aerial bombing in order to get at a few enemy fighters, now a drone flies in and lets fly a single missile against a single house where militants are gathered. Yes, sometimes such attacks hit the wrong house, but by any historical comparison the rate of civilian deaths has fallen dramatically.

So far has this trend come, and so much do we take it for granted, that a single errant missile that killed ten civilians in Afghanistan was front-page news in February 2010. This event, a terrible tragedy in itself, nonetheless was an exception to a low overall rate of harm to civilians in the middle of a major military offensive, one of the largest in eight years of war. Yet, these ten deaths brought the U.S. military commander in

Afghanistan to offer a profuse apology to the president of Afghanistan, and the world news media to play up the event as a major development in the offensive. The point is not that killing ten civilians is OK, but rather that in any previous war, even a few years ago, this kind of civilian death would barely have caused a ripple of attention.

Civilian deaths, in sizable numbers, used to be universally considered a necessary and inevitable, if perhaps unfortunate, by-product of war. That we are entering an era when these assumptions no longer apply is good news indeed. Also, although the proportion of civilians to military killed in wars has not changed over the centuries, the nature of that killing has changed, from deliberate massacre of civilians up through World War II to mostly inadvertent and indirect civilian deaths more recently.

In summary, the 90-10 claim rests on erroneous World War I data wrongly compared with incompatible 1980s data. Notwithstanding variations from one war to another, there is no evidence showing a change in the overall military-to-civilian ratio for war deaths over the past hundred years. The best guess is that the ratio remains something like 50-50.

II. The Congo War Killed 5.4 Million People—Not

If you Google the terms *Congo* and *5.4 million* you will find seventeen thousand Web pages telling you that the war in the Congo in 1998–2003 killed 5.4 million people. The 5.4 million figure is widely repeated, often with the added "fact" that this makes the Congo War "the world's most deadly since the end of World War 2." These facts fill the first paragraph of Wikipedia's entry on the Congo War. The number gains authority from its seeming precision, with a decimal point. But in fact it is wrong, not even very close. And you do not have to be a statistician to understand why.

THE IRC STUDY

It all started with the International Rescue Committee (IRC), an NGO that does fine humanitarian work around the world and raises funds for its work in the Congo. An epidemiologist working for the IRC (now at

Columbia University), Les Roberts, carried out surveys in Congo over several years to estimate mortality in the conflict-ridden east of the country. Roberts and his collaborators "estimate that about 3.9 million people have died as a result of the conflict between August, 1998, and April, 2004." (The war formally ended in 2003.) Later surveys—although only the 2004 one was published—continued to estimate the "excess deaths" from Congo's elevated mortality rate, and add them to the total number of deaths. The most recent such estimate was 5.4 million in 2008, and rising.

Unlike the very high estimates Roberts did of war deaths in Iraq after 2003, mentioned in Chapter 9, the Congo estimates did not create controversy and quickly became embedded as truths in the public discourse. *New York Times* columnist Nicholas Kristof in 2010 used the IRC figures as attention-getting starting points for his columns. However, while his columns focus on small-scale human stories of direct violence, especially rape and torture, the large-scale numbers he presents, from the IRC, are indirect deaths, caused by war's secondary effects on malnutrition, disease, and other public health concerns, rather than direct deaths caused by war violence. This is an important distinction, because the direct violence that Kristof describes is actually fairly localized and small-scale, but the indirect deaths claimed by the IRC are huge. (The IRC estimated that even during the war years, only 10 percent of excess deaths were caused directly by violence, a fraction that would be much lower by today.)

COMPARING TO AN UNKNOWN

Researchers have criticized the IRC survey on several grounds, such as for sampling in especially violent areas and extrapolating the results to larger regions less affected by violence. But the big issue is the data the IRC did *not* measure, namely the mortality rate in eastern Congo *before* war began in 1996. The deaths attributed to the war are calculated from the mortality rate during and after the war compared with the rate before the war. But neither the IRC nor anyone else knows what the "before" number is.

The IRC researchers arbitrarily used the average mortality rate for all of sub-Saharan Africa—18 per thousand annually—as representing Congo's rate before the war. But this is a very bad choice, because clearly

Congo's mortality rate was already much worse than the African average before the wars ever broke out in 1996. This is because Congo is much poorer than the average African country, which itself is none too rich.

How much poorer is Congo than Africa as a whole? In the World Bank's recent listing of the GDP per person in 210 countries, Congo ranked dead last, with $280 per person per year, well under a dollar a day. That is the average per person for a country of 60 million people. The same GDP number for sub-Saharan Africa as a whole was $1,950. Clearly, these income differences created high mortality in the Congo compared with sub-Saharan Africa as a whole—war or no war.

The researchers also extend the war deaths estimate forward year by year as the war itself recedes into the past (notwithstanding localized outbreaks ever since). Their idea is that the war shocked the mortality rate up from the African average to a high level, which has remained elevated ever since because of the residual impact of the war. But this is not the case—Congo's mortality rate was *rising* before the wars began in 1996 and *falling* after the war ended in 2003. The only indirect deaths that derive from the war would be those during the temporary additional rise in mortality during the war years themselves. We do not have a good estimate of that, but looking at the available numbers and estimates, the total war deaths is clearly much more like 1–2 million than the claimed 5.4 million and counting.

Congo's mortality rate was similar to the African average soon after independence in 1960. In the late 1970s there was a sharp and sustained drop in the price of copper, Congo's major export, on world markets. Also, Mobutu nationalized industry and kicked out foreign investors. The GDP began a long decline that lasted into the late 1990s and cut the income per person in half. In those years mortality began to rise, even as the African average continued to fall. This was before the war started.

By the time the war broke out in 1996, mortality was already elevated in the poor eastern part of the country, and presumably the war made it worse still (most wars do). The arrival of the UN and humanitarian NGOs somewhat countered this effect—for instance, war refugees could be conveniently vaccinated—but undoubtedly the overall effect of the war was to increase mortality. The IRC surveys show a drop by about one-third in the mortality rate in the conflict-ridden east of the country in 2001–02, even though the war was still continuing there. Perhaps the arrival of humanitarian aid helped. After 2003 when the war officially ended and violence became more localized, the rate dropped steadily but more gradually, and in 2007 was about half the rate during the war.

When the Vancouver group recalculated excess deaths using different estimates instead of the African average, the numbers changed a lot. For the subperiod 2001–07, they revised the IRC estimate of 2.8 million down to 0.9 million. Both numbers have a large "confidence interval," a statistical term meaning that the real numbers could be way above or below the estimates of 2.8 million or 0.9 million.

The *New York Times* headline when the new IRC survey came out in 2008, was "Congo's Death Rate Remains Unchanged Since War Ended in 2003, Survey Shows." This is completely untrue! Congo's death rate went down impressively and steadily in those five years, just no faster than the African average went down (and the African rate went down more than in the past thanks to HIV/AIDS drugs).

A peer review by an "interagency initiative hosted by WHO," charged with providing impartial information on mortality in crisis areas, concluded that mortality in eastern Congo was indeed elevated (though less than the IRC researchers claimed) but that the war in 1998 did not cause a sharp spike in mortality. The "crucial difference" between the IRC study and a contradictory study by Belgian researchers "is not so much the mortality level, but that [the Belgians] do not believe that the very high mortality levels arrived with the war."

In short, a lot of Congolese people have died too young. The big causes of these deaths were colonialism, poverty, Mobutu, and the price of copper. War also undoubtedly added to the toll, but nowhere close to 5.4 million.

NOT THE DEADLIEST

A final note: Even if the Congo War *had* indirectly killed 5.4 million people, that would not make it the deadliest conflict since World War II. Using the IRC's criteria for indirect war deaths, that distinction goes to the Korean War, which began in 1950 and has never officially ended. A truce has held since 1953, but the war locked in place a terrible situation in North Korea that continues to kill. As a rough estimate, the war itself killed somewhere close to 3 million people, and by one estimate another 5–6 million starved during it. The North Korean government has since killed, by one estimate, something on the order of another 1.5 million people, in various purges and in concentration camps. In the late 1990s, the terrible condition of the North's economy culminated in another famine that killed perhaps 3 million more. Along the way, the economic condition of North Korea, where every resource goes to the military and the government, raised mortality for decades. Add that in and the total approaches 15 million people.

In terms of direct deaths from violence, the Congo War ranks seventh since World War II ended. Considering that other wars higher on the list were also in very poor countries with poor public health systems (China, Korea, Afghanistan, Cambodia), there is no solid reason to believe that the ratio of indirect to direct deaths was higher in Congo than in these other devastating wars. My best guess is that in indirect deaths, as in direct ones, Congo would rank about seventh.

III. An Epidemic of Sexual Violence Is Raging Unabated in Congo—Not

Related to the issue of mortality in eastern Congo is that of sexual violence there. First let us agree on the aspects of this problem that are indisputable: Many thousands of women and girls (and fewer men and boys) suffered sexual violence during the war in 1996–2003, during the sporadic outbreaks of fighting since 2003, and during postconflict phases in areas where life is still insecure despite the end of active fighting. These rapes and other violent attacks were perpetrated mainly by armed men, from the government army and various rebel factions, sometimes as a deliberate policy to terrorize civilians and other times as a result of poor discipline. Responding to these large-scale crimes received too little attention and resources until recent years, when the response by the international community has sharply increased. For example, NGOs such as Human Rights Watch and Oxfam, leading politicians such as Hillary Clinton (who traveled to eastern Congo in 2009 to address the problem), and UN agencies from the Security Council to the population fund and

UNICEF, all actively engaged the problem of rape in eastern Congo in 2008–10. Wartime sexual violence, in Congo and elsewhere, is a serious war crime and must be treated as such.

THE HARVARD STUDY

Still, the question is, with the war largely over and outbreaks of fighting gradually diminishing, is the problem of rape getting better, staying the same, or getting worse? In 2010, the top UN official for humanitarian affairs, John Holmes, flew into eastern Congo and declared that "sexual violence is as bad as ever" there. The *New York Times* story reporting his trip noted that "a recent study showed that it was not just the myriad armed groups haunting the hills who were preying upon women. The number of rapes by civilians has increased 17-fold in recent years."

This recent study was sponsored by a humanitarian NGO and carried out by medical researchers at Harvard. The NGO pitched the results as "Sexual violence on rise in DR Congo." The second sentence says, "The study shows a shocking 17-fold increase in rapes carried out by civilians between 2004 and 2008." *The New York Times*, evidently, reported the story right from this press release without reading the report.

The Harvard researchers' actual report tells a completely different story. The purpose of the study was to evaluate trends in sexual violence in eastern Congo over a five-year period, 2004 to 2008, starting the year after the war officially ended. The researchers studied a single hospital, Panzi Hospital, in Bukavu, in South Kivu Province, where the majority of patients are rape survivors receiving care under the hospital's Swedish-funded "Victims of Sexual Violence Program," which provides them with medical, psychological, and economic assistance. The researchers reviewed intake interviews on about 4,000 women, representing about half the total treated for sexual violence in 2004–08. The interviews indicated the type of incidents and perpetrators for each case, although data were far from complete.

Of all these cases, just over half the assailants were identified as soldiers—and these included nearly all the cases of gang rape and sexual slavery, which were common among military-perpetrated rapes. Another 42 percent were committed by unspecified assailants, and only 6 percent by "civilians." This last category, a very small minority of the total, was where the seventeen-fold increase took place. These cases rose from 6 individuals in 2004 to 104 in 2008.

But what about the far larger numbers of military and unspecified perpetrators? The picture is quite the opposite. Sexual assaults by armed combatants *decreased* by 77 percent from 2004 to 2008. And those by unspecified assailants *decreased* by 92 percent. Looking at all sexual violence cases in this study—military, civilian, and unspecified combined—the total numbers drop year by year, from 1,064 in 2004 to 272 in 2008, a total *decrease of three-quarters* of the total. (The decrease is steady over the years and therefore does not seem to be just a drop-off after the open fighting in Bukavu in 2004.) Gang rapes, which were the majority of assaults in 2004, dropped by 84 percent. Sexual slavery, a smaller category, dropped by about 60 percent. The headline should read, "Sexual Violence Falls Dramatically in DR Congo!" Of course, this conclusion would rest on shaky ground, since the study did not have a representative sample of women in the area—but at least the conclusion would accurately reflect what the study found.

The "shocking" rise in civilian rapes is portrayed by the report as implying "a normalization of rape among the civilian population, suggesting the erosion of all constructive social mechanisms that ought to protect civilians. . . ." But is even this civilian increase real? The "unspecified" cases, 42 percent of the total, were those for which women gave no identifying information about the assailant, and thus include both civilian and military rapes—and these unspecified rapes dropped sharply. If you do the math, it turns out that if as few as 20 percent of the unspecified rapes were civilian, the seventeen-fold increase in civilian rapes would disappear and there would be no increase at all in civilian rapes.

Previous reports considered trends through time even less carefully than the Harvard researchers did. A report by the UN secretary-general in 2008 that focuses on children simply says that a high rate of new rape cases persists where fighting was taking place in the Kivus, "while the number of reported cases in post-conflict zones seems to have decreased." A report by Human Rights Watch in 2009 reported that "as fighting intensified in North Kivu in 2008, so did the cases of sexual violence." This makes sense—where fighting increases, so does sexual violence, and where it ends (such as near Panzi Hospital) sexual violence decreases.

WORST IN THE WORLD?

The UN Population Fund refers to an "epidemic of sexual violence" in the Congo, saying that "the prevalence of rape in this region has been described as the worst in the world." The UN special representative on sexual violence called the country the "rape capital of the world." There is unfortunately a lot of rape around the world, so some data would be useful in assessing this claim that Congo is the worst. In early 2010, the Population Fund released an estimate of "sexual violence committed by warring factions," mostly by the Rwandan Hutu militia that fled to Congo after the Rwandan genocide, but also by government troops. The Fund also "noted that humanitarian agencies have praised the Government for its efforts to end rape committed by its troops, but believe that much more can be done. . . ." It reported that sexual violence had become "endemic," with an estimated 8,000 women raped in 2009. A previous report found 16,000 cases in 2008 countrywide (a larger area than the 2009 estimate covers, apparently).

Human Rights Watch, however, criticizes these estimates as representing "only a small percentage of the total reported cases." For instance, in South Kivu in 2008 the UN Population Fund reported fewer than 3,000, whereas a local provincial commission reported more than 10,000. It is unclear whether this is an unusual case, or representative of remaining pockets of conflict, or representative of the whole country. The UN Population Fund numbers thus may be understated but are a useful starting point.

Obviously 8,000 rapes in the eastern Congo in 2009 is 8,000 too many, but to put it in perspective, the most conflict-riven provinces, the Kivus and Orientale, in 2002 contained something like 15–20 million people, of whom more than 10 million were age twelve or older. So 8,000 rapes equates to something on the order of magnitude of one case per thousand population twelve and older. Maybe it is really several per thousand, not one, but that is the approximate range.

By comparison, U.S. crime statistics show rape rates dropping from 2.5 per thousand in 1973 to 0.8 in 2008—the same general range of incidence as the Congo. For other countries, the World Health Organization counted the percent of women sixteen and older who said they had been sexually assaulted in the previous five years, based on international crime victim surveys. The figure ranged from below 1 percent in the Philippines and Botswana to 6 percent in Albania and 8 percent in Brazil, with a median across twenty countries of around 3 percent. The 8,000 rapes in eastern Congo in a year would equate to something like 1 percent on this scale (which is for a five-year period and a somewhat different age range). Again, perhaps the real Congo rate is several times higher but that would still leave it near the international average.

The point is not the accuracy of these estimates, which are probably low for various reasons, but rather just that 8,000 rapes *sounds* like a war-induced epidemic but might not differ that much from the sexual violence that goes on in peacetime around the world. By contrast, when the Congo War was at its height, there is ample evidence that sexual violence increased sharply and that gang rape accounted for most cases. In South Kivu in 1996–2003, almost 80 percent of reported rapes in one study were perpetrated by more than one attacker—an indicator of rapes carried out by armed groups. Wartime rapes may also be more brutal, although sexual violence anytime constitutes torture, so perhaps this distinction should not be overemphasized.

As the Population Fund mentions, the government *is* implementing measures, imperfectly, to address the problem. Also many NGOs, international organizations including the UN, and national governments are working on the problem of sexual violence in eastern Congo. Finally, the levels of overall violence in eastern Congo have been much lower overall than in 1998–2003. So it should not be hard to believe that sexual violence has diminished since then. To say that Congo's sexual violence has not improved, and is still the worst in the world, is to say that no good came of the efforts of the UN, the international community, and NGOs to address this problem, and that the end of most fighting did not affect it either. One wonders why the NGOs would even continue their work in the Congo in that case.

OVERSIMPLIFYING THE VIOLENCE

A recent Swedish analysis criticized the oversimplified portrayal of a Congolese epidemic of sexual violence used as a weapon of war. The reality is much more complex, and hinges on serious problems with integrating militia fighters into the national army, which itself had been severely corrupted during the Mobutu years. Since 2003, the army has seen "the constant addition of new armed units to be integrated. . . . Hence, the army is undergoing constant reorganisation," with armed factions being broken apart to the platoon level, given at most three months of training, and re-formed into new army units. In North Kivu Province in 2009, some 12,000 soldiers from several militia groups were integrated in this way, with no training, "all in the middle of ongoing military operations." The resulting low level of discipline in the army became even worse because of the "widespread use of alcohol and drugs" by the fighters both before and after their integration into the army, and the fact that they were badly paid, if at all.

With a decades-long history of bad civil-military relations, in which governments used the military to oppress the population, the conflict-ridden parts of the country have seen "extreme violence" against civilian men and women, with rape being only one item on a list of crimes and atrocities. "One problem with the exclusive focus on sexual violence is that it tends to downplay the ways in which sexual violence is not only (or simply) . . . a war against women. . . ." Men and boys also suffer from sexual attacks, and women from nonsexualized assaults.

Another problem with the heavy emphasis on sexual violence is that "vast resources from international organisations [are] earmarked for various services to rape survivors," such as access to medical care or direct financial assistance. Because these basic needs are often lacking for the general population, "destitute women and girls who are not rape survivors sometimes present themselves as rape victims" to gain access to them. For example, women with fistulas related to childbirth cannot receive medical help unless they present themselves as rape survivors. In addition, services provided only to rape survivors often include "food aid, training/education, and credit. . . ." Some local women's rights groups have criticized the focus on sexual violence to the exclusion of other problems, but say that because of "the interests of donors . . . it is very difficult to get funding for projects dealing with other forms of violence." Women's problems ranging from domestic violence to war atrocities to inheritance and property rights, get lost in the scramble for rape-related funding, as the donors "are mostly interested just in sexual violence . . . ," in the words of a Congolese activist.

RECENT MASS RAPE INCIDENTS

Misunderstandings about the scope and nature of the rape problem distort effective responses. This problem occurred in 2010 when a militia group went on a four-day rampage in a remote area of eastern Congo and gang-raped about 300 women. The UN had some peacekeepers twenty miles away who did not know about the attacks and did not respond to stop them. After information about this atrocity came to light, *The New York Times* ran four news articles about it in late August and early September, followed by a large color photo and article above the fold on page one in early October. Readers may not have realized that the series of headlines about war rapes in Congo in this period were all about the same incident. In the October attention-grabber, the first hint that this was not a new incident came several paragraphs into the article, after a present-tense headline, a photo caption, and a graphic description of a rape scene.

The article quotes feminist author Eve Ensler (*The Vagina Monologues*): "Congo is the U.N.'s crowning failure." Really? The fact that a forward base of peacekeepers did not manage to prevent or respond to a war atrocity can certainly be chalked up as a failure, but one of many failures and successes that must be weighed together. As we have seen, the UN does not have a perfect record in the Congo; it made mistakes and suffered setbacks. In this case it was ineffective. But the point that is completely lost in the frenzy of finger-pointing about this rape attack is that this kind of atrocity is much less common now than during the war a decade earlier, when the UN arrived. This was a single atrocity with hundreds of victims, on the scale of, say, the Oklahoma City bombing. The UN's failure to eliminate all atrocities is not a "crowning failure," or even its biggest failure, which would probably be Rwanda where the UN pulled out and let extremists massacre more than half a million people (and rape many of them).

In early 2011, another series of rape attacks occurred in eastern Congo, with at least five incidents and more than 150 victims. This time, the attacks took place in a remote, inaccessible region where peacekeepers were not present. So again, the UN's "failure" seems to be a lack of resources to be everywhere in a vast country with few roads and little infrastructure.

The recent mass rapes were not carried out with impunity. In October 2010, the UN arrested the chief of staff of the rebel group, the man accused of coordinating the 2010 attacks. He faces a trial by the Congolese government. And in the 2011 attacks, the government prosecuted the accused soldiers and sentenced their commanding officer to twenty years in prison.

SUCCESS OR FAILURE?

The UN does not have the resources and personnel to effectively enforce the rule of law in a country of 60 million extremely poor people with dysfunctional government, army, and police. Military planners can tell you how many troops would be needed for this purpose in this size country, and it runs into the hundreds of thousands—many times more than the 20,000 the UN has sent there. Our governments have not given the UN enough money and troops to succeed, certainly not enough to stop the sporadic atrocities that still plague eastern Congo.

Think of it this way. The ratio of population to peacekeepers in Congo, about 3,000:1, would mean that my nice little New England college town, population around 30,000—currently patrolled by nearly fifty police officers—would instead have about ten peacekeepers. Now imagine that you burn most of our property, homes, colleges, and commerce to the ground, reducing the population to near-starvation levels of poverty, with some displaced from their homes. Also, give groups of young men automatic weapons and the ability to get rich using them to control what wealth is left. Now tell me how well our ten peacekeepers are going to do in preventing horrendous crimes from occurring. By the way, they get paid a pittance, do not speak the local language here, and have poor equipment and information.

If the UN accomplishes most of what it came to accomplish in the Congo—end the fighting and begin the government on a path to progress—but leaves some things undone such as eliminating militias that occasionally commit atrocities, is that failure? It comes back to the question I raised in the prologue: "Compared to what?" The security situation in eastern Congo is terrible, all right, but still not as terrible as five years ago, before the UN shifted its focus to civilian protection. It is not nearly as terrible as in the all-out war years of 1998–2003. And it would be hard to be nostalgic for the earlier period of Mobutu's dictatorship, either, when the economy shrank by half, much less the seventy brutal years of Belgian colonialism. So, no, we should not rest while mass rapes and other atrocities continue to occur anywhere, but our judgments of success and failure must rest on the big picture and not spectacular, attention-grabbing episodes.

THE MORAL DILEMMA

NGOs have used both the 5.4 million deaths and the epidemic of sexual violence to show how bad the Congo situation is, to motivate people to help. They seem to have succeeded at this laudable goal. The IRC authors themselves noted in 2006 that "following the release of the 2000 survey results, total humanitarian aid increased by over 500% between 2000 and 2001. The United States' contribution alone increased by a factor of almost twenty-six. It is probably fair to assert that the mortality data played a significant role in increasing international assistance." They write that the 2004 survey, claiming 38,000 "excess deaths" monthly, even though the war had ended, "helped to keep the humanitarian situation in DRC before donors and was probably a factor in the 45% increase in total aid between 2004 and 2005." But they also note that aid remains far below needed levels, at about $11 a year per person in the affected population.

Thus, mortality and rape estimates for the Congo present a real moral dilemma. On the one hand, exaggerated figures apparently actually did draw the world's attention to a forgotten conflict and thereby helped save lives. On the other hand, making science serve political ends, even desirable ones, usually does not end well. And what happens to the international community's ability to respond to wars and crises effectively if *every* humanitarian need (and there are many in this world) shortcuts science and data in the service of big emotional appeals designed to win donors?

Interestingly, a similar question arose in 2010 when new data showed a sharp worldwide drop in deaths of women during childbirth. The research showed that lower pregnancy rates, higher incomes, more education, and an increase in trained birth attendants paid off in a drop from 526,000 maternal deaths in 1980 to 343,000 in 2008. Good news—but "some advocates for women's health tried to pressure *The Lancet* [the journal publishing the results] into delaying publication of the new findings, fearing that good news would detract from the urgency of their cause." The *Lancet* editor disagreed, saying that "actually these numbers help their cause, not hinder it." As one of the researchers—epidemiologist Christopher Murray at the University of Washington—noted, "there has been a perception of no progress," but in fact "some of the policies and programs pursued may be having an effect, as opposed to all that effort with little to show for it." On a radio program, the *Lancet* editor elaborated that the research would counter the idea that donors were throwing away "good money after bad [with] nothing to show for it." As it turned out, their investment had "made a huge difference."

In the end, does it matter if "only" 1 or 2 million people died as a result of the Congo War, making it not the deadliest since World War II but only one of the bad wars of our times? Would we conclude that Congo does not need the world's help as much as if 5 million had died? Actually, I doubt that anyone would find Congo less deserving if we accepted a more realistic, lower mortality estimate. What draws people to help are the human stories such as Nicholas Kristof tells, of women raped, families destroyed, people living in misery. War at any scale is a catastrophe that deserves a response.

Similarly, the NGO's motive for playing up the "rise" in sexual violence in the Congo was a good one—to draw attention to the problem so that the international community responds more forcefully and so that donors give them more money to carry out their programs to help rape survivors in eastern Congo. However, the effect may be the opposite. *The New York Times* reports that "Eastern Congo is stuck in a rut of violence, and the United Nations is concerned that donors and Western governments are getting tired of the steady stream of bad news that spews out of this vast nation." (But does bad news spew out of Congo because things are not improving, or because NGOs and reporters play up bad news and ignore good news?) Why should donors put money into the Congo if the situation is getting worse, or no better, despite years of international assistance—including the world's largest and most expensive peacekeeping mission—and despite a specific focus on sexual violence there in recent years?

As tempting as it is to draw attention and money to the Congo by alarmism, it is scary to see this approach play out toward its logical conclusion of radical steps such as pulling out the UN or instituting a foreign military occupation of the Congo. Listen to some readers' comments on the *New York Times* website in 2010 in response to Kristof's column about the 6.9 million dead (and still rising) and the ongoing epidemic of sexual violence: "Congo would be better off as a colony. . . . How else might this horror be stopped?" "If what you say is substantially true . . . then the Congo is truly hell on earth. The only way to bring civility to such a place would be to install a brutally punitive, but fair, military occupation." "Has anyone . . . tried to determine if Africa and Africans have been better or worse off since colonial rule ended?" "Every single person who is under the UN umbrella is collaborating to this crime with their silence." These four comments appear in just the first ten posts in response to the Kristof column.

Finally, although the issue is complex, I detect an element of racism in the popular discourse portraying Congo as a place of uncontrolled brutality. It is "darkest Africa," with black men as rapists and people so uncivilized that they commit atrocities all the time. One would hardly be surprised to read that a rebel militia had captured a white foreign humanitarian and boiled her in a big pot of water for dinner. The suggestions to put Congo back under colonial rule—made with no apparent awareness of their irony—are understandable given this level of misunderstanding and stereotyping about the Congo.

11

WARS OF THE WORLD

The Fires Still Smoldering

The gory headlines are right about one thing—war remains a serious problem in our world. However much humanity has accomplished in the past, much work remains to do in the future. Wars still kill.

I. The State of the World

Where do we stand, then, in terms of wars in progress? (This snapshot as of early 2011 will change in details in the coming years, but at the moment the overall situation has not changed much in several years.)

ABSENCE OF INTERSTATE WAR

The most important thing to notice is what you do *not* find in 2011—interstate wars, between uniformed government armies with heavy weapons. Around the world, almost all nations maintain capable military forces. Those forces contain some 20 million soldiers worldwide, several million of them in designated combat units. They are armed to the teeth with guns, planes, ships, missiles, submarines, helicopters, drones, flamethrowers, bayonets, nuclear weapons, and every other conceivably useful means of destruction. They are full-time, trained personnel. But nowhere in the world are those military forces fighting each other.

This absence of interstate war is relatively new, and still imperfect, but is the single most important cause of decreasing levels of war over recent decades. It represents a triumph for the international system, with the UN at its center, based on states' sovereignty and territorial integrity.

Taking interstate wars off the table has rid us, for the most part, of large battles with heavy weapons such as tanks and artillery, which are hugely lethal and destructive (think of the so-called "shock and awe" bombing of Baghdad in 2003). Along the spectrum of war types—from terrorism at the low end through civil war up to interstate wars and global nuclear war at the high end—we have cut away progressively at the top layers, the most destructive ones, over several generations.

The Democratic Peace

Many researchers credit the decline of interstate war to the "democratic peace" theory, which says that democracies rarely fight each other, although they fight nondemocracies. This simple, easily understood theory has spawned a profusion of statistical studies seeking to slice and dice the phenomenon every which way to see if it holds up and what causes it. But political scientists do not agree on the causes of the democratic peace. "We know it works in practice. Now we have to see if it works in theory!"

Democracy turns out to be a tricky thing to measure, because no democracy is perfect (the phrase *Bush v. Gore* comes to mind), yet even totalitarian governments hold elections and claim to be democratic. The least democratic country in the world, North Korea, has the word *Democratic* in its official name.

One plausible theory that does not hold up is that democracies are more peaceful in general (not just to each other). In fact, democracy can promote war by amplifying ethnic and nationalist forces. Early liberal theorists such as Paine and Kant believed that selfish autocrats caused wars, whereas the common people, who bear the costs, would be loath to go to war. But history does not support this view, as the common people often have clamored for war and even forced their leaders into it.

Yale political scientist Bruce Russett, a major figure in this field, and coauthor John Oneal, describe a "Kantian peace" based on three mutually supporting trends that the philosopher Immanuel Kant had linked to peace. The three—democracy, economic interdependence (especially international trade), and the growth of international organizations— reinforce each other in a "virtuous circle," with each also reinforcing peace and being reinforced by peace. Thus, while any one component, such as democracy alone, might not sustain a general peace, the combination proves robust. (The connection to Kant is tenuous, especially concerning democracy, but that is beside the point.) Classical liberals advocated both democracy and free trade as ways to increase peace.

Russett and Oneal's statistical analysis confirms that economic interdependence, including trade, lowers the chance of a militarized dispute between two countries. Economic interdependence and democracy in turn create a need for—and then support the success of—international law and organizations, such as the UN. These organizations reduce war by mediating conflicts, making information more transparent, and shaping social norms. Since 1945, rapid growth has occurred in the number of international organizations, the number of democracies, and trade as a percent of the world economy.

In thinking about economic interdependence as a source of peace, democratic peace researchers have focused on trade. John Stuart Mill wrote in 1848 that "the great extent and rapid increase in international trade [is] the principal guarantee of the peace of the world." But recently some researchers have suggested that the democratic peace is at heart a "capitalist peace" based not only on trade itself but on the declining importance of territory and the integration of capital markets.

Economic development may play an important role in the democratic peace, though that role is somewhat unclear. Military historian Azar Gat finds the economic explanation better than the democratic one. "For example, . . . economically developed democracies are far more likely to be peaceful towards one another than are poor democracies. In fact, the democratic peace phenomenon between poor democracies has been found to be weak at best." However, this seems to apply only to very low income levels. Historically, before the industrial revolution—admittedly a very long time ago—democracies fought each other, as when Athens fought Syracuse in 415–413 B.C. This and other examples show that the democratic peace is not an absolute rule but just a strong regularity. Rising wealth through time seems to reinforce the democratic peace, but not substitute for it as Gat and some others imply.

Economic development goes with the emergence of strong states. Over the past five centuries, the "processes of state formation in Europe . . . were attended by wars, revolutions, rebellions, and massacres," writes political scientist Kalevi Holsti. Poorer parts of the world have not completed this process. They have weak states that appear authoritarian but whose actual reach "is seriously limited by local centers of resistance, by bureaucratic inertia and corruption, and by social fragmentation along religious, ethnic, tribal, factional, and cultural lines."

It is hard to tell whether democracy causes peace because there is only one world, evolving through time, and no control group. Being democratic leads two countries to be more peaceful to each other, but a third factor, such as economic prosperity, could cause both democracy and peacefulness toward other democracies. Maybe democracies do not fight because they trade a lot or because they tend to be well-established countries. Despite these uncertainties, the most convincing explanation of reduced interstate war seems to be, as Russett and Oneal argue, a combination of democracy, economic interdependence, and (most important, in my view) the development of international organizations, including the UN.

Territory

A major element in the decline of interstate wars is the stability of international borders, which historically have been a major issue of contention and cause of wars. "The decline of successful wars of territorial aggrandizement during the last half century is palpable. In fact, there has not been a case of successful territorial aggrandizement since 1976." Evolving norms following each World War and in the period since have emphasized "respect for states' territorial integrity before self-determination for ethnic communities."

Of 227 conflicts in 1946–2004, 60 percent were over territory. "Above all, the struggle over territory is generally recognized to be the most pervasive form of conflict." Similarly, in 1648–1713 in Europe, "contests over territory constitute the most significant source of war. . . ." Of twenty-two wars in that period, more than half had a territorial issue at stake. In 1713–1815, territory again was the most frequent issue leading to war. Colonial competition was far less important. But by the time of 1815–1914, territory declined in importance and "problems of state creation" rose to the top of the list of issues wars were fought over, as the nineteenth century was "the era of nation-state creation and . . . of the destruction of empires." In the period between the World Wars, "territory remained the single most important source of international conflict." And even in the 1945–89 years, "territory remains . . . a significant and continuing source of international conflict." Nonetheless, "since Napoleon's defeat there has been a gradual decline in the prominence of this issue." The importance of territory as a source of war fell by about half from its peak in the eighteenth century to the Cold War according to Holsti.

Peace researcher Kenneth Boulding suggested in 1978 that the "first plank" in a peace policy should be "the removal of national boundaries from political agendas." Actually, since he wrote that more than thirty years ago, the number of attempts to change international borders has been minuscule, especially compared with historical experience. That alone is persuasive evidence that the nature of armed conflict is changing profoundly.

FIVE MIDSIZED WARS

With interstate wars absent, *all* the armed conflicts in the world today are civil wars. In each of them, a national government is fighting against insurgent forces, which often operate out of uniform and do not follow the laws of war. In a few cases, notably Afghanistan and Iraq, foreign forces are fighting in support of the government. In no case is a foreign government sending troops to fight *against* a government in a civil war, which would pit the two state armies against each other. At most, foreign governments might covertly provide economic or military assistance to the insurgents, or give them sanctuary on the foreign country's territory, as for instance Chad and Sudan do with each other's rebels.

Before considering what we know about civil wars in general—their causes, their character, and their termination—let us look at who is fighting, where, and why.

In 2009, six civil wars exceeded 1,000 battle-related deaths per year. With the end of the war in Sri Lanka in 2009, five remain. They are Pakistan, Afghanistan, Iraq, Somalia, and Congo. (In 2011, Libya would join the list.) Of these, Afghanistan and Iraq, where America is at war, are the deadliest and most expensive. Four of the five are majority-Muslim countries where governments are fighting Islamist insurgents.

These five biggest wars are not actually very big. They are *midsized wars* by historical standards. No *large wars*, those that kill by the millions, are in progress. In terms of people killed, the five biggest wars today really do not stack up against the biggest of the Cold War—Korea and Vietnam—and pale in comparison with the killing rates of the World Wars. Just from an American perspective, the more than 50,000 U.S. deaths in Vietnam far exceed the fewer than 10,000 U.S. deaths in Iraq, Afghanistan, the War on Terror, and 9/11 combined—precious though each of those lives is.

The data for the latest available year, 2008, show nearly 50,000 battle-related deaths worldwide, with half coming from Iraq (lower by 2011) and Sri Lanka (ended in 2009). Another quarter come from Afghanistan and Pakistan. By all evidence the total was no higher in 2009 and 2010, although the data are not in. By comparison, during all the time since 1946 the world total battle deaths fell below 50,000 in only four years.

Let us take a quick trip along an arc from Pakistan to Congo that includes these five wars, to get a basic overview of the main wars now in progress. Start in the tribal areas of Pakistan along the Afghan border. American military operations in recent years have degraded al Qaeda's leadership, killing Osama bin Laden and dozens of mid-level militant leaders, but have yet to decisively defeat the organization and its affiliates around the world. This remote mountainous area contains many sympathizers and supporters of this kind of jihad.

Unmanned U.S. drones fly around the region and blow up gatherings of Islamist radicals if they can find them. In several areas, such as the Swat Valley, the Pakistani army has fought to take back control from the Pakistani Taliban, at least driving the militants out of population centers. In other areas, the Pakistani Taliban or other militant groups have more or less full control of their locales, and use them as bases to set off bombs across Pakistan from time to time. A different but loosely allied set of radical Islamist groups, including the Afghan Taliban, use the Pakistani tribal areas as a base to attack across the border into Afghanistan.

Not only do the extreme terrain and remoteness of this region make it difficult to fight these militants, but Pakistani politics are complicated as well. The government, an imperfect democracy in a divided country with wildly anti-American sentiments, receives substantial American support but does not condone U.S. drone attacks nor officially allow U.S. forces to operate within Pakistan. The Pakistani army, which ran the country until a few years ago under a pro-American military dictatorship, has an arsenal of dozens of nuclear weapons, used as a deterrent against India but also posing a theoretical, if slim, possibility that al Qaeda could get its hands on one.

Today's war lies under the shadow of the Soviet occupation of Afghanistan in 1979–89, and the American operations to oppose it. Today's enemies of America were in some ways a creation of the United States in the 1980s, when those Islamist militants fought the Soviets with U.S. support. Then, as now, Pakistan provided them a haven, and they streamed through the mountains into Afghanistan carrying U.S.-supplied weapons, including sophisticated Stinger shoulder-fired antiaircraft missiles. It worked; the Soviets left; the Soviet Union collapsed. And the United States just walked away, leaving a mess behind. One piece of that mess is the close connection between Pakistan's intelligence service and some militant groups fighting in Afghanistan. Some Pakistani officials continue to see these Afghan militants as a possible avenue of influence in Afghanistan in the future, even though they are fighting against the Americans.

To punish Pakistan for going nuclear, the United States froze delivery of F-16 fighter jets for years, without returning Pakistan's payment (the dispute has since been resolved). And to protect U.S. textile workers, the United States has kept high tariffs on Pakistan's main export, clothing. Pakistan remains a large, very poor country, and government services have barely reached outlying areas. Devastating floods in 2010 made things even worse.

However, although Pakistanis generally hate America and put little faith in Pakistan's government, they definitely do not want the Taliban to run the country. The fragile government—elected after an inspiring lawyers' campaign against the dictatorship and then the assassination of opposition leader Benazir Bhutto—remains the best hope for political progress in Pakistan. Who could blame Pakistanis if they feel angry? They have been let down by everyone, from the world's superpower to their own military and civilian leaders.

In a nutshell, that is the crazy war in Pakistan. A bevy of armed fanatics in one part of the country; a pile of nuclear weapons in another. America paying a government to root out militants, allow supply convoys into Afghanistan, and turn a blind eye to U.S. drone attacks, even while that government has secretly supported militants who attack U.S. soldiers in Afghanistan. There is no UN, no NATO, no peacekeepers, and precious little economic assistance. The government tried a cease-fire a few years ago but the Pakistani Taliban used it to extend control over sizable regions (which rallied the population behind the government and led to a government military offensive).

Now hop on one of those NATO supply convoys moving from a Pakistani port along switchbacks through the mountains into Afghanistan. These convoys come under attack fairly regularly. They and other convoys within Afghanistan were in the news in 2010 because a new report confirmed that security for them is provided by local companies under contract. Those companies sometimes pay the militants protection money to not attack the convoys. Thus U.S. money helps fund the Taliban. A more important source of Taliban money is opium production, very much tied up with Afghanistan's corrupt political economy. Afghan opium supplies 90 percent of the world's heroin. The Afghan Taliban moralistically condemns the drug, then uses huge profits from it to fund the insurgency.

Here in Afghanistan is the important war, to which Pakistan is mostly a sideshow. Everyone is here—the United States, NATO, the UN, humanitarian NGOs. The international community has taken a stand here, in support of the legitimate government (democratically elected, albeit in flawed elections), and against allowing Afghanistan to again become a safe haven for al Qaeda. The U.S. forces in Afghanistan are part of a NATO operation that includes substantial forces from Britain and other countries, operating under a UN mandate. In 2001, the Americans arrived to help overthrow the Taliban government. When this succeeded, the United States lost interest in Afghanistan as it had after the Soviets left, and turned its attention to a problematic adventure in Iraq. The Taliban regrouped and gained strength. In 2010 the United States escalated the size of its force in an attempt to make a counterinsurgency strategy work. Meanwhile a murky layer of tribal politics out of public view held the possibility that shifting allegiances and deals could change the war's course.

Continuing west from Afghanistan, we jet over Iran, a great source of tension in the region because of its nuclear program and its active support of terrorist organizations on Israel's borders. But Iran is not at war so we continue on and land in Iraq. The war there was several times larger than Afghanistan's, but has wound down substantially in recent years. Iraq has had a hard time of it for decades. The brutal dictatorship of Saddam Hussein favored his Sunni group and repressed both the Shiites (a majority of the population) and the Kurds, whom he massacred with poison gas at one point. The country's oil resources made it a middle-income country (not as poor as Pakistan and Afghanistan) but at the cost of corruption and authoritarianism. The 1980s were lost to a vast, costly, pointless war with Iran, and the 1990s to an era of UN-mandated economic sanctions after Saddam occupied Kuwait and sparked the 1991 Gulf War.

Iraq's programs to develop weapons of mass destruction (nuclear, chemical, and biological) were supposed to end after that war, but Saddam used delay and trickery until everyone believed he still had these capabilities. As it turned out, after the U.S. invaded and overthrew Saddam in 2003 without UN authorization, he did not. Then the Americans botched the occupation of the country so badly that looting and massive corruption were followed by years of insurgency against the Americans, scandals involving U.S. forces' behavior, and conflict between Sunnis and Shiites that escalated to civil war in 2006–07.

Only in the last few years, as the U.S. military has learned from this school of hard knocks, have things improved. Violence levels have fallen greatly, U.S. forces have been drawn down rapidly, and the Iraqi national army and police are taking on greater roles. Continuing political problems, such as the months of delays in forming a government after elections, and continuing economic problems (notably the lack of reliable electricity in most places) create conditions for possible reversals of recent progress. However, the Iraq situation is far better in 2011 than a few years ago.

From Iraq's southern port city we can hop a ship and follow the oil tankers out of the Persian Gulf. The never-ending stream of tankers from Saudi Arabia, Iraq, Iran, and other neighbors constitutes the vital artery of the world's major economies, from Europe to America to China, and in return flow vast sums of money concentrated in a few hands in a conflict-prone region. We will not follow the tankers to the rich countries, however, but peel off south of the Gulf and turn right for the Horn of Africa.

This path takes us, along with the tens of thousands of ships using the Suez Canal each year, into the area haunted by Somali pirates. From small boats they board large ships, overpower the crew, and sail to the northern Somali shore where they hold the ships and crew for million-dollar ransom payments (which usually do arrive). This is not a civil war or even a political action; it is strictly business, capitalizing on Somalia's weak government. This northern part of Somalia is otherwise fairly peaceful, although a group there in 2010 made an alliance with the Islamist militants in the rest of the country and may destroy that peace. Another large piece of northern Somalia, called Somaliland, operates independently in practice (it had a different colonial history) and is quite peaceful, relatively stable economically, and democratic. The main problem is with the central and southern part of Somalia, including most of the population, the capital city, and the port.

Somalia has a national government that includes moderate Islamists and other important constituencies and clans. The government has international recognition, UN approval, U.S. military backing, and protection provided by about 5,000 African Union (AU) peacekeepers, mostly Ugandan. But the government controls only a few blocks of the capital, around the presidential palace, and has only limited number and quality of armed forces under its control. Most of the country, and most of the capital, is controlled by a virulent Islamist faction called Al Shabab, affiliated with al Qaeda, and another Islamist faction. Al Shabab rules by fear, and its brand of Islamic law, such as amputating limbs and banning soccer, does not have popular support. In 2010, the group went international with a lethal bombing of civilians watching World Cup soccer in Uganda (which supplies AU troops in Somalia). As in Afghanistan, the religious motivations occupy one political layer on top of ethnic (or in Somalia's case, clan) groupings and conflicts.

The United States had a taste of complex Somali politics around the

1993 *Black Hawk Down* incident, and does not care to repeat the experience. The UN left after the United States did. As in Afghanistan, we are paying the price today in Somalia for mistakes made decades ago in failing to secure peace. Several years ago the Islamists won control of the capital and nearly the whole country, providing half a year of peace, albeit under harsh rule. But when they went to grab the last piece, where the official government was holed up near the Ethiopian border, the Ethiopians came in with a big force, smashed the Islamist militias, and restored Somalia's government in the capital. This turned out to be a fleeting victory, however. Partly because of long-standing conflicts between Somalia and Ethiopia, the invading troops were unwelcome, and the Islamists ran an increasingly deadly insurgency against them. Eventually the Ethiopians gave up and went home, leaving the Somali government with its few blocks of control and triggering the AU to send in peacekeepers to protect it there. Periodically the government promises a military offensive to expand its toehold, and periodically the AU peacekeepers lose Somali hearts and minds by shelling densely populated neighborhoods, but otherwise Somalia is stuck in a rut with no clear path forward.

From the capital, Mogadishu, take a car west to Nairobi (Kenya), then Kampala (Uganda) and Kigali (Rwanda), and just across the Congolese border to Bukavu, capital of South Kivu Province. This is where Panzi Hospital found fewer rape cases in the five years after the war ended in 2003 (as Chapter 10 described). Continue on into the Congo for a hundred-some miles, assuming you have four-wheel drive, and you arrive in remote mining areas where militias—Mai Mai and the Rwandan genocide perpetrators—control illegal mines and export minerals by small plane to Goma, where international buyers take over. This is the epicenter of the past and continuing troubles in eastern Congo.

The Rwandan militia has thousands of fighters and has persisted despite the efforts of both the Congolese national army and the Rwandan army (when it crosses the border to attack them). In recent years it has lost strength and some fighters have returned to Rwanda under UN repatriation programs. But violence continues. In 2010 the Rwandan militia attacked a small plane operated by Goma Express, one of fifteen planes a day to land at the airstrip of a mine controlled by Mai Mai militia. They stole $60,000 and took the Indian copilot hostage, though the pilot got away with the plane. Periodic military offensives bring misery to the Kivus, where conflict has proven surprisingly persistent (largely because of the mineral wealth that can sustain armed groups).

Various groups operate in eastern Congo and even those now officially integrated into the national army still cause mayhem. A rebel group from Uganda, the Lord's Resistance Army, whose memorable characteristic is its heavy use of child soldiers and its wanton massacres of civilians, has also made use of lawless eastern Congo as a safe haven (see Chapter 6). But the Rwandan militia is the main remaining security threat (along with a shakily integrated and poorly trained national army). So we end this short voyage in the eastern Congo, the poorest area of the poorest country on earth.

Looking back over these five midsized wars, some commonalities may be found. First, of course, each is a civil war, pitting a government against one or more armed insurgent groups. Second, in each case a reasonably legitimate, if flawed, government is fighting against some truly bad characters—al Qaeda, the Taliban, Iraqi suicide bombers, al Shabab, and the perpetrators of the Rwandan genocide. (I was surprised the first time I read the World Bank study on civil wars, coauthored by Collier, that the takeaway message seemed to be to support governments and suppress rebels—but upon reflection this actually makes some sense.)

Third, the kinds of issues being fought over are mostly similar. These are not wars of secession by a region, but wars over the type and control of government in each country. (In Congo, however, the Rwandan militia has no hope of regaining control of Rwanda, and has morphed into something closer to organized crime.) As a rule, the insurgents are unpopular with the population, although the governments to a lesser extent are also unpopular. The rebels are trying to shoot their way into power, or at least retain a sustainable "tax base," be it a population or an opium or mineral production area.

Fourth, the wars have strong international participation, though in different ways and to varying degrees. In Pakistan (the least internationalized), the United States hits militants with drones. In Afghanistan, NATO fights throughout the country. In Iraq, the U.S. presence has been pervasive. In Somalia, the African Union has troops on the ground to protect the government. And in the eastern Congo the UN's largest peacekeeping mission tries to bring stability and end the remaining fighting.

Of these five civil wars, Afghanistan is the most important, not only because it is the deadliest and most expensive but because of the investment of the international community on the government side. A lot is at stake there. (Pakistan may be the scariest because of nuclear weapons and the size, poverty, and anti-Americanism of the country, but I have emphasized that we should proceed from realities, not fears.)

ELEVEN SMALL WARS

Of the rest of the world's armed conflicts that killed at least 25 people in 2009, the Uppsala researchers list eleven as "major." I will call them "small wars," though of course they are not small if you are in the middle of one. Most have persisted for decades. Of these, six are disputes over control of the national government or over the form of governance—in *Sudan*, *Uganda*, *Colombia*, *Peru*, *the Philippines*, and the U.S. conflict with *al Qaeda*. The other five are disputes over territories where rebels want independence or autonomy. These tend to be more ethnically based. They are in Indian-controlled *Kashmir*, Burma's *Karen* region, the island of *Mindanao* in the Philippines, the *Kurdish* part of Turkey, and *Palestine*/Israel.

UN peacekeeping is largely absent in the five midsized and eleven small wars. Among the five, the UN has missions, but not peacekeepers, in Afghanistan and Iraq. Pakistan is fighting its war on its own, without the UN. In Somalia, a very inadequate African Union force does a very inadequate job of peacekeeping. Only Congo, among the five largest current wars, has a UN peacekeeping force. Of the eleven small wars, the UN has peacekeepers only in Sudan, as part of the hybrid mission with the AU. Thus the great majority of today's active wars have no peacekeepers and no UN mission.

The Israel-Palestine conflict deserves special attention. While not very lethal in absolute terms, it holds tremendous symbolic importance for a very important world region and thus has outsized consequences, more than any of the other major armed conflicts. Negotiations, ceasefires, frameworks and agreements, along with outside international diplomats, continue to come and go as they have for decades. The United States and the international community need to step up their game and get to the critical step of actually creating a viable Palestinian state— easier said than done, but nonetheless critical to the world's prospects.

In addition to the five wars and eleven major armed conflicts, the Uppsala researchers list nineteen smaller, minor armed conflicts that each killed at least 25 people in 2009. (Wars drop on and off this list, but it is a snapshot.) Conflicts over governments were in *Algeria* (with Mali, against a regional al Qaeda), *Central African Republic, Chad, India* (one of five Indian armed conflicts), *Iran, Nigeria,* and *Yemen* (where "al Qaeda of the Arabian Peninsula" has become famous for such tactics as the failed "underwear bomber"). Those over territories were in *Angola*'s Cabinda enclave, two areas in *Burma,* two in *Ethiopia,* three in *India,* and one each in *Mali, Pakistan* (Baluchistan), *Russia* (south), and *Thailand* (south).

Recent government offensives in Colombia, Burma, and the Philippines seem to be gaining the upper hand over rebels, with some potential for either military victories or peace agreements on government terms. In Nigeria and Thailand, very small insurgencies in outlying regions seem to be growing, and in India several small guerrilla wars fester.

POSTWAR TRANSITION ZONES

Now think about these wars on a world map. You can see *zones of war,* or hot spots on a map of wildfires, so to speak. The hottest streak is the arc from Pakistan to Congo that we have just traveled. Moving out to smaller fires that simmer in a larger area, the major armed conflicts still occupy a distinct zone of active warfare.

Beyond that zone, while the world's attention remains mostly on the active wars remaining in the world—especially, for Americans, those in Iraq and Afghanistan, where U.S. soldiers fight—at least twice as many countries in the world are in postwar transitions. Their wars have ended, but their problems are not over. These postwar societies face great difficulties as they navigate treacherous routes to healing war-induced divisions, rebuilding economic and social institutions, and in most cases grappling with deep poverty worsened by the destruction of years of war. They are trying, with help from outsiders, to keep the peace and put the society back together.

These postwar societies almost all cluster in five large *postwar transition zones.* Occasionally these wars reignite, as the conflict in Georgia did for five days in 2008, but mostly they enjoy a tenuous stability held in place by UN and other international organizations' peace operations. The five postwar transition zones and the main wars of the past twenty years that have ended in them are: Southern and Central Africa (Angola, Namibia, Mozambique, South Africa, Rwanda, Burundi); Southeast Asia (Sri Lanka, Nepal, the Philippines, Aceh/Indonesia, East Timor); Central America (Guatemala, El Salvador, Nicaragua, Panama, Grenada); West Africa (Nigeria, Liberia, Sierra Leone, Ivory Coast); and the Balkans through Central Asia (Bosnia, Croatia, Kosovo, Chechnya, Azerbaijan, Tajikistan, Georgia). That adds up to a lot of ended wars to celebrate, and conversely a lot of potential trouble spots that could reignite if the international community takes its eye off the ball.

Despite their great difficulties, the world's postwar transition zones represent great progress in reducing war. Looking at the zones where war has receded since the Cold War ended, one is reminded of a cancer going into remission rather than spreading, or an epidemic winding down.

THE ZONE OF PEACE

Beyond the zones of war and postwar transition is a large outer *zone of peace* where war has been absent for decades. It includes most of Europe, East Asia, South America, and (more ambiguously) perhaps North America and Russia. The absence of recent war in this zone does not guarantee that peace will continue into the future in these regions, but consider some reasons for hope.

East Asia bears much responsibility for the decrease in major wars since the Cold War years. The region saw the deadliest wars after 1945—the Chinese civil war, Korea, and Vietnam—and those were picnics compared with Japan's occupations before 1945. But no substantial war has occurred in East Asia since 1979. Subsequent wars elsewhere in the world, as horrible as they were, did not compare in scale with the big Cold War–era East Asian wars.

China, lately a feared potential rival of the United States, follows a declared "peaceful rise" strategy and has not fought a single military battle in twenty-five years. Japan has not fought one in sixty years. And Europe, which for centuries generated many of the world's most destructive wars, has built an extremely stable peace as it transformed itself over decades into the European Union. In 2007, the border between Germany and Poland, scene of centuries of violent contention and the starting line for World War II in 1939, withered away with not a checkpoint left behind, as Poland joined the borderless zone within the EU known as the Schengen Area. Any historian or political scientist familiar with Europe knows that what has happened there over the decades since the World Wars is something completely new and enormously important in the history of the world.

Latin America had a number of active wars two decades ago, but now war is limited to the cocaine-funded remote areas in Colombia and Peru. Even there, Peru's war has largely ended since the rebel leader was jailed almost twenty years ago. Top leaders of the Colombian rebel army have been killed in recent years and the insurgency has lost steam. In 2008, the chief foreign backer of the Colombian rebels, neighboring Venezuelan president Hugo Chávez, called on them to give up guerrilla war. In part, he cited the changed character of the region: "At this moment in Latin America, an armed guerrilla movement is out of place," Chávez said.

Sherlock Holmes, in a famous story, noted the "curious incident of the dog in the night-time." But, came the response, the dog did nothing in the night-time. Sherlock replied, "That was the curious incident." (Since it did *not* bark, the dog must have known the intruder.) Similarly, we need to pay attention not only to what happens in the world, but also to what does not happen. The peaceful areas of the world are the dog that did not bark. If I tell you to take special note of the war in China, you may say, "but there is no war in China." *That* is what you should take note of.

All is not rosy in the world's zone of peace, of course. Even though most of these countries have not experienced war for decades, they remain heavily armed. Indeed they contribute the strong majority of the world's armed forces. The countries at peace also spend the lion's share of the world's military budgets. Potential flashpoints such as Taiwan remain unresolved, and war remains very much a part of the vocabulary of international relations.

In addition, some of the countries at "peace" have interventionary armies fighting beyond their borders, notably the United States, Britain, and other NATO members in Afghanistan and Iraq. Other countries at peace, such as Canada and Australia, have sent combat troops on peacekeeping missions in volatile and violent societies. Countries in the zone of peace also suffer terrorist attacks, although terrorism kills at lower levels than war.

In one sense there is no zone of peace because we remain armed and ready. The English philosopher Thomas Hobbes wrote that war "consisteth not in actuall fighting; but in the known disposition thereto during all the time there is no assurance to the contrary." By this standard the whole world remains in a "state of war." Similarly, we have not reached what Immanuel Kant called "permanent peace" as opposed to a lull between wars. Across a broad range of human societies studied by anthropologists and historians, even the most peaceful can return to terrible warfare. No peace yet has been permanent. Perhaps someday, if peace keeps increasing, we could make it permanent. This book, however, is not about that day.

Today's wars present hard challenges to peacemakers. Still, with effort and resources, the coming years present a tremendous opportunity to sustain and reinforce the trend toward fewer and smaller wars worldwide, thereby potentially achieving a more stable, peaceful world.

II. Understanding Civil Wars

All of today's wars are civil wars. How do civil wars get started? What distinguishes them from other kinds of war? How do they end? Researchers have gained valuable general insights into each of these questions.

WHY CIVIL WARS HAPPEN

Civil wars have various proximal "causes" in the sense of issues in dispute such as territory. Underlying these, however, are the deeper conditions that put a country at risk of having a civil war begin. Economist Paul Collier led the World Bank's effort to understand these conditions, using a database of civil wars from 1950 to 2000. He reminds readers in the zone of peace that "the consequences of civil war spill over to the rich world in the form of epidemics, terrorism, and drugs."

The conditions favorable to civil wars breaking out are not simple—there are many theories. One study seeking to sort out conflicting results on the causes of civil wars concluded that the onset of civil wars correlated with large populations, low incomes, low economic growth rates,

recent political instability, immature democracy, small military establishments, rough terrain, and war-prone, undemocratic neighbors. However,
of all these factors, one belongs at the top of the list—low incomes.

Economic Development

Civil war experts Michael Doyle and Nicholas Sambanis write that the
"most robust empirical finding in the literature" on civil war is that "low
levels of per capita income . . . significantly exacerbate the risk of civil
war." Stanford's James Fearon independently reaches the same conclusion: "Per capita income is the single best predictor of a country's odds
of civil war outbreak, empirically dominating other factors . . . such as
level of democracy, degree of ethnic or religious diversity, . . . or level of
income inequality." Geographically, all today's wars are in the poorer
regions of the world.

Economic development—people having more wealth in the future
than the past—supports peace. In China, the "peaceful rise" strategy has
succeeded because prosperity and peace have proven mutually reinforcing. Georgian president Mikheil Saakashvili's decision to stop fighting
Russia in 2008, when he was losing badly, also reflects the appeal of prosperity over war. "We had a choice here," he said. "We could turn this
country into Chechnya . . . [or] stay a modern European country. Eventually we would have chased them away, but we would have had to go to
the mountains and grow beards. That would have been a tremendous
national philosophical and emotional burden." The lesson here seems to
be that when prosperity beckons, war looks unattractive. Modern leaders such as Saakashvili would rather sit in the city drinking cappuccino
than live as bearded insurgents in the mountains bearing an emotional
burden. Understandably! This is a good thing for world peace.

One study estimated the probability that a typical country would
experience a new armed conflict within five years, based on its annual
GDP per capita. The odds dropped from 15 percent at $250 per person to
8 percent at $500, 4 percent at about $1,200, and 1 percent at $5,000. The
reason poverty generates wars may not be just about the grievances of
the poor, by the way. Collier suggests that poverty limits a government's
tax revenues and thus its capability to defend the country from rebels.

Income does not explain everything, however. Although poor countries were at higher risk for civil wars in 2002—about a third of countries
with incomes below $500 a person fought an armed insurgency compared

with 6 percent of countries above that income level—still two-thirds of poor countries were not at war. "Why aren't the rest of the impoverished people of the world rising up?" Clearly poverty alone does not cause everyone to take up arms. Still, the stark difference in war-proneness in moving up from very low income levels suggests that economic development assistance is one of the most effective means available to prevent wars.

The Conflict Trap

In what the World Bank study calls a "conflict trap," wars hold back economic development and poverty breeds wars. The World Bank sees countries that develop their economies successfully as enjoying a virtuous circle in which rising income reduces war risk, and peace facilitates economic growth. But a group of "marginalized" low-income countries, with negative economic growth in the 1990s and dependence on primary commodity exports, had an estimated risk of civil war about ten times higher than average. Half of that increased risk was due to the most important factor, their low income. These fifty-two marginalized countries have just over a billion people, compared with about 4 billion people in seventy-one "successful developers" at much lower risk for war. The conflict trap is one of four problems that, in Collier's view, threaten to make the "bottom billion" poorest people diverge more and more from the rest of the world economy over the coming two decades, "forming a ghetto of misery and discontent."

Also keeping countries trapped in war is the fact that a country that has had a war is two to four times more likely to have another, even taking all other factors into account. So not only is it important to help countries get out of poverty and the other conditions that present a risk for war, but it is also important to try to prevent a slide into actual war in those countries at risk.

In both marginalized countries and less desperate ones, war risk is higher after an existing war has recently ended than before a war has occurred—about 2 percent risk versus 11 percent after a war in a marginalized country, and less than 1 percent versus about 4 percent in the case of a successfully developing country, according to Collier. Thus, both failure in economic development and a recent history of war put a country at risk of an outbreak of fighting. This implies that, without effective outside help, the war-prone countries could stay war-prone for decades to come.

Collier calls civil war "development in reverse." He estimates the total cost of a typical civil war at around $60 billion. Wars leave countries about 15 percent poorer on average than before the war, and reduce growth by more than 2 percent per year. Costs, both economic and health-related, linger for years afterward. Neighboring countries also suffer losses, as refugees stream in, arms races accelerate, security decreases, and investment in the region declines. (He finds no direct increased risk of war, however, as a result of being next to a country at war.)

Peace alone does not ensure development, as proven by peaceful but impoverished Malawi, for example. But, overall, about three-quarters of the bottom-billion people have recently been, or still are, in a country at war.

Other Risk Factors

Income is hardly the only cause implicated in the outbreak of civil wars, though. Two independent statistical analyses of data on civil wars around the world in 1965–99 and 1945–99, respectively, found similar conclusions. Risk factors that made wars more likely in Collier's study were dependence on primary commodity exports, funding available from diaspora communities, and the involvement of the superpowers during the Cold War. Geographically dispersed countries, in which the government has a hard time extending its control (such as in the Congo) are more likely to have civil wars. So are countries that have been at war recently. And so are poor countries with lower education rates and faster population growth. Slow or negative economic growth also raises the risk of civil war. In the second analysis, Stanford political scientists James Fearon and David Laitin found that, after controlling for income level, the chance of civil war was not raised by ethnic and religious diversity. Rather, the factors that increased war risk were poverty (weakens governments, helps rebel recruitment), political instability, rough terrain, and large population.

The Resource Curse

In addition to low income and low economic growth, a third major economic factor makes wars more likely to break out—dependence on primary commodity exports. It, too, has robust support in the research literature as a cause of civil wars.

The "resource curse" refers to the paradox by which countries with plentiful exportable primary resources, such as oil, find their economic development held back. The problem goes back into history, and was known at one point as "Dutch disease" because the Dutch economy suffered after the discovery of natural gas. A big rise in exports in one sector, such as Dutch natural gas, causes the country's currency to rise, which depresses exports of other sectors. The manufacturing and agricultural sectors suffer, and the economy thus becomes increasingly dependent on the natural resource exports. However, prices for these exports fluctuate unpredictably—oil prices dropped by three-quarters in 2008–09, for instance—so the economy becomes vulnerable to a crash. (In Congo, a crash in copper prices in the 1970s triggered a major economic decline.) Meanwhile the sudden glut of income from the resource export brings its own problems, including opportunities for corruption and for unwise government spending, and strengthens dictators.

Primary commodity exports can be bad for development, but not always. For instance, in Sierra Leone, diamonds fueled war and held back development, but in Botswana, diamond exports played a critical role in successful, rapid, and peaceful economic growth.

A review of fourteen studies on civil war and natural resources found that oil specifically made war more likely, especially secessionist war. "Lootable" resources such as diamonds, timber, or drugs did not increase the chances of war, but did make wars last longer, as they sustained armed groups. Other primary exports, such as legal agricultural products (coffee, bananas, etc.), did not affect the course of civil wars. Despite the drop in the number of wars around the world in recent years, wars in countries with oil exports have resisted the trend to some extent and now make up about a third of the total, by one estimate.

Democracy, a help to interstate peace, yields more complex results for civil wars. Partial democracies appear to be at higher risk not only during a transition period, such as from authoritarianism to partial democracy, but also if they persist in an intermediate character for years. And even stable democracies are war-prone in very poor countries, according to Collier.

Ethnic Conflict

In the post–World War II period, ethnic conflicts have "caused more misery and loss of human life" than any other kind of war. Ted Gurr, an expert on minority groups and ethnic politics worldwide, refers to a "tsunami of ethnic and nationalist conflict that swept across large parts of Eurasia and Africa in the early 1990s." This period, however, represented a peak after years of increase throughout the Cold War. After the early 1990s, ethnic and nationalist wars "decreased sharply," from more than thirty in the early 1990s to fewer than twelve in 2002.

At the root of ethnic conflicts, Gurr argues, is "the assertion of peoples' cultural identities," leading groups to seek "collective recognition, rights, and autonomy from governments that often have reacted to these demands as threats to civic identity and state security." Thus, "most of the ethnic wars of the last half century have been fought over issues of group autonomy and independence." Collier notes that in the poorest countries, "ethnic identity usually trumps national identity. . . . Policy choices get crowded out by identity."

Subethnic identity can also trump ethnic identity. Somalis, who share a language and culture, "claim to be the descendants of a single founding father" and the society "has traditionally been viewed as an ethnically homogenous state. . . ." However, the six major clans and their subclans fell into a brutal war that continues today.

Most ethnic wars since 1960 have in fact resulted in "increased autonomy for the groups that fought them." Out of fifty-seven conflicts Gurr studied, thirty led to greater regional autonomy, power sharing, or independence. Seven were stalemated, but almost all with de facto autonomy. Eight were successfully suppressed by the government without substantial concessions, and twelve continued as of 1999. Autonomy agreements usually de-escalate the fighting, but not always completely or permanently. Ethnic wars rarely win outright independence (Bangladesh and Eritrea being the exceptions—now joined by South Sudan).

Most ethnic groups do not turn to armed rebellion. Barbara Harff and Ted Gurr, in the "Minorities at Risk" project, mapped "275 sizable groups that have been targets of discrimination or are organized for political assertiveness or both." These groups are spread across the world's regions rather equally. A strong majority have never experienced a substantial armed rebellion, although most resent their condition and try to improve it through political action.

The relationship between ethnic divisions and civil war is ambiguous and complex in the research literature. High ethnic fractionalization in a society does not make war more likely, but other aspects such as ethnic polarization and the overlap of ethnicity with class may do so. Ethnicity may make mobilization of people into a rebellion easier (by increasing trust and cohesion within the group), and therefore enable civil war in societies with a few polarized ethnic groups that are geographically concentrated. But Collier, like Fearon and Laitin, found no connection between political repression of minority groups and the risk of war. Nor did intergroup hatreds, income inequality, or colonial history affect the chances for war. Norwegian researchers looked at the risk of civil war to countries whose neighbors had a civil war, using the Uppsala data for 1950–2001. They found the risk did not come from just sharing a border, but rather from "transnational ethnic ties" especially in the context of secessionism.

In the view of political scientists Donald Rothchild and David Lake, stable and peaceful ethnic relations depend on minority groups feeling secure. "Confidence-building measures undertaken by local elites and governments are the most potent instruments to secure minority rights," but international invention can also be appropriate and effective. Both, however, are temporary, imperfect solutions. "There is no form of insurance sufficient to protect against the dilemmas that produce collective fears and violence." In stable democracies, elections can play a positive role, but elsewhere their implications can be "troubling," since they may shut minority groups out unless mechanisms are in place to "ensure some minimal representation." Even in the mature democracy of the United States, for example, African-Americans by population would have thirteen seats out of one hundred in the Senate, but currently have zero because they are a minority in each state.

THE CHARACTER OF CIVIL WAR FIGHTING

Moving from the causes of civil wars to how they are fought, we can see why civil wars have a reputation as distinctive in character.

Individual Motives

Yale political scientist Stathis Kalyvas explores motives of participants in many civil wars in various times and places, with particular reference to the Greek civil war after World War II. He finds that political causes and ideologies often form a relatively superficial layer resting atop deeply personal motivations. Local populations vary their allegiances to military organizations based on expedience, and individuals within those populations use a war as an opportunity to settle personal conflicts, such as those based on debts or love triangles.

Irregular war creates zones of varying control by armed groups. Whereas interstate wars are generally conventional and result in more or less exclusive control of territory on each side of front lines, civil war generally involves a great asymmetry between government and rebel forces, leading to guerrilla tactics that blur control. The government may control an area by day and the guerrillas by night. "The boundaries separating two (or more) sides in an irregular war are blurred and fluid. . . . Irregular war fragments space." The most important zone in civil wars is that of "contested control," more than zones of government or insurgent control.

When a faction, either the government or a rebel group, gains firm control of a territory, the population there has strong incentives to collaborate with that faction, regardless of the population's initial or "true" preferences. ("In fact, ordinary people caught in the whirlwind of violence and war are . . . less than heroic.") Decisions by individuals to actually join armed groups are, similarly, "often nonideological," being based on such considerations as "access to looted luxury items and women" or, conversely, fear of punishment for desertion or nonparticipation.

The warring parties use violence against the civilian population to induce collaboration at lower cost. They kill their opponents in the local population to set an example for others. For example, a peasant in Zimbabwe explained that guerrillas murdered someone who was helping the government in order to show that "they had the power to do anything and instill fear so that none would repeat the mistake."

But only the local population, not the occupying military force, knows who the opponents really are. As an American soldier in Afghanistan put it regarding a particular village, "Two out of ten people here hate you and want to kill you. You just have to figure out which two." Or as an American fighting in Vietnam in 1968 put it, "Wherever I went and young Vietnamese men would look at me I grew scared. There really was no way to tell who was who. You could be in a room with one and not know whether he was really a Charlie or not." (That American was John Kerry, later a U.S.

senator.) Kalyvas notes that "the inability to tell friend from enemy is a recurring element of irregular war. . . ." Thus, civilian support is a necessity for either the government or rebels to achieve victory.

This "identification problem" of telling friend from foe gives individuals in the population the opportunity to denounce their personal enemies and get them killed by one of the armed parties—and individuals appear surprisingly ready to do this when the chance arises, according to Kalyvas. "Hence civil war is so violent at least partly because it provides opportunities for indirect violence." Those personal enemies, however, can counterdenounce the denouncer to the other armed party. Some of these denunciations may be accurate and some false. "Revenge is probably the most recurrent feature in descriptions of violence in civil war, often leading to the metaphor of blood feud or vendetta."

Kalyvas finds that where one party has firm control, it can identify defectors itself, and counterdenouncers do not have access to the rival armed party to carry out retaliation, so violence is lower. And where the two sides have about equal control, people fear denouncing their enemies because of the high likelihood of counterdenunciation. Thus, "denunciation leading to selective violence will be most likely where one actor exercises dominant but incomplete control."

Indiscriminate violence, for example against a neighborhood suspected of sheltering rebels, is cheaper than selective violence but counterproductive in "winning hearts and minds." Nonetheless, if one side is very strong in an area and lacks the information needed for selective violence, it can effectively deter collaboration with the other side by punishing a whole group.

In the cycles of denunciation-driven violence, Kalyvas finds that "intimacy is essential rather than incidental to civil war . . . ; it divides families, pitting brothers and sisters, parents and children, against each other." This puzzles us only because we assume, wrongly, that relationships within neighborhoods or families are inherently peaceful when, in fact, in peacetime people simply have few opportunities to express their hatreds of each other. This characteristic of intimacy "endows civil war with its particularly abhorrent character." As one writer put it, "A civil war is not a war, but a disease. The enemy is internal. One almost fights against oneself."

These personal motives appeared in the early weeks of the 1994

Rwandan genocide, when some Hutu assailants "abus[ed] their license to kill, such as by slaying Hutu with whom they had disputes. . . ." Conversely, some Hutu "allow[ed] Tutsi to escape injury in return for money, sexual favors or other considerations." Self-interest also operated as a motive: "Officials often directed assailants first to pillage property, guaranteeing them immediate profit as they accustomed themselves to attacking their neighbors." Thus, a variety of private motives underlay actions embedded in the larger campaign of genocide.

Rebellion as Organized Crime

Economist Paul Collier views rebels as "rational economic agents" and their wars "not as the ultimate protest movements but as the ultimate manifestation of organized crime." Grievances do not cause conflicts, in his view, but rather "a sense of grievance is deliberately generated by rebel organizations." The true motive is greed, not grievance, as rebels resemble bandits, pirates, or gangsters more than opposition politicians. Thus, what matters is not motivations but "whether the [rebel] organization can sustain itself financially."

"Indeed, at one level the history of the nineties is the story of how the international community has attempted to confront and control warlords—Saddam Hussein; Slobodan Milosevic, . . . Pol Pot and Hun Sen in Cambodia; Mohammed Aideed in Somalia; Foday Sankoh . . . in Sierra Leone; General Raoul Cédras of Haiti; Jonas Savimbi . . . in Angola; Laurent Kabila . . . in Zaire/Congo; and many others from Kabul to Kurdistan . . . who have . . . held autocratic and destructive if not criminal sway over the peoples they control."

War reporter Chris Hedges concludes that "the ethnic conflicts and insurgencies of our time, whether between Serbs and Muslims or Hutus and Tutsis, are not religious wars. They are not clashes between cultures or civilizations, nor are they the result of ancient ethnic hatreds. They are manufactured wars, born out of the collapse of civil societies, perpetuated by fear, greed, and paranoia, and they are run by gangsters. . . ." These mundane causes of war are wrapped in a "veneer" of ideology and myth that obscure the nature of the wars. Hedges harshly criticizes his own profession, the press, for perpetuating wartime myths.

Some researchers take rebels' stated grievances more seriously. "Civil wars are often the final acts of decades of the slow agony of political and social discrimination, of hunger, of endless poverty, of little hope, so little that the risk of death while fighting seems better than slow death under unacceptable conditions," writes political scientist Patrick Regan. It is not absolute poverty that causes people to take up arms, in this view, but relative poverty induced by discrimination.

And individual motives for participating in an insurgency can be altruistic. Yale political scientist Elisabeth Wood found that among the leftist rebels in El Salvador whom she met, "emotional and moral motives were essential." The rebels cited such motives as "that we not be seen as slaves." Wood examines the dilemma of individual rebels, who stand to lose more than they gain (violence, jail), even if the group they represent gains land or power. Explaining this participation, which seems irrational at the individual level, the rebels told Wood that by rebelling they asserted their "dignity" and fulfilled "moral commitments and emotional engagements."

Collier finds that the actual motivation of participants in a rebellion may vary—religious for some, psychopathological for others. He finally decides that motives do not matter, and proposes the "feasibility hypothesis" of civil wars focusing on "how rebellion happens rather than on what motivates it." To sustain a civil war requires "rebel organizations that can kill and be killed on a large scale and yet survive for years." This requires both a militarily weak government and rebel access to money.

Diaspora communities—those living in another country but with ethnic, national, or family ties back home—can serve as one source of money for rebels. These communities may contribute to war outbreaks because they harbor "romanticized attachments" to their group of origin. They usually have more money than their compatriots back home, and distance shields them from the consequences of rebellion. Tamils living outside Sri Lanka were a source of financial support for the Tamil Tigers, as were Irish-Americans during the Northern Ireland conflict, among others. But diasporas can also play a positive role after wars, especially in supporting economic development.

HOW CIVIL WARS END (AND STAY ENDED)

Wars end in different ways. Some end in victory (e.g., Angola, Chechnya, Algeria, Rwanda, Sri Lanka), some in frozen cease-fires (Taiwan, Korea, Cyprus, Bosnia, Georgia), some in international administration (Cambodia, East Timor, Kosovo); some in negotiated power-sharing (Nicaragua,

Nepal, Aceh), and some in reconciliation (South Africa, Northern Ireland). During the Cold War, military victory in civil wars produced more stable peace than a negotiated settlement, but also was more likely to lead to genocide. Negotiated settlements were more inclusive but less stable than military victory because parts of transitional governments retained war-making powers while rebel groups may have lost their ability to fight. Since the Cold War, fewer civil wars, about half, have ended in victory and the rest in settlements.

The central issue in settling civil wars, in political scientist Barbara Walters's view, is not just negotiating terms but the more difficult task of "designing credible guarantees" that each side will implement the agreed terms. Because of this problem of credibility, "third-party enforcement or verification of the post-treaty implementation period is critical for success." She sees the end of civil wars as a three-part process—starting negotiations, compromising on terms, and implementing terms. The third of these phases is most difficult because even parties that want to end the war "worry that their enemy will take advantage of them after they sign a peace agreement and begin to demobilize." In Walters's view, this problem explains why, although nearly two-thirds of the seventy-two civil war negotiations in 1940–92 led to signed bargains, only 43 percent of them were ever implemented.

Doyle and Sambanis agree: "A critical difficulty in negotiating an end to civil wars is that negotiated agreements are often not credible. . . . International peacebuilding operations . . . can help provide information that resolves any uncertainty about the parties' commitment to a peace settlement or the likelihood of military victory in a new cycle of hostilities." Taking into account the presence of peacekeepers, Doyle and Sambanis find that "a comprehensive peace agreement implemented through a peace operation has an even better success rate" than a victory. Thus, "peacebuilding trumps military victories."

There are exceptions, however, where success has come despite the absence of outside guarantees. In Central America, peace agreements have been implemented relying more on shared norms such as a liberal history, economic integration, and the presence of democratic neighbors. In the hills of Bangladesh, parties implemented peace terms with no peacekeepers to help out. Still, statistically the presence of peacekeepers improves the odds.

Preventing War Recurrence

As we have seen, a major risk factor for civil war is a recent history of civil war. A sizable number of peace settlements break down—about half in the 1990s, though considerably fewer in the 2000s. Thus, a central goal in ending civil wars is to prevent recurrences.

After a war, Collier proposes, several factors increase the risk of renewed fighting. First, rebels have built up capable organizations by obtaining money, weapons, and recruits, and have gained military experience. Second, norms against using violence have been weakened by the war. Third, political allegiances may have become polarized during the conflict. After a violent conflict, primary commodity exports remain a potent risk factor for war renewal, but the government has the option to mitigate this risk by bringing rebels into the government to share the spoils, so to speak. Ethnic dominance also remains a key factor, and here outside guarantees such as UN peacekeepers can help. Even though grievances do not typically affect the outbreak of war, Collier argues, they need to be taken into account in postwar settlements, by which time rebels are trying to transition to opposition politicians and long-repeated grievances may have taken on a life of their own.

Regarding economic growth, Collier notes that countries tend to grow quickly when a civil war ends, bouncing back from the conflict, and this mitigates against a renewal of war. After a typical fifteen-year civil war, in the first five years of peace economies grew an average of 6 percent a year in Collier's analysis. However, after a war, governments' military budgets typically are double their levels before the war, which is a drag on economic growth.

In recovering economically after a civil war, market processes alone may not suffice, because those processes would naturally concentrate new growth in the capital city and the areas controlled by the government, likely leaving out rural areas controlled by rebels. Because the risk of war recurrence is high during the decade after a civil war, Collier advises governments to direct economic development to ensure fairness and not just its overall generation of wealth.

Collier argues that "the conflict trap has two points of intervention: postconflict and deep prevention." He favors the postconflict point, since about half of civil wars were relapses after a cease-fire in the period he studied. In postconflict societies, trade cannot grow much because of distorted economic conditions. Foreign aid is more useful but only if sustained for a decade rather than dumped in quickly for a few years and then stopped. External security assistance should also last a decade: "Security in postconflict societies will normally require an external military presence for a long time." The government's own military should be reduced, and its police increased, during this decade while robust external forces guarantee security.

Not to take anything from Collier's two intervention points, but a third should not be forgotten. In between prevention and peacebuilding comes "peacemaking" through active negotiation and occasionally the threat or use of force to bring warring parties to the table and get them to produce a cease-fire agreement, followed by agreements on transitional governments and constitutional arrangements. Someone needs to go in during a shooting war and get the parties to negotiate terms and get to a cease-fire. It might be a diplomat—such as Count Bernadotte in his little white plane—or a Catholic charity, an ex-president, someone from the UN, or a government, or an NGO. But somebody needs to make this work, and everything depends on it.

Spoilers

The problem of "spoilers" has been mentioned several times in the preceding discussions. Most peacekeeping operations have to confront "local parties [who] continue jockeying for position and advantage long after formal peace talks have ended and accords have been inked. Terms are reinterpreted; promised facilities are not provided . . . ; and weapons and troops fail to show up at agreed assembly points."

Whereas many leaders of governments and major armed factions may genuinely want to enjoy the benefits of peace and, for example, positions in a transitional government—notwithstanding a need for security guarantees before they lay down arms—other actors may be fundamentally unready for peace. Smaller groups may not have been a party to talks or may not have received incentives adequate to make it worth stopping the fight. Even major leaders may have made deals insincerely or might not like how events develop afterward, as when Ivory Coast's president lost a long-delayed election and used violence to cling to power until ousted by force in 2011. In the 1990s, "time and again, well-meaning bodies that sought to play a role—the UN itself, NATO, the European Union, the

Organization for Security and Cooperation in Europe (OSCE)—were stopped by the blunt fact that peacekeeping is impossible if there exist powerful, angry forces who prefer fighting to compromise." As we have seen, the presence of spoilers was a major difference between the successful and failed cases of UN peacekeeping in the early 1990s.

The problem of spoilers is especially acute in conflicts where military control can bring wealth to local groups, as in the Congo (various minerals), Sierra Leone (diamonds), and Afghanistan (opium). "Factions that have access to high-value commodities such as precious gems, minerals, or narcotics are likely to maintain the extraction and trading networks that they established during the war unless those networks are severed by superior countervailing local power."

Postwar Trauma and Denial

After wars, societies are traumatized, above and beyond the physical death, injury, destruction, and cost. As one survivor of the war in Bosnia put it, "It is as if I see life through pieces of a mirror that lies in fragments." One source finds the "psychological [aftermath] of war [to] have striking similarities across cultures and types of trauma."

Chris Hedges, who spent fifteen years as a war reporter in places like El Salvador and Bosnia, writes that "even with its destruction and carnage [war] can give us . . . purpose, meaning, a reason for living." But the myth of war as meaningful "rarely endures for those who experience combat." "In combat the abstract words of glory, honor, courage . . . are replaced by the tangible images of war, the names of villages, mountains, roads, dates, and battalions that mean nothing to the outsider but pack enormous emotional power and fear to those caught up in the combat. Once in a conflict, we are moved from the abstract to the real, from the mythic to the sensory. . . . We have nothing to do with a world not at war. . . . There is no world outside the unit. It alone endows worth and meaning."

One way to deal with trauma is denial—put the war behind, never look back, and move on. South African–born sociologist Stanley Cohen writes that denial occurs when "people, organizations, governments or whole societies are presented with information that is too disturbing, threatening, or anomalous to be fully absorbed or openly acknowledged. The information is therefore somehow repressed, disavowed, pushed aside, or reinterpreted. . . . Denial is understood as an unconscious defence mechanism for coping with guilt, anxiety, and other disturbing emotions aroused by reality." Denial causes societies to repeat "stupid destructive things" without even realizing they are repetitions.

Denial plays an important role in our confusion about whether war has been getting better or worse in recent years. Precisely because we remain in denial about past traumas, we cannot accurately compare them with today's situation.

Sometimes denial is literal, such as when the government of Sudan states that attacks on civilians in Darfur did not occur. Other times, denial is interpretive—for example, the attacks occurred but they are not what they seem; the government was not involved, or the attacks targeted rebel bases. A third type acknowledges acts but claims they were justified. Sometimes all three types occur together: The massacre did not take place, anyway it was accidental, and the victims got what they deserved!

In 1981, members of the U.S.-trained Atlacatl Brigade of the government army of El Salvador massacred 794 people, including many small children. "The essential facts of the massacre were known and disclosed almost immediately. *The New York Times* published photos and a credible report." However, officials in the Salvadoran and American governments "came up with elaborate linguistic tricks and prevarications to deny the whole story. . . ." Only eleven years later, when the mass graves were exhumed and testimony taken by El Salvador's Truth Commission, did the story reemerge.

But "denial is always partial; some information is always registered. This paradox or doubleness—knowing and not-knowing—is the heart of the concept." Sometimes, and this is especially true during and after wars, "societies arrive at unwritten agreements about what can be publicly remembered and acknowledged. . . . [For example,] the media image of the Gulf War was a masterpiece of collusive denial. . . . Nor did the public really want to know more." Given the past suffering of societies around the world, even those "that seem relatively tranquil now are still dealing with terrible histories of atrocities and social suffering." When a war ends in a society such as Sierra Leone, individual memories of the traumatic events do not disappear even though the official discourse may sweep them under the carpet. In a society such as China, at peace for decades, memories of famines and civil wars still lurk. Even in the prosperous and democratic United States of America, below the surface run dark currents of repressed memories such as of slavery and the genocide of native peoples.

Some societies after wars have used truth commissions (discussed in Chapter 3) to counter denial. "The Truth Commission, an institution created only in the last two decades, is the most resonant symbol for the uncovering and acknowledging of past atrocities. . . . The South African Truth and Reconciliation Commission (TRC) . . . report is one of the great moral documents of our time, because of its commitment to truth as a moral value in itself." However, most other truth commissions fall short of the South African standard.

In sum, the problem of stability after a civil war, of preventing a new outbreak of fighting, is multidimensional. As Doyle and Sambanis observe, stable participatory polities require a shared national identity, state institutions, a large middle class, and a growing economy, but "these are just what are missing in the typical post–civil-war environment. . . ." Continued and more vigorous support from the international community will be needed to stabilize today's postwar transition zones and keep them from slipping back into war.

The world stands at a hopeful but ambiguous stage in managing and reducing armed conflict. Successes in ending interstate and other large wars have not fully trickled down to the smaller but brutal civil wars that remain. The dynamics of those civil wars suggest that the two most important things the international community can do to help are to promote economic development and to use peacekeeping to offer security guarantees after cease-fires.

12

WHAT WE CAN DO

A New Global Identity

The progress that humanity has made toward ending war has come about not through inevitable, natural, or magical changes, but through the long, hard work of people seeking peace. The job is not finished. However, not only have the number and size of wars decreased in recent years, but our concept of war and military force is changing. The job of soldiers used to be, and still is to some extent, to kill and destroy. Nowadays, however, their job is, as often, to build and protect.

I. Soldiers for Peace

The 150,000 deployed peacekeeping troops in the world—about 100,000 UN and 50,000 non-UN—make up one of the two great interventionary armies in the field today. The other one is the U.S. military force in Iraq and (with NATO) Afghanistan, together fielding a roughly similar number of troops. The head of UN peacekeeping sees it that way, calling his forces from 118 countries "the second largest deployed army in the world."

One difference between these two armies of similar size is that the U.S. military gets more public attention than do peacekeeping forces. Another difference is in their budgets. At about $8 billion a year, peacekeeping costs roughly about 1 percent of the U.S. military budget. Given this size disparity, the deployment of 100,000 UN peacekeepers in fourteen missions around the world is an impressive military feat. Of course, the words of General Dallaire in Rwanda in 1994 apply to the whole world of peacekeeping today: "Give me the means and I can do more."

Despite these differences, U.S. military operations and UN peacekeeping are converging in some striking ways. As we have seen, peacekeeping has gotten more robust, as the international community has come to the realization that certain spoilers in rough neighborhoods respond better to attack helicopters than to nice words. UN officials and member states alike have begun to put teeth into the efforts to secure hard-won peace agreements when the actions of a few threaten to unravel them.

At the same time, U.S. forces have undergone a dramatic, if underappreciated, change in mission since the Cold War ended, from conventional combat operations to counterinsurgency. In Afghanistan, U.S. officers drink tea with village elders, army engineers build irrigation works, and anthropologists deploy with military forces to help them understand local cultures. U.S. "female engagement teams" send women Marines to engage Afghan women in village spheres that are off-limits to male soldiers—not because the U.S. military has gotten "nicer," not because men couldn't blast their way into Afghan compounds, but because the soft approach works better. The idea of tank phalanxes blazing away to conquer territory and topple governments seems anachronistic. When such an approach was last used, in Iraq in 2003, the results were not just inefficient but downright counterproductive for U.S. foreign policy goals.

Americans used to send soldiers "over there" to conquer and defeat the enemy. Now we send soldiers to put themselves in harm's way to maintain peace, to establish conditions for political and economic progress, to be diplomats and educators rather than just "grunts." In this way, U.S. soldiers have become more like UN peacekeepers than either perhaps realizes. Then, too, Americans used to fight alone, even if helped by allied nations, but today they are more integrated than ever with forces from NATO allies in Afghanistan (and, in 2011, Libya), including serving under foreign commanders or commanding foreign troops. Again—just like UN peacekeepers.

The convergence of U.S. and UN forces is likely to extend, in a small way, to a modest convergence in funding in the coming years as well. As demands on UN peacekeeping continue to grow, and the world grudgingly extends more money for those purposes, so will the U.S. government grudgingly realize that it must shrink its military budgets. Spending levels above those of the Cold War are not only unsustainable in a deficit-ridden federal budget, but unnecessary in a world of fewer wars and less use for traditional military operations. As countries count their pennies, the bargain price of peacekeeping becomes a big attraction while the insane price of industrialized war will make it unappealing. It is not that a rich country such as the United States cannot afford to fight an all-out war against a mortal threat with all the technology it can muster. Rather, it does not need to. Mortal threats are in remission, and money spent on military forces gets the most bang for the buck in operations that resemble, well, peacekeeping.

PAYING FOR WHAT WE WANT

Take out seven hundred-dollar bills and lay them on the table in front of you. If you are an average American household, this is your monthly share of U.S. military spending. Now take out two one-dollar bills and put them on the table. That is what the same household pays for UN peacekeeping. The missions described in this book, the hundreds of thousands of lives *not* being lost in wars anymore, cost the average American household two dollars a month.

Now imagine how your life would change if that two dollars a month were doubled—not much, if you are like most Americans. Then imagine how the lives of millions of people in conflict areas would change if the world's peacekeeping budget were doubled. The change would be substantial. Not only would many thousands of people have greater security, perhaps returning home if displaced, or being able to travel to markets. But also greater peace could spark broad social change in a virtuous circle of economic development, better governance, and the rule of law. Those two dollars could dramatically improve millions of lives.

We have seen that starving peacekeeping missions of needed resources is the rule, not the exception. The dysfunctional formula of big mandates and small budgets has proven surprisingly resilient despite repeated calls to change it, such as in the Brahimi Report. By contrast, the successful missions—such as in Sierra Leone—have, in the end, gone in strong, with large numbers of peacekeepers relative to the population size and usually backed up by robust forces from great powers or regional organizations.

In assessing the UN's difficulties in meeting the new demands of the post–Cold War era twenty years ago, Pérez de Cuéllar emphasized the problem of limited resources. The UN, he found, was not adequately prepared to implement Council decisions to use force in internal conflicts because it lacked "adequate funding, managerial staff, and command and control procedures for peace enforcement operations" as well as "appropriately trained troops in sufficient numbers and with the necessary equipment . . . ," among other deficiencies. UN peacekeepers sometimes act with incredible bravery, but are seriously outgunned.

Two decades later, in 2009, UN experts again worried that the new expansion of peacekeeping, in terms of numbers and the scope of missions, was not being matched by commitments from governments in troops and money. The total number of soldiers, police, and civilians in UN peacekeeping missions grew from 40,000 in 2000 to 113,000 in 2009, but resources devoted to the tasks did not keep pace. "Peacekeeping has been pushed to the wall," said one. "There is a sense across the system that this is a mess—overburdened, underfunded, overstretched."

Peacekeepers and UN personnel around the world face considerable danger, made worse by the inadequate resources available to them. A 2008 study found them more likely to be attacked in recent years than in past decades. "All of us who work for the U.N., we continue to think of ourselves as good guys, and just because you have the [UN] flag, wherever you go you will be all right. We need to realize that our flag is not enough protection." Before the 1990s, and notwithstanding exceptions such as the first Congo intervention, civilian UN and aid workers "used to be 'off-limits,'" but then they became frequent "targets." In 1999, rebels in Burundi murdered the UNICEF representative and the World Food Program logistics officer, just a day after a UN official was murdered in Kosovo and a month after a UN doctor was murdered in Somalia. During the Angola war, in 1998, a UN plane was shot down with all killed, including the Special Representative of the Secretary-General. The son of the pilot took another UN flight to search for the wreckage, and that plane, too, was shot down with all killed—twenty-three people altogether.

Ideas for radically changing the UN's funding levels and mechanisms have foundered. The "Tobin tax," proposed by the late Nobel Prize–winning economist James Tobin, would raise substantial funds to support the UN. It would apply a very small tax to international foreign exchange transactions, which constitute a very high volume of financial flows, trillions of dollars a day. Debate continues about how to implement such an idea, originally conceived as a way to dampen volatility and speculation in currency markets, as well as who would administer it and how the proceeds would be used. Proposals have included funding the UN, economic development in poor countries, global warming measures, or the creation of a kind of insurance fund against financial collapses. Britain, France, and Canada have all, at some point, supported some variation of such a tax. The Tobin tax could raise hundreds of billions of dollars a year, far more than would be needed to supercharge the current few billions devoted to peace operations. But its economic effects are uncertain and it seems politically impractical. In 2001 it received the kiss-of-death endorsement of Fidel Castro. I would not want higher peacekeeping budgets to have to wait for grand schemes such as the Tobin tax to be agreed and implemented.

AN INSTITUTION WORTH INVESTING IN

It is not just the peacekeeping department that is worthy of dramatically increased support. The UN as a whole can make our world much more peaceful and healthy, if only we would let it. A former Australian foreign minister writes, "It is not widely appreciated just how many different roles are played by the multiple departments, programs, organs, and agencies within the UN system, how many of them have performed outstandingly for many decades, and how very little, comparatively, it all costs." The UN "family" taken together, including peacekeeping and affiliated agencies such as the WHO, costs less than $20 billion a year. In addition to the 100,000 or so peacekeepers sent by national militaries, the UN system employs about 100,000 people, fewer people than the workforce of Starbucks coffee.

The small size of countries' permanent missions to the UN reflects the relatively low priority the UN has. As of 2004, the United States had 128 professionals working at the UN, Russia had eighty-three, China sixty-five, Britain thirty-eight, and France twenty-nine. Nonpermanent members of the Security Council typically had smaller missions still. Bangladesh, a top contributor of UN peacekeepers in the world and a country of 160 million people, had 8 professionals in its delegation to the UN when it last served on the Security Council in 2001.

The Secretariat lacks some basic administrative machinery that even small national governments take for granted. For instance, "unlike an actual head of state, the UN secretary-general does not have a plane of his own." Kofi Annan traveled through Africa "in a jet lent by the emir of Qatar. . . ." Everything the secretary-general needs, he has to beg or borrow from national governments. As Kofi Annan put it in 1999, "With no enforcement capacity and no executive power beyond the organization, a secretary-general is armed only with tools of his own making." Yet, with this limited tool kit, the secretary-general must take on the world's intractable problems, with time pressing. "Everything I touch is a race against time—to save lives, to stop killing," said Annan.

It took decades of work to establish even today's limited freedom of action by the secretary-general. We have seen how Dag Hammarskjöld built up the power and prestige of the office after the great powers believed he would be a passive administrator. Critics of the UN object to exactly that effort to give some power to the office. One complained that "the UN secretary-general has been transformed from an administrative officer into someone with the pretension and grandiosity of a head of state."

In late 1954 and early 1955, Hammarskjöld defused a crisis between communist China and the United States. Chinese nationalists on Taiwan still held China's UN seat, and the UN had just officially fought on one side of the Korean War, with China on the other side, so the UN would not seem the best choice as mediator when China shot down an American airplane and took the crew prisoner. Hammarskjöld, however, asked to come to China in his own capacity as secretary-general, not as a representative of the Security Council. This was a new idea—that "the secretary-general had an affirmative obligation to act when peace and security were threatened." The prisoners were eventually released. In contrast to the original vision of the UN as a collective security organization, and its history in the Korean War, a new role emerged: What the UN "had lost in coercive power it had regained through its unique, suprapartisan status."

The 1960–61 Congo problem was "a major test of the authority and independence of the secretary-general and the UN secretariat." Here the secretary-general learned that the veto power of the five permanent Security Council members gave him "considerable freedom of interpretation" in carrying out the Council's mandates, since stopping him would require all five to agree. Over the subsequent years, one government or another has found itself annoyed by the secretary-general's actions, but overall the powers of the office have not been abused. On the contrary, more freedom of action and more resources would let the secretary-general do more to limit and prevent violent conflicts around the world.

THREE THOUSAND FIVE HUNDRED FIREFIGHTERS

In 1960, the UN put 3,500 peacekeepers from four countries on the ground in the Congo in four days. Why, fifty years later, does it take months? Are our airplanes so much slower than the ones they used in 1960? Are we poorer, or have smaller armed forces to draw on? No, clearly the blockage, so to speak, is in the political plumbing.

A recurring idea to solve this problem is to give the UN standing peacekeeping capabilities. Staff and equip the fire department before a fire breaks out. "Perhaps someday this sensible notion will actually be implemented." Here is a modest proposal: Just do it! Standby peacekeepers are not so complicated, so expensive, or such a threat to almighty national sovereignty as to warrant the foot-dragging that this proposal always seems to elicit.

You might think that U.S. public opinion would be a big barrier to enlarging the powers of the UN in this way, but the opposite is true. In a 2007 poll, 72 percent of Americans supported "having a standing UN peacekeeping force selected, trained and commanded by the United Nations." In fact, creating a standing peacekeeping force controlled by the UN is supported by strong majorities, a more than two-to-one ratio of supporters to opponents, in all the Permanent Five countries. Those expressing opposition to the idea make up only 24 percent in the United States, 25 percent in France, 22 percent in Russia, and 25 percent in China. (Britain was not polled.)

While we are at it, why not populate this standing peacekeeping force, under UN command and flying the UN flag, with major troop contributions from the Permanent Five members of the Security Council? The leadership of the P5 would give the force real clout, politically and militarily. The P5 are, in fact, the five most powerful militaries in the world, which is why they have their status on the Security Council. Any force with soldiers from these five countries would have to be taken very seriously indeed by armed parties in a conflict area. And the United States possesses unique global transport capabilities that would be crucial to the success of a quick-deploying force. (The bulk of peacekeeping funds already come from the P5.)

The P5 members uniquely could feel comfortable with a permanent UN force, since they could veto any proposed use of it. No P5 country will ever have to send its soldiers on a mission it does not support. As a side benefit, the participation of P5 military personnel might help the great powers get along, since they would be working on a good project together, somewhat like the effect of outer space cooperation in easing Cold War tensions.

Troops from the current large troop-contributing countries, such as Bangladesh, would be incorporated into the standing force as well. Those countries' militaries have precious peacekeeping experience, the countries need the revenue, and the troops cost considerably less to maintain in the field than those from Europe or North America. Furthermore, a standing peacekeeping force need not do all the UN peacekeeping. The present system of slowly assembling contributions from many countries could still supply most of the needs. But while this happens, the standing force should be able to deploy to places where a few thousand peacekeepers are needed right away, pending the creation of a conventional peacekeeping mission some months later. Ralph Bunche's deployment of 3,500 in four days would make a good target to emulate.

The history of peacekeeping has repeatedly and undeniably shown that delays in responding to peacekeeping requests are a huge drag on the success of the whole enterprise. In Sierra Leone, as we have seen, a fast response in 1997 might have saved years of subsequent war. In case after case, stumbles and setbacks have resulted from delays in deployment.

Finally, if we are to have a UN standby force with troops from the Permanent Five Security Council members, why not activate the moribund Military Staff Committee, with officers from those five countries, to take up one of the roles the Charter intended for it?

Is this so much to ask? In a world where peacekeeping plays a critical role in maintaining the world's substantial progress toward peace, and where rapid deployment would tangibly improve outcomes, a standing UN force would offer great benefits at very low cost. The UN's founders gave the Permanent Five special status, not just to talk and pass resolutions, not just to cast vetoes, but to shoulder responsibility for world peace and security. If they refuse, they are not great powers but wimps. In a world of 20 million soldiers, a trillion dollars in military expenditures, and missiles that can blow up anything on earth in thirty minutes, I am talking about 3,500 peacekeepers in four days. The citizens support it, the world needs it, and the great powers can easily afford it.

Beyond this modest step, peacekeeping capabilities and budgets could be greatly expanded in future years. The "baseline" of peacekeeping forces worldwide in the post–Cold War era, about 100,000, "has been inadequate for the tasks at hand." Two recent studies cost out the options for expanding these capabilities. The first, by military policy expert Michael O'Hanlon, finds the costs of a large standby force from industrialized countries would be "very expensive" but "not astronomical." The second, by the RAND Corporation, finds that costs run ten times higher in a mission that must impose a solution by force compared to one operating with the consent of all parties. For a poor country of 5 million, such as Sierra Leone, a "light peacekeeping" mission needs 8,000 international troops, 1,000 police, and $500 million. A "heavy peace enforcement" mission needs 65,000 troops, 8,000 police, and $14 billion. In each case other costs, such as humanitarian, governance, and development expenses, add another billion dollars. Not to belabor any particular set of figures, the point is that peacekeeping can be realistically planned and budgeted instead of being improvised and funded on the cheap.

WAR PREVENTION

The main focus of this book, as of UN peacekeeping itself, is on actions by the international community to end wars and keep them from restarting. However, we have seen at several points that conflict prevention is another important tool to increase peace, one whose potential has not been realized. It is easier to prevent a war than to end one that has already started. "Once war starts, mistrust and hostility increase, and ending the war through negotiation becomes harder."

An ounce of prevention is worth a pound of cure, as the saying goes. Dag Hammarskjöld in 1960 was already advocating a "switch to . . . preventive action from corrective action." Kofi Annan said the same thing forty-two years later: "I have pledged to move the United Nations from a culture of reaction to a culture of prevention." He proposed making "prevention . . . the cornerstone of the collective security system of the United Nations in the twenty-first century."

The Carnegie Commission on Preventing Deadly Conflict concluded that of the $200 billion spent in the 1990s intervening in Bosnia, Somalia, Rwanda, Haiti, Cambodia, El Salvador, and the Gulf War, about two-thirds could have been saved by taking a preventive approach. Early-warning systems could draw policy makers' attention to conflicts before they blow up.

But as Annan notes, "existing problems usually take precedence over potential ones and, while the benefits of prevention lie in the future and are difficult to quantify, the costs must be paid in the present." Thus, the focus of the Security Council "remains almost exclusively on crises and emergencies," and the Council normally becomes "involved only when violence has already occurred on a large scale." Among other recommendations, Annan suggests earlier attention to conflicts, when preventive measures can be effective. Usually, by the time a conflict reaches the Security Council, the chance for "early" prevention has passed.

Ideally, the deployment of peacekeepers before the outbreak of violence would allow a preventive approach. This has actually happened three times in UN history—in Macedonia (1995–99), Central African Republic (1998–2000), and Haiti (several operations since 1993). In each case, the threat of war receded, yet the rarity of this kind of preventive deployment "suggests that the international community has been reluctant to expend the political and financial capital required for a peace operation without the clear case for deployment that is made by open conflict," as Annan complains.

A good example of successful conflict prevention (though not by the UN) occurred in Estonia in 1993, shortly after the breakup of the Soviet Union, which had left behind ethnic populations that did not follow new international borders. The city of Narva was located in Estonia but populated almost entirely by Russians, who had suddenly become an ethnic and linguistic minority in the new Estonian state. They voted in a referendum to secede, and the Estonian government threatened force to keep them from doing so. Russia in turn warned that it would use force to protect Narva if Estonia attacked it. The toothless Organization for Security and Cooperation in Europe (OSCE) had created a High Commissioner for National Minorities, and that individual went to Estonia and fashioned an agreement whereby the referendum was considered a statement of aspirations rather than an action plan, and the Estonian government backed off its threats of force. The outcome was a lot cheaper than a war, and even a lot cheaper than a peacekeeping mission after war occurred.

Similarly, preventive conflict resolution was quite successful in Macedonia in 1993, where the UN deployed its first preventive peacekeeping mission. After Croatia and Bosnia, the international community was eager to avoid another war in the former Yugoslavia. The mission guaranteed Macedonia's territorial integrity and supported the Macedonian government, which included both of the rival ethnic groups. Despite several serious crises in the ensuing years, Macedonia avoided war because of political accommodation among the leaders of conflicting communities. And in Bosnia, one study estimated, intervention in early 1992 would have cost $11 billion over four years, instead of the $54 billion eventually spent on the intervention there.

If this way of thinking sounds like discussions of preventive medicine and health care costs, it is no accident. Medical researcher and policy expert David Hamburg, a psychiatrist by background, was on the faculty at Stanford Medical School in the 1960s when a group there began rethinking diseases such as heart attacks and diabetes, focusing on prevention and not just treatment. Today we take for granted that any successful public health approach to these kinds of diseases must involve education of the public to adopt lifestyle changes such as in diet, exercise, and smoking. But these were new ideas at the medical school, where doctors had always just treated diseases after they showed up, sometimes too late to do much good.

Hamburg went on to become a leading policy adviser on medical issues, including from 1975 as president of the medical institute of the National Academy of Sciences which advises the government. He promoted the prevention approach to tackle challenging issues of adolescent health and other health policy problems. Then in 1983, when public concern about nuclear war had risen during the first Reagan Administration,

Hamburg took over as head of the Carnegie Corporation, a major foundation, and redirected it toward prevention of nuclear war. Then he instigated the Carnegie Commission on Preventing Deadly Conflict, which applied the prevention approach to the broader problem of war in the world. Finally, he turned to the prevention of genocide, arguing that most genocides are preceded by plentiful signs of what is coming, so that timely intervention could keep genocides from occurring. "Altogether," Hamburg concluded in 2002, "it is clear that there has been a burst of prevention activity in the early years of the twenty-first century that stands in dramatic contrast to the early years of the 1990s. . . ."

We need to develop the tools of war prevention. It is much cheaper than waiting for wars to break out.

AMERICAN LOYALTY BEYOND AMERICA

The UN's work for peace, whether through improved prevention activity or expanded peacekeeping, depends critically on U.S. support. America is the host country and leading contributor, yet Americans have long held mixed feelings about the UN. Near the end of World War II, more than 80 percent of Americans favored entry into a "world organization with police power to maintain world peace." A secret State Department poll showed a similar number supported committing U.S. military forces to the UN to help keep peace. But in the first of several swings in opinion, "by 1950, a Gallup poll found that only 27 percent of Americans thought that the UN was doing a good job." In 1965, the U.S. secretary of state shouted at the UN secretary-general, "Who do you think you are, a country?"

During the Reagan Administration, U.S. conservatives portrayed the UN "as a haven for Communist spies, as an institution inherently inimical to American interests, and as a profligate organization, badly administered, whose budget was decided by a majority that contributed very little to cover it." Pérez de Cuéllar reluctantly concluded "that these forces were aiming at U.S. withdrawal from the United Nations" and that some members of the administration shared this aim. As the United States withheld its UN dues over a number of years, by 1986 the UN "was literally on the brink of bankruptcy" despite budget cuts of $30 million annually. By 1988 the United States owed almost half a billion dollars.

After 1994, when Republicans won control of the U.S. Congress, "the

UN was a rich target, both substantively and symbolically," for their criticism. Boutros-Ghali "made the perfect hate object." In 1996, Republican
presidential candidates found strong crowd responses to their attacks
on the UN, for instance roaring their approval of Senator Phil Gramm
when he said, "I will NEVER send Americans into combat under UN command!" (At the time Americans made up about 5 percent of UN peacekeepers, none in combat operations.)

Congress withheld more UN dues. The Senate Foreign Relations Committee, chaired by Jesse Helms of North Carolina, was a center of opposition to the UN. During the Clinton Administration, Madeleine Albright,
first as UN ambassador and then secretary of state, "spent years holding
Jesse's hand and appealing to his chivalrous southern impulses in hopes
of persuading him to stop holding up peacekeeping missions and diplomatic postings and budget bills." Kofi Annan also tried to win over Helms,
but although "Helms's manner toward Annan was always polite . . . he
would not budge."

In 1999, the Senate finally confirmed, as U.S. ambassador to the UN,
Richard Holbrooke, the person who had banged heads together to push
through the Dayton Agreement and end the war in Bosnia. With great
personal energy and skillful diplomacy, he worked out the deals that
would bring the United States back into the fold, carry out reforms in the
institution, and ensure success in the crucial peacekeeping missions then
under way. But the tone shifted again in 2001. "The Bush team seemed
not so much hostile to the UN as scarcely aware of its existence." Despite
a period of working through the UN after the 9/11 attacks, the Bush Administration broke with the UN over Iraq and bypassed the international
organization in going to war in 2003. In 2008, presidential candidate John
McCain proposed to bypass the UN altogether with a new League of
Democracies, a fairly radical idea that reflects a deep lack of trust in the
UN. Opponents in the Congress have also continued to advocate against
the UN.

The current U.S. ambassador to the UN, Susan Rice, has helped the
Obama Administration to reengage America with all parts of the UN. In
2009 the United States caught up with its arrears, and President Obama
even said some nice things about the UN. However, in the 2010 elections
that shifted U.S. politics again to the right, some leading candidates criticized the UN and even called for U.S. withdrawal. So Americans have had

trouble settling down over the years and taking a consistent position on the international organization that they created and continue to host. But without Americans, there would never have been a UN.

II. Nations and Peoples United

The UN was founded on national sovereignty and continues to be at the mercy of national governments that are its members. This is not going to change anytime soon, and humanity's efforts for peace need to operate within that framework.

A CLUB OF STATES, NOT PEOPLE

Some observers find the UN too "state-centric" to respond to the challenges of our time. Many critics of the UN point out that it is not democratic. The UN does not consist of the people of the world, but of the states of the world, the national governments. Large and small countries get treated equally, and on the other hand permanent Security Council members get preferential status denied to other large, important countries. These criticisms miss the point. These are not flaws in the UN system but innate elements of its design. It would not work without them.

The UN is rooted in a system of states that evolved over centuries—a formal, symbolic system in which members all enact certain rituals, such as having a flag, an anthem, and a seat in the UN. The system protects and strengthens existing governments, sometimes at the expense of the world's people, some of whom have poor governments and lack basic rights. The interstate system follows the principle of sovereignty—that states do not interfere in each other's domestic affairs.

The interstate system divides the entire world and, almost as an afterthought, its people, into 193 units, each with a recognized government. States have rights; individuals traditionally do not. The system supports the government's right to control all the territory in its state. The places where no state holds control of a territory—such as the tribal areas of Pakistan or the south of Somalia—are generally places of trouble.

The costs of this system are well known, and we have encountered plenty of them in this book. Petty dictators get to take the stage and speechify at the General Assembly, as when Venezuelan president Hugo Chávez equated U.S. president George W. Bush with the devil, declaring that he could still smell the sulfur in the room from Bush's earlier speech. Human rights abusers have purview over upholding human rights. Heavily armed great powers control efforts on disarmament. The most reasonable and timid attempts to diminish violence or curb abuses in tiny, poor countries are loudly denounced as infringements on sovereignty. Lightly scratch any UN activity, and below a superficial layer of humanity and idealism you will find a thick bedrock of cold, hard national interests. These costs of the interstate system on which the UN rests are sometimes amusing and sometimes annoying, but mostly they are distracting—from the hard, important work of doing what we *can* do within that system to promote peace. As should be obvious from the mass of evidence in this book, we can do a lot. We should do more.

The interstate system, despite its problems, gets you a lot. It contains and potentially reduces the very large-scale violence that can take place between entire nations, where individuals do not know each other and do not expect to interact in the future. By contrast, in face-to-face settings individuals know each other personally and create social hierarchies reflecting status and access to resources. Individuals can use reciprocity and personal relationships to limit violence. What the interstate system does is to transpose a large-group dynamic, relations among nations, onto a small-group, personal setting. The members of the club, leaders of states, can sit in the UN General Assembly and operate as a community, with its status hierarchy and in-group rituals. This does not always keep wars from breaking out anyway but has been successful in limiting violence in interstate wars.

SOVEREIGNTY AND THE RESPONSIBILITY TO PROTECT

Although the UN recognizes each member state's sovereignty on its own territory, over the years a counterconcept has developed, that there are limits to sovereignty when governments commit mass atrocities against their own people. Gareth Evans, former Australian foreign minister, coined the phrase *responsibility to protect*, R2P for short, while on the commission that introduced the concept. He argues that "mass atrocities are the world's business . . . ; sovereignty is not a license to kill." Evans emphasizes that R2P should be used preventively, to head off mass atrocities before they happen. The responsibility to protect citizens from mass atrocities belongs to the national government first and foremost, and falls to the international community only when that government fails to do so. Military intervention against the wishes of the government should be only a last resort. And when intervention occurs, it should be by the UN. But ultimately there must be a limit to what governments may do to their people. The 2011 NATO air attacks in Libya, under a UN authorization to protect civilians, followed this model closely. (The outcome was uncertain as this book went to press.)

The R2P concept is a tricky one because it involves judgment of what kind of atrocities might trigger it. The Russian foreign minister used "responsibility to protect" to justify Russia's war against Georgia to protect the breakaway Georgian province of South Ossetia in 2008. "We exercised the responsibility to protect," he said. Russia can justify its actions in Georgia to protect a secessionist province by reference to NATO's actions in Kosovo in 1999. You can say that Kosovo was different because of Yugoslavia's history. But then who really can make those judgment calls about when intervention is justified or not? And the answer should be the Security Council.

The Security Council, however, does not generally agree on the issues of sovereignty versus a humanitarian intervention to stop atrocities. Russia, China, and newly independent developing countries all reject interference in their own internal affairs based on human rights concerns, and therefore oppose that kind of intervention elsewhere. Western states, especially the United States, Britain, France, and Canada, and humanitarian NGOs, support intervention to protect populations (unless it is too costly or inconvenient).

The UN Charter says, "Nothing contained in the present Charter shall authorize the United Nations to intervene in matters which are essentially within the domestic jurisdiction of any state." However, this principle is trumped by the enforcement measures allowed under Chapter VII when the Security Council acts on a threat to *international* peace and security. Thus, in practice, the international community can infringe sovereignty by declaring an internal situation—presumably a serious one such as genocide or massive starvation—to constitute a threat to international peace. Sometimes this rings true, as when Saddam Hussein's attacks on Kurds in the north of Iraq after the Gulf War sent masses of them fleeing over the mountains toward Turkey. In other cases, the international threat seems a bit more contrived.

"Humanitarian intervention" includes robust peace enforcement missions as well as traditional military interventions undertaken for humanitarian reasons, and even, in some definitions, nonmilitary actions such as economic sanctions and criminal prosecutions.

The conflict between human rights and sovereignty came to a head in Kosovo in 1999. The proponents of intervention there argued that Serbian actions against Kosovo Albanians constituted either ongoing or imminent genocide, which required a response. However, Security Council action was ruled out by both Russia (Serbia's traditional ally) and China (a champion of sovereignty because of sensitivities about Taiwan and Tibet). Various concerns made intervention by the EU, OSCE, or the United States impractical. "Faced with a genuine dilemma, the members of NATO decided, not implausibly . . . , that intervention was the lesser of two evils," concludes human rights scholar Jack Donnelly. The justification for intervening, however, troubled Donnelly, who had lived through the U.S. intervention in Vietnam, because "it has considerable potential for partisan abuse. . . . Caution is in order. The presumption always ought to be against intervention not authorized by the Security Council. But that presumption may in rare cases be overcome."

Historically, humanitarian intervention long predates the UN. The concept has a "historical pedigree . . . in the various measures taken by the European powers in the nineteenth century to curb supposed abuses within the Ottoman Empire." Political scientist Gary Bass shows that "over a century ago, it was a known principle that troops should sometimes be sent to prevent the slaughter of innocent foreigners." Human rights rhetoric played an important role in forming foreign policy, especially in Victorian Britain, as during the antislavery movement and the "mass uproar against vicious Belgian colonial rule in the Congo." Britain's government cared about Greeks oppressed by Turks, as did Russia's about Bulgarian Slavs massacred by the Ottomans and France's about Christians in Syria. Furthermore, today's heated debates—about universal human rights, about sovereignty as a shield for oppression of minorities, and about altruistic interventions that mask imperialistic designs—"were voiced loud and clear throughout the nineteenth century." The calls for interventions in that century did not align with imperialism, nor were they limited to efforts by Christians to protect other Christians where threatened overseas. The key force driving humanitarian intervention in nineteenth-century Europe was the rapid rise of a free press, which reported on atrocities overseas and thus sparked public outcries for action by democratic governments that responded to public opinion.

Norms regarding human rights have evolved in recent decades. Traditionally, notwithstanding Bass's observations about the nineteenth century, human rights have been considered "a profoundly *national*, not international, issue." During the Cold War, "it was widely accepted . . . that the use of force to save victims of gross human rights abuses was a violation of the [UN] Charter." But "a new norm of UN-authorized humanitarian intervention developed in the 1990s." In 1999, Secretary-General Kofi Annan supported the concept of humanitarian intervention if "fairly and consistently applied." He told the General Assembly, "The state is now widely understood to be the servant of its people, and not vice versa." The concept of humanitarian intervention was consistent with the spirit of the UN Charter, he argued.

But member states did not appreciate this weakening of their sovereignty, which contrasted with the positions taken by previous secretary-generals. The Group of 77 (G77), a bloc of developing countries, "formally repudiated the doctrine of humanitarian intervention as an unacceptable violation of state sovereignty." Not only did former colonies not want interference in their internal affairs—if they murder their own citizens, it is nobody else's business—but they did not trust the Security Council, on which they had little say, to make decisions about intervention. Actually, Annan claimed in his 1999 annual report, "the failure to intervene was driven more by the reluctance of Member States to pay the human and other costs of interventions, and by doubts that the use of force would be successful, than by concerns about sovereignty." The next year, Canada's prime minister set up the commission that developed the concept of R2P, and in 2005 the UN formally endorsed it.

In 2008, after the Burmese government turned down international aid to hard-hit cyclone victims and the international community refused to intervene by force to help them, former secretary of state Madeleine Albright wrote that sovereignty was on the rise again and humanitarian intervention moribund. The U.S. invasion of Iraq had given international military interventions in violation of sovereignty a bad name. The 2011 Libya intervention, however, showed that the R2P still has life.

ONE WORLD, ONE HUMANITY

Despite the resilience of sovereignty against humanitarianism, the people of the world, and not just their governments, are players in this game. The UN is an organization of states, not individuals, yet it has a place in our individual lives. Paul Kennedy, a historian at Yale who has long studied and worked with the UN, calls the image of blue-helmeted peacekeepers "one of the highest expressions of our common humanity and a testimony to human progress." Conor O'Brien wrote in 1962 that "the United Nations, with all its defects, is the most hopeful political institution that human beings have developed." Pérez de Cuéllar sees the years in which the UN has existed as "years of fundamental enlargement of human expectations . . . , a time of unparalleled human advancement, something often obscured by the perils that have accompanied it."

Since I was a kid, American children have carried cardboard boxes around on Halloween to trick-or-treat for UNICEF. "The UNICEF box was more than just a vehicle for collecting spare change," writes anthropologist Robert Rubinstein. "It was a symbol that . . . stood for the entire United Nations." The UN in turn "represented the emergence of an institutional embodiment of a moral force for the development of a better world . . . These meanings were crystallized and condensed into the little cardboard boxes, carried about by school children. . . ."

Today, peacekeeping stands as the most important symbol of the UN, represented in the public imagination by "the symbolic artifacts of peacekeeping—images of blue berets, white vehicles with large black UN letters painted on them, and, of course, the United Nations flag. . . ." However, the view of the UN as a moral force for good has been challenged by a myth of the UN as "an inefficient, ineffective, corrupt, and bureaucratically moribund institution." Bureaucratic and inefficient it may be, but the UN is not only a moral force but *our* moral force. It belongs to all of us—Americans especially—and we should let nobody steal it from us.

The UN is both an ideal of what the world can be, and a practical tool for bringing us closer to that ideal.

The UN flag belongs not to an institution nor to any national government, but to humanity. I say, go online and buy one, three by five feet, for about six dollars, and fly it. My New England college town flies the UN flag (not on the same flagpole as the American flag) in front of Town Hall. Why not? Our country *does* belong to it. If you do not want to fly the UN flag every day, how about once a year on May 29—the day the first peacekeeping mission began in 1948—which has been observed in recent years as the International Day of United Nations Peacekeepers. It would not hurt to pause once a year and pay tribute to all peacekeepers and especially the 2,500 or so who have died in the course of their missions.

There is an organization Americans can join to support the UN. The United Nations Association of the USA has 20,000 members. Compare that with other big important causes of our time—1.3 million members in the Sierra Club, for example—and it is clear that support for the UN is underdeveloped.

PASSING THE WORLD DOWN THROUGH THE GENERATIONS

In her 101-year-long life, my grandmother saw amazing changes in the world. Born near the end of the nineteenth century, she remembered the first automobile to come through her town in upstate New York, with people circling it in wonder asking, "Where's the horse?" She witnessed the advent of radio and then television and finally computers, which she considered pure magic. A lifelong feminist, Zionist, and activist in progressive causes, she saw women win the right to vote; the civil rights movement; the Holocaust and the founding of the state of Israel; the rise of communism and its fall; the creation of the League of Nations, its failure, and then the United Nations. Toward the end of this long life, she told me that the most important thing was this: She had seen two world wars and her greatest fear was a third one.

Grandma's fear did not come to pass. Writers sometimes talk about the Cold War as a "third world war" and Islamic terrorism as a fourth, but these are metaphors. My grandmother, who saw the real thing twice, knew the difference. She died peacefully, in a world that had not experienced a world war for generations.

What might my own grandchildren say about me in another fifty years? "He was born in the remote past, before space flight and the Internet. In his early decades, two superpowers kept thousands of nuclear weapons on hair-trigger alert, so that a mistake could have destroyed the world in a flash. Back then, the great powers fought big interventionary wars in places like Vietnam, Afghanistan, and Iraq, while bloody civil wars held back the economic development of many poor countries in Africa and Asia. The United Nations lacked the resources to accomplish its key missions, and the world's countries tackled global problems like AIDS, global warming, and terrorism with great difficulty and many missteps." I would reply that at least we did not have world wars in my lifetime! Step by step.

So let us move history forward another step, and another. We may not achieve "true" peace, or "permanent" peace, or "just" peace, but we can increasingly achieve what the world needs most—a peace that stops the shooting and opens the door to a future.

Should we let ourselves feel hopeful when there is still so much wrong in the world and so much left to do? What if you were trying to rescue someone trapped in a car underwater? After much effort, you have finally attached a chain, albeit precariously, and used a winch to raise the car almost to the surface. Would you become complacent and take a lunch break? Or would the prospect of success focus you on putting every effort into completing the operation without the chain slipping off? Would it be immoral to shout, "Almost there! Keep going!" to the winch operator?

Today, bit by bit, we are dragging our muddy, banged-up world out of the ditch of war. We have avoided nuclear wars, left behind world war, nearly extinguished interstate war, and reduced civil wars to fewer countries with fewer casualties. We are almost there.

Notes

Chapter 1

Page
3 *Kirkuk*: Zoepf and Dagher 2008.
3 *Proxy battles*: Slackman 2009.
3 *Beirut clash*: *New York Times* 1980a,b; Associated Press 1980.
4 *Diminished dramatically*: This paragraph is adapted from Goldstein and Pevchouse 2011: 83.
4 *Cuéllar*: Pérez de Cuéllar 1997: 14, 13, 7; Sivard 1982 gives a list of wars in progress then.
5 *Chemical weapons*: White phosphorus, whose recent use has raised controversy, is not classified as a chemical weapon in the main body of the chemical weapons convention. See fas.org/programs/bio/factsheets/whitephosphorus.html.
6 *Interlude before new. . . . wars*: Goldstein 1991: 324 suggests that an upcoming lull in war could offer a chance to break the cycle of recurrent great-power wars. See also Goldstein 1988: 349–50.
6 *Angell*: Angell 1910: vii.
8 *French UN peacekeepers*: Rieff 1995: 150–51.
9 *Mature understanding*: Worldpublicopinion.org 2007: 9–10, 5.
10 *War was a common occurrence*: Blight and McNamara 2001: 21.
10 *May well be underestimates*: Blight and McNamara 2001: 26.
10 *UN Charter*: Blight and McNamara 2001: 153, 154.

Chapter 2

13 *Data-set on battle-related deaths*: These and later battle-death data are from PRIO version 3.0; see Lacina and Gleditsch 2005 and www.prio.no/CSCW/Datasets/Armed-Conflict/Battle-Deaths/. Midpoint of low and high estimates used when no "best estimate" given.
13 *Extremely lethal*: O'Hanlon 2003: 27; see also Sivard 1993: 20.
13 *IDPs appeared to jump*: See, e.g., the graph on p. 7 of UNHCR 2009.
14 *Newly displaced. . . . return home*: UNHCR data; UNHCR 2009: 19–21; see also Harff and Gurr 2004: xii.
14 *Child soldier recruitment*: Polgreen 2008c.
14 *Global Peace Index*: Accessed 6/8/10 at www.visionofhumanity.org/gpi-data/#/2010/scor/.
14 *Brookings*: Livingston et al. 2010.
15 *Peace factors*: Kriesberg 2007: 99–101, 113.
15 *Intractable*: Crocker, Hampson, and Aall 2005: 3–4.
16 *Fatality totals by war*: PRIO battle-death data, see Lacina and Gleditsch 2005; Bethany Lacina, personal communication, October 2010.
18 *War on terrorism*: Allison 2004.
18 *Mind-boggling 30,000*: Data from Federation of American Scientists and National Resource Defense Council, reported in *New York Times*, April 8, 2010.

18 *Fallen in just twenty-five years*: In addition, each side has several thousand weapons waiting in line to be dismantled.
18 *U.S. tactical nuclear*: Norris and Kristensen 2011.
18 *Storage facilities*: Norris and Kristensen 2009: 86.
18–19 *Incredible accomplishment*: Easterbrook 2003: 70.
19 *Doomsday clock*: Bulletin of the Atomic Scientists 2007.
19 *Total number of refugees*: UNHCR 2000: 310. Higher numbers mentioned earlier include
internally displaced persons.
19–20 *Warned West Point cadets*: Shanker 2011.
20 *Global turmoil*: Mearsheimer 1990: 6; Kaplan 1994; Brzezinski 1993; see also Cooper 2003:
vii, 5, 25, 83.
20 *Ghastly and persistent*: Collier 2009: 7, 3, 4; O'Hanlon 2003: 2.
20 *Mention that violence is decreasing*: Crocker, Hampson, and Aall 2007; Brown 2007: 39;
King 2007: 115; Gurr 2007: 133, 134, 151; Urquhart 2007: 265; O'Hanlon 2007: 323; Freedman
2007: 261.
20 *No less dangerous*: Solomon 2007: xi; Crocker, Hampson, and Aall 2007: 6.
21 *Rape of Nanking*: Chang 1997; Rummel 1991: 6–7; see also Slim 2008: 236.
21 *Aerial bombardment*: Slim 2008: 56–57.
21 *Dresden. . . . raid*: Taylor 2004: 448.
21 *Fifty German cities. . . . Tokyo*: Slim 2008: 57; Downes 2008: 116–17.
22 *Burning flesh*: Downes 2008: 116.
22 *Bombed sixty-four Japanese cities*: Downes 2008: 117.
22 *Bomber Command*: Markusen and Kopf 1995: 12, 13.
22 *Passchendaele*: Quigley 1966: 231.
22 *British naval blockade*: Markusen and Kopf 1995: 30; Downes 2008: 84 estimates half a
million German deaths and a similar number of Austrians.
23 *Most war-torn century*: Ferguson 2006: iv, 647; Valentino 2004: 1; Carnegie Commission
1997: 11; Luard 1986: 394.
23 *No scientific basis*: Payne 2004: 10–11.
23 *Incidentally China*: Rummel 1991: 3.
23 *Many writers equate*: Holsti 1996: 36; Ferguson 2006: lxxi, 596; see also Brzezinski 1993:
4–5, 7.
23 *87 million war deaths*: Brzezinski 1993: 9. Leitenberg 2006: 8 has 136–149 million total.
24 *Relative tranquility*: Schroeder 2006: 36–40 calls the eighteenth and nineteenth centuries
peaceful, but he focuses on Austria, Germany, and Russia, not worldwide.
24 *Political science databases*: Levy 1983: 113; Payne 2004.
24 *Taiping*: McEvedy and Jones 1978: 167 show a population decline of 20 million in 1850–75.
24 *Yunnan Province*: Rummel 1994: 53.
24 *Confederate general*: Quoted in Markusen and Kopf 1995: 27.
25 *Percent of GDP in Western countries*: Gat 2006: 524–27.
25 *Erosion of. . . . rules of conduct*: Jackson 1999: 49; 123, 124, 130, 137, 139.
25 *As the war dragged on*: Jackson 1999: 149, 150, 153, 155.
25–26 *Atrocities were not uncommon*: Downes 2008: 156–77; Midlarsky 2005: 33; Jackson
1999: 11.
26 *Dahomey*: Forbes 1851.
26 *Massacre is not*: Slim 2008: 3, 46.
26 *Deliberately intended*: Slim 2008: 39, 40.
26 *Warfare and genocide*: Markusen and Kopf 1995: 21; see also Holsti 1991: 84, 102, 142.
26 *Thirty Years' War*: Wedgwood 1938: 525, 511, 516; Markusen and Kopf 1995: 24; Friedrichs
1997: 188, 189.
27 *Mortality among the civilian population*: Wedgwood 1938: 516, 512–13.
27 *Those Germans who survived*: Parker 1997: 170; Friedrichs 1997: 192, 188.
27 *Losses in battle*: Parker 1997: 182, 183.
27 *Frequent brutality*: Friedrichs 1997: 187.
27 *Manchu*: McEvedy and Jones 1978: 167, 52; see also Goldstone 1993: 390–91.
27 *Experts have puzzled*: Heijdra 1998: 436–37; Peterson 2002: 5; Rowe 2002: 475; Myers and
Wang 2002: 565.

27 *Brutality of colonial wars*: Wills 1998: 358; Cook 1998: 1, 5; see also Slim 2008: 101.

28 *Conquistadors*: Cook 1998: 3.

28 *Las Casas. . . . Devastation caused by diseases*: Cook 1998: 2, 10–11.

28 *Warfare. . . . was extremely prevalent*: Luard 1986: 25.

28 *English warfare*: Prestwich 1996: 11, 115, 4.

28 *Limoges*: Jean Froissart, quoted in Prestwich 1996: 219.

28–29 *Not easy to reconcile*: Prestwich 1996: 219, 231, 318, 161, 296.

29 *Destruction of the property and lives*: Prestwich 1996: 240, 242, 243; see also Tuchman 1978: 81, 83.

29 *Actual battles*: Prestwich 1996: 328, 330–32, 239.

29 *Siege warfare saw the worst atrocities*: Prestwich 1996: 303; Eckhardt 1989: 94; Bradbury 1992: 298, 329; see also Downes 2008: 19.

30 *Alençon*: Bradbury 1992: 53–54; see also 321.

30 *Massacres and mutilations*: Bradbury 1992: 319, 322.

30 *The Crusades*: Slim 2008: 47; Bradbury 1992: 319, 192, 195, 318, 297.

30 *War between groups that hated each other*: Bradbury 1992: 331; see also 227, 320; 323–24.

31 *Outside Europe*: Bradbury 1992: 319.

31 *Genghis Khan*: Rummel 1994: 49; Man 2004: 200 estimates that Samarkand's population was reduced by more than 250,000.

31 *Urgench. . . . Nishapur*: Man 2004: 174; Rummel 1994: 46.

31 *Mongols killed. . . . in Merv*: Rummel 1994: 49; Slim 2008: 48. Note that Rummel also refers to "Meru Chahjan," leading others to add this as a different city, but Meru is another name for Merv.

31 *Pearl of Central Asia*: Man 2004: 174, 176.

31 *Khan's biographer*: Man 2004: 177–80.

32 *In China, the Mongol's scale of killing*: Rummel 1994: 49–51; Man 2004: 254, 262.

32 *Campaign to Europe*: Bradbury 1992: 319; Slim 2008: 48–49; Man 2004: 267; Markusen and Kopf 1995: 23; see also Rummel 1994: 50.

32 *Toynbee*: Quoted in Markusen and Kopf 1995: 24; also in Rummel 1994: 50–51.

33 *Not the only massacring army*: Rummel 1994: 60, 63.

33 *An Shi Rebellion*: Sorokin 1925/1967: 199–200; Parker 1903: 25–26; McEvedy and Jones 1978: 167; Twitchett 1979: 453–63, esp.455; Peterson 1979; 478, 485.

33 *Byzantium*: Eckhardt 1992: 63.

33 *Normal part of medieval war*: Bradbury 1992: 325, 324, 327.

34 *Pinker*: Pinker 2007: 19; see Pinker 2011.

34 *Carthage*: Quoted in Markusen and Kopf 1995: 23.

34 *Raping of women*: Slim 2008: 60, 61, 234; Anderlini 2007: 30–31; see Wood 2009; Goldstein 2001: 362–71.

34 *Looting was the norm*: Slim 2008: 94, 96–97.

35 *Dynastic transitions*: McEvedy and Jones 1978: 167.

35 *Assyrian Empire*: Markusen and Kopf 1995: 22; Dupuy and Dupuy 1993: 10, 11.

35 *Sumerian. . . . Uruk*: Guilaine and Zammit 2005: 1–3.

35 *Eastern Mediterranean*: Guilaine and Zammit 2005: 4; Dupuy and Dupuy 1993: 4; but see Eckhardt 1992: 145, 169.

36 *Downward trend*: Levy 1983: 131, 132.

36 *Upward trend*: Eckhardt 1992: 130–31, 108, 127, 128.

36 *No trend*: Sorokin 1937: 347; Sarkees, Wayman, and Singer 2003; Clark 2007: 128.

36 *Gat*: Gat 2006: 535.

36 *Nearly triple*: Markusen and Kopf 1995: 32–33; see Eckhardt 1991: 438; 440.

36 *One recent analysis*: Sarkees and Wayman 2010: 562, 567, 569, 3; but see Lacina and Gleditsch 2005: 155; see also Schroeder 2006: 36–40; Väyrynen 2006; Thompson 2006.

36 *Luard*: Luard 1986: 395, 396, 399, 5, 9–10.

36 *Various scholars have tried*: White 2003 provides exemplary source notes and a variety of estimates; see also Wright 1942/1965: 1542, 665, 243–44 n.64, 658–61, 245; Gat 2006: 131–32; Wedgwood 1938: 516.

37 *4 billion total deaths*: Summation of annual data from White 2003.

37 *1.5 percent of deaths*: The 4 billion total deaths may be an underestimate, which would make the war deaths an even smaller percentage; Steven Pinker, personal communication, October 2010.

37 *Corresponding guesses*: Eckhardt 1991: 438, from McEvedy and Jones 1978.

37 *Nine European countries*: Sorokin 1937: 273, 341; reprinted in Wright 1942/1965: 656.

37 *Greek and Roman. . . . guessy*: Sorokin 1937: 47, 346–47, 295, 296, 297, 303.

38 *Not so uniquely bloody*: Ferguson 2006: 649–53.

38 *Common and deadly*: LeBlanc 2003: 8; see also Martin and Frayer eds. 1997.

38 *Thirty-one hunting-gathering societies*: Ember 1978: 444.

38 *Time and time again*: LeBlanc 2003: 154; see also Keeley 1996; Gat 2006: 131; Payne 2004: 76–77.

38 *Estimates of hunter-gatherers' mortality*: Gat 2006: 129–30; See also Clark 2007: 125; LeBlanc 2003: 150, 151. LeBlanc 2003: 127 reports a "25 percent warfare death rate" for the Murngin.

39 *Southern California*: LeBlanc 2003: 9, 154.

39 *Archaeology in North America*: Krech 1994: 14; LeBlanc 2003: 199; see also Bamforth 1994; Gat 2006: 130–31; Chacon and Mendoza eds. 2007.

39 *Detailed evidence from archaeology*: LeBlanc 2003: 12–13, 6, xi, xii, xiii, 223, 230.

40 *Three continents*: LeBlanc 2003: xii–xiii, 126, 154.

40 *Embedded projectile points*: Keeley 1996: viii.

40 *LeBlanc argues that tribal societies*: LeBlanc 2003: 155, 186, 187, 198, 191, 217, 218.

40 *At the state level*: LeBlanc 2003: 191, 193–94.

40 *Talheim*: Guilaine and Zammit 2005: 86, 87.

41 *Austria. . . . Mannheim. . . . France*: Guilaine and Zammit 2005: 91–93, 241–49, Appendix 1 by Maryvonne Naudet and Raymond Vidal.

41 *Grave site in Sudan*: Guilaine and Zammit 2005: 67–72.

41 *Rock paintings*: Gat 2006: 27–29, 18; see also LeBlanc 2003: 114.

41 *These Australians*: Gat 2006: 17–18.

41 *Neolithic men*: Dupuy and Dupuy 1993: 1.

42 *Neanderthals*: LeBlanc 2003: 96–97.

42 *Deep-seated forces*: Goldstein 1988.

Chapter 3

45 *Win the peace*: Ruggie 1996: 28–29.

46 *Dumbarton Oaks*: Hilderbrand 1990: 67; Ruggie 1996: 28–34; see also doaks.org/about/the_dumbarton_oaks_conversations.html.

46 *Temporary headquarters*: Rosenthal 1995; Meisler 1995: 34.

46 *Bunche. . . . main architect*: Urquhart 1993: 22; see also www.library.ucla.edu/bunche.

46–47 *Bunche. . . . childhood. . . . professorship*: Urquhart 1993: 134–35.

47 *Win the confidence of postcolonial leaders*: Urquhart 1993: 221–22.

47 *UNSCOP. . . . lightweight*: Urquhart 1993: 142.

47 *They were to visit Palestine*: Urquhart 1993: 142, 144.

47 *UNSCOP first went to Jerusalem*: Urquhart 1993: 143, 288.

48 *Terrible mess of things*: Urquhart 1993: 146.

48 *Appointing a special representative*: Meisler 1995: 39; Kennedy 2006: 80.

48 *Chartered a DC-3*: Urquhart 1993: 159, 160.

48 *Appointed Chief Representative*: Urquhart 1993: 249, 168, 171.

49 *Shot him dead*: Urquhart 1993: 178, 180.

49 *Created a new enterprise*: Urquhart 1993: 160–61, 169; UNSC 50, S/801, May 29, 1948.

49 *Principle was to remain neutral*: Urquhart 1993: 161, 170, 185.

50 *Painted its vehicles*: Urquhart 1993: 161.

50 *Early UN peacekeeping missions*: Urquhart 1993: 161.

50 *The 1,000 armed UN guards*: Urquhart 1993: 161–62, 203.

51 *150 military observers*: http://www.un.org/depts/dpko/missions/untso/background.html, accessed 6/23/09.

51 *Nobel Peace Prize*: Urquhart 1993: 231.

51 *Not everyone appreciated*: Urquhart 1993: 235, 247.
51 *President Truman*: Urquhart 1993: 247.
51 *Soviet Union was no friend*: Pérez de Cuéllar 1997: 7, 8.
52 *By May 1954*: Urquhart 1993: 253–55.
52 *Severest test*: Urquhart 1972: 6–7.
52–53 *Someone weak*: Linnér 2008: 29; Urquhart 1972: 15.
53 *Exemplify the ideal*: Linnér 2008: 28; Traub 2006a: 10.
53 *Back on the job*: Urquhart 1993: 265.
53 *Lester Pearson*: Urquhart 1993: 265–67.
54 *Troubling. . . . disturbing*: Kennedy 2006: 82.
54 *Masterpiece*: Urquhart 1993: 267; see also Bellamy, Williams, and Griffin 2004: 99; Diehl
        2008: 42–45.
54 *Landmark event*: Kennedy 2006: 81, 82; see also Doyle and Sambanis 2006: 12.
54 *Teasing him*: Sir Brian Urquhart, personal communication, September 2010.
54 *Corporal. . . . noncontroversial countries*: Urquhart 1993: 266, 270, 267.
54 *Commonwealth*: Kennedy 2006: 83.
54 *New principles and rules*: Urquhart 1993: 266.
54–55 *Many details stood between*: Urquhart 1993: 172–73, 269.
55 *Signature look*: Rubinstein 2008: 72.
55 *Fully independent*: UNEF n.d.
55 *Supply of food*: Urquhart 1993: 269; see also Rubinstein 2008: 22, Traub 2006a: 12.
55 *Bunche's conference room*: Urquhart 1993: 268, 269.
55–56 *Moving quickly was paramount*: Urquhart 1993: 268, 270.
56 *Status-of-forces*: UNEF n.d.
56 *Fly only the UN flag*: Urquhart 1993: 271–72.
56 *Holy trinity*: Diehl 2008: 57; see also UNDPKO 2008: 31.
56 *Later undermine UNEF*: UNEF n.d.
56 *Political rhetoric*: Rubinstein 2008: 22.
56 *Purely temporary*: UNEF n.d.
57 *Spraying the minaret*: Rubinstein 2008: 35.
57 *Frontline of a moral force*: Urquhart 1993: 271, 289, 272.
58 *Used violence freely*: Stanley 1879: 276; see also Driver 2001: 137.
58 *Brutal efficiency*: Urquhart 1993: 303.
58 *Leopold's personal rule*: Hochschild 1998.
59 *Leaderless mass*: Urquhart 1993: 310.
59 *Two weeks before independence*: Urquhart 1993: 308; Urquhart 1972: 401.
59 *Two weeks after independence*: Urquhart 1972: 408.
60 *Swiftness in arrival*: Quoted in Urquhart 1993: 312.
60 *Miraculously short time*: Urquhart 1972: 401, 402.
60 *Onusians*: O'Brien 1962: 10–11.
61 *Quite unlike anything*: Urquhart 1972: 402.
61 *Mandate was more expansive*: See Diehl 2008: 45–47.
61 *First aid to a wounded rattlesnake*: Urquhart 1993: 312, 319, 320, 322.
61 *Belgian channels to communicate*: Urquhart 1972: 418–19.
61 *Irish diplomat*: O'Brien 1962. On his later controversial writings, see *Guardian* 2009.
62 *Extraction of minerals for profit*: O'Brien 1962: 65.
62 *Stakes were high*: Gibbs 1993.
62 *Shinkolobwe*: Zoellner 2009: 43, 50.
62 *Big-power politics*: Nkrumah 1960.
63 *UN would not take sides*: Urquhart 1972: 425; O'Brien 1962: 98.
63 *Three or four heads*: Linnér 2008: 25.
63 *Short of clarity*: Urquhart 1972: 403; see also Bellamy, Williams, and Griffin 2004: 156–57.
63 *Hammarskjöld flew to Katanga*: Urquhart 1972: 427, 436.
64 *Justify foreign intervention*: See, e.g., Donnelly 2003: 179–80, 254–58.
64 *Senseless slaughter*: Urquhart 1972: 438.
64 *Central government split*: Urquhart 1972: 443, 452–53; Urquhart 1993: 337.
64 *Khrushchev. . . . ill-concealed glee*: Urquhart 1972: 459, 462, 486.

64–65 *Even more isolated*: Urquhart 1972: 490.
65 *The "Congo Club"*: O'Brien 1962: 204, 51.
65 *Three Americans*: O'Brien 1962: 50, 52, 53.
65 *Back in the Congo*: Urquhart 1993: 328, 329, 337.
66 *Small apartment building*: Urquhart 1972: 410.
66 *Crisis-ridden*: Urquhart 1993: 338.
66 *Accused the UN of complicity*: Urquhart 1993: 338, 340; Urquhart 1972: 506.
66–67 *Passivity. . . . some joker in the UN*: Urquhart 1972: 506, 507; Urquhart 1993: 339.
67 *Atmosphere of horror*: Urquhart 1972: 508, 509.
67 *Massacred 44 peacekeepers*: Kennedy 2006: 84.
67 *By spring of 1961*: Urquhart 1972: 515, 524.
67 *Skilled personnel*: Urquhart 1972: 518, 519, 525, 341.
67 *UN shop in Katanga*: O'Brien 1962: 98; Urquhart 1993: 346.
67–68 *Used massive atrocities*: O'Brien 1962: 146, 149.
68 *Operation Rumpunch*: O'Brien 1962: 220–21; see also Urquhart 1972: 556.
68 *Indian and Swedish UN contingents*: O'Brien 1962: 252–53, 1; Urquhart 1972: 567.
68 *Squalid battle*: Urquhart 1993: 342.
69 *Encirclement of the Palace*: O'Brien 1962: 256, 257.
69 *UN's military headquarters*: O'Brien 1962: 270–71, 273, 276.
69 *Foreign press pounded*: O'Brien 1962: 266; Urquhart 1972: 572–73; Urquhart 1993: 343.
69 *Toxic brew*: O'Brien 1962: 278, 276.
69 *Nuanced document*: Urquhart 1993: 326.
70 *Appointment of O'Brien*: O'Brien 1962: 41.
70 *An Irish diplomat*: O'Brien 1962: 41–42; see Urquhart, 1972: 548.
71 *Propellor DC-6*: Urquhart 1972: 587–93.
71 *Sabotage theories*: Rösiö 1993.
71 *Hit the wrong plane*: Sir Brian Urquhart, personal communication, September 2010.
71 *Suspicions ran high*: O'Brien 1962: 286–87; see also *New York Times* 1992; Rösiö 1993; Gibbs 1993.
71 *21 UN soldiers killed*: Urquhart 1993: 349–50.

Chapter 4

73 *Foreseen transformational change*: Rosenau 1990.
74 *Positively triumphant*: Barnett 2002: 22.
74 *From 1948 to 1988*: Kennedy 2006: 91.
74 *Agenda for Peace*: Boutros-Ghali 1992: 8, 11.
74 *Peace-enforcement*: Boutros-Ghali 1992: 25, 26; see Pugh 2007.
75 *Killing 140,000*: PRIO data; Lacina and Gleditsch 2005.
76 *Underfunded and underpowered*: Kennedy 2006: 94; see Howard 2008: 37–40.
76 *Most vicious fighting*: Howard 2008: 37, 38.
76 *Final shootout*: BBC News 2002.
76 *Not rate much press*: A *New York Times* article on p. 6, a paragraph next day on p. 9, and a few short paragraphs the third day on p. 12.
77 *Somalia, the mission began*: Howard 2008: 23–25; budget is for UNASOM I and II.
77 *Mission morphed*: Howard 2008: 25; see also Diehl 2008: 50–52.
77 *Mandate. . . . was deeply conflicted*: Howard 2008: 26–27; see Doyle and Sambanis 2006: 152.
78 *Black Hawk Down*: Bowden 1999; also a 2001 movie.
78 *Pivotal role*: Rubinstein 2008: 4, 8.
78 *Ended the starvation*: Doyle, Johnstone, and Orr 1997: 5.
78 *Proved totally ineffective*: Kennedy 2006: 104.
79 *Solid support*: Howard 2008: 29, 87, 89, 50.
79 *Honest and energetic*: Des Forges 1999: 45, 46.
79 *The rebels gained ground*: Des Forges 1999: 96, 4, 109.
79 *UNAMIR was created*: Howard 2008: 29; Des Forges 1999: 17.

79 *Success at low cost. . . . budget was not approved*: Des Forges 1999: 18, 131–33.
80 *Accords were actually implemented*: Des Forges 1999: 131.
80 *Operate without adequate resources*: Bellamy, Williams, and Griffin 2004: 131.
80 *You'll get your APCs*: Dallaire 2003: 331–32.
80 *Definitive account*: Des Forges 1999: 1, 2, 5.
81 *Sent a telegram*: Howard 2008: 32; Des Forges 1999: 18.
81 *Narrowest possible interpretation*: Des Forges 1999: 19, 172, 174–75.
81 *Chaotic, spontaneous*: Barnett 2002: 110.
81 *Plane was shot down*: Des Forges 1999: 6, 181.
81 *Massive but systematic campaign*: Des Forges 1999: 8, 10, 215.
81 *In the first days*: Des Forges 1999: 206–08, 212.
81–82 *At one church. . . . little success*: Des Forges 1999: 212, 297.
82 *Clergy*: Des Forges 1999: 245–47.
82 *Half a million persons*: Quotes are from Des Forges 1999: 15–16.
82 *Uppsala*: Sundberg 2009: 17.
82 *On a much smaller scale*: Des Forges 1999: 692.
82 *Brutally massacred. . . . crippling*: Howard 2008: 32.
82 *Give me the means*: Both quoted in Des Forges 1999: 598.
83 *Cupboards were bare*: Dallaire 2003: 264.
83 *Contingent from Bangladesh*: Dallaire 2003: 272–73.
83 *On the fifth day*: Dallaire 2003: 289–90.
83 *And then departed*: Des Forges 1999: 7; see also 606.
83 *Running out of ammunition*: Barnett 2002: 100.
83 *Toward the apocalypse*: Dallaire 2003: 293.
83 *Drastically scale back*: Dallaire 2003: 291, 295.
83–84 *Dallaire later estimated*: Des Forges 1999: 22, 607.
84 *Already in the capital*: Des Forges 1999: 606, 608.
84 *Stopped the massacres*: Quoted in Des Forges 1999: 607.
84 *Objective was forgotten*: Quoted in Des Forges 1999: 600.
84 *Attempts were subverted*: Howard 2008: 32.
84 *Jamming*: Des Forges 1999: 25.
84 *Avoid the word*: Des Forges 1999: 19, 595; Barnett 2002: 3.
84 *One bright spot*: Dallaire 2003: 296, 297.
84–85 *Mille Collines*: Dallaire 2003: 302.
85 *Bravery of the Tunisians*: Dallaire 2003: 302, 296.
85 *Captain from Senegal*: Des Forges 1999: 610.
85 *Ultimately, the UN just pulled out*: Des Forges 1999: 617, 618, 22.
85–86 *When evacuating UN peacekeepers*: Des Forges 1999: 611, 610.
86 *Bad timing*: Howard 2008: 29; see also Barnett 2002: 13; Traub 2006a: 53.
86 *A more traditional approach*: Both quoted in Barnett 2002: 116, 74.
86 *Sad ending*: Des Forges 1999: 23; Prunier 1999: 301, 302.
86 *We were manipulated*: Des Forges 1999: 24, 668–81, 681, 687–88.
86 *English-speaking*: Des Forges 1999: 117–19, 670.
87 *Tribunal for Rwanda*: Des Forges 1999: 738, 739, 761; BBC News 2008b.
87 *Bosnia*: That is, the Republic of Bosnia and Herzegovina.
87–88 *Many times in the war years*: For a contrary view, see Gibbs 2009.
88 *Defend Bosnia's integrity*: Picco 1999: 297.
88 *No secret of his distaste*: Traub 2006a: 43; Picco 1999: 37.
89 *Safe areas*: Traub 2006a: 50, 44, 47.
89 *Scenes from hell*: Quoted in Meisler 2007: 115.
90 *Dayton*: Daalder 2000.
90 *Most important test*: Shawcross 2000: 147.
91 *In 2005, . . . considerable progress*: Cousens and Harland 2006: 49.
91 *Equivalent of post-traumatic*: Traub 2006a: 124.
91 *Stories of success*: Howard 2008: xi. Doyle and Sambanis (2006: 21) list as failures Somalia, Bosnia, Rwanda, and Cyprus, and list as successes Congo, El Salvador, Cambodia, Croatia, Brcko (in Bosnia), and East Timor.

92 *UN's first return*: Durch 2006a: 3.
92 *Differed from all previous*: Howard 2008: 52.
92 *First of five*: Fortna and Howard 2008: 293.
92–93 *Finally began in 1989*: Howard 2008: 53–56, 64, 67.
93 *South Africa tried to subvert*: Krasno 2003a: 48–49.
94 *The remarkable cooperation*: Howard 2008: 77–80; Krasno 2003a: 47–48.
94 *Tight timetable*: Howard 2008: 81, 83.
94 *Success stories*: Krasno 2003a: 25.
94 *El Salvador the UN came in*: Howard 2008: 92, 97, 129.
95 *Key figure*: Howard 2008: 99, 98.
95 *Had a clear mandate*: Howard 2008: 101–03.
95 *Truth Commission*: Howard 2008: 108.
96 *UN's police work*: Howard 2008: 112–14.
96 *Land reform*: Howard 2008: 118–21.
96 *Similarly, elections*: Howard 2008: 122–25; Wood 2000; Wood 2003a: 30.
97 *Mixed results. . . . peace talks began*: Howard 2008: 131–32, 137.
97–98 *The mission lasted eighteen months*: Howard 2008: 138.
98–99 *An immediate. . . . hostages four times*: Howard 2008: 144–49, 151–52, 155.
99 *The Khmer Rouge withdrew*: Howard 2008: 139, 167–73.
99 *UNTAC did not end political violence*: Howard 2008: 171, 173, 176.
99–100 *The experience gained*: Howard 2008: 231–33, 258, 245–46, 249–51, 225; Boothby 2003: 121–23, 127, 129.
100 *Paradigm-setting*: Doyle, Johnstone, and Orr 1997: 2, 20.
100–01 *The UN mission in Mozambique*: Howard 2008: 179, 184–85, 189.
101 *Sant-Egidio*: Giro n.d.
101 *Offered itself as mediator*: Howard 2008: 191.
101 *Both sides asked the UN*: Howard 2008: 187.
101–02 *An overtaxed, divided*: Salomons 2003: 83, 96.
102 *High degree of autonomy*: Howard 2008: 198–99, 196.
102 *Assessed that money could*: Howard 2008: 197, 199; Salomons 2003: 112.
102 *Another trust fund*: Howard 2008: 202; Salomons 2003: 109–10.
102–03 *After the UN departed*: Salomons 2003: 111; Howard 2008: 219–21.
103 *The two sets side by side*: 1990 population data from UN Population Division 2009.
104 *In addition to the consent*: Howard 2008: 8, 10, 15, 16, 19; Doyle and Sambanis 2006: 2; see also Autesserre 2010: 8.
104 *Cultural learning that must occur*: Rubinstein 2008: 36, 107.
104 *Peace missions also need*: Rubinstein 2008: 37, 51, 89; see also 138.
105 *Made a database*: Fortna 2008: 2, 3, 11; Fortna's dataset is an expanded version of Doyle and Sambanis's.
105 *Evidence is overwhelming*: Fortna 2008: 6, 9–10, 106, 116.
105 *Resounding yes*: Fortna and Howard 2008: 289; Fortna 2008: 125.
105 *Several pathways*: Fortna 2008: 9, 102.
105–06 *Despite these positive outcomes*: Fortna 2008: 24, 44; see also Regan 2000: 39; Fortna and Howard 2008: 290; Collier 2009: 84.
106 *Separate but parallel*: Collier 2009: 83, 95.
106 *Very good value*: Collier 2009: 96, 97, 99.
106 *Reversion to war*: Collier 2009: 75, 88.
106 *Markedly improved*: Griffin 2003: 214.
106 *Built a data-set*: Doyle and Sambanis 2006: 72, 126; see Durch 2006a: 13–16.
106–07 *Roland Paris*: Paris 2004: 19, 6, ix, 5, 89, 95, 111, 113, 145–46, 223.
107 *The case of Nicaragua*: Paris 2004: 139, 118–20; Paris 2009a: 58.
107–08 *Daniel Ortega*: BBC News 2006.
108 *To Paris's credit*: Paris 2009b: 108.

Chapter 5

109 *Famine to feast*: Weiss et al. 2007: 76.
109 *Launched just two. . . . guessed*: Durch 2006a: 5, 28.

110 *Roller-coaster ride*: Meisler 2007: 25, 43, 44, 53.
110 *With the rapid expansion*: Meisler 2007: 59, 60.
110 *Steamroller. . . . euphoria*: Quoted in Meisler 2007: 61.
110–11 *In February 1993*: Meisler 2007: 64–65, 69, 71, 76, 107, 110.
111 *Far overshadowed. . . . flies commercial*: Meisler 2007: 115, 117.
111 *Turn the UN key*: Meisler 2007: 117.
111 *Historic decision*: Traub 2006a: 64.
111 *Gutsy performance*: Shawcross 2000: 181.
111 *Shipping a rival*: Meisler 2007: 120.
111–12 *France agreed to support Annan*: Meisler 2007: 140, 142–43.
112 *Most popular figure*: Traub 2006a: xi.
112 *Grey-haired African men*: William Shawcross quoted in Meisler 2007: 227.
112 *Muppets*: Meisler 2007: 204, 211.
112 *After the September 11*: Meisler 2007: 207, 275, 4, 3.
112 *Hiccuped, coughed*: Traub 2006a: xii.
112–13 *Vieira de Mello*: Power 2008.
113 *Blew it up*: BBC News 2003. Reports that Vieira de Mello said "Don't let them pull the UN out" to rescuers while he was dying under the rubble are doubtful; see Power 2008: 499–500.
113 *The worst day*: Traub 2006a: 196; see Power 2008: 451–95.
113 *Discouragement*: Meisler 2007: 264; ; see also Traub 2006a: 197.
113 *Zombies*: Power 2008: 506.
113 *Depressed funk*: Meisler 2007: 282–83.
113 *More than hang on*: Durch 2006a: 30.
113 *Annan's tenure*: Meisler 2007: 316, 317.
114 *Various missions use*: Durch 2006a: 7.
114 *Do not fit neatly*: Bellamy, Williams, and Griffin 2004: 13.
114–15 *More complex*: Fortna and Howard 2008: 285; Rubinstein 2008: 19; 34, 17; see Doyle and Sambanis 2006: 14–15.
115 *In addition to peacekeeping*: Mingst and Karns 2007: 89.
115 *Greater institutional capacity*: Bellamy, Williams, and Griffin 2004: 49, 50.
115–16 *The report calls for*: Brahimi et al. 2000.
116 *Regarding headquarters staff*: Brahimi et al. 2000: 32, 30.
116 *Would dream of*: Traub 2006a: 128.
116 *Refined recommendations on deployment times*: Durch 2006b: 589; see also Bellamy, Williams, and Griffin 2004: 50–51.
116 *Golden hour*: Dobbins et al. 2007: 15.
116 *Start from scratch*: Urquhart 2007: 274–75; see Weiss et al. 2007: 128.
116–17 *Deployment now takes*: Durch 2006b: 589; see also Rubinstein 2008: 29.
117 *Other major, recurring problems*: Durch 2006b: 576, 588; see also Bellamy, Williams, and Griffin 2004: 171, 183.
117 *UN doubled the staff*: Fortna and Howard 2008: 289.
117 *Little progress has been made*: Durch 2006a: 9.
117 *Following up on the Brahimi*: Weiss et al. 2007: 106, 115.
118 *Killed off the idea*: Weiss et al. 2007: 114.
118 *They control two-thirds*: Goldstein and Pevehouse 2011: 197.
118 *Peacebuilding Commission*: Weiss et al. 2007: 117, 118.
119 *Less than $100 million*: Source: UN Peacebuilding Fund, accessed 2009 at www.unpbf. org/. I calculated per capita data using UN population data.
119 *UN again restructured*: UN 2008; Weiss 2009: 197.
119 *Shaky organizational ground*: Weiss et al. 2007: 17.
119–20 *Bureaucracy can be convoluted*: UN DPKO 2008: 94–100; Brahimi et al. 2000; Autesserre 2010: 88.
120 *Unabashedly undemocratic*: Barnett and Finnemore 2004: 172.
120 *Ad hoc, political*: Bellamy, Williams, and Griffin 2004: 14.
120 *Kept vague*: Rubinstein 2008: 27.
120 *If a crisis erupts*: Stephen Stedman, quoted in Traub 2006a: 313.
120 *Conflict with DPA*: Bellamy, Williams, and Griffin 2004: 49.

120 *UN's internal problems*: Pérez de Cuéllar 1997: ix, x.
120 *Walk on water*: Boothby 2003: 131.
121 *Pivotal position*: Collier et al. 2003: 160–61; Dobbins et al.: 28–31.
121 *Swedish study*: Nilsson 2008.
121 *May have knowledge*: Kalyvas 2006: 392.
121 *UN study*: Muggah 2005; see also Toft 2009.
121 *Most DDR processes*: Swedish Ministry for Foreign Affairs 2006: 33, 34, 40.
122 *Reform the security sector*: Dobbins et al. 2007: 34–36; Hansen and Wiharta 2007.
122 *Police Mission*: EUPM website www.eupm.org/Overview.aspx.
123 *Truth Commissions have been*: Dobbins et al. 2007: 96; see Hayner 2001.
123 *South African TRC*: Cobban 2007: 9–12.
124 *Work took six years*: Cobban 2007: 112, 194–95, 202, 239.
124 *Unsettle listeners*: Payne 2008: 2; see Hayner 2001: 5, 183–205.
124 *No other country has adopted*: Payne 2008: 3, 4–5, 279.
124 *What kind of peace*: Anderlini 2007: 153–54.
125 *Within the UN*: Durch 2006a: 34–36.
125 *Budget is divided*: Durch 2006a: 38.
125 *In terms of the size*: Diehl 2008: 87–91.
125–26 *Today's UN missions draw on*: Daniel and Wiharta 2008: 1; Daniel, Heuel, and Margo 2008: 29, 35; Heldt 2008: 21, 23.
126 *Top fourteen contributing*: Accessed 3/6/11 at www.un.org/en/peacekeeping/contributors/2011/jan11_1.pdf.
126 *Four South Asian countries*: Banerjee 2008: 188.
127 *Bangladesh has specialized*: Banerjee 2008: 187–95.
127 *Military Staff Committee*: Weiss et al. 2007: 17.
127 *About 50,000 more*: Sidhu 2007: 222.
127 *UN had organized sixty-eight*: Diehl 2008: 66.
128 *Two types*: Heldt 2008: 14, 10–12, 22–23; see Weiss et al. 2007: 120; Daniel and Wiharta 2008: 1.
128 *Success rates*: Heldt and Wallensteen 2006: 34–36.
128 *UN Charter proposes*: Pugh and Sidhu 2003: 3, 1.
128 *Multinational Force and Observers*: Rubinstein 2008: 25.
128–29 *Some regional organizations*: Coleman 2007: 8.
129 *Single nation-state*: Coleman 2007: 9.
129 *ECOWAS intervention*: Malan 2008: 91.
129 *In sixteen other cases*: Coleman 2007: 10, 56, 57.
129 *In terms of one central, new*: Howard 2008: 300.
130 *New military doctrine*: Durch 2006a: 12.
130 *On call force*: European Union 2007.
130 *ESDP. . . . unproblematic*: Giegerich 2008: 120–21, 126.
130 *Greatest potential*: Evans 2008: 183.
130 *Rapid Reaction Force*: Bellamy, Williams, and Griffin 2004: 43.
130–31 *SHIRBRIG*: Goldstein and Pevehouse 2011: 249; Bellamy, Williams, and Griffin 2004: 149.
131 *The European or American*: Durch 2006a: 31, 33.
131 *Other important regional*: Diehl 2008: 71–74.
131 *One problem with "subcontracting"*: Bellamy, Williams, and Griffin 2004: 225.
131–32 *Less international legitimacy*: Coleman 2007: 2–4.
132 *Overwhelming consensus*: Evans 2008, quoted in Coleman 2007: 3.
132 *Club members*: Coleman 2007: 3, 19, 38.
132 *For instance, the intervention of ECOWAS*: Coleman 2007: 73, 78–79, 82.
132 *Similarly, in 1998 Angola*: Coleman 2007: 152, 151–55.
133 *African regional organizations*: Malan 2008: 90, 99.
133 *AU forces in Somalia*: Malan 2008: 100.
133 *Most useful tool*: Malan 2008: 109, 115.
133 *Also, in Asia*: Heldt 2008: 9, 16.
134 *Lack basic capabilities*: Malan 2008: 93, 94; Whitworth 2004.

134 *AU mission in Darfur*: Malan 2008: 97.
134 *For the wrong reason*: Dobbins et al. 2007: 10–12.
134 *The United States, France*: Malan 2008: 102–07.
135 *So subcontracting*: Weiss 2009: 134.

Chapter 6

137 *A major success*: Collier 2009: 85.
137 *Immediately horrible*: Shawcross 2000: 38, 40.
137 *Journalists have questioned*: See the summary in Rayman 2008.
137 *Other child soldiers*: Farah 2000.
138 *Sudden noises*: Beah 2007: 5.
138 *When Beah was twelve*: Critics say this happened in 1995 and Beah's subsequent story took place over just a few months, not years.
138 *Total confusion*: Beah 2007: 9.
138 *Things changed rapidly*: Beah 2007: 29.
138 *Signature atrocity*: Slim 2008: 59; see also 158, 224.
138 *Terrified of boys our age*: Beah 2007: 37.
139 *Easy as drinking water*: Beah 2007: 121–22, 124.
139 *World's worst. . . . manipulated*: Deng 2001.
139 *One researcher. . . . armed conflicts*: Singer 2001.
139 *Followed orders better*: Berman and Labonte 2006: 189.
139 *Chadian*: Polgreen 2008c.
140 *Work here is done*: Beah 2007: 128.
140 *UNICEF staff were happy*: Beah 2007: 129–30, 137, 138. Beah describes a lethal fight among recently demobilized boys from the RUF and government sides, but apparently exaggerates it; see Rayman 2008.
140 *Be rehabilitated*: Beah 2007: 161, 168–69, 181.
140 *Post reporter*: Farah 2000.
140 *Victims or perpetrators*: Berman and Labonte 2006: 190.
141 *Mercedes-Benzes*: Beah 2007: 187.
141 *Conflict diamonds*: Berman and Labonte 2006: 141; Renner 2002: 7; Collier et al. 2003: 143.
141 *Foreign armies*: Avant 2005: 82–98.
141 *Gurkhas*: Berman and Labonte 2006: 145.
141–42 *Executive Outcomes*: Avant 2005: 84–88, 91.
142 *One visitor*: Shawcross 2000: 203–04.
142 *Sandline*: Avant 2005: 93, 95.
142 *RUF would be transformed*: Berman and Labonte 2006: 147.
143 *Timetable*: Berman and Labonte 2006: 147.
143 *Fire brigade*: Tharoor 1995–96: 63; Shashi Tharoor quoted in Meisler 2007: 70.
143 *Evidence surfaced*: Berman and Labonte 2006: 147, 148.
144 *ELOWAS. . . . ran out of money*: Berman and Labonte 2006: 149–58.
144 *Butchery paid off*: Smillie and Minear 2004: 32.
144 *UN sent a force of 6,000*: Berman and Labonte 2006: 183–84.
145 *Difficult time fielding*: Berman and Labonte 2006: 167, 170.
145 *Most dangerous. . . . fiasco*: Traub 2006a: 119.
145 *Came apart in 2000*: Former UNAMSIL military official quoted in Berman and Labonte 2006: 179–80.
145 *Drinking, fistfights*: Smillie and Minear 2004: 34.
145 *Bosnia redux*: Traub 2006a: 120.
146 *Critical one-week*: Berman and Labonte 2006: 181, 182.
146 *Children armed*: Singer 2001.
146 *Near impunity*: Smillie and Minear 2004: 34.
146 *Undermined the rebel*: Berman and Labonte 2006: 182, 178.
146 *Degree of contempt*: Bellamy, Williams, and Griffin 2004: 38; see Collier 2007b: 128.
146 *Britain's success showed*: Berman and Labonte 2006: 201; see Traub 2006a: 121.

146 *On the 10th anniversary*: BBC World News [TV], May 18, 2010.
147 *Major sex scandal*: Smillie and Minear 2004: 40, 41, 49.
147 *Serve as a model*: UN DPKO, 2005; see also Berman and Labonte 2006: 192–94.
147 *The UN successfully*: UN DPKO 2005.
147 *Rarely met half*: Smillie and Minear 2004: 23.
148 *The UN had somewhat more success*: UN DPKO 2005.
148 *Initially disasters*: Kennedy 2006: 108.
148 *Integrated Office*: UN DPKO 2005.
149 *Fourteen rounds*: Zartman 2005: 51.
149 *Plenty of signs*: Polgreen 2007a.
149 *UN-occupied neutral zone*: BBC News 2010a.
150 *Generally stable*: Ban 2009.
150 *Lost Boys*: Jal 2009.
150–51 *Court of Arbitration*: Otterman 2009.
152 *Dual mission*: Traub 2006a: 267, 240.
152 *One single helicopter*: Hoge 2007.
152–53 *Ongoing in other regions*: On recent peace operations worldwide, see Center on International Cooperation 2010, sponsored by the UN DPKO Best Practices Section.
153 *Honestly meant*: Kennedy 2006: 88.
154 *LeRoy*: Erlanger 2009.
155 *Aouzou Strip*: Azevedo 1998: 124–27.
156 *Isaksson*: Charlotte Isaksson, personal communication, January 2010.
156 *All the help it could get*: European Union 2006, 2007.
157 *Kleptocracy*: Transparency International, Seize Mobutu's Wealth. . . . [Press release.] Berlin, May 15, 1997; Transparency International 2004.
158 *Near complete collapse*: worldbank.org "Country Brief," "last updated October 2008."
158 *Cuban communist*: Guevara 2000.
159 *Persistent attacks*: Roessler and Prendergast 2006: 235.
159 *Dramatic military gains*: Roessler and Prendergast 2006: 236.
159 *Engulfed the Congo*: Roessler and Prendergast 2006: 236.
160 *Certainly one motivation*: UN Security Council 2002.
160 *Congo Desk*: Roessler and Prendergast 2006: 241.
160 *Uganda pursued a less*: Roessler and Prendergast 2006: 241, 243.
161 *When Laurent Kabila still*: Renner 2002: 27, 30.
161 *Offshore oil wells*: Renner 2002: 30.
161 *Self-financing. . . . $5 billion*: Roessler and Prendergast 2006: 242.
161 *Commissioned a report*: UN Security Council 2002.
161 *Late 2008, a reporter*: Polgreen 2008d.
162 *Two dozen peace initiatives*: Roessler and Prendergast 2006: 243.
162 *Enormous military pressure*: Roessler and Prendergast 2006: 245.
162 *Was paralyzed*: Roessler and Prendergast 2006: 247, 262.
163 *The Lusaka signatories*: Roessler and Prendergast 2006: 230, 248, 249.
163 *The UN was hardly*: Roessler and Prendergast 2006: 230, 246, 249, 248, 257, 259.
163–64 *For years the UN held down*: Roessler and Prendergast 2006: 256–57, 260, 265, 266; see Lynch 2000.
164 *The situation changed abruptly*: Roessler and Prendergast 2006: 250–55.
164 *Substantial progress occurred*: Roessler and Prendergast 2006: 269, 270.
165 *In Kisangani*: Roessler and Prendergast 2006: 271–72.
165 *Beyond these specific*: Roessler and Prendergast 2006: 272, 273, 277.
165 *At the end of 2002*: Roessler and Prendergast 2006: 231, 278.
165 *Smaller, splinter militias*: Roessler and Prendergast 2006: 278, 255, 269, 279, 276–77; see U.S. Department of State 2004.
165–66 *Ituri district*: Roessler and Prendergast 2006: 279, 281, 283.
166 *Operation Artemis*: Roessler and Prendergast 2006: 231, 285, 284.
166 *The Ituri crisis finally*: Roessler and Prendergast 2006: 231–32, 295.
167 *Mandate was further expanded*: MONUC n.d.
167 *The UN force was drawn*: Roessler and Prendergast 2006: 232, 299; see also 254.

167 *During the Bukavu crisis*: Traub 2006a: 341–42.
167 *Main rival*: Gettleman and Mwassi 2006.
167 *Savimbi*: Noble 1992.
167–68 *Some fighting erupted*: Economist Paul Collier makes too much of this incident; see Collier 2009: 85.
168 *He was arrested*: Simons 2008; BBC News 2009b.
168 *Trouble continued*: Polgreen 2007b, 2008b.
168 *The UN learned*: Traub 2006a: 349.
168 *In 2008, an offensive*: Gettleman 2008; Gettleman and MacFarquhar 2008.
168 *Civilians threw rocks*: Polgreen 2008e.
169 *Resigned abruptly*: New York Times 2008.
169 *Leaders of Congo and Rwanda sat down*: Gettleman 2009a.
170 *The bad news*: IRIN 2009; BBC News 2009a; Gettleman 2009b; Oxfam International 2009.
170 *Clinton*: McCrummen 2009.
170 *One other group*: Onyiego 2010.
170–71 *Mandated MONUC to shift*: UNSC Resolution 1856, December 22, 2008.
171 *Autesserre knows*: Autesserre 2008; Autesserre 2010. Autesserre, personal communication 2009.
171 *Among her criticisms*: Autesserre 2010: 84.
171 *Pack of cookies*: Autesserre 2010: 41.
171 *Autesserre talked*: Autesserre 2010: 1.
172 *Autesserre's central criticism*: Autesserre 2010: 8, 177.
173 *Clearly too small*: Autesserre 2010: 18.
173 *Just as in 1961*: Autesserre 2010: 87.
173 *Deplored a lack of financial*: Autesserre 2010: 87, 182, citing Englebert and Tull 2008: 130.
174 *MONUC's multinational nature*: Autesserre 2010: 88.
174 *Language barriers. . . . Bukavu*: Autesserre 2010: 89, 126.
174 *Soldiers themselves*: Autesserre 2010: 89–90.
175 *Pacification*: Mountain 2009.
175 *Averted*: Collier 2009: 98; see Autesserre 2010: 4, 14, 266.
175 *Helped nineteen million*: UN News Service 2010c.
175 *MONUSCO*: UN News Service 2010b.

Chapter 7

177–78 *Visit Angola. . . . UNITA girls*: Gerald Bender, personal communication, 2010.
178 *CIA officer*: Stockwell 1991: 144.
179 *Integral part of today's*: Weiss 2009: 9.
179 *Most underestimated*: Picco 1999: 3–7; see Pérez de Cuéllar 1997: 105; Meisler 2007: 38.
179 *Cyprus*: Picco 1999: 16, 18, 27.
179–80 *Taught Picco. . . . Geneva*: Picco 1999: 23, 30, 34, 33.
180 *Nodding off*: Picco 1999: 22, 25.
180–81 *Picco's concept*: Picco 1999: 40–44.
181 *Quietly negotiated*: Picco 1999: 49.
181–82 *Gorbachev. . . . long leash*: Picco 1999: 52, 54, 55.
182 *New independence*: Picco 1999: 61, 72.
182 *Pin the Iranians down*: Picco 1999: 71, 77.
182 *Push both sides hard*: Picco 1999: 81, 27, 85, 90.
183 *Down to the wire*: Picco 1999: 94, 95.
183 *Owed us one*: Picco 1999: 99, 104, 3–7, 105, 249; 201, 209, 220.
183 *Toughest part*: Picco 1999: 129, 128, 180, 188, 193, 208, 194.
184 *Rent a plane*: Picco 1999: 213–16.
184 *Hostage mission cost*: Picco 1999: 233–34.
184 *Left the UN convinced*: Picco 1999: 274–87; 296.
185 *Madagascar in 2002*: Murphy 2006: 315–17.
185 *Entrenched in the social fabric*: Harbom and Wallensteen 2007: 625.
185 *Ripe for resolution*: Zartman 2005: 10–11; see also Rubinstein 2008: 23.

185 *Costly catastrophes*: Rubinstein 2008: 11.
185 *Having reached the point*: Iklé 1991: 2; 17–18, 59, 60, 66, 72; see also Reiter 2009.
186 *Solves the dilemma*: Rubinstein 2008: 24.
186 *Soft stalemate*: Zartman 2005: 11, 12, 16.
186 *Form of third-party*: Zartman and Touval 2007: 437, 438, 453.
186–87 *Requires multiple attempts*: Bercovitch 2005: 102, 112, 118.
187 *Rhodes*: Urquhart 1993: 201.
187 *Preeminent international actor*: Whitfield 2007: 40.
187 *Exactly the type*: Ramsbotham, Woodhouse, and Miall 2005: 4, 6–7.
187 *Advocates of conflict resolution*: Ramsbotham, Woodhouse, and Miall 2005: 12, 14, 26.
188 *Bernadotte Academy*: See folkebernadotteacademy.se.
188 *Warning and insights*: Hamburg 2002: 88.
188 *Russia and Eastern Europe*: Hamburg 2002: 92–95.
188 *Human dignity*: Lindner 2006.
188–89 *Aceh province*: Aall 2007: 478–79.
189 *The trouble with NGOs*: Whitfield 2007: 42.
189 *Plethora*: Prantl 2006: 3.
189 *Go by the name. . . . governance*: Whitfield 2007: 2.
189 *These informal arrangements date*: Whitfield 2007: 3–4; see also Prantl 2006; Krasno
       2003b; Jones 2002.
189–90 *The first to operate*: Prantl 2006: 17, 159–208, 95–158, 18; Whitfield 2007: 1–2.
190 *In recent cases*: Prantl 2006: 18–19, 209–48.
190 *Some wars are more likely*: Whitfield 2007: 8, 14, 45.
191 *Annan has suggested*: Annan 2002: 27
191 *Humanitarianism makes up*: Weiss 2009: 89, 87, 90.
192 *Water purification*: Shawcross 2000: 16.
192 *Cuny got started*: Shawcross 2000: 17; see also Edwards 1999: 92.
192 *It did not go smoothly*: Quoted in Shawcross 2000: 17.
192 *Never seen again*: Anderson 1996.
193 *Cuny's fate is becoming*: Stoddard, Harmer, and DiDomenico 2009: 1, 3, 4, 10.
193 *British humanitarian*: Foley 2008, 4, 5.
193 *More problems than it has solved*: Quoted in Malcomson 2008.
193 *Necessary evil*: Foley 2008: 233, 234.
193–94 *Recently the lines*: Smillie and Minear 2004: 151–53, 9.
194 *Food aid in Somalia*: Gettleman and MacFarquhar 2010.
194 *Kept many people alive*: Shawcross 2000: 23.
194 *70 percent. . . . captured*: Edwards 1999: 91; see Gibbs 2009; Seybolt 2007: 278.
194 *Deteriorated rapidly*: Smillie and Minear 2004: 28–29.
194–95 *Bureaucratic budgeting*: Smillie and Minear 2004: 137–38, 144–45, 43.
195 *Remains messy*: Overseas Development Institute, 2010.
195 *No humanitarian regime*: Smillie and Minear 2004: 3, 7; see Polman 2010: 158.
195–96 *Of the ninety NGOs*: Smillie and Minear 2004: 43–45, 49.
196 *Transition from short-term*: Smillie and Minear 2004: 46, 47.
196 *Unlike membership dues*: Smillie and Minear 2004: 7–8, 171.
196 *ICRC historically*: Finnemore 1996: 69–88.
196–97 *Had a budget. . . . funds*: ICRC 2010: 91–93, 450.
197 *Women's peace activism*: Anderlini 2007: xii, 5, 55, 6.
197 *Five-year follow-up. . . . shepherded*: Anderlini 2007: 6–7.
197 *Implementation of 1325*: Mazurana, Raven-Roberts, and Parpart eds. 2005.
197–98 *Fewer than 2 percent*: Weiss 2009: 117–118.
198 *Such women were active*: Anderlini 2007: 34.
198 *In Liberia*: Anderlini 2007: 56–57; Sirleaf 2009.
198 *However, more often than not*: Anderlini 2007: 35, 40, 6, 43, 54, 58.
199 *Different philosophy*: Anderlini 2007: 41.
199 *Government amnesty*: Reuters 2009; Nossiter 2010.
199 *Vital role in South Africa's*: Anderlini 2007: 43.
199 *Women as actors in*: Quoted in Anderlini 2007: 106–08.

200 *Conflict early-warning*: Anderlini 2007: 28, 30; Clinton 2009: 42.
200 *After a war, women*: Anderlini 2007: 29, 93–95, 102.
200–01 *Recent initiatives to include women*: Anderlini 2007: 95, 100–02.
201 *Literally saw things*: Julie Mertus quoted in Anderlini 2007: 166.
201 *First prosecution*: Anderlini 2007: 166–68.
201 *Acquaint myself*: Linnér 2008: 30.
201 *Although recent attention*: Rehn and Sirleaf 2002: 56; Clinton 1998.
201–02 *Women and children*: Goldstein 2001: 399–401; Carpenter 2006.
202 *Quite the contrary*: Carpenter 2006; Kristof 2010d; see Save the Children 2003b.

Chapter 8

204 *NFP*: See nebraskanforpeace.org/history.
205 *Billion people have risen*: Dugger 2009.
205 *Billion people remain*: Collier 2007b.
206 *Peace Development Fund*: Accessed 9/30/09 at peacedevelopmentfund.org/page/pro-gramareas.
206 *Prairie Peace Park*: See www.peacepark.us/site/. Site description from Google Maps street view.
207 *A third approach*: Accessed 9/29/09 at fcpeace.com, centerofpeace.org, and thepeacecenter.info.
208 *The pope argued*: Pope Paul VI 1972; see also Cortright 2008: 262; Toft 2009: 11–12.
208 *"True" peace*: See Cortright 2008: 6–7; Doyle and Sambanis 2006: 73; Regan 2000: ix; Boulding 1978: 135.
208 *Oppose abortion*: Pope John Paul II 1999; see also Pope John Paul II 1995.
209 *Group of 20*: Urbina 2009.
210 *William Penn*: DeBenedetti 1980: 8–10; on Quaker pacifism in Britain see Brock 1972: 255–366.
210 *Conversely, patriotic fervor*: DeBenedetti 1980: 18, 20, 21.
211 *After the War of 1812*: DeBenedetti 1980: 28–29, 33, 36–37, 32.
211 *Women constituted*: DeBenedetti 1980: 48, 46.
211 *Only the Massachusetts*: Cortright 2008: 30.
211 *Tennyson*: Tennyson 1874: 54; Kennedy 2006: xi.
211–12 *Ladd. . . . London. . . . Brussels*: DeBenedetti 1980: 46–47.
212 *Idea of arbitration*: Cortright 2008: 49–51.
212 *Antislavery movement*: DeBenedetti 1980: 48–49.
212 *Universal Brotherhood*: DeBenedetti 1980: 52–53; see also Cortright 1980: 33.
212–13 *Two evils. . . . Kansas. . . . APS collapsed*: DeBenedetti 1980: 55, 32.
213 *Eventually shattered*: Cortright 2008: 35.
213 *Longtime leader*: Cortright 2008: 3, 13.
213 *Two distinct schools*: Cortright 2008: 36.
213 *Cortright traces*: Cortright 2008: 37, 260, 261.
213 *Socialists have rarely*: Cortright 2008: 262, 268.
214 *Trotsky*: D'Amato 2002.
214 *Socialists completely rejected*: Quoting Cortright 2008: 263, not Passy.
214 *New wave of American*: DeBenedetti 1980: 61, 67.
214 *Peace efforts before World War I*: DeBenedetti 1980: 66, 75.
214 *Americans also drew strength*: Cortright 2008: 40–43, 8–9.
215 *Germany*: Chickering 1975.
215 *Growth spurt*: DeBenedetti 1980: 79, 81–84; see also Cortright 2008: 50.
215 *James. . . . Addams*: DeBenedetti 1980: 88.
215 *Socialist Congresses*: Callahan 2004.
215 *Empowerment of women*: Cortright 2008: 70.
216 *Collapsed and fractured*: Cortright 2008: 10.
216 *Punished by the government*: DeBenedetti 1980: 102–05.
216 *Turning point*: Payne 2004: 66.
216 *This paradox*: DeBenedetti 1980: xiii.

216–17 *Insanity of warfare. . . . Wilson's work*: DeBenedetti 1980: 109–11, 106; see also Cortright 2008: 47.

217 *Far more popular in Europe*: Cortright 2008: 61, 64–65, 59, 56–57.

218 *After Wilson failed. . . . led by women*: DeBenedetti 1980: 112, 114, 115.

218 *Jail them. . . . college. . . . Peace Ballot*: Cortright 2008: 72, 73, 77–78.

218 *Conceptual evolution*: Cortright 2008: 271.

218 *Old issues again*: Cortright 2008: 68, 88.

219 *Korean War*: DeBenedetti 1980: 155.

219 *Kremlin's*: Cortright 2008: 279.

219 *From the ashes*: On the evolution of transnational peace activism over the Cold War decades see Evangelista 1999.

219 *Atomic scientists*: Wittner 2009.

219 *Social scientists. . . . SANE*: DeBenedetti 1980: 144–45, 157, 163; Cortright 2008: 128–31, 134.

219 *Women Strike*: Swerdlow 1989; Cortright 2008: 136.

220 *Merchants of death*: Cortright 1980: 93, 94, 97–99.

220 *No precedent in history*: Cortright 2008: 11.

220 *World federalism*: Cortright 2008: 116–17.

220 *Most sustained*: Cortright 2008: 157, 18.

221 *Outpouring*: DeBenedetti 1980: 185.

221 *Could not convert*: DeBenedetti 1980: 186; Cortright 2008: 18, 157, 160.

221 *Each element*: Cortright 2008: 157–59.

221 *New left*: Cortright 2008: 162.

221–22 *Second Cold War. . . . Western Europe*: Cortright 2008: 140, 145, 148.

222 *Day After*: See www.imdb.com/title/tt0085404/.

222 *Dampen the bellicose*: Cortright 2008: 141, 142–43, 145, 148; Cutter, Holcomb, and Shatin 1986; Meyer 1990; see also Solo 1988.

222–23 *Bosnia. . . . Kosovo*: Cortright 2008: 280, 289–90.

223 *10 million people*: Cortright 2008: 18, 2, 172, 175, 277.

224 *At the time of the European*: Holsti 1991: 81, 107, 161, 164.

224 *Attitudes shifted completely*: Holsti 1991: 327.

224–25 *Evolution of international norms*: Finnemore 2003: 2, 3, 49, 83; see Crawford 2002.

225 *Clear trend*: Finnemore 2003: 19. Fettweis 2010 appeared too late to include here.

225 *In 1918*: Coleman 2007: 43.

225 *Aristotle*: Payne 2004: 17.

225 *Two hundred years ago*: Crawford 2002: 175, 320, see 176–84, 320–23.

225 *Human sacrifice. . . . dueling*: Forsberg 1997; Mueller 1989; Mueller 2006b: 66.

225 *Normal part*: Payne 2004: 30–31, 171, 185–86.

226 *Coups. . . . terrorism*: Payne 2004: 113, 144, 146.

226 *Land mines*: Information from icbl.org.

227 *Remnants*: Mueller 2004; Mueller 2006b: 66–74; see Van Crevald 2006: 97.

227 *Attitudes about violence*: Payne 2004: 54, 56, 141.

227 *Restraints on killing*: Slim 2008: 19.

227–28 *Norms against violent civil*: Payne 2004: 174–76, 179, 180.

Chapter 9

231 *Enticingly*: Crawford 1987.

231 *SIPRI*: SIPRI 2010.

231 *Route to ending war*: Boulding and Forsberg 1998: 13–26.

232 *Imagine that we had*: On "social data stations" see Ramsbotham, Woodhouse, and Miall 2005: 41.

232 *Scour journalists'*: For the UCDP Battle Deaths Dataset, see www.pcr.uu.se/research/UCDP/; see also Lacina, Gleditsch, and Russett 2006: 676–78; on the Lacina battle death data-set see Lacina and Gleditsch 2005.

232 *Factiva*: Harbom and Wallensteen 2007: 628; UCDP 2010; see also Gleditsch et al. 2002; UCDP/PRIO 2009; Collier 2009: 4–5.

232 *Contested incompatibility*: UCDP 2009; Harbom and Wallensteen 2007: 625.
233 *Nonstate. . . . one-sided*: Sundberg 2009; see Human Security Report Project 2007: 37.
233 *PRIO*: Nils Petter Gleditsch, Bethany Lacina, Stein Tønnesson, Andrew Mack, personal communication, October 2010.
234 *Clodfelter*: Clodfelter 2008; Clodfelter, personal communication 2010.
235 *Indirect deaths are those*: Slim 2008: 90, 98, 99, 103; see Leitenberg 2006: 5–6.
235 *Depend on a counterfactual*: See Lacina and Gleditsch 2005: 149.
236 *Every reason to expect*: Mack 2007: 531. For a contrary view see Shaw 2005.
236 *New wars*: Kaldor 2006 vs. Melander, Öberg, and Hall 2009; see also Sarkees and Wayman 2010: 559; Lacina and Gleditsch 2005: 154.
236 *Quickly defies*: Lacina and Gleditsch 2005: 148; see also Collier 2009: 4.
237 *Have become rare*: Wallensteen and Sollenberg 1996: 356; Harbom and Wallensteen 2009: 578, 579.
237 *Djibouti*: BBC News 2008a.
237 *Georgia and its breakaway*: Harbom and Wallensteen 2009: 579–80.
237 *Diminished as well*: Levy 2002: 351.
238 *Trend has flattened out*: Hewitt, Wilkenfeld, and Gurr 2007; Harbom and Wallensteen 2009.
238 *Ripple of interest*: Easterbrook 2005; Mack 2005; Tierney 2005; Noah 2005; Sands 2005; Kaplan 2006; Traub 2006b; Arquilla 2006.
239 *Steady downward trend*: Wilson and Gurr 1999; see also Goldstein 2002.
239 *Not seem to get through*: Mack 2007: 523, 524; see also Human Security Centre 2005: 18.
239 *Selection bias*: Licklider 2005: 37.
239 *Reporting the worst*: Boulding 1978: 83.
240 *Plenty of images*: Payne 2004: 13; see also Taleb 2007: 112, 55, 80, 100.
240 *Bleeds, it leads*: See Boulding 1978: 83.
240 *Progress Paradox*: Easterbrook 2003: 35, 36.
240–41 *Much more peaceful*: Payne 2004: 7.
241 *Chronological bias*: He used this nice phrase at a conference, but calls it "presentism" in Payne 2004: 8.
241 *Tendency to assume*: Payne 2004: 68, 8, 9.
241 *Takes to task*: Payne 2004: 14, 9, 69, 267 n.3; Richardson 1960: 112, 128; Luard 1986: 23.
242 *Glorify violence*: Pinker 2007: 20.
242 *Lack moral concern*: Payne 2004: 10–11.
242 *High-decibel*: Easterbrook 2003: 100.
242 *Followers and donations*: Pinker 2007: 20.
242 *The generation*: Toynbee 1954: 322.
243 *Researchers in Vancouver*: Human Security Centre 2005: 17, 36, 28, 41, 42, 44.
244 *One area where things*: Human Security Report Project 2007: 28, 38–39, 35, 36, 42, 43.
244 *Number of terrorist attacks*: Human Security Report Project 2007: 2–3. See also Carle 2008; Mueller 2006a; Allison 2004.
244 *Attributes the positive trends*: Human Security Report Project 2007: 153–55, 10.
245 *University of Maryland*: Gurr, Marshall, and Khosla 2000: ii, 1, 2, 22.
245 *Showed modest progress*: Gurr, Marshall, and Khosla 2000: 4–6; Uppsala conflict database.
245 *Almost half. . . . Beyond these 33*: UCDP website, accessed 6/6/10 at www.pcr.uu .se/publications/UCDP_pub/UCDP_PRIO_ArmedConflictDataset_V4_2010.xls.
246 *Slight uptick*: Hewitt, Wilkenfeld, and Gurr 2010: 1.
246 *Scenes of carnage*: Pinker 2007: 20; see Pinker 2011.
246 *Recently, both the Maryland*: Harbom and Wallensteen 2007: 623, 625; Hewitt, Wilkenfeld and Gurr 2007.
247 *Multinationalization*: Gleditsch 2008.
247 *Fundamental way unsolved*: Hewitt, Wilkenfeld, and Gurr 2007; Lacina and Gleditsch 2005: 155.
247 *Interdisciplinary community*: Boulding 1978: 131.
248 *Minuscule operation*: Boulding 1978: 120, 121, 143.

248 *Paltry resources*: Deutsch 1965: xi.
248 *Sorokin*: Sorokin 1937: 268, 269.
249 *Iraq Body Count*: www.iraqbodycount.org, accessed 11/7/10; see also Hicks et al. 2010: 1586.
249 *Lancet*: Burnham et al. 2006; see also Roberts et al. 2004: 1861; Johnson et al. 2008.
249 *Science of casualty*: Asher 2009.
249 *Several epidemiologists*: Obermeyer, Murray, and Gakidou 2008: 1; Murray et al. 2002: 346, 348; Murray and Lopez 1996.
250 *New Murray article*: Obermeyer, Murray, and Gakidou 2008: 6.
250 *Considerable uncertainty*: Obermeyer, Murray, and Gakidou 2008: 7.
250 *Gleditsch*: Bohannon 2008.
250 *Bosnia*: BBC News 2007. Incidentally, the Oxford Research Group, a British NGO, has begun a "Recording Casualties of Armed Conflicts" project to apply this Bosnia-style person-by-person approach to wars worldwide.
250 *Spagat*: Spagat et al. 2009; see Asher 2009.
250 *Seattle group claims*: Obermeyer, Murray, and Gakidou 2008: 3–6.
251 *Returned the favor*: Human Security Report Project 2009: 21.
251 *Thanks to these efforts*: Dugger 2009.
251 *In countries at war*: Human Security Report Project 2009: 23, 22.

Chapter 10

254 *Norman Cousins*: Jongman and van der Dennen 1988: 200–02; see also Payne 2004: 271 n.19.
255 *Repeat this claim*: Paris 2004: 1; Doyle and Sambanis 2006: 4; Collier et al. 2003: 17; Carnegie Commission 1997: 11.
255 *These and other works*: Kaldor 2006: 9; Blight and McNamara 2001: 21; Krippner and McIntyre eds. 2003: 1; Greitens 2001: 149.
255 *One political scientist*: Holsti 1996: 37.
255 *Another source*: Ramsbotham, Woodhouse, and Miall 2005: 72; UNICEF 1992: 26; Save the Children 2003a: 9.
255 *Chain of citations*: Paris's 2004: 1 cites three sources. The third of these, Kaldor 1999: 9, does not say what Paris does, and does not give a source for what she does say. Paris's second source is Collier et al. 2003: 17, which cites Cairns 1997, which cites Jongman and Schmid 1996: 25, Ahlström 1991, and Watkins 1995: 43, which gives no source. Jongman and Schmid cite Cranna 1994: xvii, who does not say what Jongman and Schmid do. Paris's first source is UNDP 1994: 47, mis-cited by Paris as UNDP 2002: 85. UNDP 1994 cites Ahlström 1991.
255 *First is*: UNDP 1994: 47; see also Smith 1994.
255 *Second is*: Ahlström 1991.
255 *Influential report*: UNICEF 1996a.
255–56 *Machel*: Machel 1996: paragraph 24; see also UNICEF 1996b.
256 *UN put the claim*: UN 1997.
256 *Actually say*: Ahlström 1991: 8, 19.
257 *Book that lists*: Beer 1981: 37.
257 *Short monograph*: Wood 1968: 24.
257 *Unknown origin*: Wood 1968 cites Wright 1942, but although Wright 1942: 664 gives estimates of military deaths in World War I there is almost nothing on civilian casualties. Wright cites Nickerson 1934 and Ayres 1919, which says nothing about civilian deaths (see p. 119).
257 *On this basis*: Nickerson 1934: 110–11.
257 *Lower than the range cited by most*: Lacina and Gleditsch 2005: 146.
257 *Lower than the historical*: Wright 1942/1965: 245
258 *Hasty conclusions*: Sollenberg 2006: 1; Sollenberg, personal communication, 2008.
258 *Book on civilians*: Downes 2008: 1.
258 *Respected epidemiologists*: Murray et al. 2002: 348.
258 *Tabulated civilian*: Eckhardt 1992: 254, 255, 90, 91.
258 *The 20th century itself*: Eckhardt 1992: 254.
258 *Strange idea*: Slim 2008: 71.

258–59 *Some wars kill*: Wedgwood 1938: 516; Rabb ed. 1981; Wright 1942/1965: 244.
259 *In African conflicts*: Lacina and Gleditsch 2005: 159; Human Security Centre 2005: 128, 129.
259 *Healthy life lost*: Ghobarah, Huth, and Russett 2004.
259 *Smart bombs*: Slim 2008: 58.
259 *Single errant missile*: Chivers and Nordland 2010.
260 *Seventeen thousand web pages*: Accessed at google.com 6/28/10.
260 *World's most deadly*: Coghlan et al. 2006: 44.
260–61 *It all started*: Coghlan et al. 2006; for earlier survey results see Roberts et al. 2003; for later results see Coghlan et al. n.d.
261 *Embedded as truths*: Kristof 2010a, b, c; Coghlan et al. n.d.: 13.
261 *Extrapolating the results*: Human Security Report Project 2009: 36–48; Spielmann 2010.
261 *All of sub-Saharan Africa*: Coghlan et al. 2006: 49.
262 *Same GDP number for sub-Saharan*: World Bank data; purchasing power parity adjusted. Accessed 6/28/10 at siteresources.worldbank.org/DATASTATISTICS/Resources/GNIPC.pdf.
262 *Surveys show a drop*: From about 65 to 43 deaths per thousand population.
263 *Half the rate during the war*: Coghlan et al. n.d.: 13.
263 *Vancouver group recalculated*: Human Security Report Project 2009: 45; the Vancouver researchers did not try to reestimate the first two IRC surveys, before 2001, which they considered too unreliable.
263 *Remains Unchanged*: Polgreen 2008a.
263 *Peer review*: Pedersen 2009: 21.
263 *Belgian researchers*: Lambert and Lohlé-Tart 2008.
263 *Korean War*: Human Security Report Project 2009: 26–27.
264 *Has since killed*: Rummel 1997: 377; see also economic data from World Bank and CIA World Factbook.
264 *Clinton*: BBC News 2009c.
265 *John Holmes*: Gettleman 2010a.
265 *NGO pitched the results*: Oxfam International 2010.
265 *Completely different story*: Harvard Humanitarian Initiative 2010: 7, 8.
265 *Of all these cases*: Harvard Humanitarian Initiative 2010: 13, 19.
266 *But what about the far larger*: Harvard Humanitarian Initiative 2010: 18–20.
266 *Normalization of rape*: Harvard Humanitarian Initiative 2010: 2.
266 *Previous reports considered*: Arieff 2009: 18; UN Security Council 2008: 8; Human Rights Watch 2009: 15.
267 *Rape capital*: BBC News 2010b.
267 *Population Fund*: UNFPA 2008; UN News Service 2010a.
267 *South Kivu in 2008*: Human Rights Watch 2009: 14.
267 *15–20 million people*: World Bank 2005: 11.
267 *U.S. crime statistics*: U.S. Bureau of Justice Statistics 2010.
267–68 *World Health Organization*: Krug et al. eds. 2002: 151.
268 *Congo War was at its height*: Réseau des Femmes pour un Développement Associatif 2005.
268–69 *Swedish analysis*: Baaz and Stern 2010: 16, 18, 19, 24.
269 *With a decades-long*: Baaz and Stern 2010: 42, 43.
269 *Another problem with the heavy emphasis*: Baaz and Stern 2010: 53–55.
270 *Attention-grabber*: Gettleman 2010b.
270 *In early 2011*: Gettleman 2011.
271 *Not carried out with impunity*: United Nations 2010; Bloomberg News 2010; Gettleman 2011.
272 *IRC authors themselves*: Brennan, Despines, and Roberts 2006; see also Roessler and Prendergast 2006: 229, 236.
272 *Women during childbirth*: Grady 2010; Richard Horton on National Public Radio, "Here and Now," April 14, 2010.
273 *Rut of violence*: Gettleman 2010a.
273–74 *Readers' comments*: Accessed 6/28/20 at community.nytimes.com/comments/kristof. blogs.nytimes.com/2010/02/06/your-comments-on-my-sunday-congo-column/.
274 *Uncontrolled brutality*: See Autesserre 2010: 75.

Chapter 11

276 *Many researchers credit*: Rummel 1994: 2, 16.
276 *Works in theory*: Lipson 2003: 1.
276 *Democracy turns out*: Collier 2009: 2.
276 *One plausible theory*: Gat 2010: 89, 95–96; Cortright 2008: 302.
277 *Virtuous circle*: Russett and Oneal 2001: 24–28; 35–39, 127–29.
277 *Statistical analysis confirms*: Russett and Oneal 2001: 163–65.
277 *Rapid growth*: Gleditsch 2008: 700.
277 *Focused on trade*: Mill 1848/1902: 136; see also Gartzke 2007: 170, 166–67; McDonald 2009.
277 *Weak at best*: Gat 2010: 91.
277 *Low income levels*: Russett 2010.
278 *Syracuse*: Gat 2010: 92.
278 *Rising wealth*: See Russett 2010 versus Gat 2010: 87, 91, 92, 598; Kacowicz 1995; Mousseau 2000: 472.
278 *Economic development goes*: Holsti 1996: 116, 16–17, 41, 147, 150–51, 183, 185.
278 *Maybe democracies*: Kacowicz 1995.
278 *Territorial aggrandizement*: Zacher 2001: 244, 245.
278 *Of 227 conflicts*: Gleditsch 2007: 180; see also Vasquez and Henehan 2010.
278–79 *Similarly in 1648–1713. . . . Cold War*: Holsti 1991: 47, 87, 95, 143, 217, 281, 307.
279 *First plank*: Boulding 1978: 109.
280 *In 2009, six civil wars*: Uppsala/PRIO data; Harbom and Wallensteen 2010a.
285 *Mai Mai*: Reuters 2010.
287 *List eleven*: Harbom and Wallensteen 2010b; see also Harbom, ed. 2010.
289 *Zone of peace*: This zone of peace is considerably larger than that envisioned by Singer and Wildavsky 1996 as including only developed democracies; see also Ramsbotham, Woodhouse, and Miall 2005: 62.
289 *East Asia bears*: Stein Tønnesson, Personal communication, September 2010.
289–90 *Germany and Poland*: Kulish 2007.
290 *Chávez*: Romero 2008.
290 *Sherlock*: Doyle 1894: 22, 26.
290 *All is not rosy*: Kal Holsti sees more gradations in zones; see Holsti 1996: 148; see also Kupchan 2010; Deutsch et al. 1957.
290 *Terrorism kills*: Mueller 2006a; Human Security Report Project 2007.
291 *Hobbes*: Hobbes 1651/1996: 88–89.
291 *Spill over*: Collier 2007b: 126.
291 *The conditions favorable*: Hegre and Sambanis 2006.
292 *Most robust*: Doyle and Sambanis 2006: 34.
292 *Best predictor*: Fearon 2008: 293.
292 *Saakashvili*: Chivers and Schwirtz 2008.
292 *One study estimated*: Cited in Mack 2007: 526; see also Stewart and FitzGerald 2001a: 2.
292 *Tax revenues*: Collier 2009: 206.
293 *Why aren't the rest*: Regan 2009: 23–24, 35.
293 *Conflict trap*: Collier et al. 2003: 1, 101–03; Collier 2007b: 7, xi.
293 *Also keeping countries*: Collier et al. 2003: 104; see also Collier 2007b: 27.
293 *In both marginalized*: Collier et al. 2003: 107; Collier 2007b: 35.
294 *Development in reverse*: Collier et al. 2003: 2, 106; Collier 2007b: 27; Collier 2007a: 211; see Stewart and FitzGerald 2001b: 230–32, 240–41.
294 *About three-quarters*: Collier 2007b: x, 17.
294 *Two independent statistical*: Collier 2007a: 200–02; Fearon and Laitin 2003.
294 *Primary commodity exports*: Wood 2003b; Collier 2007a: 205; Ron 2005; Lujala, Gleditsch, and Gilmore 2005.
294–95 *Resource curse*: Drelichman and Voth 2008; see Ross 2008.
295 *Botswana*: Collier et al. 2003: 126.
295 *Review of fourteen studies*: Ross 2004; see Ross 2006, Fearon 2005; Ross 2008.
295 *More complex results*: Hegre et al. 2001; see also Mansfield and Snyder 2005; Gat 2010: 89; Ottoway 2007: 603, 604; Fortna and Howard 2008: 294.

295 *In very poor countries*: Collier 2009: 20–21, 49.
295 *Caused more misery*: Harff and Gurr 2004: 1, xii.
296 *Tsunami*: Gurr 2000: xiii, 203, 204, 211.
296 *At the root*: Gurr 2000: 3, 195; Collier 2009: 51, 56; see also Lake and Rothchild 1998: 5–6.
296 *Somalis*: Keller 1998: 278.
296 *Most ethnic wars since 1960*: Gurr 2000: 197, 223, 203.
296 *275 sizable groups*: Harff and Gurr 2004: 3–5.
296 *Relationship between ethnic divisions*: Wood 2003b: 251–52; see Collier 2007a: 201–213.
296–97 *Fractionalization. . . . mobilization*: Doyle and Sambanis 2006: 37–39.
297 *Political repression*: Collier 2007b: 23, 25; Fearon and Laitin 2003.
297 *Norwegian*: Buhaug and Gleditsch 2008: 230.
297 *Confidence building. . . . minimal representation*: Rothchild and Lake 1998: 203 209, 210.
298 *Irregular war creates zones*: Kalyvas 2006: 11–12, 88, chapters 3–5.
298 *Warring parties use violence*: Kalyvas 2006: 12, 111, 145, 45, 46, 28, 27.
298–99 *But only the local*: Kalyvas 2006: 89, 92.
299 *Dominant but incomplete*: Kalyvas 2006: 14, 59, 174.
299 *Cycles of denunciation*: Kalyvas 2006: 147–49, 167, 330, 332, 338, 333.
299 *Not a war, but a disease*: Antoine de Saint-Exupéry, quoted in Kalyvas 2006: 334.
299–300 *These personal motives appeared*: Des Forges 1999: 10, 11, 90.
300 *Rational economic agents*: Collier 2007a: 216; 198, 199; see also Hultman 2008.
300 *Control warlords*: Shawcross 2000: 29.
300 *War reporter*: Hedges 2002: 20, 22.
300 *Some researchers take*. Kegan 2000: 0, 10 ??
301 *And individual motives*: Wood 2003a: 2, 12, 18, 227–28.
301 *Feasibility*: Collier 2009: 135, 132, 133.
301 *Diaspora communities*: Collier 2007a: 210; Collier et al. 2003: 162–63.
301–02 *Wars end in different ways*: Licklider 1995; Toft 2009: 6, xi, 5.
302 *The central issue*: Walter 2002: 3, 4, 6.
302 *Peacebuilding trumps*: Doyle and Sambanis 2006: 48, 45, 5.
302 *In Central America*: Peceny and Stanley 2001.
302 *Hills of Bangladesh*: Fortna 2008: 50–55.
303 *After a war*: Collier 2007a: 211–13.
303 *Regarding economic growth*: Collier 2007a: 215; Collier 2007b: 27.
303 *In recovering economically*: Collier et al. 2003: 166.
303 *Two points of intervention*: Collier 2007b: 177–78.
304 *Not to take anything*: Francesch et al. 2008: 19; see also Fisas 2010.
304 *Continue jockeying*: Durch 2006b: 595; see also Stedman 2002.
305 *Blunt fact*: Kennedy 2006: 98.
305 *High-value commodities*: Durch 2006b: 595.
305 *Pieces of a mirror*: Hedges 2002: 119.
305 *Striking similarities*: Krippner and McIntyre 2003: 4; see also Shay 1994.
305 *Spent fifteen years*: Hedges 2002: 3, 38, 40.
305–06 *One way to deal*: Cohen 2001: 1, 5, 6, 119.
306 *Denial is literal*: Cohen 2001: 7, 103.
306 *Atlacatl*: Cohen 2001: 135–36.
306 *Denial is always partial*: Cohen 2001: 22, 11, 117.
307 *Truth Commission*: Cohen 2001: 227.
307 *What are missing*: Doyle and Sambanis 2006: 19.

Chapter 12

308 *The second largest*: Erlanger 2009.
310 *Surprisingly resilient*: Shawcross 2000: 299; Kennedy 2006: 110 ; Bellamy, Williams, and Griffin 2004: 8.
311 *In assessing the UN's*: Pérez de Cuéllar 1997: 16–17, 36–37.
311 *Pushed to the wall*: MacFarquhar 2009a; see Banerjee 2008: 187.

311 *Flag is not enough*: MacFarquhar 2008.

311 *Plane was shot down*: Shawcross 2000: 403, 38.

312 *Tobin tax*: Diehl 2008: 113; Castro 2001.

312 *Australian*: Evans 2008: 176.

312–13 *Permanent missions*: Prantl 2006: 75; Data from globalpolicy.org/security/data/tab-sec.htm.

313 *Plane of his own*: Traub 2006a: 221.

313 *No enforcement. . . . race against time*: Shawcross 2000: 34, 45.

313 *Power and prestige*: O'Brien 1962: 64.

313 *Pretension and grandiosity*: Babbin 2004: 196.

313 *In late 1954*: Traub 2006a: 11.

314 *Test of the authority*: Urquhart 1993: 336.

314 *Considerable freedom*: O'Brien 1962: 269.

314 *Sensible notion*: Weiss 2009: 180.

314 *U.S. public opinion*: Worldpublicopinion.org 2007: 9–10, 5.

316 *Military policy expert*: O'Hanlon 2007: 323, 321, 328, 319–28.

316 *RAND*: Dobbins et al. 2007: 4–5, 258, 6, 256.

316 *Once war starts*: Doyle and Sambanis 2006: 43.

317 *Ounce of prevention*: Urquhart 1972: 524; Annan 2002: 2, 11; Stares and Zenko, 2009.

317 *$200 billion*: Cited in Annan 2002: 1–2.

317 *Early-warning*: Carnegie Commission 1997: 43–48; see also Edwards 1999: 109.

317 *As Annan notes*: Annan 2002: 1, 19, 35, 27.

317 *Annan complains*: Annan 2002: 45; see Melander, Möller, and Öberg 2009.

317–18 *OSCE*: Ramsbotham, Woodhouse, and Miall 2005: 127–29, 110–12.

318 *Cost $11 billion*: Zartman 2005: 203, 204.

318 *Medical researcher*: Hamburg 2002: x; Stanford Prevention Research Center n.d.

318 *Hamburg went on*: Carnegie Commission on Preventing Deadly Conflict 1997; Hamburg 2008; Hamburg 2002: 308.

319 *State Department poll*: Ruggie 1996: 33.

319 *Who do you think*: Traub 2006a: 8, 16.

319 *During the Reagan*: Pérez de Cuéllar 1997: 9, 10, 12.

319–20 *After 1994*: Ruggie 1996: 7.

320 *Jesse Helms*: Traub 2006a: 131–35; see also Shawcross 2000: 33.

320 *Richard Holbrooke*: Traub 2006a: 136–38, 143.

320 *Tone shifted again*: Traub 2006a: 153; see Bolton 1994; Weiss 2009: 2; Doyle and Sambanis 2006: 2.

320 *Obama Administration*: MacFarquhar 2009b; UNA-USA 2010.

321 *State-centric*: Weiss 2009: 2, 19.

321 *192 units*: Garrett 1999: 30.

322 *Personal setting*: See Long and Brecke 2003.

322 *Limits to sovereignty*: Holsti 1996: 191.

323 *World's business*: Evans 2008: 5, 11, 175.

323 *Breakaway Georgian*: Malcomson 2008: 13.

323 *Security Council, however*: Bellamy, Williams, and Griffin 2004: 3; see also Garrett 1999: 67.

323 *UN Charter says*: See Donnelly 2003: 243.

324 *Humanitarian intervention*: Thakur 2007: 399; Mingst and Karns 2007: 109–10; Garrett 1999: 4, viii; see also Zartman 2005: 1.

324 *Came to a head in Kosovo*: Donnelly 2003: 258, 259.

324–25 *Long predates*: Garrett 1999: 9; Bass 2008: 3–8.

325 *Profoundly national. . . . 1990s*: Wheeler 2000: 1, 8; see also Donnelly 2003: 179, 242; Seybolt 2007: 270.

325 *Annan supported the concept*: Quoted in Traub 2006a: 100.

325 *Potential weakening. . . . driven more*: Wheeler 2000: 285, 300.

325 *G77*: Traub 2006a: 101; see Marten 2004.

325 *Set up the commission*: International Commission on Intervention and State Sovereignty 2001.

325–26 *In 2008*: Albright 2008.
326 *Despite the resilience*: Kennedy 2006: 77; O'Brien 1962: 3; Pérez de Cuéllar 1997: 3.
326 *Trick-or-treat*: Rubinstein 2008: 1–2.
326 *Symbolic. . . . moribund*: Rubinstein 2008: 3.
327 *International Day*: UN 2008.

References

Aall, Pamela. "The Power of Nonofficial Actors in Conflict Management." In Chester A. Crocker, Fen Osler Hampson, and Pamela Aall, eds. *Leashing the Dogs of War: Conflict Management in a Divided World*. Washington, D.C.: U.S. Institute of Peace Press, 2007: 477–96.

Ahlström, Christer. *Casualties of Conflict: Report for the World Campaign for the Protection of Victims of War*. Uppsala, Sweden: Department of Peace and Conflict Research, Uppsala University, 1991.

Albright, Madeleine K. "The End of Intervention." *New York Times*, June 11, 2008: A29.

Allison, Graham T. *Nuclear Terrorism: The Ultimate Preventable Catastrophe*. New York: Times Books/Henry Holt, 2004.

Anderlini, Sanam Naraghi. *Women Building Peace: What They Do, Why It Matters*. Boulder: Rienner, 2007.

Anderson, Scott. "What Happened to Fred Cuny?" *New York Times Magazine*, February 25, 1996.

Angell, Norman. *The Great Illusion: A Study in the Relation of Military Power in Nations to Their Economic and Social Advantage*. New York: Knickerbocker Press, 1910.

Annan, Kofi A. *Prevention of Armed Conflict: Report of the Secretary-General*. New York: United Nations, 2002.

Arieff, Alexis. "Sexual Violence in African Conflicts." Washington, D.C.: Congressional Research Service, 2009.

Arquilla, John. "Realities of War." *San Francisco Chronicle*, April 30, 2006: E1.

Asher, Jana. "Developing a Science for Recording, Estimating Casualties." *AMSTATNEWS: The Membership Magazine of the American Statistical Association*. December 1, 2009.

Associated Press. "Shiite Rivals Fight in Beirut." *New York Times*, April 18, 1980: A8.

Autesserre, Séverine. "The Trouble with Congo: How local disputes fuel regional conflict." *Foreign Affairs* 87 (3), May–June 2008: 94–110.

Autesserre, Séverine. *The Trouble with the Congo: Local Violence and the Failure of International Peacebuilding*. Cambridge, UK: Cambridge University Press, 2010.

Avant, Deborah D. *The Market for Force: The Consequences of Privatizing Security*. Cambridge, UK: Cambridge University Press, 2005.

Ayres, Leonard P. *The War with Germany: A Statistical Summary*. Washington, D.C.: Government Printing Office, 1919.

Azevedo, Mario. *Roots of Violence: A History of War in Chad*. Abingdon, UK: Gordon & Breach, 1998.

Baaz, Maria Eriksson, and Maria Stern. *The Complexity of Violence: A Critical Analysis of Sexual Violence in the Democratic Republic of Congo (DRC)*. [Sida Working Paper on Gender-based Violence]. Stockholm: Swedish International Development Cooperation Agency [Sida], 2010.

Babbin, Jed. *Inside the Asylum: Why the UN and Old Europe Are Worse Than You Think*. Washington, D.C.: Regnery, 2004.

Bamforth, Douglas B. "Indigenous People, Indigenous Violence: Precontact Warfare on the North American Great Plains." *Man* 29, 1994: 95–115.

Ban Ki–moon. Twenty–first progress report of the Secretary-General on the United Nations Operation in Côte d'Ivoire. UN Security Council S/2009/344. July 7, 2009.

Banerjee, Dipankar. "South Asia: Contributors of Global Significance." In Donald C. F. Daniel, Patricia Taft, and Sharon Wiharta, eds. *Peace Operations: Trends, Progress, and Prospects.* Washington, D.C.: Georgetown University Press, 2008: 187–202.

Barnett, Michael. *Eyewitness to a Genocide: The United Nations and Rwanda.* Ithaca: Cornell University Press, 2002.

Barnett, Michael, and Martha Finnemore. *Rules for the World: International Organizations in Global Politics.* Ithaca: Cornell University Press, 2004.

Bass, Gary J. *Freedom's Battle: The Origins of Humanitarian Intervention.* New York: Knopf, 2008.

BBC News. "Savimbi 'Died with Gun in Hand.'" February 25, 2002. Accessed at news.bbc.co.uk/2/hi/africa/1839252.stm.

BBC News. "Ortega Wins Nicaragua Election." November 8, 2006. Accessed 4/19/10 at news.bbc.co.uk/go/pr/fr/-/2/hi/americas/6117704.stm.

BBC News. "Bosnia War Dead Figure Announced." June 21, 2007. Accessed 5/29/10 at news.bbc.co.uk/go/pr/fr/-/2/hi/europe/6228152.stm.

BBC News. "France Backing Djibouti in 'War.'" June 13, 2008a. Accessed 6/6/10 at news.bbc.co.uk/go/pr/fr/-/2/hi/africa/7453063.stm.

BBC News. "Rwanda Genocide Mastermind Jailed." December 18, 2008b. Accessed 5/14/09 at news.bbc.co.uk/2/hi/africa/7789039.stm.

BBC News. "DR Congo Hutu Gunmen 'on Rampage.'" February 19, 2009a. Accessed at news.bbc.co.uk/go/pr/fr/-/2/hi/africa/7900319.stm.

BBC News. "Congo's Bemba to Stand ICC Trial." June 16, 2009b. Accessed at news.bbc.co.uk/go/pr/fr/-/2/hi/africa/8101809.stm.

BBC News. "Clinton Demands End to Congo Rape." August 11, 2009c. Accessed at news.bbc.co.uk/2/hi/8194836.stm.

BBC News. "Ivory Coast Sets New Election Date." August 5, 2010a. Accessed at www.bbc.co.uk/news/world-africa-10884545.

BBC News. "UN Official Calls DR Congo 'Rape Capital of the World.'" April 28, 2010b. Accessed at news.bbc.co.uk/2/hi/8650112.stm.

Beah, Ishmael. *A Long Way Gone: Memoirs of a Boy Soldier.* New York: Farrar, Straus and Giroux, 2007.

Beer, Francis A. *Peace against War: The Ecology of International Violence.* San Francisco: W. H. Freeman, 1981.

Bellamy, Alex J., Paul Williams, and Stuart Griffin. *Understanding Peacekeeping.* Cambridge, UK: Polity, 2004.

Bercovitch, Jacob. Mediation in the Most Resistant Cases. In Chester A. Crocker, Fen Olsen Hampson, and Pamela Aall, eds. *Grasping the Nettle: Analyzing Cases of Intractable Conflict.* Washington, D.C.: U.S. Institute of Peace, 2005: 99–122.

Berman, Eric G., and Melissa T. Labonte. "Sierra Leone." In William J. Durch, ed. *Twenty-First-Century Peace Operations.* Washington, D.C.: U.S. Institute of Peace, 2006: 141–228.

Blight, James G., and Robert S. McNamara. *Wilson's Ghost: Reducing the Risk of Conflict, Killing, and Catastrophe in the 21st Century.* New York: PublicAffairs, 2001.

Bloomberg News. "Democratic Republic of Congo: Arrest of Rebel Leader in Hundreds of Rapes." *New York Times,* October 6, 2010: A14.

Bohannon, John. "War Deaths Grossly Underreported—Study." *ScienceNOW* Daily News. June 20, 2008.

Bolton, John. Speech at "The Global Structures Convocation," February 3, 1994, New York. Transcript accessed 2009 at www.democracynow.org/2005/3/31/john_bolton_in_his_own_words.

Boothby, Derek. "The Application of Leverage in Eastern Slavonia." In Jean Krasno, Bradd C. Hayes, and Donald C. F. Daniel. *Leveraging for Success in United Nations Peace Operations.* Westport, CT: Praeger, 2003: 117–40.

Boulding, Elise, and Randall Forsberg. *Abolishing War: Dialogue with Peace Scholars.* Cambridge, Mass.: Boston Research Center for the 21st Century, 1998.

Boulding, Kenneth E. *Stable Peace.* Austin: University of Texas Press, 1978.

Boutros-Ghali, Boutros. *An Agenda for Peace: Preventive Diplomacy, Peacemaking and Peacekeeping.* New York: United Nations, 1992.

Bowden, Mark. *Black Hawk Down: A Story of Modern War*. New York: Atlantic Monthly Press, 1999.

Bradbury, Jim. *The Medieval Siege*. Boydell Press, 1992.

Brahimi, Lakhdar, et al. Report of the Panel on United Nations Peace Operations. UN document A/55/305 S/2000/809. New York: UN, 2000.

Brennan, Richard J., Michael Despines, and Leslie F. Roberts. "Mortality Surveys in the Democratic Republic of Congo: Humanitarian Impact and Lessons Learned." *Humanitarian Exchange Magazine* #35, November 2006. Accessed 5/26/10 at www.odihpn.org/report.asp?id=2838.

Brock, Peter. *Pacifism in Europe to 1914*. Princeton, N.J.: Princeton University Press, 1972.

Brown, Michael E. "New Global Dangers." In Chester A. Crocker, Fen Olsen Hampson, and Pamela Aall, eds. *Leashing the Dogs of War: Conflict Management in a Divided World*. Washington, D.C.: U.S. Institute of Peace Press, 2007: 39–52.

Brzezinski, Zbigniew. *Out of Control: Global Turmoil on the Eve of the Twenty-First Century*. New York: Robert Stewart [Scribner], 1993.

Buhaug, Halvard, and Kristian Skrede Gleditsch. "Contagion or Confusion? Why Conflicts Cluster in Space." *International Studies Quarterly* 52, 2008: 215–33.

Bulletin of the Atomic Scientists. Doomsday Clock: Timeline. 2007. Accessed 6/5/09 at www.thebulletin.org/content/doomsday-clock/timeline.

Burnham, Gilbert, Riyadh Lafta, Shannon Doocy, and Les Roberts. "Mortality after the 2003 Invasion of Iraq: A Cross-Sectional Cluster Sample Survey." *The Lancet* 368, October 21, 2006: 1421–28.

Cairns, Edmund. *A Safer Future: Reducing the Human Cost of War*. Oxford, UK: Oxfam Publications, 1997.

Callahan, Kevin J. "The International Socialist Peace Movement on the Eve of World War I Revisited: The Campaign of 'War against War!' and the Basle International Socialist Congress in 1912." *Peace and Change* 29 (2), 2004: 147–76.

Carle, Glenn L. "Overstating Our Fears." *Washington Post*, July 13, 2008: B7.

Carnegie Commission on Preventing Deadly Conflict. *Preventing Deadly Conflict: Final Report*. New York, Carnegie Corporation, 1997.

Carpenter, R. Charli. *Innocent Women and Children: Gender, Norms, and the Protection of Civilians*. Aldershot, Hampshire, UK: Ashgate, 2006.

Castro, Fidel. Key address by Dr. Fidel Castro Ruz, President of the Republic of Cuba, at the World Conference against Racism, Racial Discrimination, Xenophobia and Related Intolerance. Durban, South Africa. September 1, 2001. Accessed 4/4/10 at www.un.org/WCAR/statements/0109cubaE.htm.

Center on International Cooperation. [Benjamin C. Tortolani et al.]. *Annual Review of Global Peace Operations 2010*. Boulder: Lynne Rienner, 2010.

Chacon, Richard J., and Rubén G. Mendoza, eds. *North American Indigenous Warfare and Ritual Violence*. Tucson: University of Arizona Press, 2007.

Chang, Iris. *The Rape of Nanking: The Forgotten Holocaust of World War II*. New York: Basic Books, 1997.

Chickering, Roger. *Imperial Germany and a World Without War: The Peace Movement and German Society, 1892–1914*. Princeton, N.J.: Princeton University Press, 1975.

Chivers, C. J., and Rod Norland. "Errant U.S. Rocket Strike Kills Civilians in Afghanistan." *New York Times*, February 15, 2010: A1.

Chivers, C. J., and Michael Schwirtz. "Georgian President Vows to Rebuild Army." *New York Times*, August 25, 2008: A5.

Clark, Gregory. *A Farewell to Alms: A Brief Economic History of the World*. Princeton, N.J.: Princeton University Press, 2007.

Clinton, Hillary. Speech at First Ladies' Conference on Domestic Violence (As Delivered), San Salvador, El Salvador, November 17, 1998. Accessed at the National Archives at clinton3.nara.gov/WH/EOP/First_Lady/html/generalspeeches/1998/19981117.html.

Clinton, Hillary. "Hillary Clinton Talks about the Obama Administration's Plans to Push Women's Rights Issues on the International Stage" [Interview by Mark Lander]. *New York Times Magazine*, August 23, 2009: 41–43.

Clodfelter, Micheal. *Warfare and Armed Conflicts: A Statistical Encyclopedia of Casualty and Other Figures, 1494–2007*. Third edition. Jefferson, NC: McFarland, 2008.

Cobban, Helena. *Amnesty after Atrocity?: Healing Nations after Genocide and War Crimes.* Boulder: Paradigm, 2007.

Coghlan, Benjamin, Richard J. Brennan, Pascal Ngoy, David Dofara, Brad Otto, Mark Clements, Tony Stewart. "Mortality in the Democratic Republic of Congo: A Nationwide Survey." *The Lancet* 367, January 7, 2006: 44–51.

Coghlan, Benjamin, et al. *Mortality in the Democratic Republic of the Congo: An Ongoing Crisis.* International Rescue Committee, undated [Jan. 2008].

Cohen, Stanley. *States of Denial: Knowing about Atrocities and Suffering.* Cambridge, UK: Polity, 2001.

Coleman, Katharina P. *International Organisations and Peace Enforcement: The Politics of International Legitimacy.* Cambridge, UK: Cambridge University Press, 2007.

Collier, Paul. "Economic Causes of Civil Conflict and Their Implications for Policy." In Chester A. Crocker, Fen Olsen Hampson, and Pamela Aall, eds. *Leashing the Dogs of War: Conflict Management in a Divided World.* Washington, D.C.: U.S. Institute of Peace Press, 2007a: 197–218.

Collier, Paul. *The Bottom Billion: Why the Poorest Countries Are Failing and What Can Be Done About It.* Oxford: Oxford University Press, 2007b.

Collier, Paul. *Wars, Guns, and Votes: Democracy in Dangerous Places.* New York: Harper, 2009.

Collier, Paul, V. L. Elliott, Håvard Hegre, Anke Hoeffler, Marta Reynal-Querol, Nicholas Sambanis. *Breaking the Conflict Trap: Civil War and Development Policy.* World Bank and Oxford University Press, 2003.

Cook, Noble David. *Born to Die: Disease and New World Conqest, 1492–1650.* Cambridge, UK: Cambridge University Press, 1998.

Cooper, Robert. *The Breaking of Nations: Order and Chaos in the Twenty-first Century.* New York: Atlantic Monthly Press, 2003.

Cortright, David. *Peace: A History of Movements and Ideas.* Cambridge, UK: Cambridge University Press, 2008.

Cousens, Elizabeth, and David Harland. "Post-Dayton Bosnia and Herzegovina." In William J. Durch, ed. *Twenty-First-Century Peace Operations.* Washington, D.C.: U.S. Institute of Peace, 2006: 49–140.

Cranna, Michael, ed. *The True Cost of Conflict.* London: Earthscan, 1994.

Crawford, Neta C. *Soviet Military Aircraft.* Lanham, Md.: Lexington Books, 1987.

Crawford, Neta C. *Argument and Change in World Politics: Ethics, Decolonization, and Humanitarian Intervention.* Cambridge, UK: Cambridge University Press, 2002.

Crocker, Chester A., Fen Olsen Hampson, and Pamela Aall. "Introduction: Mapping the Nettle Field." In Chester A. Crocker, Fen Olsen Hampson, and Pamela Aall, eds. *Grasping the Nettle: Analyzing Cases of Intractable Conflict.* Washington, D.C.: U.S. Institute of Peace, 2005: 3–32.

Crocker, Chester A., Fen Olsen Hampson, and Pamela Aall. "Leashing the Dogs of War." In Chester A. Crocker, Fen Olsen Hampson, and Pamela Aall, eds. *Leashing the Dogs of War: Conflict Management in a Divided World.* Washington, D.C.: U.S. Institute of Peace Press, 2007: 3–13.

Cutter, Susan L., H. Briavel Holcomb, and Dianne Shatin. "Spatial Patterns of Support for a Nuclear Weapons Freeze." *Professional Geographer* 38 (1), 1986: 42–52.

Daalder, Ivo H. *Getting to Dayton: The Making of America's Bosnia Policy.* Washington, D.C.: Brookings, 2000.

Dallaire, Lieutenant-General Roméo, with Major Brent Beardsley. *Shake Hands with the Devil: The Failure of Humanity in Rwanda.* Toronto: Random House Canada, 2003.

D'Amato, Paul. "Pacifism and War." *International Socialist Review,* July/August 2002. Accessed 3/10/2010 at www.isreview.org/issues/24/pacifism_war.shtml.

Daniel, Donald C. F., and Sharon Wiharta. "Introduction." In Donald C. F. Daniel, Patricia Taft, and Sharon Wiharta, eds. *Peace Operations: Trends, Progress, and Prospects.* Washington, D.C.: Georgetown University Press, 2008: 1–8.

Daniel, Donald C. F., Katrin Heuel, and Benjamin Margo. "Distinguishing among Military Contributors." In Donald C. F. Daniel, Patricia Taft, and Sharon Wiharta, eds. *Peace Operations: Trends, Progress, and Prospects.* Washington, D.C.: Georgetown University Press, 2008: 27–46.

DeBenedetti, Charles. *The Peace Reform in American History*. Bloomington: Indiana University Press, 1980.

Deng, William Deng. A Survey of Programs on the Reintegration of Former Child Soldiers. Ministry of Foreign Affairs of Japan, 2001. Accessed 8/09 at www.mofa.go.jp/policy/human/child/survey/.

Des Forges, Alison. *"Leave None to Tell the Story": Genocide in Rwanda*. New York: Human Rights Watch, 1999.

Deutsch, Karl W., et al. *Political Community and the North Atlantic Area: International Organization in the Light of Historical Experience*. Princeton University Press, 1957.

Deutsch, Karl W. "Quincy Wright's Contribution to the Study of War: A Preface to the Second Edition." In Quincy Wright. *A Study of War: Second Edition*. University of Chicago Press, 1965.

Diehl, Paul F. *Peace Operations*. Cambridge, UK: Polity, 2008.

Dobbins, James, Seth G. Jones, Keith Crane, and Beth Cole DeGrasse. *The Beginner's Guide to Nation-Building*. Santa Monica: RAND Corporation, 2007.

Donnelly, Jack. *Universal Human Rights in Theory and Practice*. 2nd ed. Ithaca: Cornell University Press, 2003.

Downes, Alexander B. *Targeting Civilians in War*. Ithaca: Cornell University Press, 2008.

Doyle, A. Conan. "Silver Blaze." In *Memoirs of Sherlock Holmes*. New York: A. L. Burt, 1894.

Doyle, Michael W., Ian Johnstone, and Robert C. Orr. Introduction. In Michael W. Doyle, Ian Johnstone, and Robert C. Orr, eds. *Keeping the Peace: Multidimensional UN Operations in Cambodia and El Salvador*. Cambridge, UK: Cambridge University Press, 1997.

Doyle, Michael W., and Nicholas Sambanis. *Making War and Building Peace: United Nations Peace Operations*. Princeton N.J.: Princeton University Press, 2006.

Drelichman, Mauricio, and Hans-Joachim Voth. "Institutions and the Resource Curse in Early Modern Spain." In Elhanan Helpman, ed. *Institutions and Economic Performance*. Cambridge, Mass.: Harvard University Press, 2008: 120–47.

Driver, Felix. *Geography Militant: Cultures of Exploration and Empire*. Hoboken, N.J.: Wiley-Blackwell 2001.

Dugger, Celia W. "Global Number of Early Childhood Deaths Falls Below 9 Million for First Time." *New York Times*, September 10, 2009.

Dupuy, R. Ernest, and Trevor N. Dupuy. *The Harper Encyclopedia of Military History: From 3,500 b.c. to the Present*. Fourth edition. New York: HarperCollins, 1993.

Durch, William J., with Tobias C. Berkman. "Restoring and Maintaining Peace: What We Know So Far." In William J. Durch, ed. *Twenty-First-Century Peace Operations*. Washington, D.C.: U.S. Institute of Peace, 2006a: 1–48.

Durch, William J. "Are We Learning Yet? The Long Road to Applying Best Practices." In William J. Durch, ed. *Twenty–First–Century Peace Operations*. Washington, D.C.: U.S. Institute of Peace, 2006b: 573–602.

Easterbrook, Gregg. *The Progress Paradox: How Life Gets Better While People Feel Worse*. New York: Random House, 2003.

Easterbrook, Gregg. "The End of War?" *The New Republic*, May 30, 2005: 18–21.

Eckhardt, William. "Civilian Deaths in Wartime." *Bulletin of Peace Proposals* 20 (1), 1989: 89–98.

Eckhardt, William. "War-related Deaths Since 3000 b.c." *Bulletin of Peace Proposals* 22 (4), 1991: 437–43.

Eckhardt, William. *Civilizations, Empires and Wars: A Quantitative History of War*. Jefferson, NC: McFarland, 1992.

Edwards, Michael. *Future Positive: International Cooperation in the 21st Century*. London: Earthscan, 1999.

Ember, Carol R. "Myths about Hunter-Gatherers." *Ethnology* 17 (4) 1978: 439–48.

Englebert, Pierre, and Denis Tull. "Postconflict Resolution in Africa: Flawed Ideas about Failed States." *International Security* 32 (4), 2008: 106–39.

Erlanger, Steven. "Europeans Transfer Chad Mission to U.N." *New York Times*, March 17, 2009: A10.

European Union [Council of, General Secretariat]. Background: DRC Elections 2006: EU Support to the DRC during the Election Process. EU press release RDC/02/EN, June 2006.

European Union [Council of]. EUFOR RD CONGO: The Mission. January 1, 2007. Accessed on the EU website 9/18/09 at www.consilium.europa.eu/uedocs/cmsUpload/The_mission.pdf.

Evangelista, Matthew. *Unarmed Forces: The Transnational Movement to End the Cold War.* Ithaca: Cornell, 1999.

Evans, Gareth. *The Responsibility to Protect: Ending Mass Atrocity Crimes Once and For All.* Washington, D.C.: Brookings, 2008.

Farah, Douglas. "Children Forced to Kill." *Washington Post*, April 8, 2000.

Fearon, James D. "Primary Commodity Exports and Civil War." *Journal of Conflict Resolution* 49 (4), 2005: 483–507.

Fearon, James D. "Economic Development, Insurgency, and Civil War." In Elhanan Helpman, ed. *Institutions and Economic Performance.* Cambridge, Mass.: Harvard University Press, 2008: 292–328.

Fearon, James D., and David D. Laitin. "Ethnicity, Insurgency, and Civil War." *American Political Science Review* 97 (1), 2003: 75–90.

Fettweis, Christopher J. *Dangerous Times? The International politics of Great power peace.* Washington, D.C.: Georgetown University Press, 2010.

Ferguson, Niall. *The War of the World: Twentieth-Century Conflict and the Descent of the West.* New York: Penguin, 2006.

Finnemore, Martha. *National Interests in International Society.* Ithaca: Cornell University Press, 1996.

Finnemore, Martha. *The Purpose of Intervention: Changing Beliefs about the Use of Force.* Ithaca: Cornell University Press, 2003. Fisas, Vincenç. *2010 Yearbook on Peace Processes.* Bellaterra, Spain: Escola de Cultura de Pau, 2010.

Foley, Conor. *The Thin Blue Line: How Humanitarianism Went to War.* London: Verso: 2008.

Forbes, Frederick E. *Dahomey and the Dahomans.* Volumes 1 and 2. London: Frank Cass, 1851 [1966].

Forsberg, Randall Caroline Watson. "Toward a Theory of Peace: The Role of Moral Beliefs." Ph.D. dissertation, Department of Political Science, Massachusetts Institute of Technology, 1997.

Fortna, Virginia Page. *Does Peacekeeping Work? Shaping Belligerents' Choices after Civil War.* Princeton University Press, 2008.

Fortna, Virginia Page, and Lise Morjé Howard. "Pitfalls and Prospects in the Peacekeeping Literature." *Annual Review of Political Science* 11, 2008: 283–301.

Francesch, Maria Cañadas, et al. *Alert 2008!: Report on Conflicts, Human Rights and Peace-Building.* Bellaterra, Spain: Escola de Cultura de Pau, 2008. See escolapau.uab.cat/english/index.php.

Freedman, Lawrence. "Using Force for Peace in an Age of Terror." In Chester A. Crocker, Fen Olsen Hampson, and Pamela Aall, eds. *Leashing the Dogs of War: Conflict Management in a Divided World.* Washington, D.C.: U.S. Institute of Peace Press, 2007: 245–64.

Friedrichs, Christopher R. "The War and German Society." In Geoffrey Parker, ed. *The Thirty Years' War.* Second ed. London: Routledge, 1997: 186–92.

Garrett, Stephen A. *Doing Good and Doing Well: An Examination of Humanitarian Intervention.* Westport, Conn: Praeger, 1999.

Gartzke, Erik. "The Capitalist Peace." *American Journal of Political Science* 51 (1), 2007: 166–91.

Gat, Azar. *War in Human Civilization.* Oxford: Oxford University Press, 2006.

Gat, Azar. *Victorious and Vulnerable: Why Democracy Won in the 20th Century and How It Is Still Imperiled.* Lanham, Md.: Rowman & Littlefield, 2010.

Gettleman, Jeffrey. "In Congo, a Little Fighting Brings a Lot of Fear." *New York Times*, November 3, 2008: A6.

Gettleman, Jeffrey. "With Leader Captured, Congo Rebel Force Is Dissolving." *New York Times*, January 25, 2009a: 10.

Gettleman, Jeffrey. "Congo: Rights Group Reports Attacks on Civilians." *New York Times*, July 3, 2009b: A11.

Gettleman, Jeffrey. "U.N. Official Fears Congo Is Overcome by Violence." *New York Times*, May 1, 2010a: A6.

Gettleman, Jeffrey. "4-Day Frenzy of Rape in Congo Reveals U.N. Troops' Weakness." *New York Times*, October 4, 2010b: A1.

Gettleman [printed as "Gettelman"], Jeffrey. "Rapes Are Again Reported in Eastern Congo." *New York Times*, February 26, 2011: A7.

Gettleman, Jeffrey, and Neil MacFarquhar. "Congo Rebels Advance; Protesters Hurl Rocks at U.N. Compound." *New York Times*, October 28, 2008: A6.

Gettleman, Jeffrey, and Neil MacFarquhar. "Somalia Food Aid Bypasses Needy, U.N. Study Shows." *New York Times*, March 9, 2010: A1.

Gettleman, Jeffrey, and Mossi Mwassi. "Challenger in Congo Vote Says He'll Contest Results." *New York Times*, November 17, 2006:

Ghobarah, Hazem Adam, Paul Huth, and Bruce Russett. "The Post-war Public Health Effects of Civil Conflict." *Social Science and Medicine* 59, 2004: 869–84.

Gibbs, David N. "Dag Hammarskjöld, the United Nations, and the Congo Crisis of 1960–1: A Reinterpretation." *Journal of Modern African Studies* 31 (1), 1993: 163–74.

Gibbs, David N. *First Do No Harm: Humanitarian Intervention and the Destruction of Yugoslavia*. Nashville: Vanderbilt University Press, 2009.

Giegerich, Bastian. "Europe: Looking Near and Far." In Donald C. F. Daniel, Patricia Taft, and Sharon Wiharta, eds. *Peace Operations: Trends, Progress, and Prospects*. Washington, D.C.: Georgetown University Press, 2008: 119–36.

Giro, Mario. "War, Mother of All Poverty: Mozambique." ["Community of Sant'Egidio and Peace."] Accessed 3/26/10 at: www.santegidio.org/en/pace/pace3.htm. Undated.

Gleditsch, Nils Petter. "Environmental Change, Security, and Conflict." In Chester A. Crocker, Fen Olsen Hampson, and Pamela Aall, eds. *Leashing the Dogs of War: Conflict Management in a Divided World*. Washington, D.C.: U.S. Institute of Peace Press, 2007: 177–96.

Gleditsch, Nils Petter. "The Liberal Moment Fifteen Years On." Presidential Address, International Studies Association, March 27, 2008, San Francisco. *International Studies Quarterly* 52, 2008: 691–712.

Gleditsch, Nils Petter; Peter Wallensteen, Mikael Eriksson, Margareta Sollenberg, and Håvard Strand. "Armed Conflict 1946–2001: A New Dataset." *Journal of Peace Research* 39 (5), 2002: 615–37.

Goldstein, Joshua S. *Long Cycles: Prosperity and War in the Modern Age*. New Haven: Yale University Press, 1988.

Goldstein, Joshua S. "A War-Economy Theory of the Long Wave." In Neils Thygesen, Kumaraswamy Velupillai, and Stefano Zambelli, eds. *Business Cycles: Theories, Evidence, and Analysis*. Basingstoke, Hampshire, UK: Macmillan, 1991.

Goldstein, Joshua S. *War and Gender: How Gender Shapes the War System and Vice Versa*. Cambridge, UK: Cambridge University Press, 2001.

Goldstein, Joshua S. "The Worldwide Lull in War." *Christian Science Monitor*, May 14, 2002: 9.

Goldstein, Joshua S., and Jon C. Pevehouse. *International Relations*, 9th edition, 2010–2011 Update. New York: Pearson Longman, 2011.

Goldstone, Jack A. *Revolution and Rebellion in the Early Modern World*. Berkeley: University of California Press, 1993.

Grady, Denise. "Maternal Deaths in Sharp Decline across the Globe." *New York Times*, April 14, 2010: A1.

Grant, James P. *See* UNICEF 1992.

Greitens, Eric. "The Treatment of Children during Conflict." In Frances Stewart and Valpy FitzGerald and Associates. *War and Underdevelopment. Volume 1: The Economic and Social Consequences of Conflict*. Oxford: Oxford University Press, 2001: 149–67.

Griffin, Michèle. "The Helmet and the Hoe: Linkages between United Nations Development Assistance and Conflict Management." *Global Governance* 9, 2003: 199–217.

Guardian, The. Conor Cruise O'Brien: "An intellectually formidable figure" [Obituary]. *The Guardian* [UK], December 19, 2008.

Guevara, Ernesto "Ché." *The African Dream: The Diaries of the Revolutionary War in the Congo*. Trans. Patrick Camiller. New York: Grove Press, 2000 [original Spanish 1965].

Guilaine, Jean, and Jean Zammit. *The Origins of War: Violence in Prehistory*. Trans. Melanie Hersey. Malden, Mass: Blackwell, 2005 [French 2001].

Gurr, Ted Robert. *People versus States: Minorities at Risk in the New Century*. Washington, D.C.: U.S. Institute of Peace Press, 2000.

Gurr, Ted Robert. "Minorities, Nationalists, and Islamists: Managing Communal Conflict in the Twenty-first Century." In Chester A. Crocker, Fen Olsen Hampson, and Pamela Aall, eds. *Leashing the Dogs of War: Conflict Management in a Divided World*. Washington, D.C.: U.S. Institute of Peace Press, 2007: 131–60.

Gurr, Ted Robert, Monty G. Marshall, and Deepa Khosla. *Peace and Conflict 2001: A Global Survey of Armed Conflicts, Self-Determination Movements, and Democracy.* College Park, Md.: CIDCM, University of Maryland: 2000.

Hamburg, David A. *No More Killing Fields: Preventing Deadly Conflict.* Lanham, Md.: Rowman & Littlefield, 2002.

Hamburg, David A., M.D. *Preventing Genocide: Practical Steps toward Early Detection and Effective Action.* Boulder: Paradigm, 2008.

Hansen, Annika S., and Sharon Wiharta. *The Transition to a Just Order—Establishing Local Ownership after Conflict.* Sandöverken, Sweden: Folke Bernadotte Academy, 2007.

Harbom, Lotta, ed. *States in Armed Conflict 2009.* Research Report, Department of Peace and Conflict Research, Uppsala University, 2010.

Harbom, Lotta, and Peter Wallensteen. "Armed Conflict, 1989–2006." *Journal of Peace Research* 44 (5), 2007: 623–34.

Harbom, Lotta, and Peter Wallensteen. "Armed Conflicts, 1946–2008." *Journal of Peace Research* 46 (4), 2009: 577–87.

Harbom, Lotta, and Peter Wallensteen. "Armed Conflicts, 1946–2009." *Journal of Peace Research* 47 (4), 2010a: 501–09.

Harbom, Lotta, and Peter Wallensteen. "Patterns of Major Armed Conflicts, 1997–2006." Appendix 2A in *SIPRI Yearbook 2010: Armaments, Disarmament, and International Security.* Oxford: Oxford University Press, 2010b.

Harff, Barbara, and Ted Robert Gurr. *Ethnic Conflict in World Politics.* 2nd ed. Boulder: Westview, 2004.

Harvard Humanitarian Initiative [Susan Bartels, Michael VanRooyen, Jennifer Leaning, Jennifer Scott, and Jocelyn Kelly]. *"Now, the World Is Without Me": An Investigation of Sexual Violence in Eastern Democratic Republic of Congo.* Cambridge, Mass.: Harvard Humanitarian Initiative, 2010.

Hayner, Priscilla B. *Unspeakable Truths: Confronting State Terror and Atrocity.* New York: Routledge, 2001.

Hedges, Chris. *War Is a Force That Gives Us Meaning.* New York: PublicAffairs, 2002.

Hegre, Håvard, Tanja Ellingsen, Scott Gates, and Nils Petter Gleditsch. "Toward a Democratic Civil Peace? Democracy, Political Change, and Civil War, 1816–1992." *American Political Science Review* 95 (1), 2001: 33–48.

Hegre, Håvard, and Nicholas Sambanis. "Sensitivity Analysis of Empirical Results on Civil War Onset." *Journal of Conflict Resolution* 50 (4), August 2006: 508–35.

Heijdra, Martin. "The Socio-Economic Development of Rural China during the Ming." In Denis Twitchett and Frederick W. Mote, eds. *The Cambridge History of China: Volume 8, The Ming Dynasty, 1368–1644, Part 2.* Cambridge, UK: Cambridge University Press, 1998: 417–578.

Heldt, Birger. "Trends from 1948 to 2005: How to View the Relation between the United Nations and Non-UN Entities." In Donald C. F. Daniel, Patricia Taft, and Sharon Wiharta, eds. *Peace Operations: Trends, Progress, and Prospects.* Washington, D.C.: Georgetown University Press, 2008: 9–26.

Heldt, Birger, and Peter Wallensteen. *Peacekeeping Operations: Global Patterns of Intervention and Success, 1948–2004.* Sandöverken, Sweden: Folke Bernadotte Academy, 2006.

Hewitt, J. Joseph, Jonathan Wilkenfeld, and Ted Robert Gurr. *Peace and Conflict 2008.* Paradigm, 2007.

Hewitt, J. Joseph, Jonathan Wilkenfeld, and Ted Robert Gurr. *Peace and Conflict 2010.* Paradigm, 2010.

Hicks, Madelyn Hsiao-Rei, Hamit Dardagan, Gabriela Guerrero Serdán, Peter M. Bagnall, John A. Sloboda, and Michael Spagat. "The Weapons That Kill Civilians—Deaths of Children and Noncombatants in Iraq, 2003–2008." *New England Journal of Medicine* 360 (16), April 16, 2009: 1585–88.

Hilderbrand, Robert C. *Dumbarton Oaks: The Origins of the United Nations and the Search for Postwar Security.* Chapel Hill: University of North Carolina Press, 1990.

Hochschild, Adam. *King Leopold's Ghost: A Story of Greed, Terror, and Heroism in Colonial Africa.* Boston: Houghton Mifflin 1998.

Hobbes, Thomas. *Leviathan.* Richard Tuck, ed. Revised Student Edition. Cambridge, UK: Cambridge University Press, 1996 [1651].

Hoge, Warren. "Lack of Donated Copters Harms Darfur Effort, U.N. Leader Says." *New York Times*, December 7, 2007: A10.

Holsti, Kalevi J. *Peace and War: Armed Conflicts and International Order 1648–1989*. Cambridge, UK: Cambridge University Press, 1991.

Holsti, K. J. *The State, War, and the State of War*. Cambridge, UK: Cambridge University Press, 1996.

Howard, Lise Morjé. *UN Peacekeeping in Civil Wars*. Cambridge, UK: Cambridge University Press, 2008.

Hultman, Lisa. *Targeting the Unarmed: Strategic Rebel Violence in Civil War*. Report No. 82, Uppsala University Department of Peace and Conflict Research, Sweden, 2008.

Human Rights Watch. *Soldiers Who Rape, Commanders Who Condone: Sexual Violence and Military Reform in the Democratic Republic of Congo*. New York: Human Rights Watch, 2009.

Human Security Centre. *Human Security Report 2005: War and Peace in the 21st Century*. Oxford: Oxford University Press, 2005.

Human Security Report Project [Andrew Mack, director and editor-in-chief]. *Human Security Brief 2007*. Vancouver, BC: HSRP, Simon Fraser University, 2007.

Human Security Report Project [Andrew Mack, director and editor-in-chief]. *Human Security Report 2009: The Shrinking Costs of War*. Vancouver, BC: HSRP, Simon Fraser University, 2009.

ICRC [International Committee of the Red Cross]. *Annual Report 2009*. Geneva: ICRC, 2010.

Iklé, Fred Charles. *Every War Must End*. Rev. Ed. New York: Columbia University Press, 1991.

International Commission on Intervention and State Sovereignty. *The Responsibility to Protect: Report of the International Commission on Intervention and State Sovereignty*. Ottowa: International Development Research Centre, 2001.

IRIN [Integrated Regional Information Networks, DRC]. DRC: Kivu Crisis Worsens with 100,000 More Displaced. July 10, 2009. Accessed 7/30/09 at UNHCR website, www.unhcr.org/refworld/docid/4a5aff9f1e.html.

Jackson, Tabitha. *The Boer War*. UK: Channel 4 Books [Macmillan], 1999.

Jal, Emmanuel, with Megan Lloyd Davies. *War Child: A Child Soldier's Story*. New York: St. Martin's Press, 2009.

Johnson, Neil, Michael Spagat, Sean Gourley, Jukka-Pekka Onnela; and Gesine Reinert. "Bias in Epidemiological Studies of Conflict Mortality." *Journal of Peace Research* 45 (5), 2008: 653–63.

Jones, Bruce D. "The Challenges of Strategic Coordination." In Stephen John Stedman, Donald Rothchild, and Elizabeth M. Cousens, eds., *Ending Civil Wars: The Implementation of Peace Agreements*. Boulder: Lynne Rienner, 2002: 89–116.

Jongman, A. J., and A. P. Schmid. "Contemporary Armed Conflicts: A Brief Survey." In Dutch Centre of Conflict Prevention (NCDO), ed. *Prevention and Management of Conflicts: An International Directory*. Amsterdam: NCDO, 1996: 25–29.

Jongman, Berto, and Hans van der Dennen. "The Great 'War Figures' Hoax: An Investigation in Polemomythology." *Bulletin of Peace Proposals* 19 (2), 1988: 197–203.

Kacowicz, Arie M. "Explaining Zones of Peace: Democracies as Satisfied Powers?" *Journal of Peace Research* 32 (3), 1995: 265–76.

Kaldor, Mary. *New and Old Wars: Organized Violence in a Global Era*. Cambridge, UK: Polity, 1999.

Kaldor, Mary. *New and Old Wars: Organized Violence in a Global Era*. 2nd edition. Cambridge, UK: Polity, 2006.

Kalyvas, Stathis N. *The Logic of Violence in Civil War*. Cambridge, UK: Cambridge University Press, 2006.

Kaplan, Fred. "What 'Peace Epidemic'?" Slate.com, January 25, 2006. www.slate.com/id/2134846.

Kaplan, Robert D. "The Coming Anarchy: How scarcity, crime, overpopulation, tribalism, and disease are rapidly destroying the social fabric of our planet." *Atlantic Monthly*, 273 (2), February 1994: 44–76.

Keeley, Lawrence H. *War before Civilization: The Myth of the Peaceful Savage*. Oxford: Oxford University Press, 1996.

Keller, Edmond J. "Transnational Ethnic Conflict in Africa." In David A. Lake and Donald Rothchild, eds. *The International Spread of Ethnic Conflict: Fear, Diffusion, and Escalation*. Princeton University Press, 1998: 275–92.

Kennedy, Paul. *The Parliament of Man: The Past, Present, and Future of the United Nations.* New York: Random House, 2006.

King, Charles. "Power, Social Violence, and Civil Wars." In Chester A. Crocker, Fen Olsen Hampson, and Pamela Aall, eds. *Leashing the Dogs of War: Conflict Management in a Divided World.* Washington, D.C.: U.S. Institute of Peace Press, 2007: 115–30.

Krasno, Jean. Leveraging "Namibian Independence." In Jean Krasno, Bradd C. Hayes, and Donald C. F. Daniel. *Leveraging for Success in United Nations Peace Operations.* Westport, Conn.: Praeger, 2003a: 25–54.

Krasno, Jean. "The Group of Friends of the Secretary-General: A Useful Leveraging Tool." In Jean Krasno, Bradd C. Hayes, and Donald C. F. Daniel. *Leveraging for Success in United Nations Peace Operations.* Westport, Conn.: Praeger, 2003b: 171–200.

Krech, Shepard III. "Genocide in Tribal Society." *Nature* 371, Sep. 1, 1994: 14–15.

Kriesberg, Louis. "Long Peace or Long War: A Conflict Resolution Perspective." *Negotiation Journal,* April 2007: 97–116.

Krippner, Stanley, and Teresa M. McIntyre. "Overview: In the Wake of War." In Stanley Krippner and Teresa M. McIntyre, eds. *The Psychological Impact of War Trauma on Civilians: An International Perspective.* Westport, Conn.: Praeger, 2003: 1–14.

Kristof, Nicholas D. "Orphaned, Raped and Ignored." *New York Times,* January 31, 2010a: 11.

Kristof, Nicholas D. "From 'Oprah' to Building a Sisterhood in Congo." *New York Times,* February 4, 2010b: A25.

Kristof, Nicholas D. "The World Capital of Killing." *New York Times,* February 7, 2010c: 12.

Kristof, Nicholas D. "The Grotesque Vocabulary in Congo." *New York Times,* February 11, 2010d: A27.

Krug, Etienne G., Linda L. Dahlberg, James A. Mercy, Anthony B. Zwi, and Rafael Lozano, eds. *World Report on Violence and Health.* Geneva: World Health Organization, 2002.

Kulish, Nicholas. "Once Volatile, Crossing Is Opening with a Whisper." *New York Times,* December 20, 2007: A4.

Kupchan, Charles A. *How Enemies Become Friends: The Sources of Stable Peace.* Princeton, N.J.: Princeton University Press, 2010.

Lacina, Bethany, and Nils Petter Gleditsch. "Monitoring Trends in Global Combat: A New Dataset of Battle Deaths." *European Journal of Population* 21, 2005: 145–66.

Lacina, Bethany, Nils Petter Gleditsch, and Bruce Russett. "The Declining Risk of Death in Battle." *International Studies Quarterly* 50, 2006: 673–80.

Lake, David A., and Donald Rothchild. Spreading Fear: The Genesis of Transnational Ethnic Conflict. In David A. Lake and Donald Rothchild, eds. *The International Spread of Ethnic Conflict: Fear, Diffusion, and Escalation.* Princeton, N.J.: Princeton University Press, 1998: 3–32.

Lambert, André, and Lohlé-Tart, Louis. D R Congo's Excess Death Toll during the 1998–2004 Conflicts: An Excess Death Estimate Based Scientifically on Demographic Methods. Brussels: ADRASS, 2008.

LeBlanc, Stephen A., with Katherine E. Register. *Constant Battles: The Myth of the Peaceful, Noble Savage.* New York: St. Martin's, 2003.

Leitenberg, Milton. *Deaths in Wars and Conflicts in the 20th Century.* Ithaca: Cornell University Peace Studies Program, Occasional Paper #29, 3rd ed., 2006.

Levy, Jack S. *War in the Modern Great Power System 1495–1975.* Lexington, Ky.: University Press of Kentucky, 1983.

Levy, Jack S. War and Peace. In Walter Carlsnaes, Thomas Risse, and Beth A. Simmons, eds. *Handbook of International Relations.* Los Angeles: Sage, 2002.

Licklider, Roy. The Consequences of Negotiated Settlements in Civil Wars, 1945–1993. *American Political Science Review* 89 (3), September 1995: 681–90.

Licklider, Roy. Comparative Studies of Long Wars. In Chester A. Crocker, Fen Olsen Hampson, and Pamela Aall, eds. *Grasping the Nettle: Analyzing Cases of Intractable Conflict.* Washington, D.C.: U.S. Institute of Peace, 2005: 33–46.

Lindner, Evelin. *Making Enemies: Humiliation and International Conflict.* Westport, Conn.: Praeger, 2006.

Linnér, Sture. "Dag Hammarskjöld and the Congo Crisis, 1960–61." In Sture Linnér and Sverker Astrom, *UN Secretary-General Hammarskjöld: Reflections and personal experiences.* The 2007 Dag Hammarskjöld Lecture, ed. Peter Wallensteen, trans. Rod Bradbury. Uppsala: X-O Graf, 2008.

Lipson, Charles. *Reliable Partners: How Democracies Have Made a Separate Peace.* Princeton, N.J.: Princeton University Press, 2003.

Livingston, Ian, Heather Messera, Michael E. O'Hanlon, and Amy Unikewicz. The States of War [Op Chart]. *New York Times,* May 31, 2010.

Long, William J., and Peter Brecke. *War and Reconciliation: Reason and Emotion in Conflict Resolution.* Cambridge, Mass.: MIT Press, 2003.

Luard, Evan. *War in International Society: A Study in International Sociology.* London: I. B. Tauris, 1986.

Lujala, Päivi, Nils Petter Gleditsch, and Elisabeth Gilmore. "A Diamond Curse? Civil War and a Lootable Resource." *Journal of Conflict Resolution* 49 (4), 2005: 538–62.

Lynch, Colum. "U.N. Holds Back Observer Mission for Congo, Citing Logistical Woes." *Washington Post,* June 15, 2000: A27.

Machel, Craça. *The Impact of Armed Conflict on Children.* [Report of the expert of the secretary-general.] UN General Assembly document A/51/306, August 26, 1996.

MacFarquhar, Neil. "U.N. Personnel Increasingly under Attack, Study Finds." *New York Times,* July 1, 2008: A13.

MacFarquhar, Neil. "In Peacekeeping, a Muddling of the Mission." *New York Times,* February 11, 2009a: A6.

MacFarquhar, Neil. "A U.S. Envoy with a Case for Why the U.N. Matters." *New York Times,* September 22, 2009b: A10.

Mack, Andrew. "Peace on Earth? Increasingly, Yes." *Washington Post,* December 28, 2005: A21.

Mack, Andrew. "Successes and Challenges in Conflict Management." In Chester A. Crocker, Fen Olsen Hampson, and Pamela Aall, eds. *Leashing the Dogs of War: Conflict Management in a Divided World.* Washington, D.C.: U.S. Institute of Peace Press, 2007: 521–34.

Malan, Mark. "Africa: Building Institutions on the Run." In Donald C. F. Daniel, Patricia Taft, and Sharon Wiharta, eds. *Peace Operations: Trends, Progress, and Prospects.* Washington, D.C.: Georgetown University Press, 2008: 89–118.

Malcomson, Scott. "When to Intervene." *New York Times Book Review,* December 14, 2008: 12–13.

Man, John. *Genghis Khan: Life, Death, and Resurrection.* New York: Thomas Dunne, 2004.

Mansfield, Edward D., and Jack Snyder. *Electing to Fight: Why Emerging Democracies Go to War.* Cambridge, Mass.: MIT Press, 2005.

Markusen, Eric, and David Kopf. *The Holocaust and Strategic Bombing: Genocide and Total War in the Twentieth Century.* Boulder: Westview, 1995.

Marten, Kimberly Zisk. *Enforcing the Peace: Learning from the Imperial Past.* New York: Columbia, 2004.

Martin, Debra L., and David W. Frayer, eds. *Troubled Times: Violence and Warfare in the Past.* War and Society, vol. 3. Amsterdam: Gordon & Breach, 1997.

Mazurana, Dyan, Angela Raven-Roberts, and Jane Parpart, eds. *Gender, Conflict, and Peacekeeping.* Lanham, Md.: Rowman & Littlefield, 2005.

McCrummen, Stephanie. "Congo's Rape Epidemic Worsens during U.S.-Backed Military Operation." *Washington Post,* August 10, 2009.

McDonald, Patrick J. *The Invisible Hand of Peace: Capitalism, the War Machine, and International Relations Theory.* Cambridge, UK: Cambridge University Press, 2009.

McEvedy, Colin, and Richard Jones. *Atlas of World Population History.* London: Penguin, 1978.

Mearsheimer, John J. "Back to the Future: Instability in Europe after the Cold War." *International Security* 15 (1), Summer 1990: 5–56.

Meisler, Stanley. *United Nations: The First Fifty Years.* New York: Atlantic Monthly Press, 1995.

Meisler, Stanley. *Kofi Annan: A Man of Peace in a World of War.* Hoboken, NJ: Wiley, 2007.

Melander, Erick, Frida Möller, and Magnus Öberg. "Managing Intrastate Low-Intensity Armed Conflict 1993–2004: A New Dataset." *International Interactions* 35, 2009: 58–85.

Melander, Erik, Magnus Öberg, and Jonathan Hall. "Are 'New Wars' More Atrocious? Battle Severity, Civilians Killed, and Forced Migration before and after the End of the Cold War." *European Journal of International Relations* 15 (3), 2009: 505–36.

Meyer, David S. *A Winter of Discontent: The Nuclear Freeze and American Politics.* Westport, Conn.: Praeger, 1990.

Midlarsky, Manus I. *The Killing Trap: Genocide in the Twentieth Century.* New York: Cambridge University Press, 2005.

Mill, John Stuart. *Principles of Political Economy: With Some of Their Applications to Social Philosophy.* Vol. 2. From the 5th London Edition. New York: Appleton, 1902 [1848].

Mingst, Karen A. and Margaret P. Karns. *The United Nations in the 21st Century.* 3rd ed. Boulder: Westview, 2007.

MONUC [UN Mission in the Congo] website. MONUC—Mandate. Accessed 9/14/09 from www.un.org/depts/dpko/missions/monuc/mandate.html.

Mountain, Ross. The United Nations Are Committed to Supporting the Congolese. . . . News feature, MONUC website (monuc.unmissions.org), June 24, 2009.

Mousseau, Michael. "Market Prosperity, Democratic Consolidation, and Democratic Peace." *Journal of Conflict Resolution* 44, 2000: 472–507.

Mueller, John. *The Remnants of War.* Ithaca, N.Y.: Cornell University Press, 2004.

Mueller, John. *Retreat from Doomsday: The Obsolescence of Major War.* New York: Basic, 1989.

Mueller, John. *Overblown: How Politicians and the Terrorism Industry Inflate National Security Threats and Why We Believe Them.* New York: Free Press, 2006.

Mueller, John. Accounting for the Waning of Major War. In Raimo Väyrynen, ed. *The Waning of Major War: Theories and Debates.* London: Routledge, 2006: 64–79.

Muggah, Robert. *Listening for Change: Participatory Evaluations of DDR and Arms Reduction in Mali, Cambodia, and Albania.* Geneva: UN Institute for Disarmament Research, 2005.

Murphy, Craig N. *The United Nations Development Programme: A Better Way?* Cambridge, UK: Cambridge University Press, 2006.

Murray, C. J. L., G. King, A. D. Lopez, N. Tomijima, and E. G. Krug. "Armed Conflict as a Public Health Problem." *British Medical Journal [BJM]* 324, February 9, 2002: 346–49.

Murray, Christopher J. L., and Alan D. Lopez. *Global Burden of Disease and Injury* (2 volumes). Cambridge, Mass.: Harvard School of Public Health on behalf of the World Health Organization and the World Bank [distributed by Harvard University Press], 1996.

Myers, Ramon H., and Yeh–Chien Wang. "Economic Developments, 1644–1800." In Willard J. Peterson, ed. *The Cambridge History of China, Volume 9: Part One: The Ch'ing Empire to 1800.* Cambridge, UK: Cambridge University Press, 2002: 563–645.

New York Times. "5 Killed in Shiite Clash in Lebanon." April 16, 1980a: A3.

New York Times. "5 Killed in Beirut Clash between 2 Militia Units." April 17, 1980b:A4.

New York Times. "Ex–U.N. Officials Question Hammarskjöld Crash." September 13, 1992: 21.

New York Times. "Commander of U.N. Peacekeepers in Congo Resigns." October 27, 2008.

Nickerson, Hoffman. *Can We Limit War?* Port Washington, N.Y.: Kennikat Press, 1934.

Nilsson, R. Anders. *Dangerous Liaisons: Why Ex-Combatants Return to Violence. Cases from the Republic of Congo and Sierra Leone.* Report No. 84, Department of Peace and Conflict Research, Uppsala University, 2008.

Nkrumah, Kwame. Letter to Canadian Prime Minister, August 12, 1960. Accessed 2/1/10 at website of Foreign Affairs and International Trade Canada [Documents on Canadian External Relations, DEA/6386–C–40].

Noah, Timothy. "The Peace Epidemic." Slate.com, December 29, 2005. www.slate.com/id/2133226.

Noble, Kenneth B. "Savimbi Meets U.N. Official on Angola Election Impasse." *New York Times,* October 10, 1992: A5.

Norris, Robert S., and Hans M. Kristensen. "Nuclear Notebook: Worldwide Deployments of Nuclear Weapons, 2009." *Bulletin of the Atomic Scientists* 65 (6), November/December 2009: 86–98.

Norris, Robert S., and Hans M. Kristensen. "Nuclear Notebook: U.S. Tactical Nuclear Weapons in Europe, 2011." *Bulletin of the Atomic Scientists* 67 (1), January/February 2011: 64–73.

Nossiter, Adam. "Group Says It Is Ending Cease–Fire in Nigeria." *New York Times,* February 1, 2010: A7.

Obermeyer, Ziad, Christopher J. L. Murray, and Emanuela Gakidou. "Fifty Years of Violent War Deaths from Vietnam to Bosnia: Analysis of Data from the World Health Survey Programme." *British Medical Journal [BMJ]* 336, 2008: 1482–86.

O'Brien, Conor Cruise. *To Katanga and Back: A UN Case History.* New York: Simon and Schuster, 1962.

O'Hanlon, Michael E. *Expanding Global Military Capacity for Humanitarian Intervention.* Washington, D.C.: Brookings, 2003.

O'Hanlon, Michael. "Expanding Global Military Capacity to Save Lives with Force." In Chester A. Crocker, Fen Olsen Hampson, and Pamela Aall, eds. *Leashing the Dogs of War:*

Conflict Management in a Divided World. Washington, D.C.: U.S. Institute of Peace Press, 2007: 319–34.

Onyiego, Michaek. "Ugandan Rebels Threaten Southern Sudan's Referendum." Voice of America, October 18, 2010. Accessed 10/27/10 at voanews.com/english/news/africa/105191669.html.

Ottaway, Marina. "Is Democracy the Answer?" In Chester A. Crocker, Fen Olsen Hampson, and Pamela Aall, eds. *Leashing the Dogs of War: Conflict Management in a Divided World.* Washington, D.C.: U.S. Institute of Peace Press, 2007: 603–18.

Otterman, Sharon. "Court Redraws Disputed Zone in Sudan in Effort to Keep North and South at Peace." *New York Times,* July 23, 2009: A6.

Overseas Development Institute [ODI], Humanitarian Policy Group. Aid and War: A Response to Linda Polman's Critique of Humanitarianism. ODI *Opinion* 144, May 2010. Accessed 6/9/10 at www.odi.org.uk/resources/download/4835.pdf.

Oxfam International. Rape, Forced Labor, Reprisal Attacks, and Torture Surge in Eastern Congo. Press release, July 14, 2009.

Oxfam International. "Sexual Violence on Rise in DR Congo." In Newsletter, e-mail distribution, April 2010.

Paris, Roland. *At War's End: Building Peace after Civil Conflict.* Cambridge, UK: Cambridge University Press, 2004.

Paris, Roland. "Understanding the 'Coordination Problem' in Postwar Statebuilding." In Roland Paris and Timothy D. Sisk. *The Dilemmas of Statebuilding: Confronting the Contradictions of Postwar Peace Operations.* London: Routledge, 2009a: 53–78.

Paris, Roland. "Does Liberal Peacebuilding Have a Future?" In Edward Newman, Roland Paris, and Oliver P. Richmond, eds. *New Perspectives on Liberal Peacebuilding.* Tokyo: United Nations University Press, 2009b: 97–111.

Parker, Edward Harper. *China Past and Present.* London: Chapman & Hall, 1903.

Parker, Geoffrey, ed. *The Thirty Years' War.* 2nd edition. London: Routledge, 1997. [Parker is the author of the sections quoted, except those cited as Friedrichs 1997.]

Payne, James L. *A History of Force: Exploring the Worldwide Movement against Habits of Coercion, Bloodshed, and Mayhem.* Sandpoint, Idaho: Lytton, 2004.

Payne, Leigh A. *Unsettling Accounts: Neither Truth nor Reconciliation in Confessions of State Violence.* Durham, N.C.: Duke University Press, 2008.

Peceny, Mark, and William Stanley. "Liberal Social Reconstruction and the Resolution of Civil Wars in Central America." *International Organization* 55 (1), 2001: 149–82, Winter 2001.

Pedersen, Jon [Health and Nutrition Tracking Service]. *Mortality from the Conflict in the Democratic Republic of Congo 1998–2006: A Reexamination.*

Pérez de Cuéllar, Javier. *Pilgrimage for Peace: A Secretary-General's Memoir.* New York: St. Martin's, 1997.

Peterson, C. A. "Court and Province in Mid- and Late T'ang." In Denis Twitchett and John K. Fairbank, eds. *The Cambridge History of China: Volume 3, Sui and T'ang China, 589–906, Part I.* Cambridge, UK: Cambridge University Press, 1979: 464–560.

Peterson, Willard J. "Introduction: New Order for the Old Order." In Willard J. Peterson, ed. *The Cambridge History of China, Volume 9: Part One: The Ch'ing Empire to 1800.* Cambridge, UK: Cambridge University Press, 2002.

Picco, Giandomenico. *Man without a Gun: One Diplomat's Secret Struggle to Free the Hostages, Fight Terrorism, and End a War.* New York: Times Books, 1999.

Pinker, Steven. "A History of Violence: We're Getting Nicer Every Day." *The New Republic,* March 19, 2007: 18–21.

Pinker, Steven. *Better Angels of Our Nature.* New York: Viking, Forthcoming, 2011.

Polgreen, Lydia. "A War Ends in Ivory Coast, but Peace, Order, and Unity Are Flickering Dreams." *New York Times,* June 10, 2007a: 14.

Polgreen, Lydia. "Resolving Crisis in Congo Hinges on Foreign Forces." *New York Times,* December 19, 2007b: A11.

Polgreen, Lydia. "Congo's Death Rate Remains Unchanged since War Ended in 2003, Survey Shows." *New York Times,* January 23, 2008a.

Polgreen, Lydia. Congo, "Rebels Sign Deal to End Eastern Conflict." *New York Times,* January 24, 2008b: A7.

Polgreen, Lydia. "Fewer Conflicts Involve Child Soldiers, Report Finds." *New York Times,* May 22, 2008c: A18.

Polgreen, Lydia. "Congo's Riches, Looted by Renegade Troops." *New York Times*, November 16, 2008d: 1.

Polgreen, Lydia. "Massacre Unfurls in Congo, Despite Nearby Aid." *New York Times*, December 11, 2008e: A1.

Polman, Linda. *War Games: The Story of Aid and War in Modern Times.* New York: Penguin, 2010.

Pope John Paul II. Evangelium Vitae [Encyclical]. March 25, 1995. Accessed 10/14/09 at www.vatican.va/holy_father/john_paul_ii/encyclicals/documents/hf_jp-ii_enc_25031995_evangelium-vitae_en.html.

Pope John Paul II. Evening Prayer of John Paul II at the Cathedral Basilica of Saint Louis. January 27, 1999. Accessed 10/14/09 at www.usccb.org/pope/prayer.htm.

Pope Paul VI. "If You Want Peace, Work for Justice." January 1, 1972. Accessed 10/14/09 at www.vatican.va/holy_father/paul_vi/messages/peace/documents/hf_p-vi_mes_19711208_v-world-day-for-peace_en.html.

Power, Samantha. *Chasing the Flame: Sergio Vieira de Mello and the Fight to Save the World.* New York: Penguin, 2008.

Prantl, Jochen. *The UN Security Council and Informal Groups of States: Complementing or Competing for Governance?* Oxford: Oxford University Press, 2006.

Prestwich, Michael. *Armies and Warfare in the Middle Ages: The English Experience.* New Haven: Yale University Press, 1996.

Prunier, Gérard. "Operation Turquoise: A Humanitarian Escape from a Political Dead End." In Howard Adelman and Astri Suhrke, eds. *The Path of a Genocide: The Rwanda Crisis from Uganda to Zaire.* New Brunswick, N.J.: Transaction, 1999: 281–306.

Pugh, Michael. "Peace Enforcement." In Thomas G. Weiss and Sam Daws, eds. *The Oxford Handbook on the United Nations.* Oxford: Oxford University Press, 2007: 370–86.

Pugh, Michael, and Waheguru Pal Singh Sidhu. "Introduction: The United Nations and Regional Actors." In Michael Pugh and Waheguru Pal Singh Sidhu, eds. *The United Nations and Regional Security: Europe and Beyond.* Boulder: Lynne Rienner, 2003.

Rabb, Theodore K., ed. *The Thirty Years' War,* 2nd ed. Lanham, Md.: 1981.

Ramsbotham, Oliver, Tom Woodhouse, and Hugh Miall. *Contemporary Conflict Resolution: The Prevention, Management, and Transformation of Deadly Conflicts.* 2nd ed. Cambridge, UK: Polity, 2005.

Rayman, Graham. "Boy Soldier of Fortune." *The Village Voice* 53 (12), March 19–25, 2008: 22–30.

Regan, Patrick M. *Civil Wars and Foreign Powers: Outside Intervention in Intrastate Conflict.* Ann Arbor: University of Michigan Press, 2000.

Regan, Patrick M. *Sixteen Million One: Understanding Civil War.* Boulder: Paradigm, 2009.

Rehn, Elisabeth, and Ellen Johnson Sirleaf. *Women, War, Peace: The Independent Experts' Assessment on the Impact of Armed Conflict on Women and Women's Role in Peacebuilding.* New York: UN Development Fund for Women, 2002.

Reiter, Dan. *How Wars End.* Princeton, N.J.: Princeton University Press, 2009.

Renner, Michael. "The Anatomy of Resource Wars." Worldwatch Paper 162. Washington, D.C.: Worldwatch Institute, October 2002.

Réseau des Femmes pour un Développement Associatif. *Women's Bodies as a Battleground: Sexual Violence against Women and Girls during the War in the Democratic Republic of Congo, South Kivu (1996–2003).* Bujumbura, Burundi: Réseau des Femmes pour un Développement Associatif, 2005.

Reuters. "Nigeria's Last Major Oil Militant Agrees to Amnesty." October 5, 2009.

Reuters. "Congo Rebels Seize Indian Pilot in Attack on Plane." July 25, 2010.

Richardson, Lewis F. *Statistics of Deadly Quarrels.* Pittsburgh: Boxwood, 1960.

Rieff, David. *Slaughterhouse: Bosnia and the Failure of the West.* New York: Simon and Schuster, 1995.

Roberts, L. [Les], M. Zantop, P. Ngoy, C. Lubula, L. Mweze, C. Mone. Elevated Mortality Associated with Armed Conflict—Democratic Republic of Congo, 2002. *Morbidity and Mortality Weekly Report* [MMWR] 52 (2), May 23, 2003: 469–71.

Roberts, Les, Riyadh Lafta, Richard Garfield, Jamal Khudhairi, and Gilbert Burnham. "Mortality before and after the 2003 Invasion of Iraq: Cluster Sample Survey." *Lancet* 364, Nov. 20, 2004: 1857–64.

Roessler, Philip, and John Prendergast. "Democratic Republic of the Congo." In William J. Durch, ed. *Twenty-First-Century Peace Operations*. Washington, D.C.: U.S. Institute of Peace, 2006: 229–48.

Romero, Simon. "Chávez Urges Colombian Rebels to End Their Struggle." *New York Times*, June 9, 2008: A8.

Ron, James. "Paradigm in Distress? Primary Commodities and Civil War." [Introduction to special journal issue.] *Journal of Conflict Resolution* 49 (4), 2005: 443–50.

Rosenau, James N. *Turbulence in World Politics: A Theory of Change and Continuity*. Princeton, N.J.: Princeton University Press, 1990.

Rosenthal, A. M. "The U.N. at 50: The History." *New York Times*, Oct. 22, 1995.

Rösiö, Bengt. "The Ndola Crash and the Death of Dag Hammarskjöld." *Journal of Modern African Studies* 31 (4), 1993: 661–71.

Ross, Michael L. "What Do We Know About Natural Resources and Civil War?" *Journal of Peace Research* 41 (3), 2004: 337–56.

Ross, Michael. "A Closer Look at Oil, Diamonds, and Civil War." *Annual Review of Political Science* 9, 2006: 265–300.

Ross, Michael L. "Blood Barrels: Why Oil Wealth Fuels Conflict." *Foreign Affairs*, May/June 2008: 2–8.

Rothchild, Donald, and David A. Lake. Containing Fear: The Management of Transnational Ethnic Conflict. In David A. Lake and Donald Rothchild, eds. *The International Spread of Ethnic Conflict: Fear, Diffusion, and Escalation*. Princeton, N.J.: Princeton University Press, 1998: 203–26.

Rowe, William T. "Social Stability and Social Change." In Willard J. Peterson, ed. *The Cambridge History of China, Volume 9: Part One: The Ch'ing Empire to 1800*. Cambridge, UK: Cambridge University Press, 2002: 473–562.

Rubinstein, Robert A. *Peacekeeping under Fire: Culture and Intervention*. Boulder: Paradigm, 2008.

Ruggie, John Gerard. *Winning the Peace: America and World Order in the New Era*. New York: Columbia University Press, 1996.

Rummel, R. J. *China's Bloody Century: Genocide and Mass Murder since 1900*. New Brunswick, N.J.: Transaction, 1991.

Rummel, R. J. *Death by Government*. New Brunswick, N.J.: Transaction, 1994.

Russett, Bruce. "Capitalism *or* Democracy?: Not So Fast." *International Interactions* 36 (2), 2010: 198–205.

Russett, Bruce, and John R. Oneal. *Triangulating Peace: Democracy, Interdependence, and International Organization*. New York: Norton, 2001.

Salomons, Dirk. "Probing the Successful Application of Leverage in Support of Mozambique's Quest for Peace." In Jean Krasno, Bradd C. Hayes, and Donald C. F. Daniel. *Leveraging for Success in United Nations Peace Operations*. Westport, Conn.: Praeger, 2003: 81–116.

Sands, David R. "Warfare Waning across the World." *Washington Times*, June 27, 2005.

Sarkees, Meredith Reid, Frank Whelon Wayman, and J. David Singer. "Inter-State, Intra-State, and Extra-State Wars: A Comprehensive Look at Their Distribution over Time, 1816–1997." *International Studies Quarterly* 47, 2003: 49–70.

Sarkees, Meredith Reid, and Frank Whelon Wayman. *Resort to War: A Data Guide to Inter–State, Extra–State, Intra–State, and Non–State Wars, 1816–2007*. Washington, D.C.: CQ Press, 2010.

Save the Children. *State of the World's Mothers 2003: Protecting Women and Children in War and Conflict*. Westport, Conn.: Save the Children, 2003a.

Save the Children. U.S. Congress Should Put Women and Children First in Setting Priorities for Humanitarian Assistance in War Zones. [Press Release.] October 14, 2003b.

Schroeder, Paul W. The Life and Death of a Long Peace, 1763–1914. In Raimo Väyrynen, ed. *The Waning of Major War: Theories and Debates*. London: Routledge, 2006: 33–63.

Seybolt, Taylor B. *Humanitarian Military Intervention: The Conditions for Success and Failure*. Oxford: Oxford University Press, 2007.

Shanker, Thom. "Gates Warns Against Wars Like Iraq and Afghanistan." *New York Times*, February 26, 2011: A7.

Shaw, Martin. *The New Western Way of War: Risk-Transfer War and Its Crisis in Iraq*. Cambridge, UK: Polity, 2005.

Shawcross, William. *Deliver Us from Evil: Peacekeepers, Warlords, and a World of Endless Conflict.* New York: Simon & Schuster, 2000.

Shay, Jonathan. *Achilles in Vietnam: Combat Trauma and the Undoing of Character.* New York: Atheneum, 1994.

Sidhu, Waheguru Pal Singh. "Regional Groups and Alliances." In Thomas G. Weiss and Sam Daws, eds. *The Oxford Handbook on the United Nations.* Oxford: Oxford University Press, 2007: 217–32.

Simons, Marlise. "Congolese Faces Charges of Atrocities." *New York Times*, July 5, 2008: A5.

Singer, Max, and Aaron Wildavsky. *The Real World Order: Zones of Peace / Zones of Turmoil.* Rev. Ed. Chatham, N.J.: Chatham House, 1996.

Singer, P. W. "Caution: Children at War." *Parameters: U.S. Army War College Quarterly*, Winter 2001–02 [c 2001]: 40–56.

SIPRI [Stockholm International Peace Research Institute]. *SIPRI Yearbook 2009: Armaments, Disarmament, and International Security.* Oxford: Oxford University Press, 2010.

Sirleaf, Ellen Johnson. Madame President [interview], *New York Times Magazine*, August 23, 2009: 16.

Sivard, Ruth Leger. *World Military and Social Expenditures 1982.* Washington, D.C.: World Priorities, 1982.

Sivard, Ruth Leger. *World Military and Social Expenditures 1993.* Washington, D.C.: World Priorities, 1993.

Slackman, Michael. "American-Backed Alliance Appears to Win in Lebanon." *New York Times*, June 8, 2009: A7.

Slim, Hugo. *Killing Civilians: Method, Madness, and Morality in War.* New York: Columbia University Press, 2008.

Smillie, Ian, and Larry Minear. *The Charity of Nations: Humanitarian Action in a Calculating World.* Bloomfield, Conn.: Kumarian, 2004.

Smith, Dan. War, Peace, and Third World Development. [Background Paper for 1994 UN Human Development Report.] Oslo: International Peace Research Institute, Oslo: 1994.

Sollenberg, Margareta. Civilian Consequences of War: A Review of the Literature. Draft, Uppsala University Department of Peace and Conflict Research, January 2006.

Solo, Pam. *From Protest to Policy: Beyond the Freeze to Common Security.* Cambridge, Mass.: Ballinger, 1988.

Solomon, Richard H. Foreword. In Chester A. Crocker, Fen Olsen Hampson, and Pamela Aall, eds. *Leashing the Dogs of War: Conflict Management in a Divided World.* Washington, D.C.: U.S. Institute of Peace Press, 2007: ix–xi.

Sorokin, Pitirim A. *The Sociology of Revolution.* New York: Howard Fertig, 1967 [1925].

Sorokin, Pitirim A. *Social and Cultural Dynamics, vol. 3, Fluctuation of Social Relationships, War, and Revolution.* New York, Bedminster, 1937 [1962 reprint].

Spagat, Michael, Andrew Mack, Tara Cooper, and Joakim Kreutz. "Estimating War Deaths: An Arena of Contestation." *Journal of Conflict Resolution* 53 (6), 2009: 934–50.

Spielmann, Peter James. "Review of Congo War Halves Death Toll." Associated Press, January 20, 2010.

Stanford Prevention Research Center. History. No date. Accessed 4/10/10 at prevention.stanford.edu/about/history.html.

Stanley, Henry M. *Through the Dark Continent: The Sources of the Nile around the Great Lakes of Equatorial Africa and down the Livingstone River to the Atlantic Ocean.* Vol. 1. New York: Harper, 1879.

Stares, Paul B., and Micah Zenko. *Enhancing U.S. Preventive Action.* New York: Council on Foreign Relations, 2009.

Stedman, Stephen John. Introduction. In Stephen John Stedman, Donald Rothchild, and Elizabeth M. Cousens, eds., *Ending Civil Wars: The Implementation of Peace Agreements.* Boulder: Lynne Rienner, 2002: 1–42.

Stewart, Frances, and Valpy FitzGerald. Introduction: Assessing the Economic Costs of War. In Frances Stewart and Valpy FitzGerald and Associates. *War and Underdevelopment. Volume 1: The Economic and Social Consequences of Conflict.* Oxford: Oxford University Press, 2001a: 1–20.

Stewart, Frances, and Valpy FitzGerald. "The Costs of War in Poor Countries: Conclusions and Policy Recommendations." In Frances Stewart and Valpy FitzGerald and Associates.

War and Underdevelopment. Volume 1: The Economic and Social Consequences of Conflict. Oxford: Oxford University Press, 2001b: 225–45.

Stockholm International Peace Research Institute; *see* SIPRI.

Stockwell, John. *The Praetorian Guard: The U.S. Role in the New World Order.* Boston: South End Press, 1991.

Stoddard, Abby, Adele Harmer, and Victoria DeDomenico. Providing Aid in Insecure Environments: 2009 Update. HPG Policy Brief 34. London: Humanitarian Policy Group, Overseas Development Institute, 2009.

Sundberg, Ralph. Revisiting One-sided Violence: A Global and Regional Analysis. UCDP Paper No. 3. Uppsala University: Department of Peace and Conflict Research, 2009.

Swedish Ministry for Foreign Affairs. *Stockholm Initiative on Disarmament Demobilisation Reintegration: Final Report.* Stockholm, 2006.

Swerdlow, Amy. "Pure Milk, Not Poison: Women Strike for Peace and the Test Ban Treaty of 1963." In Adrienne Harris and Ynestra King, eds., *Rocking the Ship of State: Toward a Feminist Peace Politics.* Boulder: Westview, 1989: 225–37.

Taleb, Nassim Nicholas. *The Black Swan: The Impact of the Highly Improbable.* New York: Random House, 2007.

Taylor, Frederick. *Dresden: Tuesday, February 13, 1945.* New York: HarperCollins, 2004.

Tennyson, Alfred. *The Works of Alfred Tennyson. Vol. 3: Locksley Hall, and Other Poems.* London: Henry S. King, 1874.

Thakur, Ramesh. Humanitarian Intervention. In Thomas G. Weiss and Sam Daws, eds. *The Oxford Handbook on the United Nations.* Oxford: Oxford University Press, 2007: 387–403.

Tharoor, Shashi. "Should UN Peacekeeping Go 'Back to Basics'?" *Survival* 37 (4), 1995–96.

Thompson, William R. The Democratic Peace and Civil Society as Constraints on Major Power Warfare. In Raimo Väyrynen, ed. *The Waning of Major War: Theories and Debates.* London: Routledge, 2006: 209–38.

Tierney, John. "Give Peace a Chance." *New York Times,* May 28, 2005: A23.

Toft, Monica Duffy. *Securing the Peace: The Durable Settlement of Civil Wars.* Princeton, N.J.: Princeton University Press, 2009.

Toynbee, Arnold J. *A Study of History,* Vol. 9. Oxford: Oxford University Press, 1954.

Transparency International. *Global Corruption Report 2004.* Berlin: Transparency International, 2004.

Traub, James. *The Best Intentions: Kofi Annan and the UN in the Era of American World Power.* New York: Farrar, Straus and Giroux, 2006a.

Traub, James. "Wonderful World?" *New York Times Magazine,* March 19, 2006b: 13.

Twitchett, Denis. "Hsüan-tsung (Reign 712–56)." In Denis Twitchett and John K. Fairbank, eds. *The Cambridge History of China: Volume 3, Sui and T'ang China, 589–906, Part I.* Cambridge, UK: Cambridge University Press, 1979: 333–463.

Tuchman, Barbara W. *A Distant Mirror: The Calamitous 14th Century.* New York: Knopf, 1978.

UCDP [Uppsala Conflict Data Program]. Codebook for the UCDP Battle-Deaths Dataset: Definitions, Sources, and Methods forUCDP Battle-Death Estimates. Version 5.0. July 1, 2009. Accessed 3/5/11 at www.pcr.uu.se/digitalAssets/15/15912_UCDP_Battle-related _deaths_dataset_codebook_v5_2009.pdf.

UCDP [Uppsala Conflict Data Program]. UCDP Database: www.ucdp.uu.se/database, Uppsala University. Accessed June 3, 2010 at www.ucdp.uu.se/database. June 2010 update.

UCDP/PRIO [Uppsala Conflict Data Program and Centre for the Study of Civil Wars, International Peace Research Institute, Oslo.] *UCDP/PRIO Armed Conflict Dataset Codebook. Version 4-2009.* Uppsala: UCDP, 2009.

United Nations. 60 Years of United Nations Peacekeeping. 2008. Accessed 8/4/09 at www.un .org/events/peacekeeping60/60years.shtml.

United Nations. War on Civilians. In "United Nations Cyberschoolbus / Global Bytes" [online], January 13, 1997. Accessed at www.un.org/pubs/cyberschoolbus/dailyfax/df9701ix .htm.

United Nations. Recent Arrests in Mass Rape Cases in Democratic Republic of Congo May Help "Turn Tide against Impunity," Security Council Is Told. SC/10055. UN Dept. of Public Information, October 14, 2010.

UNA-USA [United Nations Association of the United States of America]. U.S.-UN Funding Update. Accessed 8/5/10 at unausa.org/Page.aspx?pid=1633.

UNDP [UN Development Programme]. *Human Development Report 1994: Deepening Democracy in a Fragmented World*. New York: Oxford University Press, 1994.

UNDP [UN Development Programme]. *Human Development Report 2002: Deepening Democracy in a Fragmented World*. New York: Oxford University Press, 2002.

UNDPKO [Department of Peace Keeping Operations]. UNAMSIL End of Mission Press Kit. Accessed 8/09 at www.un.org/Depts/dpko/missions/unamsil/press_kit.htm. UN, 2005.

UNDPKO [Department of Peace Keeping Operations]. *United Nations Peacekeeping Operations: Principles and Guidelines* [Capstone Doctrine]. UN: 2008.

UNEF [UN Emergency Force]. Background. Posted on UNEF mission website. No date. Accessed 6/24/09 at www.un.org/depts/dpko/co_mission/unef1backgr2.html.

UNFPA [UN Population Fund]. Legacy of War: An Epidemic of Sexual Violence in DRC. Website "Feature Story," November 26, 2008. Accessed 5/31/10 at www.unfpa.org/public/cache/offonce/news/pid/1399.

UNHCR [High Commissioner for Refugees]. *The State of the World's Refugees 2000: Fifty Years of Humanitarian Action*. New York: UN, 2000.

UNHCR. *2008 Global Trends: Refugees, Asylum-Seekers, Returnees, Internally Displaced and Stateless Persons*. New York: UN, 2009.

UNICEF [UN Children's Fund]. *The State of the World's Children 1992*. [James P. Grant, principal author.] New York: Oxford University Press, 1992.

UNICEF [UN Children's Fund]. *The State of the World's Children 1996*. ["Children in War" section. New York: UNICEF: 1996a.

UNICEF. Impact of Armed Conflict on Children. [Press release for Machel report.] Accessed 10/5/08 at unicef.org/graca/summry.htm. 1996b.

UN News Service. More than 8,000 Women Raped Last Year by Fighters in Eastern DR Congo—UN. Press release, February 8, 2010a. Accessed 2/10/2010 at un.org/apps/news/story.asp?NewsID=33703.

UN News Service. Security Council Agrees to Convert UN Mission in DR Congo into Stabilization Force. Press release, May 28, 2010b. Accessed 6/7/10 at un.org/apps/news/story.asp?NewsID=34841.

UN News Service. DR Congo improves education, child survival but greater efforts needed—UN. Press release, October 6, 2010c. Accessed 10/27/10 at un.org/apps/news/story.asp?NewsID=36354.

United Nations Population Division. *World Population Prospects: The 2008 Revision*. New York: UN, 2009. Accessed at data.un.org 10/27/10.

UN Security Council. *Final report of the Panel of Experts on the Illegal Exploitation of Natural Resources and Other Forms of Wealth of the Democratic Republic of the Congo*. UN S/2002/1146.

UN Security Council. *Report of the Secretary-General on Children and Armed Conflict in the Democratic Republic of the Congo*. UN S/2008/693.

U.S. Bureau of Justice Statistics. Key Facts at a Glance: Violent Crime Trends. U.S. Department of Justice website 2010. Accessed 2/10/10 at bjs.ojp.usdoj.gov/content/glance/tables/viortrdtab.cfm.

U.S. Department of State. Congo, Democratic Republic of the: Country Reports on Human Rights Practices, 2003. Feb. 25, 2004. Accessed 3/19/2010 at www.state.gov/g/drl/rls/hrrpt/2003/27721.htm.

Urbina, Ian. In Pittsburgh, Thousands Stage a Peaceful March for Multiple Causes. *New York Times*, Sept. 26, 2009: A9.

Urquhart, Brian. *Hammarskjold*. New York: Knopf, 1972.

Urquhart, Brian. *Ralph Bunche: An American Life*. New York: Norton, 1993.

Urquhart, Brian. Limits on the Use of Force. In Chester A. Crocker, Fen Olsen Hampson, and Pamela Aall, eds. *Leashing the Dogs of War: Conflict Management in a Divided World*. Washington, D.C.: U.S. Institute of Peace Press, 2007: 265–76.

Valentino, Benjamin A. *Final Solutions: Mass Killing and Genocide in the Twentieth Century*. Ithaca: Cornell University Press, 2004.

Van Creveld, Martin. "The Waning of Major War." In Raimo Väyrynen, ed. *The Waning of Major War: Theories and Debates*. London: Routledge, 2006: 97–112.

Vasquez, John A., and Marie T. Henehan. *Territory, War, and Peace: An Empirical and Theoretical Analysis*. London: Routledge, 2010.

Väyrynen, Raimo. "Introduction: Contending Views." In Raimo Väyrynen, ed. *The Waning of Major War: Theories and Debates*. London: Routledge, 2006: 1–30.

Wallensteen, Peter, and Margareta Sollenberg. "The End of International War? Armed Conflict 1989–95." *Journal of Peace Research* 33 (3), 1996: 353–70.

Walter, Barbara F. *Committing to Peace: The Successful Settlement of Civil Wars*. Princeton, N.J.: Princeton University Press, 2002.

Watkins, Kevin. *The Oxfam Poverty Report*. Oxford, UK: Oxfam, 1995.

Wedgwood, C. V. *The Thirty Years War*. London: Jonathan Cape, 1938.

Weiss, Thomas G. *What's Wrong with the United Nations and How to Fix It*. Cambridge, UK: Polity, 2009.

Weiss, Thomas G., David P. Forsythe, Roger A. Coate, and Kelly-Kate Pease. *The United Nations and Changing World Politics*. 5th ed. Boulder: Westview, 2007.

Wheeler, Nicholas J. *Saving Strangers: Humanitarian Intervention in International Society*. Oxford: Oxford University Press, 2000.

White, Matthew. Historical Atlas of the Twentieth Century [website]. "Last Updated: 25 March 2003." Accessed 5/9/10 at users.erols.com/mwhite28/warstats.htm; warstat0.htm; and warstat2.htm.

Whitfield, Teresa. *Friends Indeed? The United Nations, Groups of Friends, and the Resolution of Conflict*. Washington, D.C.: U.S. Institute of Peace, 2007.

Whitworth, Sandra. *Men, Militarism, and UN Peacekeeping: A Gendered Analysis*. Boulder: Rienner, 2004.

Wills, John E., Jr. Relations with Maritime Europeans, 1514–1662. In Denis Twitchett and Frederick W. Mote, eds. *The Cambridge History of China: Volume 8, The Ming Dynasty, 1368–1644, Part 2*. Cambridge, UK: Cambridge University Press, 1998: 333–75.

Wilson, Ernest J., III, and Ted Robert Gurr. "Fewer Nations Are Making War." *Los Angeles Times*, August 22, 1999.

Wittner, Lawrence S. *Confronting the Bomb: A Short History of the World Nuclear Disarmament Movement*. Palo Alto, C.A.: Stanford University Press, 2009.

Wood, David. Conflict in the Twentieth Century. [Adelphi Papers #48.] London: Institute for Strategic Studies, 1968.

Wood, Elisabeth Jean. *Forging Democracy from Below: Insurgent Transitions in South Africa and El Salvador*. Cambridge, UK: Cambridge University Press, 2000.

Wood, Elisabeth Jean. *Insurgent Collective Action and Civil War in El Salvador*. Cambridge, UK: Cambridge University Press, 2003a.

Wood, Elisabeth Jean. "Civil Wars: What We Don't Know." *Global Governance* 9, 2003b: 247–60.

Wood, Elisabeth Jean. "Armed Groups and Sexual Violence: When Is Wartime Rape Rare?" *Politics and Society* 37 (1), 2009: 131–61.

World Bank. *Education in the Democratic Republic of Congo: Priorities and Options for Regeneration*. Washington, D.C.: World Bank, 2005.

Worldpublicopinion.org. "World Publics Favor New Powers for the UN. May 9, 2007" [cowritten with the Chicago Council on Global Affairs]. College Park, MD: Program on International Policy Attitudes, University of Michigan. May 9, 2007. Accessed 6/2010 at www.worldpublicopinion.org/pipa/articles/btunitednationsra/355.php

Wright, Quincy. *A Study of War*. Second ed., with a Commentary on War since 1942. University of Chicago Press, 1965 [1942].

Zacher, Mark W. "The Territorial Integrity Norm: International Boundaries and the Use of Force." *International Organization* 55 (2), 2001: 215–50.

Zartman, I. William. *Cowardly Lions: Missed Opportunities to Prevent Deadly Conflict and State Collapse*. Boulder, C.O.: Rienner, 2005.

Zartman, I. William, and Saadia Touval. "International Mediation." In Chester A. Crocker, Fen Olsen Hampson, and Pamela Aall, eds. *Leashing the Dogs of War: Conflict Management in a Divided World*. Washington, D.C.: U.S. Institute of Peace Press, 2007: 437–54.

Zoellner, Tom. *Uranium: War, Energy, and the Rock that Shaped the World*. New York: Viking, 2009.

Zoepf, Katherine, and Sam Dagher. "A Decline in Deaths in Iraq Is Not Enough for a Family." *New York Times*, November 3, 2008: A9.

Acknowledgments

For hosting seminars on the subject of this book, I thank Yale University, the University of Maryland, American University, the University of Wisconsin, and Robert Jay Lifton's mass violence seminar at Harvard. Thanks also to participants in the City College of New York 2008 conference on the end of war (in memory of Randy Forsberg), and especially to its lead organizer, Neta Crawford. I also learned from the participants at the 2009 International Studies Association panel and dinner on the decline of war, and from my conversations with the researchers at PRIO in Norway and Uppsala University in Sweden, with members of the Human Security Report Project in Vancouver, and with Steven Pinker at Harvard. Jane Huber and other writers at Oxfam America gave me useful comments on early chapter drafts. My literary agent, Fredrica S. Friedman, contributed her vision, experience, creativity, and patience in helping to shape this long and ambitious project. At Dutton, my editor, Stephen Morrow, provided valuable guidance and suggestions, and Stephanie Hitchcock lent superb professional assistance during the book's progress toward publication. Thanks also to Jamie McDonald, Christine Ball, Carrie Swetonic, and Alan Walker at Dutton. The University of Massachusetts library facilitated my research. Thanks for ideas and suggestions go to Andrew Mack, Bruce Russett, Nils Petter Gleditsch, Peter Wallensteen, Lotta Harbom, Margareta Sollenberg, Gerdis Wischnath, Joseph Hewett, John Mueller, Charli Carpenter, Peter M. Haas, Laura Reed, Craig Murphy, Séverine Autesserre, Page Fortna, John Steinbruner, David Hamburg, Paul Kennedy, Brian Urquhart, Shibley Telhami, Charlotte Isaksson, Gerald Bender, Yoav Freund, Jon Pevehouse, Hannah Meyers, Elena Stone, Dora B. Goldstein, Andra Rose, Solomon Goldstein-Rose, Ruth Goldstein-Rose, and others with whom I have spoken about this topic over the years.

Index

Afghanistan
  and al Qaeda, 112
  civilian casualties in, 259–60
  current state of, 280, 282–83, 286, 287
  fatalities in, 16, 280
  and humanitarian aid, 193
  identifying enemies in, 298
  Obama's escalation of war in, 224
  peace negotiations in, 180
  Soviet occupation of, 4, 16, 43, 281
  UN missions in, 287
  U.S. troops in, 13, 14–15
  warlords and chiefdoms of, 40
Africa
  peacekeeping missions in, 148–55
  civilian casualties in, 259
  history of war in, 4, 41
  regional organizations in peace
    operations, 133–35
  resources devoted to, 136, 137
  trends in wars, 14, 15
African Union (AU), 76, 133–35, 141, 152,
  285, 287
Ahlström, Christer, 255, 256–57
Ahtisaari, Martti, 93
Aideed, Mohamed, 77–78, 103
al Qaeda. *See* Qaeda
al Shabab. *See* Shabab
Albright, Madeleine, 111, 320, 326
American Peace Society (APS), 211–13, 214
An Lushan, 33
ancient warfare, 34–35
Anderlini, Sanam, 197, 198, 201
Angell, Norman, 6, 7
Angola, 75–77
  and Congo, 164
  and consent of the parties, 104
  demobilization and reintegration in, 121
  economy in, 177–78
  fatalities in, 16

  success of peacebuilding in, 107
  as UN failure, 75–77, 103
Annan, Kofi, 110–13
  on abilities of secretary-general, 313
  achievements of, 113
  on African conflicts, 137
  and Bosnia, 89
  and Congo, 164
  and Darfur, 152
  and Helms, 320
  and humanitarian aid, 325
  on legitimacy, 132
  on prevention, 317
  secretary-general position, 111–12
  and Sierra Leone, 145
  undersecretary-general appointment,
    110–11
  and U.S. occupation of Iraq, 112–13
  on the World Court, 191
Arab Higher Committee, 47
Arab-Israeli Conflict (1947–49), 47–49
arbitration, 90, 150–51, 212, 214–15, 220
archaeological evidence of warfare,
  39–40, 41
Argentina, 24, 123
arms embargoes, 115
Asia, 19
Assyrian Empire, 35
Athens, 34, 278
Australia, 38, 41
Austria, 41
Autesserre, Séverine, 119–20,
  171–72, 173–74
Aztec civilization, 27–28, 33

Bangladesh, 83, 85, 126–27
Ban Ki-moon, 113, 152
Bass, Gary, 324, 325
Beah, Ishmael, 137–40, 143
Beirut, Lebanon, 1–3

Belgium
  and Congolese independence,
    57, 58, 59, 63, 66
  and ONUC forces, 70
  and Rwanda, 81, 82, 83–84, 85
  troops in Congo, 59, 63–64, 68
  and uranium deposits of Congo, 62
  in World War I, 22
Bemba, Jean-Pierre, 167–68
Bender, Gerald, 76, 177–78
Bercovitch, Jacob, 186–87
Berlin Wall, 73
Bernadotte, Folke, 48–49, 50, 54–55
Blight, James, 9–10
Bolivia, 123
border stability, 278–79
Bosnia, 87–91
  bombing missions in, 88, 89, 111
  and the Dayton Agreement, 90, 91
  humanitarian aid to, 194
  Kofi Annan's role in, 111
  security sector reform in, 122
  success of peacebuilding efforts in, 107
  as UN failure, 103
Boulding, Kenneth, 239, 248, 279
Boutros-Ghali, Boutros
  American attitudes toward, 320
  and Bosnia, 88, 89
  and Cambodia, 98, 99
  and Croatia, 100
  and diplomatic negotiations, 86, 184
  and Kofi Annan, 110, 111
  peacekeeping report of, 74
  and Picco, 181, 184
  and Rwanda, 81
  and Somalia, 77
Bradbury, Jim, 30, 33
Brahimi Report, 115–19, 310
Brazil, 24, 39, 55, 126
Britain
  Boer War, 25
  and Congo, 59, 70
  and Kofi Annan, 111
  and origins of the UN, 45
  and Palestine, 47–48
  peace movements in, 218
  and Sierra Leone, 146, 147
  and Suez War, 53, 54, 56
  and World Wars, 21, 22
Bunche, Ralph, 46–47
  and Arab-Israeli Conflict, 48–51
  awarded Nobel Peace Prize, 51
  and Congo, 59, 60, 61, 65, 66–67
  and Israeli-Egyptian talks, 187
  and Palestine, 47–48
  and peacemaking, 181
  and fears of communism, 52

  and Suez War, 53, 55–56
  and UNEF, 54, 55, 57
  and UNTSO, 49–51
Burma, 287, 325–26
Burundi, 15, 121
Bush, George H. W., 73–74, 77, 183
Bush, George W., 224, 276, 320, 322

Cambodia, 97–99
  and consent of the parties, 104
  fatalities in, 16
  as multidimensional peacekeeping
    operation, 100
  success of peacebuilding efforts in, 107
  UN administration of, 92
  as UN success story, 97–99, 103
Canada, 55, 84, 104–5
causality, 42–44
cease-fires, supervision of, 49, 57, 74, 80, 92,
    97, 105–6, 114, 136, 154, 164–5, 169, 178
Central African Republic, 121, 154, 317
Central America, 4
Ceylon (Sri Lanka), 54, 55
Chad, 154, 155
children, 137–40, 170, 251, 255
China
  and Cambodia, 97
  civil war, 16
  decline in warfare, 43
  dynastic transitions in, 27, 35
  Hammarskjöld's intervention with, 313
  history of war in, 22, 32, 33, 35
  Nanking massacre, 21
  and origins of the UN, 46
  and peace-and-justice argument, 205
  peace in, 289
  prosperity in, 292
  revolution of 1949, 52
  Taiping Rebellion, 24, 27
  troops contributed by, 126
  violence in, 23
civilians
  changing norms regarding, 227
  and disease, 27
  fatalities among, 36–37, 233, 253, 254–60
  inducing collaboration of, 298
  and military goals, 26
  and one-sided violence, 244
  property destruction, 29
  targeting of, 26, 311
  and terror tactics, 138
  and Thirty Years' War, 26–27
  in World-Wars era, 21–22
civil service, international, 52, 70
civil wars
  conclusions of, 301–7
  current civil wars, 280–86

decline in, 6, 43
and economic growth and recovery, 106
and fatality trends, 5, 16, 237
motives of individuals, 297–300
preventing recurrence of, 106, 303–4
risk factors for, 291–97
success rate in, 128
trends in, 247, 279, 286–87
Clinton, Bill, 84
Clinton, Hillary, 170, 200, 201, 264
Cohen, Stanley, 305
Cold War
end of, 15, 43–44, 73–74
and fatality trends, 16, 236–37
and peace movements, 219–22
post-Cold War era compared to, 16–20
and UN Security Council, 5
and uranium deposits of Congo, 62
Collier, Paul
on civil wars, 286, 291
on Congo, 175
on economic effects of war, 294, 303
on ethnic conflict, 296, 297
on motives of participants, 300, 301
on poverty, 292, 295
on recurrence of conflict, 303
on Sierra Leone, 137
on value of peacekeeping, 106, 108
on war risks, 293
Colombia, 15, 54, 55, 287, 290
Commonwealth of Independent States
    (CIS), 129, 131
concentration camps, 25, 201, 264
conflict resolution, 15, 48, 187–89
Congo, Democratic Republic of, 57–72,
    155–75
Belgian troops in, 59, 63–64, 68
Bukavu crisis, 167
colonial rule of, 58–59, 66, 274
current state of, 280, 285–86
disarmament, demobilization, and
    reintegration in, 121, 165
elections in, 167, 175
ending the war in, 162–69
ethnic violence in, 165–66
fatalities in, 16, 253, 260–64, 272–73
Hutu rebels in, 86, 158–59, 161, 165, 167,
    169, 267, 285–86
independence of, 57, 58, 59
lootable resources of, 62, 160–62, 166
multidimensional nature of, 156–57
names of, 58, 159
and Nkunda's forces, 168–69
peacekeeping operations in , 60–61,
    63–72
persistence of fighting in, 169–72, 175
poverty in, 156, 158, 162, 253, 262

progress made in, 149
resources devoted to, 136, 172–74, 175–76
road to war in, 157–60
secessionist movements, 59–60, 61–65,
    67–72, 157
sexual exploitation and violence in, 167,
    170, 174, 254, 264–74
Sierra Leone compared to, 175–76
UN operations in, 15, 156, 162–67, 168–69,
    170–72, 175, 286, 287
corporations, 208, 223–24
Cortright, David, 213, 221, 223
costs of peacekeeping operations, 125, 131,
    154, 310, 316
counterinsurgency operations, 130
countries contributing troops, 125–27
coups, 226, 244
Cousins, Norman, 254
Crawford, Neta, 225, 230–1
credibility, importance of, 179
Croatia
as multidimensional peacekeeping
    operation, 100
security sector reform in, 122
and Serbia, 89, 90, 111
success of peacebuilding efforts in,
    100, 107
UN administration of, 92, 100
Crusades, 30–31, 35
Cuba, 17, 25
Cuny, Fred, 191–92
Cyprus, 154, 179

Dallaire, Roméo, 79–85, 309
Darfur, Sudan, 26, 136, 149, 151–52, 244
Dayton Agreement, 90, 91
DeBenedetti, Charles, 211, 221
demobilization, 101, 102, 103, 121, 126
democracy and democracies
and civil wars, 295
and democratic peace theory, 43, 276–78
spread of, 15
and trends in wars, 244
in the UN operations, 120
and UN participation, 125–26
Democratic Republic of the Congo. See
    Congo, Democratic Republic of
denial, 17, 20, 123, 234, 305–7
Department of Peace Keeping Operations.
    See United Nations.
deployment of peacekeeping missions
Brahimi Report on, 115–16, 117, 310
"golden hour" window of, 116, 117
number of troops, 125
prior to outbreaks of violence, 317
time required for, 50, 116–17, 314
Des Forges, Alison, 80, 82

De Soto, Álvaro, 95
Deutsch, Karl, 248
Diagne, Mbaye, 85
diamonds, 141, 160, 295
diaspora communities, 43, 294, 301
diplomacy, 179–91
    difficulties in, 183–84
    elements of, 179–80
    by Groups of Friends, 189–90
    and hostage negotiations, 183–84
    and Iran-Iraq War, 181–83
    limitations on, 180
    persistence required in, 186–89
    Picco's experiences in, 179–84
    Resident Representatives' roles in, 184–85
    and secretary-general's role, 180–81, 182, 183–84
    and stalemates, 185–86
    timing in, 185–86
    withdrawal of diplomatic relations, 115
    and World Court, 190–91
disarmament, 99, 103, 121, 150
Disarmament, Demobilization, and Reintegration (DDR), 121, 135, 142, 144, 165, 199–201
disease, 28, 30, 235
Donnelly, Jack, 324
Doyle, Michael, 106, 108, 292, 302, 307
Dresden, Germany, 21

East Asia, 289
Easterbrook, Gregg, 18–19, 240, 242
East Timor, 92, 107, 120, 123, 155
Eckhard, Fred, 93
Eckhardt, William, 258
Economic Community of West African States (ECOWAS)
    peace enforcement operations of, 129, 132
    peacekeeping operations of, 131, 133–35
    and Sierra Leone, 141, 143–44, 145
    and Ivory Coast, 149
economics
    conflict trap, 293–94, 303
    interdependence among economies, 277, 278
    and motives of participants, 300–301
    and preventing recurrence of wars, 303–4
    recovery and growth, 106
    returns on peacekeeping, 106
    and risk factors for wars, 292–94
    and roots of war, 218
Egypt
    and Israel, 50, 187
    and Multinational Force and Observers, 128

nonviolent revolution in 2011, 228
prehistoric warfare in, 40
and Suez War, 53–54, 56
troops contributed by, 126
election administration and monitoring
    in Angola, 76
    in Cambodia, 98, 99
    and disarmament, 150
    in Ivory Coast, 150
    in Nicaragua, 107
    and Resident Representatives, 185
    UN's emphasis on, 107
El Salvador, 94–96
    denial of massacre in, 306
    fatalities in, 16
    as multidimensional peacekeeping operation, 100
    rebel party in, 5
    as UN success story, 94–96, 103, 107
epidemiologists, 248–50
Eritrea, 16, 131, 189, 191, 245, 296
Estonia, 317–18
Ethiopia, 16, 126, 131, 152, 191, 194
ethnic conflict, 87–91, 287, 295–97. See also Rwanda
Europe
    attitudes toward war, 224
    military spending in, 19
    nuclear weapons in, 18
    peace in, 289–90
    peace movements in, 213, 214
    post-Cold War era in, 20
    prehistoric warfare in, 40–41
    prosperity in, 43
European Security and Defense Policy (ESDP), 130
European Union
    and the Congo, 156, 166
    European Security and Defense Policy of, 130
    peacekeeping operations of, 130
    Rapid Reaction Force of, 130
Evans, Gareth, 322–23

fatalities, 229–43
    in current civil wars, 280
    difficulties in estimating, 248
    diminishing numbers of, 4, 5–6
    empirical data, 230–35, 236–43, 250, 251
    epidemiologists' measurements of, 248–49
    indirect deaths from war, 6, 232, 233, 235–36, 257
    mortality declines in wartime, 251
    and trends in wars, 36–38, 247, 251–52
fear of war, 10–11
Fearon, James, 292, 294, 297

Ferguson, Niall, 23, 37–38
financial assets, freezing of, 115
Finnemore, Martha, 224–25
firebombings, 21–22
Foley, Conor, 193
Folke Bernadotte Academy, 188
Forsberg, Randall, 222, 230–31, 247
Fortna, Virginia Page, 105–6, 108
France
    and Congo, 67, 166
    and Kofi Annan, 111–12
    and origins of the UN, 46
    and Rwanda, 79, 83, 84, 85–87
    and Suez War, 53, 54, 56

Gat, Azar, 36, 38–39, 277
genocides
    in Bosnia, 87
    in the history of war, 26, 31–32, 34, 35
    relatively rare occurrence of, 26
    in South West Africa, 92
    trends in, 26, 244
    turning point on, 90
    See also Rwanda
Georgia, 154, 237
Germany
    African colonies, 25
    and Namibia, 92
    nuclear weapons of, 18
    prehistoric warfare in, 40–41
    Thirty Years' War, 26–27
    in World War I, 22
    in World War II, 21, 22
Ghana, 62, 123, 126
Gleditsch, Nils Petter, 250
globalization, 15, 205, 208, 209, 223–24
Global Peace Index, 14
Gorbachev, Mikhail, 73–74, 181
Goulding, Marrack, 110
Great Illusion (Angell), 6
great-powers wars, 6, 7
Group of 20 (G20) 2009 summit, 209
Guatemala, 107
guerrilla warfare, 298
Gurr, Ted, 295–96

Haiti, 115, 153–54, 317
Hamburg, David, 318–19
Hamburg, Germany, 21
Hammarskjöld, Dag
    and Congo, 58, 59–61, 63–68, 69–70
    death of, 58, 70
    on prevention, 317
    and secretary-general position, 52–53, 313
    and Suez War, 53
    and UNEF, 54, 55, 56–57
    on women's societal position, 201

Harff, Barbara, 296
Harvard University, 265–66
Hedges, Chris, 300, 305
Helms, Jesse, 320
Hezbollah, 5, 153
Holbrooke, Richard, 89, 111, 320
Holmes, John, 265
Holsti, Kalevi, 278
hostage negotiations, 183–84
Howard, Lise Morjé, 91–92, 104
humanitarian assistance, 114,
    191–97, 323–26
human rights, 64, 95, 323–25
Human Security Report 2005, 243–44
Hundred Years' War, 29
hunter-gatherer societies, 38–39
Hussein, Saddam, 5, 113, 182, 283

identification of enemies, 298–99
Iklé, Fred, 185–86
impartiality, 179
Inca civilization, 27–28
India, 54, 55, 126, 154, 287
Indonesia, 188–89
Intergovernmental Authority on
    Development (IGAD), 133
International Committee of the Red Cross
    (ICRC), 84, 196–97
international community, 7–9
International Court of Justice. See World
    Court
International Criminal Court (ICC),
    122, 138, 168
interstate wars
    decline in, 6, 43, 128, 275–79
    and fatality trends, 5, 237
intractable conflicts, 15
Iran, 182, 283
Iraq
    current state of, 280, 283
    fatalities in, 16, 280
    Iran-Iraq War, 3, 4, 5, 16, 181–83, 237
    Iraq War, 15, 223–24, 244, 249, 283, 320
    oil for food scandal, 113
    sanctions against, 115
    UN missions in, 112–13, 287
    U.S. invasion of, 11, 13, 112, 326
    U.S. occupation of, 14, 112, 283, 286
Ireland, 60, 70
Isaksson, Charlotte, 156–7, 171
Islamic radicals, 200, 280–81
Israel
    Arab-Israeli Conflict, 47–49
    Israeli-Egyptian talks, 187
    and Lebanon, 153
    and Multinational Force and
        Observers, 128

Israel (cont.)
  and Palestine, 15, 182, 188, 287
  and Suez War, 53–54, 56
  UN peacekeeping missions in, 154
  and UNEF, 54–57
Italy, 83, 84
Ivory Coast, 15, 136, 149–50, 304

Japan, 21–22, 98, 220, 289
Jerusalem, 30–31, 47–48, 50
John Paul II (pope), 208
Johnson-Sirleaf, Ellen, 198
Jordan, 50, 126
justice, 204–9, 213, 218, 224

Kabila, Joseph, 164, 167
Kabila, Laurent-Désiré, 158–59, 161,
    162, 164
Kalyvas, Stathis, 297–99
Kaplan, Robert, 20
Keeley, Lawrence, 40
Kennedy, John F., 17, 53
Kennedy, Paul, 54, 78, 148, 326
Kenya, 86
Khmer Rouge, 97–99, 104
Khrushchev, Nikita, 64
King, Gary, 250
Kofi Annan International Peacekeeping
    Training Centre, 135
Korea, 16
Korean War, 51, 52, 219, 237–38, 263–64
Kosovo, 91, 92, 107, 154, 155, 324
Kriesberg, Louis, 15
Kristof, Nicholas, 201–2, 261, 273, 274

Laitin, David, 294, 297
Lake, David, 297
land mines, 226–27
language barriers, 174
Latin America, 24, 39, 290
League of Nations, 45, 88, 217, 220
Lebanon, 4, 5, 57, 153
LeBlanc, Stephen, 38, 39–40
legitimacy concerns, 131–32
Liberia, 107, 136, 149, 198
Libya, 155, 228, 280
Lie, Trygve, 47
Linnér, Sture, 60, 61
Lord's Resistance Army (LRA), 170, 286
Luard, Evan, 36, 241–42
Lumumba, Patrice, 59, 64, 65–67, 69, 158

Macedonia, 317, 318
Machel, Graça, 256
Mack, Andrew, 239
Madagascar, 185
Man, John, 31–32

Mandela, Nelson, 112
McCarthy era, 51
McNamara, Robert, 9–10
Mearsheimer, John, 20
media, 239–40, 242
mediation, 179–80, 186–89. See also
    arbitration, diplomacy
medieval war, 28–33
Mediterranean, 35
Mesopotamia, 35
Mexico, 27–28
Middle Ages, 28–33
military power in the world, 118
Millennium Development Goals, 113
Milosevic, Slobodan, 91
Minear, Larry, 194, 195, 196
Miyet, Bernard, 112
Mobutu, Joseph, 64, 66, 72, 157, 262
Mongols, 27, 31–33, 35
motives for warfare, 39, 297–301
Mozambique, 16, 100–103, 107, 123, 180
Mueller, John, 227, 228
multidimensional peacekeeping
    operations, 100, 129, 156–57
Multinational Force and Observers, 128
multinationalization of military operations,
    246–47
Murray, Christopher, 249–50, 273
Muslim population, 24, 35, 87
myths about wars, 253–74

Namibia, 92–94, 103, 104
Native Americans, 27–28, 39
NATO (North Atlantic Treaty Organization)
    and Afghanistan, 247, 282, 286, 290,
        308–9
    and Bosnia, 88, 90–91, 100, 192
    in Cold War era, 52
    and dual-key system for bombing
        missions, 111
    and Kosovo, 190, 193, 223, 259, 320, 324
    regional peace operations of, 127–32
    and uranium deposits of Congo, 62
natural resources, 294–95
Nazis, 22, 35
Neanderthals, 41–42
Nebraskans for Peace (NFP), 204–5
Nepal, 126, 198–9, 201, 289
NGOs (non-governmental organizations),
    15, 104, 188–89, 191, 194, 272
Nicaragua, 5, 107
Nigeria, 126, 143–44, 192, 199
Nkrumah, Kwame, 62
norms
    about peace and human rights, 15,
        42, 224
    about war and use of force, 224–26

North Korea, 52
Norway, 54, 55
nuclear weapons, 17–20, 42–43, 206,
    219–20, 221–22
number of wars, 5–6, 234–35. *See also*
    trends in violence and wars

Obama, Barack, 223–24, 320
O'Brien, Conor Cruise, 61–62, 67–70, 71, 119,
    326
O'Hanlon, Michael, 316
oil companies, 208–9, 223–24
Oneal, John, 277, 278
one-sided violence, 244
Organization of African Unity, 131, 133, 162
organized crime, 300–301
Ortega, Daniel, 107–8
Ottoman Turks, 31, 324

Paine, Thomas, 210
Pakistan, 55, 126, 154, 280–81, 286, 287
Palestine, 15, 47–49, 181–2, 184, 188,
    198, 287
Palestine Liberation Organization (PLO),
    1–2, 4, 153
Panama, 123
Paraguay, 24
Paris, Roland, 106–7
Paris Peace Accord, 97
Paul VI (pope), 208
Payne, James, 227, 240–42
peace
    eight "peace factors," 15
    graduations in, 3–4
    relative peace of modern era, 34
    trends in, 6
    UN's conflict-management
        approach to, 74
    zones of, 289–91
Peace and Conflict reports, 245–46
Peacebuilding Commission (PBC), 118–19
peacebuilding operations of the UN, 57,
    74, 119
peace enforcement operations of the UN,
    57, 74, 114, 128
peacekeeping operations of the UN
    and the Brahimi Report, 115–19, 310
    and Chapter VI and VII mandates, 114
    costs of, 125, 131, 154, 310, 316
    in current wars, 287
    effectiveness of, 105–8
    expansion in, 74, 311
    gender issues in, 156, 157, 197
    model for, 136–37
    principles of, 56
    smaller missions, 154–55
    standing force proposals, 74, 314–16

as symbol of the UN, 326
    toolbox of, 114–15
    and trends in wars, 244
    See also specific countries and missions
peacemaking operations of the UN, 74,
    181, 304
peace movements, 203–28
    in Cold War era, 219–22
    and growing desirability of peace, 224–28
    history of, 209–10
    justice focus in, 204–9, 213, 218, 224
    nineteenth century movements, 210–14
    in post-Cold War era, 222–24
    and the Quakers, 209–10
    support for UN peacekeeping
        operations, 207
    in World-Wars era, 214–19
peace researchers, 247–48
Peace Research Institute, Oslo (PRIO), 233,
    236, 247, 259
Pearson, Lester, 53
Pérez de Cuéllar, Javier, 4–5, 51, 120, 179,
    180–82, 311, 319
Peru, 123, 287, 290
Peterson, C. A., 33
Petraeus, David, 91
Philippines, 27, 214, 287
Picco, Giandomenico, 179–84
Pinker, Steven, 34, 242, 246
post-Cold War era
    and Bosnia, 87, 90
    Cold War era compared to, 16–20
    expansion in peacekeeping in, 74
    and fatality trends, 4, 236
    nature of peace operations during,
        114–15
    peace movements in, 222–24
postwar transition zones, 288–89
poverty, 205, 209, 292, 294, 301
Prairie Peace Park, 206–7
Prantl, Jochen, 190
prehistoric warfare, 38–42
Prestwich, Michael, 28–29
preventive diplomacy and peacekeeping,
    74, 114, 316–19
prosperity, 43, 292

al Qaeda, 112, 280, 281, 284, 286, 287
Quakers, 209–10, 216

RAND Corporation, 316
rape. *See* sexual exploitation and violence
Reagan Administration, 221–22
reciprocity, 179
recurrence of war, prevention of, 303–4
refugees, 13, 19, 201–2
Regan, Patrick, 301

regional organizations in peace operations, 127–32, 133–35
reintegration programs, *see* Disarmament, Demobilization, and Reintegration
Resident Representatives, 184–85
Rice, Susan, 320
Roberts, Les, 249, 261
Roman Empire, 34–35, 37
Roosevelt, Franklin D., 45
Rothchild, Donald, 297
Rousseau, Jean-Jacques, 39
Rubinstein, Robert, 104, 326
Russett, Bruce, 277, 278
Russia, 18, 131, 154, 237, 289
Rwanda, 78–87
    and Congo's natural resources, 160
    and consent of the parties, 104
    demobilization and reintegration in, 121
    genocide in, 78, 80–87, 300
    genocide perpetrators, 86, 158–59, 161, 165, 169
    Hutu rebels in Congo, 86, 158–59, 161, 165, 167, 169, 267, 285–86
    international response to, 82–86
    and Operation Turquoise, 86
    success of peacebuilding efforts in, 107
    troops contributed by, 126
    as UN failure, 103, 270
    UN operations in, 15, 78, 79–80, 82–86
    war-crimes trials for, 87, 123
    warlords and chiefdoms of, 40

Sambanis, Nicholas, 106, 108, 292, 302, 307
sanctions enforcement of the UN, 114, 115
Sandinistas, 107–8
Savimbi, Jonas, 75–76, 103
scale of war, 3, 11
Seattle research group, 249–50
security companies for hire, 141–42
Security Council, UN. *See* United Nations Security Council
Security Sector Reform (SSR), 121–4, 148, 156, 172
Senegal, 126
September 11th terrorist attacks, 13, 112, 280, 320
Serbia, 87–91, 100, 111. *See also* Bosnia, Croatia, Kosovo
sexual exploitation and violence
    in Congo, 167, 170, 174, 254, 264–74
    and Gender Advisor positions, 156
    in history of war, 25, 34
    in Rwanda, 81
    scandals, 119, 147, 156, 167
    in Sierra Leone, 147
    trends in, 34, 267–68

as war crime, 201
    and zero-tolerance policy of UN, 119
Al Shabab, 284, 286
siege warfare, 29–30, 33
Sierra Leone, 137–48
    and British intervention, 146, 147
    current state of, 280
    and decrease in UN spending, 119
    diamonds of, 141, 295
    disarmament, demobilization, and reintegration program, 147, 200
    foreign forces in, 141–42
    humanitarian aid to, 194, 195–96
    international response to, 143, 144
    peace agreements, 142–43, 144, 145, 147
    sex scandal in, 147
    success of, 107, 137, 149, 175–76
    truth commission for, 123
    UN operations in, 15, 144–46, 147–48, 315
    war period of, 137–42, 143
size of wars, 5–6
slavery, 26, 34, 225, 265, 266
Slim, Hugo, 26
Smillie, Ian, 194, 195, 196
socialism, 213–14
Sollenberg, Margareta, 258
Somalia, 77–78
    and cultural barriers in peacekeeping, 104
    current state of, 280, 284, 286, 287
    ethnic conflict of, 296
    and humanitarian aid, 193, 194
    intractable status of, 15
    Kofi Annan's role in, 110, 111
    as UN failure, 77–78, 103
    U.S. Army Rangers killed in, 78, 86, 285
    warlords and chiefdoms of, 40
Sorokin, Pitirim, 37, 248
South Africa
    apartheid in, 4, 123
    Boer War, 25
    and Namibia, 92–93
    troops contributed by, 126
    truth commission for, 123–24
    women's political participation in, 199
South America, 33, 289
Southern African Development Community (SADC), 129, 132, 133, 134
South Korea, 52
South West Africa, 25, 92. *See also* Namibia
sovereignty issues, 56, 64, 92, 322–26
Soviet Union
    Afghanistan occupation by, 4, 16, 43, 281
    attitude toward the UN of, 181
    and Cambodia, 97
    collapse of, 16
    and Congo, 64, 66, 67, 70

and nuclear fears, 17–20
and origins of the UN, 45–46
proxy wars of, 43
and Suez War, 54
and United States, 4
and uranium deposits of Congo, 62
Spagat, Michael, 250
Spain, 25, 27, 28, 41
spiritual peace, 207
spoilers, 116–17, 304–5
Sri Lanka (formerly Ceylon), 15, 16, 55, 280
Standby High Readiness Brigade
    (SHIRBRIG), 130–31
starvation, 30, 235
Sudan
    border dispute in, 150–51
    current state of, 287
    fatalities in, 16
    and humanitarian aid, 193
    intractable status of, 15
    prehistoric warfare in, 41
    progress made in, 149
    secession of South Sudan, 151
    southern Sudan, 136
    UN operations in, 150–51
    warlords and chiefdoms of, 40
Suez War, 53–57
Syria, 57, 154

Taliban, 259, 280–83, 286
Taylor, Charles, 138
Tennyson, Alfred, 211
territory, struggles over, 278–79
terrorism
    declines in, 226, 244
    fatalities from, 4, 290
    September 11th attacks, 13, 112
    war on, 18, 280
Thirty Years' War, 26–27, 37, 259
Tobin tax, 312
Toynbee, Arnold, 32, 242
transition period, postwar, 148–49
Traub, James, 53, 89, 145
trauma of war, 242, 305–7
travel bans, 115
trends in violence and wars, 12–44
    ancient warfare, 34–35
    assessment of, 9–10
    attitudes toward violence, 227
    and causality questions, 42–44
    Cold War era vs. post-Cold War era,
        16–20
    consolidation in, 246–47
    cycles of violence, 124–25
    decreases in, 20, 42, 236–43, 275–79
    empirical data, 230–35, 236–43
    and fatalities, 36–38

Maryland researchers on, 245–46
Middle Ages, 28–33
nineteenth century, 24–25
prehistoric warfare, 38–42
sixteenth to eighteenth centuries, 26–28
twentieth century vs. previous centuries,
    23–33
twenty-first century vs. the 1990s, 13–15
Uppsala researchers on, 245, 246
Vancouver Group on, 243–44
World Wars vs. post-World War era, 21–22
troop contributing countries, 125–27, 134
Truman, Harry, 51
Trusteeship Division of the UN, 46–47, 92
truth commissions, 95, 123–25, 307
Tunisia, 84–85, 228
Turkey's Kurdish region, 287
Tutu, Desmond, 123
Twitchett, Denis, 33

Uganda
    and Congo, 160, 164–65, 166
    current state of, 287
    demobilization and reintegration in, 121
    fatalities in, 16
    and Lord's Resistance Army (LRA),
        170, 286
    truth commission for, 123
    UN operations in, 15
Unarmy, 177–202
    and humanitarian assistance, 191–97
    scope of, 178–79
    and women's political participation,
        197–202
    See also diplomacy
UNHCR (UN refugee agency), 94, 195
UNICEF (United Nations Children's Fund),
    140, 251, 255, 326
UNITA (Angolan rebels), 75–76, 178
United Nations
    and "Agenda for Peace" report, 74
    America's relationship with, 8–9, 51–52,
        319–21
    and anti-communist fears, 51–52
    arming of peacekeepers, 53–54
    budgetary issues of, 79
    bureaucracy of, 69–70, 88–9, 110, 119–20,
        171, 174, 182, 184, 195, 326
    charter of, v, 10, 46
    civil administration by, 92, 98, 100
    on civilian casualties, 255–57
    conflict management approach of, 74
    and consent of the parties, 103–4
    critics of, 171–72, 313, 319–20, 321
    Department of Peace Keeping Operations
        (UNDPKO), 115, 120
    development program (UNDP), 121

United Nations *(cont.)*
   dual-key system for bombing
      missions, 111
   effectiveness of, 44, 105–8
   election emphasis of, 107
   failures of, 8, 90, 103–8 *(see also* Angola;
      Bosnia; Rwanda; Somalia)
   flag of, 50, 56, 311, 327
   headquarters of, 46, 51, 59, 65, 71, 81–2,
      84, 89, 95, 116
   interstate system of, 321–22
   Military Staff Committee, 127, 315
   Millennium Development Goals, 113
   monitoring missions of, 154–55
   moral authority of, 326
   multidimensional peacekeeping
      operations of, 100
   and non-UN peacekeeping missions,
      127–32
   observers from, 49–51, 57
   origins of, 45–47
   and peace movements, 207
   postwar missions of, 56–57
   reforms of, 115–19
   and refugees, 19, 94
   resources of, 69, 80, 115, 117, 152, 175–76,
      271, 309, 310–12, 313
   and responsibility to protect (R2P),
      322–23, 325–26
   secretary-generals of, 47, 53, 111–12,
      180–82, 313–14
   staff of, 116, 117, 119–20
   standing force proposals for, 74, 314–16
   and strength of forces, 90–91
   successes of, 10, 91, 103–8 *(see also*
      Cambodia; El Salvador; Mozambique;
      Namibia)
   and targeting of aid workers, 311
   as transition authority, 98
   transparency emphasis in, 113, 120
   value of, 312–14
   World Court, 190–91
   and world federalists, 220
   See also peacekeeping operations of the
      UN; *specific divisions*
United Nations Emergency Force
   (UNEF), 53–57
United Nations Security Council
   and Africa peacekeeping, 137, 152
   authorization of missions, 48, 50, 54,
      71, 76, 77, 94–7, 109, 115, 117, 143, 190,
      223, 317, 323–5
   and Cold War end, 5, 74, 110, 179
   and Congo, 60, 63–5, 67, 70, 163–7,
      170, 175
   and costs of peacekeeping, 125
   diamond embargo, 141

   failures in response to Rwanda and
      Bosnia, 80–89
   permanent members (P5), 47, 54, 154,
      191, 314–16
   purpose of, 115, 118
   reforms of, 10, 117–18, 321
   and regional organizations'
      peacekeeping, 128, 132
   and secretary-general, 53, 111, 181–2,
      313–14
   summit of members, 74, 181
   women and gender issues, 156, 197, 264
United Nations Transition Assistance
   Group (UNTAG), 93–94
United Nations Truce Supervision
   Organization (UNTSO), 49–51, 57, 154
United States
   and Afghanistan, 13, 14–15
   anti-communist fears, 51–52, 219
   and Bosnia, 89–90, 91
   and budgetary issues of the UN, 79,
      319–20
   and Cambodia, 97
   changing norms in, 227–28
   Civil War, 24, 212–13
   and Congo, 59, 62, 66, 72, 164
   dominance of, 15
   and foreign civil wars, 86
   Iraq War, 11, 13, 14, 112, 320, 326
   and Kofi Annan, 111–12
   and Korean War, 52
   and Kosovo, 91
   military's mission changes, 309–10
   military spending of, 19–20
   nuclear fears in, 17–20
   and origins of the UN, 45–6
   and Palestinian state, 287
   and peacekeeping operations, 314
   peace movements in, 207, 210–14, 215–18
   proxy wars of, 43
   relationship with the UN, 8–9, 51–52, 117,
      319–21
   and Rwanda, 78, 79, 80, 81, 84, 85
   and Somalia, 77–78, 111
   and Soviet Union, 4
   and Suez War, 53
   trends in violence and wars, 13
   troops contributed by, 127
   UN bashing in, 111, 320
   and UNEF, 54
   U.S. Army, 19–20, 309
   in World War II, 21, 22
University of Maryland, 245–46, 247
University of Washington, 249–50
Uppsala Conflict Data Project, 232–33
   on civilian casualties, 236
   on interstate wars, 237

methods of, 232–33, 235
resources of, 247
role of, 240
on Rwandan genocide, 82
on trends in armed conflicts, 245, 246
Urquhart, Brian, 47, 55, 57, 68, 71, 116
Uruguay, 24, 126
U.S. Institute of Peace, 15, 20

Vancouver Group, 243–44, 247, 251–52, 263
Vieira de Mello, Sergio, 112–13
Vietnam
    antiwar movement, 203, 220–21
    and Cambodia, 97
    and doomsday clock, 19
    fatalities in, 16, 234, 237–38
    identifying enemies in, 298–99

Walter, Barbara, 302
war crimes, 82, 140, 168, 170, 244, 265
war crimes tribunals, 87, 89, 91, 122–23, 201
Western Sahara, 154
Whitfield, Teresa, 187, 189

Wieschhoff, Heinz, 65, 71
women, 197–202
    peace movement participation of, 211,
        215–16, 218
    political participation of, 15
    See also sexual exploitation and violence
Wood, Elisabeth, 301
World Bank, 121
World Court, 190–91, 212, 217
World Summit (2005), 117–18
World War I, 10, 22, 216–17, 220, 257
World War II
    fatalities in, 10, 21, 26, 238, 259
    and origins of the UN, 45
    and peace movements, 218–19, 224
    violence in, 21–22

Yugoslavia, 87, 97, 115, 123

Zaire. See Congo
Zartman, I. William, 185
Zeid Report, 119
Zoellner, Tom, 62